T0325042

Critical Approaches to Data Engineering Systems and Analysis

Abhijit Bora
Assam Don Bosco University, India

Papul Changmai
Assam Don Bosco University, India

Mrutyunjay Maharana
Xi'an Jiatong University, China

A volume in the Advances
in Computer and Electrical
Engineering (ACEE) Book Series

Published in the United States of America by
    IGI Global
    Engineering Science Reference (an imprint of IGI Global)
    701 E. Chocolate Avenue
    Hershey PA, USA 17033
    Tel: 717-533-8845
    Fax: 717-533-8661
    E-mail: cust@igi-global.com
    Web site: http://www.igi-global.com

Library of Congress Cataloging-in-Publication Data

CIP Pending
ISBN: 979-8-3693-2260-4
EISBN: 979-8-3693-2261-1

This book is published in the IGI Global book series Advances in Computer and Electrical Engineering (ACEE) (ISSN: 2327-039X; eISSN: 2327-0403)

British Cataloguing in Publication Data
A Cataloguing in Publication record for this book is available from the British Library.

All work contributed to this book is new, previously-unpublished material.
The views expressed in this book are those of the authors, but not necessarily of the publisher.

For electronic access to this publication, please contact: eresources@igi-global.com.

Advances in Computer and Electrical Engineering (ACEE) Book Series

ISSN:2327-039X
EISSN:2327-0403

Editor-in-Chief: Srikanta Patnaik, SOA University, India

MISSION

The fields of computer engineering and electrical engineering encompass a broad range of interdisciplinary topics allowing for expansive research developments across multiple fields. Research in these areas continues to develop and become increasingly important as computer and electrical systems have become an integral part of everyday life.

The **Advances in Computer and Electrical Engineering (ACEE) Book Series** aims to publish research on diverse topics pertaining to computer engineering and electrical engineering. **ACEE** encourages scholarly discourse on the latest applications, tools, and methodologies being implemented in the field for the design and development of computer and electrical systems.

COVERAGE

- Electrical Power Conversion
- Optical Electronics
- Chip Design
- Power Electronics
- Algorithms
- VLSI Fabrication
- Applied Electromagnetics
- Qualitative Methods
- Computer Science
- Sensor Technologies

IGI Global is currently accepting manuscripts for publication within this series. To submit a proposal for a volume in this series, please contact our Acquisition Editors at Acquisitions@igi-global.com or visit: http://www.igi-global.com/publish/.

Titles in this Series

For a list of additional titles in this series, please visit:
http://www.igi-global.com/book-series/advances-computer-electrical-engineering/73675

Applications and Principles of Quantum Computing
Alex Khang (Global Research Institute of Technology and Engineering, USA)
Engineering Science Reference • copyright 2024 • 491pp • H/C (ISBN: 9798369311684)
• US $300.00 (our price)

Emerging Trends in Cloud Computing Analytics, Scalability, and Service Models
Dina Darwish (Ahram Canadian University, Egypt)
Engineering Science Reference • copyright 2024 • 468pp • H/C (ISBN: 9798369309001)
• US $300.00 (our price)

Principles and Applications of Quantum Computing Using Essential Math
A. Daniel (Amity University, India) M. Arvindhan (Galgotias University, India) Kiranmai
Bellam (Prairie View A&M University, USA) and N. Krishnaraj (SRM University, India)
Engineering Science Reference • copyright 2023 • 237pp • H/C (ISBN: 9781668475355)
• US $275.00 (our price)

NeutroGeometry, NeutroAlgebra, and SuperHyperAlgebra in Today's World
Florentin Smarandache (University of New Mexico, USA) and Madeline Al Tahan (Abu
Dhabi University, UAE)
Engineering Science Reference • copyright 2023 • 264pp • H/C (ISBN: 9781668447406)
• US $270.00 (our price)

Principles and Theories of Data Mining With RapidMiner
Sarawut Ramjan (Thammasat University, Thailand) and Jirapon Sunkpho (Thammasat
University, Thailand)
Engineering Science Reference • copyright 2023 • 319pp • H/C (ISBN: 9781668447307)
• US $255.00 (our price)

For an entire list of titles in this series, please visit:
http://www.igi-global.com/book-series/advances-computer-electrical-engineering/73675

701 East Chocolate Avenue, Hershey, PA 17033, USA
Tel: 717-533-8845 x100 • Fax: 717-533-8661
E-Mail: cust@igi-global.com • www.igi-global.com

Table of Contents

Detailed Table of Contents

    Md Sakir Ahmed, Department of Computer Applications, Assam Don
        Bosco University, India
    Abhijit Bora, Assam Don Bosco University, India

This study is focused on the possible application of hybrid models as well as their usage in the detection of diabetes. This study focuses on various machine learning algorithms like Decision Trees, Random Forests, Logistic Regression, K-nearest neighbor, Support Vector Machines, Gaussian Naive Bayes, Adaptive Boosting Classifier, and Extreme Gradient Boosting as well as the usage of Stacking Classifier for the preparation of the hybrid model. An in-depth analysis was also made during this study to compare the traditional approach with the hybrid approach. Moreover, the usage of data augmentation and its application during an analysis has also been discussed along with the application of hyperparameter tuning and cross-validation during training of the various models.

    Lakshmi Haritha Medida, R.M.K. Engineering College, India
    Kumar, BVC Institute of Technology and Science, India

Data analytics, in the context of big data, presents numerous challenges that organizations must overcome to harness the full potential of their data. Risk managers may face a number of obstacles in their efforts to gather and apply analytics. Fortunately, there is a solution. This chapter addresses some of the major problems with data analytics and the probable solutions. The main issues covered in this study are data volume, real-time analytics, data validation, poor data quality, lack of support, ambiguity, financial restrictions, talent scarcity, and security. It will need a holistic strategy that includes strategic planning, modern technology, and cooperative efforts to address these difficulties. Organizations must traverse these challenges to extract valuable insights and make educated choices from their data, from adopting scalable infrastructures for data processing to developing a competent staff and putting in place strong security measures.

Chapter 3
Gypsy Nandi, Assam Don Bosco University, India
Yadika Prasad, Assam Don Bosco University, India

Technological advancement has now allowed researchers to overcome barriers that exist in the research of marine animals. While traditional methods provided limited insights and relied heavily on sound signals, the advent of sophisticated image and video- capturing devices has made it possible to collect data on marine animals in their natural habitat. This has allowed research into the detection and classification of marine animals underwater to rapidly rise in the last few decades. Computer vision and deep learning have given unprecedented results in this field in recent years yielding efficient results with low computational power. This chapter discusses the trends in the evolution of techniques used in underwater marine animal detection. This chapter also serves as a valuable resource in the field of marine research for researchers and practitioners alike to better understand the capabilities and limitations of specific areas. It will help in the further enhancement of techniques in the area of marine animal detection.

Chapter 4
Saurav Bhattacharjee, Kamrup Polytechnic, India
Sabiha Raiyesha, Kamrup Polytechnic, India

Weather forecasting is a scientific method that involves the prediction of atmospheric conditions at a specific geographic location. The increased volatility over the last decade is owing to an enormous rise in water used for irrigation application throughout agricultural area, much of which evaporates, necessitating accurate forecasting in order to take essential safeguards. In this chapter, an attempt is made to predict the average temperature and maximum temperature through machine learning models. The daily temperature data from 1970 to 2022 were collected from the National Centre of Environmental Information (NCEI). The ARIMA model is used to predict the weather data sets of Tezpur, Assam. Previous conventional models are insufficient to predict forecasting precisely. So statistical models and auto-regressive models are programmed and compared.

Chapter 5
Critical Approaches to Data Engineering Systems Innovation and Industry Application Using IoT 64

Naren Kathirvel, Anand Institute of Higher Technology, India
Kathirvel Ayyaswamy, Department of Computer Science and
Engineering, Panimalar Engineering College, India
B. Santhoshi, St. Anne's Arts and Science College, India

The IoT influence presents new design and implementation challenges in a variety of fields, including seamless platform integration, context-based cognitive network integration, new mobile sensor/actuator network paradigms, architectural domains for smart farming, infrastructure, healthcare, agriculture, business, and commerce. Applications for automation in the internet of robotic things (IoRT) are numerous and are developing quickly. IoRT blends the strength of robots and the internet of things (IoT), resulting in creative solutions for a range of sectors. While ensuring the authenticity of the content in this introduction, the authors shall investigate the wide range of IoRT automation applications. IoRT automation refers to a broad range of endeavors that use connected gadgets, sensors, and autonomous machinery to improve production, efficiency, and safety across a variety of industries. These regions are general categories into which these programs can be placed: Industry 4.0 and manufacturing

Chapter 6
Data Insight Unveiled: Navigating Critical Approaches and Challenges in Diverse Domains Through Advanced Data Analysis 90

K. Sudha, RMD Engineering College, India
C. Balakrishnan, S.A. Engineering College, India
T. P. Anish, RMK College of Engineering and Technology, India
T. Nithya, Rajalakshmi Institute of Technology, India
B. Yamini, SRM Institute of Science and Technology, India
R. Siva Subramanian, RMK College of Engineering and Technology, India
M. Nalini, S.A. Engineering College, India

Data engineering solutions have become important in our quickly evolving technological world for handling and analysing the massive volumes of data generated every day. The chapter examines data engineering systems exponential expansion and data analysis's growing importance across businesses. It highlights data-driven healthcare's transformational influence on patient care and treatment advances, while noting privacy and ethical issues. The research analyses data categorisation techniques, focusing on machine learning and deep learning for healthcare and agricultural decision support systems. The story expects AI and blockchain integration in emerging decision support systems. Data analysis in clinical trials, precision healthcare decision-making, and agricultural applications are also covered. The conclusion is that data analytics improves weather prediction accuracy and gives useful insights for scholars and practitioners navigating the complex world of data analysis.

Chapter 7
    Sabiha Raiyesha, Assam Don Bosco University, India
    Papul Changmai, Assam Don Bosco University, India

Educational institutes have ample potential and good scope to generate solar energy. As these institutes function during daytime, the generated energy can be used in order to meet the electricity requirements of the campus. It can both be designed to work as grid-connected and off-grid mode using the unused rooftops of these institutes. In this study, a 90 kWp grid connected solar photovoltaic system for Kamrup Polytechnic in Baihata Chariali has been designed at the proposed rooftop. It simulated using PVsyst version 7.0.9 simulation tool. The annual energy generation from simulation for the 90 kWp grid connected 12675 kWh with a performance ratio of 73.1%. Economic analysis of these PV systems has also been performed to determine the annual levelised cost of energy production which is found to range from about Rs 3.170/kWp for 90 kWp PV system. This work summarizes the estimation of electrical load in Kamrup polytechnic, the design of PV system, the simulation results, performance analysis, as well as economic analysis for grid connected PV system.

Chapter 8
    Sagar Saikia, National Institute of Technology, Meghalaya, India
    Jonti Deuri, Assam Don Bosco University, India
    Riya Deka, NERIM Group of Institutions, India
    Rituparna Nath, NERIM Group of Institutions, India

Diabetes is a prevalent and chronic health condition affecting millions globally. Diabetes is caused by a combination of many factors including obesity, excessive blood glucose levels, abnormal cholesterol levels, family history, physical inactivity, bad food habits, and other causes. Frequent urination, increased thirst, increased hunger, and loss of weight are the common symptoms of diabetes. A person having diabetes has heavy risks of heart disease, kidney disease, nerve damage, diabetic retinopathy, brain stroke, foot ulcer, etc. These risks factors can be reduced by early detections of disease. The big challenge for the health care industries nowadays is to give a more precise result which could easily predict whether a patient is having or diagnosed with such disease.

Chapter 9

Jonti Deuri, Assam Don Bosco University, India
Dhanjit Gogoi, Assam Secratariate, India
Sagar Saikia, National Institute of Technology, Meghalaya, India

The agricultural sector is undergoing frequent transformation and the inclusion of data analysis techniques have the potential to revolutionize the traditional farming practices. In recent years, use of data analysis methodologies with farming has become very important, as it can make farming more sustainable and efficient in the future. The main objective of this chapter is to explore and establish a comprehensive data analysis methodology for sustainable farming. The relationship between data-driven approaches and the advancement of commercially and environmentally sound and economically viable agricultural practices are explored. By combining computer science and engineering with farming knowledge, this new method aims to change how farming can be done in an advanced way and wants to use resources better, grow more crops, and encourage sustainable farming.

Chapter 10

Rituparna Nath, NERIM Group of Institutions, India
Arunima Devi, NERIM Group of Institutions, India

Classification is a supervised machine learning technique which is used to predict group membership for data instances. For simplification of classification, one may use scikit-learn tool kit. This chapter mainly focuses on the classification of Iris dataset using scikit-learn. It concerns the recognition of Iris flower species (setosa, versicolor, and verginica) on the basis of the measurements of length and width of sepal and petal of the flower. One can generate classification models by using various machine learning algorithms through training the iris flower dataset, and can choose the model with highest accuracy to predict the species of iris flower more precisely. Classification of Iris dataset would be detecting patterns from examining sepal and petal size of the Iris flower and how the prediction was made from analyzing the pattern to form the class of Iris flower. By using this pattern and classification, in future upcoming years the unseen data can be predicted more precisely. The goal here is to gain insights to model the probabilities of class membership, conditioned on the flower features. The proposed chapter mainly focuses on how one can train their model with data using machine learning algorithms to predict the species of Iris flower by input of the unseen data using what it has learnt from the trained data.

Chapter 11

Arunjyoti Das, National Informatics Centre, India
Abhijit Bora, Assam Don Bosco University, India

The internet of things (IoT) is a network of physical objects with sensors, software, and network connectivity built in to enable data collection and sharing. It has led to an exponential increase in data generation, necessitating the development of effective statistical analysis for a range of IoT applications. Predictive analytics is an essential procedure that converts unprocessed data into meaningful insights. To improve decision-making and enhance IoT application performance, it is crucial to create innovative data processing methods and predictive analytical models that can handle the volume and complexity of IoT data. Microservices-based strategies can be implemented to create scalable, reusable, and effective IoT-based analytics solutions.

Chapter 12

Lianmuansang Samte, Assam Don Bosco University, India
Aditya Kumar Rabha, Assam Don Bosco University, India
Bhargav Kalpa Hazarika, Assam Don Bosco University, India
Gypsy Nandi, Assam Don Bosco University, India

Near-Earth objects (NEOs) are asteroids or comets that have their orbits in close proximity with Earth. Some objects amongst these are known to be potentially hazardous and pose a risk of collision. This chapter developed four supervised machine learning algorithms, namely, logistic regression, random forest, support vector machine, and XGBoost, for the detection and classification of hazardous near-earth objects. Two datasets were utilised, the first taken from the Kaggle website, and the second generated from NASA's JPL Small-Body database. Feature importance analysis of these datasets was done by analysing the Shapley values of the individual features in both datasets. This chapter concludes by finding all models to have performed sufficiently well, with XGBoost found to be the best and most consistent performing across both datasets. Additionally, both min and max diameter, and the absolute magnitude features for the Kaggle dataset, and the H and moid features for the JPL dataset were found to be the most impactful features for classifying hazardous near-earth objects.

Chapter 13

Jesif Ahmed, Assam Don Bosco University, India
Papul Changmai, Assam Don Bosco University, India

In typical Indian organisational settings, users usually rely on the traditional electrical grid and costly, environmentally harmful diesel generators to supply electricity for regular, emergency backup, and transient services. In addition to offering a chance to supply electricity to relocated people, integrating solar capacity into the current grid can result in considerable cost and carbon reductions. Utilising computational energy system modelling and the analysis of monitored demand data, we assess the savings made possible by the integration of solar (160 kW) capacity into the current supply grid of Assam Power Distribution Co. Ltd. (APDCL, India) at the Azara campus of Assam Don Bosco University, India. The authors discover that, over a five-year period, the renewable infrastructure significantly lowers costs and CO_2 emissions. In order to cut costs and emissions and pave the way for sustainable energy practices, organisations should look into ways to integrate renewable energy sources into their current electrical infrastructure and maximise their performance once installed.

Pranjit Kakati, Assam Don Bosco University, India
Abhijit Bora, Assam Don Bosco University, India

With the rapid advancement and usage of technology like smart devices, sensors, IoT devices etc. the cloud computing technology is facing challenges of high response time, latency, high load on network due to explosion of data in the recent times. Edges computing technology emerges as solution for this down sides of Cloud computing by bringing the computation and processing of Cloud computing to the edge of the network i.e closer to the source of data. The application developed to run in Edge computing uses Microservices due to its advantages of lightweight, independent deployment, loosely coupled and scalability characteristics. In the research community, the deployment of microservices using microservice design patterns and analysis of performance metrics is an important discussion point. Here, a novel methodology will be proposed in edge computing environment using microservice orchestration. Here, the details of Edge computing and microservice architecture using microservice design patterns will be discussed.

Foreword

Data Engineering is evolving as a prominent tool for orchestrating systems and architectural frameworks. This book presents everything from theoretical discourse to practical implications on data engineering. It emphasizes the challenges faced in effective learning from unstructured data. With a specific focus on cloud systems, instrumentation, software modules, and global end-product usage surveys, the book extends its reach to diverse domains such as healthcare, clinical trials, telemedicine, farming, and societal needs. This book is a "must-have" for any professional and researcher working on information and knowledge management. The editors and authors of the book have done a commendable job in providing information that spans various disciplines such as information and communication sciences, computer science, information technology, renewable energy, electronics, and instrumentation.

Rohith Sangineni
School of Engineering Cardiff University, Cardiff, UK
February 2024

Preface

In the realm of modern data-driven enterprises, the significance of robust data engineering systems and insightful analysis cannot be overstated. As editors of this comprehensive reference book, *Critical Approaches to Data Engineering Systems and Analysis*, we are delighted to present a compendium that delves deep into the practical applications, methodologies, and challenges surrounding data engineering and analysis.

Data engineering is the backbone of contemporary information management, encompassing the entire lifecycle of data from collection to processing to analysis. It entails the design and implementation of systems and frameworks that facilitate the efficient handling of vast datasets, ensuring their integrity, security, and accessibility for meaningful analysis. At its core, data engineering empowers organizations to leverage their data assets effectively, driving informed decision-making and fostering innovation.

Within these pages, we aim to unlock the latent potential inherent in various data analysis techniques and methodologies. Our objective is to offer a multidimensional exploration of the landscape of data analysis, blending diverse perspectives, guidelines, and frameworks to address personalized challenges across different domains. From statistical and mathematical models to heuristic approaches and software modules, we endeavor to illuminate the path towards accurate, insightful data analysis.

The book's thematic focus spans a broad spectrum of industries and domains, reflecting the ubiquitous nature of data-driven decision-making. From healthcare and clinical trials to agriculture, renewable energy, and beyond, each chapter offers valuable insights into tailored data analysis solutions tailored to specific needs and challenges.

We invite contributions from experts and practitioners across various disciplines, aiming to enrich this compendium with diverse perspectives and innovative approaches. The topics covered include but are not limited to classification techniques, decision support systems, precision decision-making, fault tolerance, and heuristic data analysis, among others.

Our target audience comprises professionals and researchers engaged in information and knowledge management across diverse fields, including information sciences, computer science, renewable energy, and beyond. Additionally, executives and decision-makers grappling with organizational development and knowledge management will find this book to be a valuable resource.

As editors, we are committed to curating a collection that not only elucidates the intricacies of data engineering and analysis but also serves as a practical guide for professionals navigating the complex terrain of modern data-driven enterprises. We are confident that this book will serve as a beacon for those seeking to harness the transformative power of data in their respective domains.

Chapter 1: A Comprehensive Approach for Using Hybrid Ensemble Methods for Diabetes Detection

Authored by Md Ahmed and Abhijit Bora from the Department of Computer Applications at Assam Don Bosco University, India, this chapter explores the application of hybrid models in diabetes detection. The authors delve into various machine learning algorithms, including decision trees, random forests, logistic regression, and more, along with the stacking classifier technique. Through meticulous analysis, they compare traditional and hybrid approaches, shedding light on the efficacy of data augmentation, hyperparameter tuning, and cross-validation methodologies in optimizing diabetes detection models.

Chapter 2: Addressing Challenges in Data Analytics - A Comprehensive Review and Proposed Solutions

Lakshmi Haritha Medida from R.M.K. Engineering College, India, and Kumar G L N V S from BVC Institute Of Technology & Science, India, scrutinize the challenges inherent in data analytics within the realm of Big Data. Their comprehensive review identifies obstacles such as data volume, real-time analytics, and poor data quality, proposing holistic solutions encompassing strategic planning, technological advancements, and collaborative efforts to overcome these hurdles and extract actionable insights from data reservoirs.

Chapter 3: Advances in Marine Animal Detection Techniques: A Comprehensive Review and Analysis

Authored by Gypsy Nandi and Yadika Prasad from Assam Don Bosco University, India, this chapter explores the evolution of techniques used in underwater marine animal detection. The authors elucidate the transformative impact of computer vision and deep learning, facilitated by sophisticated image and video-capturing devices. By highlighting the trends in marine animal detection, Nandi and Prasad offer valuable insights into advancing research and conservation efforts in marine biology.

Chapter 4: Analysis of ARIMA Model for Weather Forecasting in Assam District

Saurav Bhattacharjee and Sabiha Raiyesha from Kamrup Polytechnic, India, delve into weather forecasting techniques, focusing on predicting average and maximum temperatures using machine learning models. Leveraging the ARIMA model and decades of temperature data, the authors seek to enhance the accuracy of weather forecasting, surpassing the limitations of conventional methods through statistical and autoregressive techniques.

Chapter 5: Critical Approaches to Data Engineering Systems Innovation and Industry Application Using IoT

Authored by Naren Kathirvel from Anand Institute of Higher Technology, India, Kathirvel Ayyaswamy from Panimalar Engineering College, India, and Santhoshi B from St. Anne's Arts and Science College, India, this chapter explores the convergence of data engineering systems and the Internet of Things (IoT). The authors delve into the challenges and opportunities presented by IoT automation applications across various industries, highlighting the transformative potential of integrating connected devices and sensors to enhance production efficiency and safety.

Chapter 6: Data Insight Unveiled: Navigating Critical Approaches and Challenges in Diverse Domains through Advanced Data Analysis

Authored by Sudha K, Balakrishnan C, Anish T P, Nithya T, YAMINI B, Siva Subramanian R, and Nalini M from various engineering colleges in India, this chapter offers a panoramic view of data analysis's exponential growth and its pivotal role in sectors such as healthcare and agriculture. The authors explore cutting-edge techniques like machine learning and deep learning, underscoring their potential to revolutionize clinical trials, precision healthcare, and agricultural practices.

Chapter 7: Design and Economic Analysis of Grid-Connected PV System in Kamrup Polytechnic

Sabiha Raiyesha and Papul Changmai from Assam Don Bosco University, India, present a detailed analysis of a grid-connected solar PV system designed for Kamrup Polytechnic, India. Through simulation and economic analysis, they showcase the performance and economic viability of solar PV integration, highlighting its potential to significantly reduce carbon emissions and energy costs, fostering sustainability in institutional settings.

Chapter 8: Diabetes Prediction Using Novel Machine Learning Methods

Authored by Sagar Saikia from NIT Meghalaya, India, Jonti Deuri from Assam Don Bosco University, India, Rituparna Nath and Riya Deka from NERIM Group of Institutions, India, this chapter focuses on employing novel machine learning techniques for diabetes prediction. The authors highlight the importance of early detection in mitigating potential complications, offering insights into improving patient care and outcomes through predictive analytics.

Chapter 9: Harvesting Insights - A Comprehensive Data Analysis Methodology for Sustainable Agri-Farming Practices

Jonti Deuri from Assam Don Bosco University, India, Dhanjit Gogoi from Assam Secretariat, India, and Sagar Saikia from NIT Meghalaya, India, delve into the synergy between data-driven approaches and sustainable agricultural practices. By combining computer science with farming knowledge, the authors aim to optimize resource utilization and crop yields, fostering a more sustainable and efficient farming ecosystem.

Chapter 10: Machine Learning Algorithms Used for Iris Flower Classification

Authored by Rituparna Nath and Arunima Devi from NERIM Group of Institutions, India, this chapter focuses on the classification of iris flower species using machine learning algorithms. By training models on the iris dataset, the authors demonstrate the predictive capabilities of various algorithms, offering insights into botanical classification and predictive modeling.

Chapter 11: Microservices Architecture for Data Analytics in IoT Applications

Authored by Arunjyoti Das from the National Informatics Centre, India, and Abhijit Bora from Assam Don Bosco University, India, this chapter explores the integration of microservices architecture with IoT data analytics. Emphasizing scalability and performance, the authors highlight the role of microservices-based strategies in developing robust and adaptable data analytics frameworks for IoT applications.

Chapter 12: NEOTracker: Near-Earth Object Detection and Analysis

Lianmuansang Samte, Aditya Rabha, Bhargav Hazarika, and Gypsy Nandi from Assam Don Bosco University, India, delve into the detection and analysis of hazardous near-Earth objects. Leveraging supervised machine learning algorithms, the authors analyze feature importance and classification performance, offering insights into mitigating risks associated with space debris.

Chapter 13: Optimizing the Benefits of Solar PV-Integrated Infrastructure in Educational Institutes and Organizational Setups in North Eastern India

Authored by Jesif Ahmed and Papul Changmai from the Department of Electrical and Electronics Engineering, Assam Don Bosco University, India, this chapter explores the economic and environmental benefits of integrating solar PV systems into institutional settings in North Eastern India. Through computational energy system modeling and economic analysis, the authors showcase the potential for cost and emissions reductions, paving the way for sustainable energy practices.

Chapter 14: Some Aspects of Data Engineering for Edge Computing Using Microservice Design Pattern

Authored by Pranjit Kakati and Abhijit Bora from Assam Don Bosco University, India, this chapter investigates the integration of microservices architecture with edge computing. Highlighting advantages in scalability and performance, the authors discuss novel methodologies for deploying microservices in edge computing environments, offering insights into optimizing data engineering solutions for edge computing applications.

As editors of this comprehensive reference book, *Critical Approaches to Data Engineering Systems and Analysis*, we are pleased to present a collection that delves deep into the practical applications, methodologies, and challenges surrounding data engineering and analysis. Data engineering serves as the backbone of modern information management, facilitating the efficient handling of vast datasets and empowering organizations to extract valuable insights for informed decision-making.

Throughout the chapters, authored by esteemed contributors from various institutions across India, we have explored a diverse array of topics spanning from healthcare and agriculture to renewable energy and space exploration. Each chapter offers unique perspectives and insights into tailored data analysis solutions, reflecting the ubiquitous nature of data-driven decision-making in today's enterprises.

From the application of hybrid ensemble methods for diabetes detection to the economic analysis of grid-connected solar PV systems, the chapters in this book highlight the transformative potential of data engineering and analysis across different domains. Whether it's predicting weather patterns, classifying marine animals, or detecting hazardous near-Earth objects, the contributions exemplify the multifaceted nature of data-driven research and innovation.

As editors, we extend our gratitude to the authors for their invaluable contributions and dedication to advancing the field of data engineering and analysis. We also invite further contributions from experts and practitioners across diverse disciplines, aiming to enrich this compendium with additional perspectives and innovative approaches.

In conclusion, we believe that this book will serve as a valuable resource for professionals and researchers engaged in information and knowledge management, offering practical insights and guidance for navigating the complex landscape of modern data-driven enterprises. We are confident that the diverse perspectives and methodologies presented in this compendium will inspire further exploration and innovation in the field of data engineering and analysis.

Abhijit Bora
Assam Don Bosco University, India

Papul Changmai
Assam Don Bosco University, India

Mrutyunjay Maharana
Xi'an Jiaotong University, China

Chapter 1
A Comprehensive Approach for Using Hybrid Ensemble Methods for Diabetes Detection

Md Sakir Ahmed

ⓘ https://orcid.org/0000-0002-7754-639X
Department of Computer Applications, Assam Don Bosco University, India

Abhijit Bora

ⓘ https://orcid.org/0009-0009-7481-0835
Assam Don Bosco University, India

ABSTRACT

This study is focused on the possible application of hybrid models as well as their usage in the detection of diabetes. This study focuses on various machine learning algorithms like Decision Trees, Random Forests, Logistic Regression, K-nearest neighbor, Support Vector Machines, Gaussian Naive Bayes, Adaptive Boosting Classifier, and Extreme Gradient Boosting as well as the usage of Stacking Classifier for the preparation of the hybrid model. An in-depth analysis was also made during this study to compare the traditional approach with the hybrid approach. Moreover, the usage of data augmentation and its application during an analysis has also been discussed along with the application of hyperparameter tuning and cross-validation during training of the various models.

DOI: 10.4018/979-8-3693-2260-4.ch001

1. INTRODUCTION

1.1 Background of the problem

With the increase in the consumption of processed foods, there has also been an increase in the number of cases of cases of diabetes. There has been a linear increase in the number of cases, affecting a vast spectrum of the global population ranging from children to adults to seasoned citizens. This sudden increase can be directly correlated to increased consumption of processed foods as per studies, however, this is not the only factor. Lack of physical activity, consumption of alcohol, smoking, and improper sleep schedules are some of the contributing factors to the rise in the number of cases. Traditional approaches for diabetes detection include urine tests, random blood sugar tests, clinical symptoms, risk assessments, etc. However, with the advent of technology emphasis needs to be given to finding newer methods to identify and assess the various risk factors as well as for early detection of diabetes. This may in turn reduce the number of cases occurring annually enabling a healthier life for the global population.

1.2 Proposed solution

This study is a brief introduction to hybrid ensemble learning models and focuses on giving a detailed overview of the possible implications of these models on early diagnosis as well as their usage for the identification of risk factors. Several machine learning algorithms like Decision Trees, Random Forest, Logistic Regression, K-nearest neighbors, Support Vector Machines, Gaussian Naive Bayes, and Adaptive Boosting Classifier can be used to diagnose diabetes as well as other diseases quite accurately. The accuracy can be further increased by stacking multiple models using a stacking classifier. These stacked models are known as hybrid models and provide better accuracy compared to just using a single classifier due to their robustness in identifying noise in the data, better hyperparameter tuning, enhanced adaptability, and improved generalization.

In this study, several traditional machine-learning algorithms were used along with hyperparameter tuning to find the best suitable parameter for the given data after which the best-performing models were stacked together along with Extreme Gradient Boosting Classifier, and their accuracy for training and testing was calculated. The observations are discussed in detail in Sections 3 and 4.

2. RELATED WORK

The HoeffdingTree algorithm was used (Mercaldo et al., 2017) to detect diabetes and showed 77% accuracy and 77.5% recall. Various machine (Al-Zebari & Sengur, 2019) learning algorithms were implemented. It was found that Logistic Regression yielded the best result with an accuracy of 77.9%, and the Coarse Gaussian SVM technique yielded an accuracy of 65.5% which was the lowest among all the algorithms. Again several machine learning models were implemented (Islam et al., 2020) and it was found that the random forest classifier gave a very high accuracy of 99.35% for the prediction of diabetes. It was also observed that (Islam and Khanam, 2021) the Gaussian Naive Bayes classifier yielded an accuracy of 79.87% for the prediction of diabetes. A web app was also developed (Pankaj et al., 2021) for the diagnosis of diabetes that uses a questionnaire rather than a medical test and utilizes machine learning algorithms to predict if a person has diabetes. Similarly, various other machine learning algorithms were implemented (Farajollahi et al., 2021) and it was found that the Adaptive Boosting Classifier yielded the highest accuracy of 81%. In another study (Mangal and Jain, 2022) it was found that Random Forest yielded an accuracy of 99% for the detection of diabetes. It was also observed (Liu et al., 2022) that the Extreme Gradient Boosting classifier yielded the best accuracy of 75% among several other algorithms and proposed that it can be used for screening individuals at high risk of Type 2 diabetes at an early stage. It was also proposed (Charitha et al., 2022) that machine learning algorithms can be used to predict Type 2 diabetes, and observed that the Light Gradient Boosting Machine yielded the highest accuracy of 91.47% . Again in another study (Bhat et al., 2022) it was found that random forest gives an accuracy of 97.75% in the detection of Diabetes Mellitus. In another study (Gowthami et al., 2023), various algorithms were implemented, namely., Logistic Regression, K-Nearest Neighbors, Decision Trees, Random Forest, and Support Vector Machines found that the Random Forest Classifier yielded the highest accuracy with an accuracy of 98% for Type 2 Diabetes Mellitus. KNN was also applied (Rathi and Madeira., 2023) to detect and test its implication regarding Diabetes Mellitus.

3. PROPOSED APPROACH

3.1 What is Machine Learning?

Within the field of artificial intelligence, machine learning is the area of study dedicated to creating models and algorithms that allow computers to learn and make choices without explicit programming. It includes giving machines the tools they need to gradually get better at a certain activity by using statistical approaches.

1. **Data Input:** To train algorithms, machine learning algorithms require a lot of data. The data that is used as input is processed by these algorithms to find patterns, connections, and trends in it.
2. **Training Algorithms:** Machine learning models gain knowledge from the supplied data during the training phase. To minimize the discrepancy between the expected and actual results in the training set, the algorithm modifies its parameters. However, this may not be enough, and as such these algorithms need to be manually tuned. This is known as hyperparameter training.
3. Types of Machine Learning:
   1) *Supervised learning:* It is the process of teaching an algorithm to translate input data to the appropriate output by using a labeled dataset.
   2) *Unsupervised Learning:* In this kind of learning, the algorithm is given unlabeled data and is required to look for correlations or patterns without direct supervision.
   3) *Reinforcement learning:* The model picks up new skills via interacting with its surroundings and getting feedback through reward or penalty.

It can be concluded that machine learning is vital to the automation of various processes, be it for making predictions, extraction of insights from data, analysis tasks for business, detection of diseases, etc., all of which have a major positive impact on the development of technology in our everyday life.

3.2 Algorithms used

For this study, seven machine learning algorithms were used namely Decision Tree (DT), Random Forest (RF), Logistic Regression (LR), K-Nearest Neighbor (KNN), Support Vector Machine (SVM), Gaussian Naive Bayes (GNB), Adaptive Boosting (AdaBoost), and Extreme Gradient Boosting (XGBoost) classifiers.

1. **Decision Tree:** A decision tree is a machine-learning technique that arranges data into a structure resembling a tree. Every internal node in the tree symbolizes a choice made based on a certain attribute, every branch denotes the decision's result, and every leaf node offers the final value or prediction. The objective of the approach is to minimize entropy and maximize information gain in classification tasks or reduce variance in regression tasks by recursively splitting the dataset based on the most useful features. Decision trees are well-known for being easy to understand, straightforward, and useful for managing both

category and numerical data. They may, however, be prone to overfitting, therefore pruning and ensemble approaches, such as Random Forests, are frequently used to improve their resilience and generalization capabilities.

2. **Random Forest:** It is an ensemble learning approach that combines the predictions of several decision trees to increase the overall robustness and accuracy of the model. A bootstrap sample of the training data and a random subset of the characteristics are used to build each decision tree in the forest. The individual tree projections are combined during prediction either by average (for regression) or voting (for classification). Randomness in data sampling and feature selection reduces overfitting and improves the model's performance in generalizing to new data. This is because of their great predictive performance, ability to handle big and complicated datasets, and resistance to overfitting, Random Forests are commonly employed for classification and regression applications.

3. **Logistic Regression:** It is a statistical technique and kind of regression analysis for estimating the likelihood of an event happening. It can also be used for binary classification. The logistic regression model converts a linear combination of input characteristics into a probability score between 0 and 1 using the sigmoid function. The link between the independent variables and the log odds of the dependent variable falling into a certain class is estimated by the model. The model's parameters are optimized using methods such as maximum likelihood estimation. Because of its ease of use, interpretability, and efficiency in capturing the likelihood of binary outcomes, logistic regression is extensively employed in a variety of sectors, including the social sciences, health, and finance.

4. **K-Nearest Neighbor:** It is a simple machine-learning technique that is utilized for tasks like item classification and outcome prediction. Visualize a graph with data points - what KNN does is that it operates by determining whose neighbors are closest to a place of interest and predicting values based on those neighbors. "K" stands for the number of neighbors taken into account. For example, if K=3, it examines the three closest neighbors. The predominant class is taken into account while classifying them. KNN in regression involves averaging the values. KNN is simple to understand but can become slower when dealing with large amounts of data since it makes no assumptions about the type or shape of the input.

5. **Support Vector Machine:** It is a powerful machine-learning approach used for classification and regression problems. It operates by determining which hyperplane in a high-dimensional space best divides data points belonging to distinct classes. The data points that are closest to the decision border are known as "support vectors". When classifying data, Support Vector Machines

(SVM) maximize the distance between support vectors of distinct classes to find the best margin. Using a kernel approach, SVM can map data into a higher-dimensional space for non-linear issues. SVM is often used in text classification, picture recognition, and other fields because it works well with complicated connections in data.

6. **Gaussian Naive Bayes:** It is a probabilistic machine learning approach for classification problems. It assumes that characteristics are regularly distributed among each class. It is known to work especially well with numerical data. This algorithm utilizes the Bayes theorem, which assumes feature independence and computes the probability of a class given a collection of characteristics. Gaussian Naive Bayes works effectively in a variety of applications, including spam filtering and natural language processing, despite the "naive" assumption of independence. Compared to more intricate algorithms, it uses less training data and is computationally efficient.

7. **Adaptive Boosting:** It is an ensemble learning technique used for classification problems. To build a powerful, precise model, AdaBoost aggregates the predictions of several weak learners or models that outperform random guessing by a small margin. AdaBoost gives weights to incorrectly categorized data points in each iteration, so that subsequently weak learners concentrate more on correctly categorizing those points. Each weak learner prediction is combined in a weighted manner to get the final prediction. AdaBoost is resistant to overfitting and especially good at enhancing the performance of weak models. Applications for it include text categorization, face identification, and a host of other areas where reliable and precise classification is essential.

8. **Extreme Gradient Boosting:** It is a sophisticated and incredibly effective machine learning technique. Extreme Gradient Boosting (XGBoost) is renowned for its quickness and effectiveness in classification and regression applications. It is a gradient-boosting extension that makes use of many decision trees as base learners. This algorithm adds weak learners repeatedly and modifies their weights in an attempt to minimize the cost function. Because of its precisness and efficient usage of computational resources it has become quite popular within the machine learning and data science community.

3.3 Preparation of the Hybrid Model

In machine learning, hybrid models are those that combine many algorithms or methods to improve overall performance and tackle particular problems. These models frequently take advantage of several methods to improve generalization, accuracy, and resilience. A hybrid model, for instance, may incorporate deep learning approaches with conventional statistical methods or decision trees with neural

Figure 1. Proposed architecture for evaluation

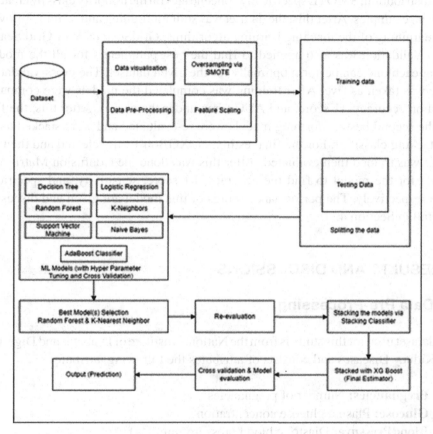

networks. The intention is to build a more potent and adaptable model by using the complimentary qualities of each constituent part. In settings with complicated and varied data, where a single algorithm might not work well in every situation, hybrid models are frequently employed. In this study, a hybrid model was prepared using the best-performing models (i.e., RF and KNN) and then stacked using the stacking classifier and XGBoost was selected as the final estimator. The proposed architecture of the following approach is shown in Figure 1.

As shown in Figure 1, for this study a diabetes dataset was taken and initial steps like data exploration, data preparation, etc were done. There was also an imbalance in the data, as one of the classes had a higher number of samples compared to the other, and as such data augmentation was applied. This was done via the usage of the SMOTE which stands for Synthetic Minority Over-sampling Technique. It is a machine learning strategy for dealing with imbalanced datasets, which are datasets in which one class is underrepresented in comparison to another. To equalize the

7

class distribution, SMOTE specifically concentrates on the minority class by creating artificial examples. After this, the dataset was split for training and testing, followed by the training of the machine learning algorithms. GridSearchCV or Grid Search Cross Validation was also applied to find the best parameters for all the models so that each one can perform optimally for the given dataset. The cross-validation value was taken as five. After training was completed the models were compared based on accuracy, f1 score, and AUC (area under the curve). After this, the first and the second best-performing models were re-evaluated and were stacked using the stacking classifier. For the final estimator, XGBoost was selected and then the model was trained then evaluated. After this was done the Confusion Matrix was plotted for the model to find the accuracy, F1 score, sensitivity, and specificity score respectively. The performance scores of this model are given and discussed in detail in Section 4.

4. RESULTS AND DISCUSSIONS

4.1 Data Pre-Processing

The dataset used for this study is from the National Institute of Diabetes and Digestive and Kidney Diseases and consists of attributes the following attributes.

1. **Pregnancies:** Number of pregnancies
2. **Glucose:** Plasma glucose concentration
3. **BloodPressure:** Diastolic blood pressure (mm Hg)
4. **SkinThickness:** Triceps skin fold thickness (mm)
5. **Insulin:** Serum insulin (mu U/ml)
6. **BMI:** Body mass index (weight in kg/(height in m)^2)
7. **DiabetesPedigreeFunction:** function
8. **Age:** Age in years
9. **Outcome:** Class variable (0 or 1)

Initially, exploratory data analysis was performed, and a histogram was plotted to visualize the data and see the trends in it, as well as to check outliers and also to get a grasp of the central tendency. After this, the heatmap was plotted to see the correlation between different variables. As seen in Figure 2. There is no significant correlation between the different variables. Due to a lesser number of independent variables, feature selection was not applied. The dataset didn't contain any missing values, however, there were inconsistencies in it, and as such the StandardScaler method was used to scale the values. StandardScaler is a machine learning preprocessing

Figure 2. Heatmap of the used dataset

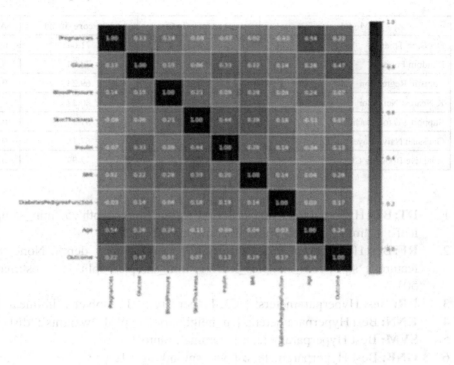

approach that helps to standardize a dataset's characteristics. It changes the data so that the standard deviation is one and the mean is zero for each characteristic. To center and scale the data, a transformation is used after determining the mean and standard deviation for every feature. StandardScaler is very helpful for ensuring that every feature contributes evenly to the model when dealing with algorithms that are sensitive to the scale of input features. It's a component of the Python sci-kit-learn toolkit that is used to boost the efficiency and performance of several machine-learning algorithms.

After this data augmentation via the SMOTE library was applied to balance the data of each class. After this, the machine learning algorithms were deployed.

4.2 Deployed Machine Learning Algorithms

As mentioned earlier seven different machine learning algorithms were deployed and for each model hyperparameter tuning with cross-validation was applied to find the best hyperparameter and to prevent problems like overfitting and underfitting. The ROC (Reciever Operating Characteristic) Curve as well as the AUC curve was plotted. The best hyperparameters obtained for each model are as follows:

Table 1. Performance of the algorithms

Model	Accuracy (in %)	F1 Score (in %)	AUC
Decision Tree	74.67	71.64	0.848
Random Forest	79.33	77.04	0.879
Logistic Regression	73.33	69.23	0.821
K-Nearest Neighbor	80.66	80.27	0.902
Support Vector Machine	74.00	57.14	0.870
Gaussian Naive Bayes	72.00	67.18	0.801
Adaptive Boosting Classifier	75.33	72.99	0.839

1. **DT:** Best Hyperparameters: { 'criterion': 'gini', 'max_depth': 5, 'min_samples_ leaf': 4, 'min_samples_split': 10, 'splitter': 'best' }
2. **RF:** Best Hyperparameters: { 'criterion': 'entropy', 'max_depth': None, 'max_ features': 'sqrt', 'min_samples_leaf': 1, 'min_samples_split': 2, 'n_estimators': 50}
3. **LR:** Best Hyperparameters: { 'C': 1, 'penalty': 'l1', 'solver': 'liblinear' }
4. **KNN:** Best Hyperparameters: { 'n_neighbors': 9, 'p': 1, 'weights': 'distance' }
5. **SVM:** Best Hyperparameters: { 'gamma': 'auto' }
6. **GNB:** Best Hyperparameters: { 'var_smoothing': 1e-05}
7. **AdaBoost:** Best Hyperparameters: { 'learning_rate': 0.1, 'n_estimators': 100}

After this, the models were re-evaluated after fitting them with the best parameters, and the following scores were obtained for each model (please refer to Table 1).

After this, a graph was plotted to show the difference in the scores graphically. The graph plotted is shown in Figure 3. The models with the highest accuracy were re-trained and the predicted values were obtained.

After re-deployment, a slight change in the F1 score was observed in both RF and KNN. The scores of both the models for training and testing are shown in Table 2.

As seen in Table 2 there is a significant difference in the training and testing accuracy for both models. This is a sign of "overfitting". A model that learns the training data too well, collecting characteristics and noise unique to that dataset but does not perform well with fresh, unobserved data, is termed as overfitting. This issue, in our case, arises due to the small size of the dataset. For the next step, we shall deploy a hybrid model and evaluate its performance.

Figure 3. Comparison of different classification algorithms

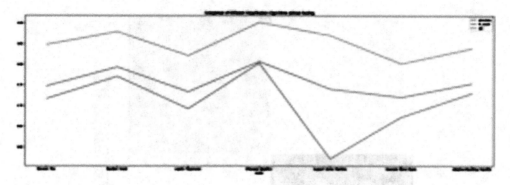

4.3 Deployed Hybrid Model

As mentioned in the earlier section, the hybrid model deployed is a combination of RF, KNN, and XGBoost where the RF and KNN are the initial estimators and XGBoost is the final estimator. K-fold cross-validation was also applied to this model to reduce data leakage, enhancing generalization as well as preventing underfitting and overfitting. The stacking classifier was used to combine the three models. It is an ensemble machine learning model that combines the results of many basic classifiers to enhance predictive performance overall. In contrast to more conventional ensemble techniques like bagging and boosting, stacking entails teaching a meta-model, also known as a higher-level classifier, how to aggregate the predictions made by the base classifiers. The stacked model was then trained and the following scores were obtained. The observed readings are given in Table 3.

Table 2. Training and testing accuracy of RF and KNN

Model Name	Training Accuracy (in %)	Testing Accuracy (in %)	F1 Score (in %)
RF	93.76	79.33	79.44
KNN	100	80.67	80.71

Table 3. Training and testing accuracy of hybrid model

	Accuracy (in %)	F1 Score (in %)
Training	77.53	77.51
Testing	78.67	78.75

Figure 4. Confusion matrix of the hybrid model

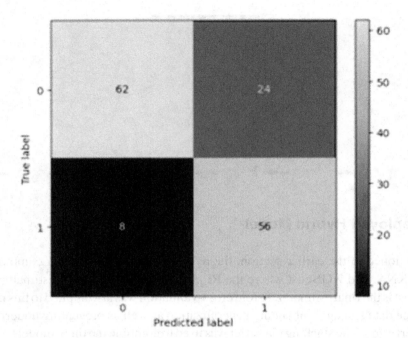

As seen from the above observation, even if there was no significant improvement in accuracy as compared to the individual classifiers, the performance of the hybrid model is significantly better due to very low accuracy between training and testing. This shows that the hybrid models are significantly better than individual classifiers as they are not very susceptible to underfitting and overfitting. Following this, the confusion matrix was also plotted and is shown in Figure 4.

From Figure 4, we can conclude that the number of True Positives obtained is 62, the number of False Positives is 24, the number of False Negative is 8 and the number of True Negative obtained is 56. These scores can also be used to evaluate the model by using the following formulae:

Accuracy = (TP + TN) / (TP + TN + FP + FN) (1)

Precision = TP / (TP + FP) (2)

Sensitivity = TP / (TP + FN) (3)

$$\text{Specificity} = TN / (TN + FP) \qquad\qquad (4)$$

For this study, the scores obtained are 0.787, 0.70, 0.875, and 0.721 for accuracy, precision, sensitivity, and specificity respectively.

5. CONCLUSION AND FUTURE PROSPECTS

This study is focused on the deployment of hybrid models and their potential implications in the field of medical science. The proposed architecture can also be re-deployed using different datasets and then tested to further expand the scope of utilization of hybrid models as well as to expand our understanding of the behavior of these models in contrast to other datasets.

As seen in this study, hybrid models are not prone to the problems the traditional machine learning algorithms face. The hybrid model showed a high degree of resilience towards underfitting and overfitting, which was found to be a prominent problem in traditional machine learning algorithms which resulted in a very high training accuracy but a relatively low testing accuracy. From this, it can be concluded that hybrid models can generalize the data more efficiently as well as are far more efficient in adapting to different data characteristics.

This study can be further expanded by using a larger dataset and integrating other advanced models, or by adding multiple estimators. Moreover, deep learning algorithms can also be incorporated with traditional machine learning algorithms. However, the dataset while using deep learning algorithms should be significantly larger as deep learning models perform much better when the provided dataset is huge. In this study, deep learning algorithms were not used due to the usage of a small dataset. It is also known that machine learning algorithms are much better at giving predictions when the dataset is small and as such they were used for this study.

REFERENCES

Al-Zebari, A., & Sengur, A. (2019, November). Performance comparison of machine learning techniques on diabetes disease detection. In *2019 1st International Informatics and software engineering conference (UBMYK)* (pp. 1-4). IEEE. 10.1109/ UBMYK48245.2019.8965542

Bhat, S. S., Selvam, V., Ansari, G. A., & Ansari, M. D. (2022). *Analysis of Diabetes mellitus using Machine Learning Techniques.* 2022 5th International Conference on Multimedia, Signal Processing and Communication Technologies (IMPACT), Aligarh, India. 10.1109/IMPACT55510.2022.10029058

Charitha, C., & Chaitrasree, A. Devi, Varma, P. C. & Lakshmi, C. (2022). *Type-II Diabetes Prediction Using Machine Learning Algorithms.* 2022 International Conference on Computer Communication and Informatics (ICCCI), Coimbatore, India. 10.1109/ICCCI54379.2022.9740844

Farajollahi, B., Mehmannavaz, M., Mehrjoo, H., Moghbeli, F., & Sayadi, M. (2021). Diabetes Diagnosis Using Machine Learning. *Frontiers in Health Informatics.*, *10*(1), 65. doi:10.30699/fhi.v10i1.267

Islam, M. T., Raihan, M., Aktar, N., Alam, M. S., Ema, R. R., & Islam, T. (2020). *Diabetes Mellitus Prediction using Different Ensemble Machine Learning Approaches.* 2020 11th International Conference on Computing, Communication and Networking Technologies (ICCCNT), Kharagpur, India. 10.1109/ICCCNT49239.2020.9225551

Islam, N. U., & Khanam, R. (2021). *Classification of Diabetes using Machine Learning. 2021 International Conference on Computational Performance Evaluation (ComPE)*, Shillong, India. 10.1109/ComPE53109.2021.9751955

Liu, Q., Zhang, M., Yifeng, H., Zhang, L., Zou, J., Yan, Y., & Guo, Y. (2022). Predicting the Risk of Incident Type 2 Diabetes Mellitus in Chinese Elderly Using Machine Learning Techniques. *Journal of Personalized Medicine, 12*(6), 905. doi:10.3390/jpm12060905 PMID:35743691

Mangal, A., & Jain, V. (2022). *Performance analysis of machine learning models for prediction of diabetes.* 2022 2nd International Conference on Innovative Sustainable Computational Technologies (CISCT), Dehradun, India. 10.1109/CISCT55310.2022.10046630

Mercaldo, F. (2017). Diabetes Mellitus Affected Patients Classification and Diagnosis through Machine Learning Techniques. *Procedia Computer Science, 112*, 2519-2528. .(https://www.sciencedirect.com/science/article/pii/S1877050917315880) doi:10.1016/j.procs.2017.08.193

Pankaj, C., Singh, K. V., & Singh, K. R. (2021). Artificial Intelligence enabled Web-Based Prediction of Diabetes using Machine Learning Approach. *2021 International Conference on Disruptive Technologies for Multi-Disciplinary Research and Applications (CENTCON)*, Bengaluru, India. 10.1109/CENTCON52345.2021.9688236

Rathi, B., & Madeira, F. (2023). Early Prediction of Diabetes Using Machine Learning Techniques. *2023 Global Conference on Wireless and Optical Technologies (GCWOT)*, Malaga, Spain. 10.1109/GCWOT57803.2023.10064682

S, G., Reddy, V. S., & Ahmed, M. R. (2023). Type 2 Diabetes Mellitus: Early Detection using Machine Learning Classification. *International Journal of Advanced Computer Science and Applications*, *14*(6). doi:10.14569/IJACSA.2023.01406127

Chapter 2
Addressing Challenges
in Data Analytics:
A Comprehensive Review
and Proposed Solutions

Lakshmi Haritha Medida
https://orcid.org/0000-0002-6400-8998
R.M.K. Engineering College, India

Kumar
https://orcid.org/0009-0001-4756-2241
BVC Institute of Technology and Science, India

ABSTRACT

Data analytics, in the context of big data, presents numerous challenges that organizations must overcome to harness the full potential of their data. Risk managers may face a number of obstacles in their efforts to gather and apply analytics. Fortunately, there is a solution. This chapter addresses some of the major problems with data analytics and the probable solutions. The main issues covered in this study are data volume, real-time analytics, data validation, poor data quality, lack of support, ambiguity, financial restrictions, talent scarcity, and security. It will need a holistic strategy that includes strategic planning, modern technology, and cooperative efforts to address these difficulties. Organizations must traverse these challenges to extract valuable insights and make educated choices from their data, from adopting scalable infrastructures for data processing to developing a competent staff and putting in place strong security measures.

DOI: 10.4018/979-8-3693-2260-4.ch002

1. INTRODUCTION

1.1 Big Data

The widespread use of technology and networked systems in the digital age has resulted in an unprecedented amount of data, which is changing how businesses function and make decisions (*Leadership Challenges in the Digital Age: Navigating Disruption - The Economic Times*, n.d.). Big Data, the term for this era of abundant data, goes beyond typical data processing skills and presents a plethora of potential as well as obstacles. Big Data is the umbrella term for enormous and varied datasets that are larger and more varied than traditional databases. This creates new opportunities for innovation, insight creation, and business transformation.

Volume, Velocity, and Variety are the three Vs that define big data as depicted in figure 1. Every day, enormous amounts of data are produced, including data from sensors, social media, and transaction records, among other sources. The extraordinary rate of data production necessitates real-time processing and analytical capabilities. Additionally, the range of data kinds—both structured and unstructured—presents a complex environment that calls for sophisticated tools and methods for insightful analysis (Elgendy & Elragal, 2014). Big Data frequently encompasses more dimensions than just the three Vs, such as value (the possible insights gained) and veracity (data correctness).

Big Data is now a driving force behind innovation, giving businesses in a variety of industries the ability to streamline operations, make wise decisions, and obtain a competitive advantage. In the corporate world, it powers data-driven strategy, predictive analytics, and tailored consumer experiences. Big Data in healthcare helps with individualized therapies and illness prediction. It helps create smart cities in the field of urban planning. Big Data is having a significant social influence on fields including science, education, and public policy, influencing the direction of a future that is increasingly data-driven.

Big Data has unique properties that demand advanced tools and frameworks to handle in order to fully realize its potential. Distributed computing frameworks such as Apache Spark and Hadoop allow massive datasets to be processed over computer clusters. Scalable storage options for a variety of data kinds are offered by NoSQL databases. Complex datasets may be analyzed with the help of advanced analytics tools and machine learning algorithms, and cloud computing platforms provide scalable and reasonably priced resources for Big Data processing.

Despite the enormous potential of big data (Hariri et al., 2019), companies still have to deal with issues including data security, privacy, and the shortage of qualified personnel. Navigating these obstacles offers chances for creativity, better decision-making, and the creation of sustainable data strategies as the environment

Figure 1. Three Vs of big data
(3 V's of Big Data - CopyAssignment, n.d.)

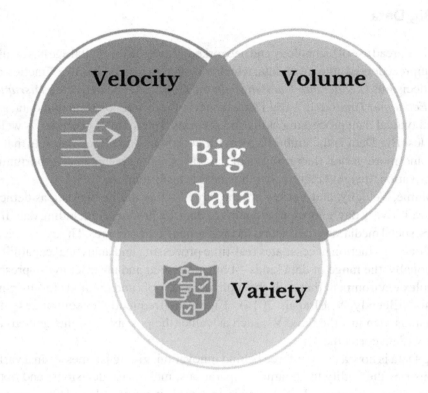

changes. An awareness of big data's revolutionary potential, a strategic approach to harnessing its capabilities for the benefit of organizations and society at large, and a comprehensive grasp of its aspects are all necessary for navigating the world of big data (*Unveiling The Future Of Big Data: Insights And Innovations – Avenga*, n.d.).

1.2 Unlocking the Potential of Big Data Analytics

In the Big Data age, enterprises must deal with an unparalleled amount of data created from many sources, including social media platforms, IoT devices, and networked systems. Organizations must overcome a distinct set of problems posed by this data explosion in order to fully realize the promise of data analytics and derive valuable insights. In-depth discussions of issues such as data validation, poor data quality, inadequate support, ambiguity, budgetary restraints, talent scarcity, and security concerns are included in this paper's examination of the complex problems that businesses encounter when implementing data analytics.

The capability of conventional data processing and storage infrastructures has been overtaken by the exponential development in the volume of data created. The proliferation of data has compelled enterprises to use scalable technologies and techniques in order to maintain the efficacy and efficiency of their analytics operations. In a setting where making decisions quickly is crucial, real-time analytics become essential. In order to analyze data in real-time and enable enterprises to react quickly to changing market circumstances and developing trends, sophisticated tools and technologies must be able to handle and understand data streams with agility.

Organizations must contend with the difficulties of verifying and guaranteeing the accuracy of their datasets, making data quality a fundamental problem in the analytics environment. Navigating and using the potential of data analytics is made more difficult by inadequate support, which includes a lack of qualified personnel and the requirement for tools that are easy to use. For efforts and expectations to be aligned across organizational levels, ambiguity in analytics targets and outcomes need a solid strategic vision and communication. The quest for efficient data analytics is made more difficult by financial limitations and a lack of skilled workers, which calls for the smart allocation of resources and ongoing skill-building programs.

The data analytics environment is further complicated by security issues. Big Data volumes' sheer size presents security difficulties, such as the requirement for real-time security analytics, data privacy concerns, and safeguards against the generation of fraudulent data. A recent report from Dun & Bradstreet revealed that businesses have the most trouble with the following three areas: protecting data privacy (34%), ensuring data accuracy (26%), and processing & analyzing data (24%) (*Data Management Study: The Past, Present, and Future of Data*, n.d.). A comprehensive and flexible strategy is necessary to effectively manage the complexities of data analytics as companies look for answers to these problems (Tsai et al., 2015). We go into each of these issues in detail in the sections that follow, offering tactics and solutions that will enable businesses to fully utilize data analytics in the constantly changing Big Data environment.

2. ADDRESSING THE CHALLENGES

2.1 The Volume of Data Being Gathered

The massive amount of data being created and gathered is one of the biggest obstacles that businesses confront in the ever-changing field of data analytics. The introduction of contemporary technology, including social media platforms, networked systems, and the Internet of Things (IoT), has resulted in an unparalleled surge in the quantity of data accessible for examination. For companies and data specialists trying to glean valuable insights from this enormous amount of data, this exponential expansion presents a formidable obstacle.

The traditional infrastructures for data processing and storage are finding it difficult to keep up with the increasing volume of data (*10 Common Data Analysis Challenges Facing Businesses | Pathstream,* n.d.). The sheer volume of data created every day is frequently too much for traditional relational databases and storage systems to handle and analyze effectively. This has forced a paradigm change in data management techniques and prompted the use of cutting-edge technology such as cloud-based solutions and distributed computing. Large datasets may be handled by organizations with ease because to scalable and flexible structures, which also guarantee that analytical processes stay responsive and adaptable even as data quantities increase.

The problem of data volume necessitates a comprehensive solution that includes strong data governance procedures in addition to technology developments. Companies need to spend money on platforms and technologies that provide real-time analytics and processing so they can quickly extract actionable insights from huge amounts of data. Furthermore, by putting in place strong data governance frameworks, the risks connected with handling large datasets are reduced and data quality, security, and compliance are guaranteed. Businesses may harness the full potential of analytics for well-informed decision-making by transforming the data flood into a strategic asset and embracing scalable technology and robust governance procedures.

2.2 Gathering Relevant Facts in Real Time

It's challenging to sift through the abundance of data and find the insights that are most urgently required. Real-time insights are becoming more and more important in the field of data analytics for companies looking to maintain their competitive edge and adapt to changing market conditions. But obtaining pertinent information in real time is a difficult task, frequently due to the speed at which data is produced and the variety of sources from which it comes. The immediacy required by some industries, including banking, healthcare, and e-commerce, where quick decision-making is crucial, is beyond the capabilities of traditional batch processing methods.

Overworked staff members might not thoroughly examine data or might just concentrate on the measurements that are simplest to gather rather than those that actually provide value. It could also be hard for an employee to obtain real-time insights into what is going on if they have to manually go through data. Decision-making can be seriously harmed by outdated information.

In order to tackle the difficulty of obtaining pertinent information quickly, companies are resorting to sophisticated technologies and techniques. The paradigm known as "stream processing (Liu et al., 2016)," which enables ongoing analysis of data as it is produced, is becoming more and more popular. With the use of this method, businesses may quickly and intelligently make decisions by gaining insightful knowledge from data streams in almost real-time. Furthermore, edge computing integration has become essential since it enables data processing closer to the point of generation, decreasing latency and increasing the speed at which insights may be obtained.

The problem of gathering the relevant facts can be resolved with the use of a data system that gathers, organizes, and automatically notifies users of trends. Workers just generate a report with their objectives input and the answers to the questions that matter most to them. Making decisions is made easier for decision-makers with real-time information and notifications. Decision-makers may be sure that any decisions **There are no sources in the current document.**they make are based on reliable and comprehensive information with real-time reports and notifications.

Furthermore, a key component of real-time data analytics is the application of Machine Learning (ML) and Artificial Intelligence (AI) algorithms. With the help of these technologies, businesses can automatically recognize patterns, anomalies, and pertinent information from streaming data, giving them access to actionable insights right when they're required (Sarker, 2021). Businesses may meet the challenge of obtaining pertinent information in real-time and make well-informed decisions in the constantly changing field of data analytics by adopting these state-of-the-art technologies.

2.3 Data Validation

Up to 75% of firms think their customer contact records include erroneous data, according to an Experian survey (*Quality Data Proves Critical to Business Performance*, n.d.). In order to make sure that judgments are based on reliable information, data validation attempts to guarantee that data sets are comprehensive, correctly structured, and deduplicated.

Data validation is becoming a more significant difficulty in the world of big data and complicated datasets. It is challenging to ensure the accuracy of the data due to the sheer amount and diversity of data sources, which can result in errors that have a substantial influence on the conclusions drawn from analytical procedures. Validating data at scale is a challenge that many organizations face, particularly when integrating data from several systems or handling real-time data streaming.

Regretfully, the process of validating data may be somewhat time-consuming, especially when done by hand. Furthermore, data may be low-quality, obsolete, or compartmentalized. As a result, if firms don't address quality concerns, all analytics efforts are either worthless or deliberately detrimental to the company's bottom line.

Open-source platforms and scripting are two methods for validating data. These call either corporate software, which can be costly, or prior expertise or coding experience. Organizations are using thorough data quality management techniques in order to meet the difficulty of data validation. This entails putting in place automated validation procedures that evaluate data at different points in time, from input to storage and analysis. Automated validation systems can identify any problems before they jeopardize the accuracy of analytical data by looking for mistakes, inconsistencies, and outliers. A framework for validation may also be established by clearly defining data quality standards and processes, which guarantee that data meets predetermined requirements for relevance, correctness, and completeness.

Moreover, there is growing popularity in incorporating ML algorithms into data validation procedures. These algorithms' capacity to recognize and automatically correct mistakes is improved by their capacity to learn from patterns and anomalies in previous data. Organizations may address the challenging task of data validation in data analytics by utilizing a blend of automated technologies, strong quality standards, and clever algorithms. This approach will eventually promote trust in the precision and dependability of the insights obtained from the datasets.

2.4 Visual Data Representation

Data is frequently best presented graphically in the form of graphs or charts in order to be easily understood and effective. Even though these tools are really helpful, creating them by hand is challenging. It is annoying and time-consuming to have to gather data from several sources and enter it into a reporting tool.

Therefore, when it comes to conquering obstacles in the data analytics industry, visual data visualization is clearly very important. Presenting information in an easily comprehensible style is essential for efficient communication and understanding due to the increasing complexity and volume of data. Deciding what insights are useful to take away from traditional tabular reports and raw data can be difficult since they can be overwhelming. Quicker and more thorough comprehension of the information at hand is made possible by visualizations, which include charts, graphs, and dashboards. They provide complicated data correlations, trends, and patterns in an elegant manner.

Report creation is made possible with the push of a mouse by robust data systems. Decision-makers and staff will have easy access to the current information they require in an engaging and instructive manner. Enterprises are spending more in sophisticated visualization tools and technology to overcome the problems with visual data display. With the use of these tools, users may create dynamic and interactive visualizations that allow them to study and engage with data in real time. Furthermore, the fusion of virtual and augmented reality technologies is expanding the possibilities for data visualization by providing immersive experiences that improve the understanding of complex information.

In addition, there's a growing trend in data visualization that uses narrative tactics. Visualizations may use narratives to emphasize important findings, give background information, and lead viewers through the data story. This narrative technique helps to communicate the relevance of discoveries to a wider audience while also making statistics more interesting. Organizations may build a data-driven culture that empowers decision-makers at all levels of the business by prioritizing visual data representation as a means of bridging the gap between complicated statistics and actionable insights.

2.5 Information From Numerous Sources

Because data streams are various and sometimes divergent, handling information from several sources is a ubiquitous difficulty in the field of data analytics (Luan et al., 2020). Organizations today get data from a wide range of sources, such as external APIs, social media platforms, internal databases, Internet of Things devices, and more. Creating a coherent and unified dataset for analysis is difficult due to the complexity of data integration, standardization, and normalization brought about by the variety of data sources. Consequently, enterprises have challenges in deriving significant insights from data that may exhibit irregularities in terms of style, structure, or quality.

Developing strong data integration solutions is necessary to tackle the problem of information from several sources. Platforms and tools for integration assist in combining data from several sources and converting it into a format that is compatible with and useful for analysis. Adoption of technologies such as data integration platforms and Extract, Transform, Load (ETL) procedures allows information to move seamlessly between systems, giving companies a more unified and complete picture of their data.

An all-inclusive, centralized system will provide staff with access to all kinds of data in one place. This not only reduces the time spent navigating between sources, but it also enables cross-comparisons and guarantees completeness of data. Furthermore, developments in federated querying and data virtualization are crucial in overcoming the difficulties posed by a variety of data sources. These technologies eliminate the need for significant data transfer or consolidation by enabling enterprises to query and analyze data in real-time. Organizations may effectively manage the intricacies of data from several sources by adopting a comprehensive strategy to data integration and utilizing cutting-edge technology. This facilitates the development of more precise and perceptive data analytics.

2.6 Inadequate or Unstructured Data

The process of gathering, storing, organizing, and managing information from diverse data sources is referred to as data management. The data sets originate from a variety of sources, including as customer evaluations, Twitter, and Internet of Things (IoT) data, and they can be either organized or unstructured.

If data is not freely available to those who require it, consolidating it into a single system will not have much of an impact. Even when they are working remotely, decision-makers and risk managers want access to all of the organization's data in order to get insight into what is going on at any given time. Information access ought to be the most straightforward aspect of data analytics.

One major obstacle in the field of data analytics is the existence of incomplete or unstructured data, which makes it more difficult for enterprises to extract valuable insights from their datasets. It might be difficult to draw trustworthy conclusions or make wise judgments when there is insufficient data available since it may be incomplete, inaccurate, or irrelevant. Conversely, unstructured data—text, photos, and videos, for example—does not follow the conventions of relational databases, which makes analysis more difficult and restricts the use of typical analytical methods.

Unstructured data offers a chance to gather deep insights that can paint a whole picture of your clients and explain why sales are declining or expenses are rising. The issue is that processing unstructured data at high speeds and quantities results in a lot of fantastic information being collected, but it also creates a lot of noise, which can mask the insights that are most valuable to your company.

By taking care of these, you may avoid Big Data problems:

- Which data must be combined?
- How many data silos must be linked together?
- What knowledge do you hope to acquire?

All these problems will be resolved with an efficient database. Authorized staff members will have secure remote access to examine or alter data, facilitating quick decision-making and illuminating organizational changes.

Advances in data preparation techniques are being utilized by businesses to tackle the problems posed by incomplete or unorganized data. By finding and fixing mistakes, adding missing variables, and standardizing formats, data cleansing and enrichment procedures are used to raise the quality of subpar data. Furthermore, computer vision and natural language processing (NLP) technologies are essential for obtaining useful information from unstructured data. These technologies let businesses integrate a variety of data formats into their analytical workflows by enabling the analysis of text, picture recognition, and video processing.

Moreover, the application of ML algorithms may assist firms in deriving insights from incomplete or unstructured datasets, especially when it comes to predictive modeling and categorization. Despite the difficulties caused by incomplete or unstructured data, these algorithms may identify patterns and correlations in the data, enabling the generation of insightful predictions and classifications. By putting these tactics into practice, businesses may unleash the hidden potential in their data, transforming seemingly difficult datasets into priceless resources for well-informed data analytics decision-making.

2.7 Inferior Data Quality

Nothing is more detrimental to data analytics than data that is not correct. Reliability is compromised in output if input is subpar. Human mistake during data input is a major contributor to erroneous data. If the analysis is applied to decision-making, this might have serious adverse effects. Asymmetrical data is another problem, when information in one system is out of date because it does not reflect changes made in another system (Leonard et al., 2013).

So, poor data quality is a prevalent issue in the field of data analytics that can have a substantial influence on the dependability and credibility of analytical results. Multiple duplications, missing values, inconsistencies, and errors are some of the ways that poor data quality can appear. These problems may surface throughout the procedures of gathering, integrating, or storing data, which might result in inaccurate assessments and poor decision-making. For companies looking to fully utilize their data assets, addressing the issue of poor data quality is essential.

These problems are eliminated with a centralized system. With obligatory or drop-down fields, data entry may be done automatically, reducing the possibility of human error. System integrations make sure that modifications made in one place are immediately reflected everywhere.

Organizations are putting comprehensive data quality management frameworks into place to fight poor data quality. These frameworks cover a wide range of tasks, including validation and enrichment as well as data cleansing and profiling. To guarantee that the data satisfies predetermined quality requirements, automated techniques and algorithms are utilized to detect and correct problems. Creating data governance procedures is also essential for preserving and improving data quality over time. Establishing unambiguous standards, regulations, and data ownership may help businesses cultivate a culture of accountability and responsibility for data quality.

Working together, IT and business stakeholders can effectively solve poor data quality. Business users frequently have important domain expertise that may help find and fix problems with data quality. Establishing data quality measures and ongoing monitoring through close collaboration makes it possible to guarantee that data is correct, consistent, and suitable for analysis. Organizations may establish a strong basis for dependable and significant decision-making by making data quality a top priority in their data analytics endeavors.

2.8 Insufficient Assistance

When an organization lacks the knowledge, experience, or resources to successfully manage the intricacies of data-driven projects, it might encounter difficulties with data analytics. This is known as inadequate help. Data analytics is a multidisciplinary profession that requires proficiency in data engineering, statistics, programming, and domain knowledge. Analytics initiatives may be hampered by a lack of qualified personnel with the know-how to analyze and draw conclusions from data. Organizations could also have trouble locating the infrastructure, technology, or tools required to support their data analytics initiatives.

Without organizational support from both upper management and lower level staff, data analytics cannot be effectively implemented. In many endeavors, risk managers will be helpless if leaders deny them the authority to take action. Other staff members are crucial as well; without their data submission for analysis or without their systems being inaccessible to the risk manager, it will be difficult to provide any useful information.

To overcome this obstacle, stress the importance of risk management and analysis to every part of the company. Other team members are more willing to collaborate if they are aware of the advantages. Change implementation can be challenging, but risk managers can successfully gain buy-in from a variety of stakeholders by communicating outcomes with ease and utilizing a centralized data analysis system.

Organizations are investing in talent development and training initiatives to cultivate a talented workforce in response to the dilemma of inadequate help. Investing in the upskilling of current staff members or employing data analytics specialists guarantees that companies have the manpower needed to handle and evaluate their data. Participating in industry-specific training programs and working with educational institutions can help close the skills gap and develop a pool of skilled data analysts.

Furthermore, the implementation of analytics tools and platforms that are easy to use is crucial in enabling non-technical stakeholders to extract insights from data. Business customers may now engage with data in a natural way thanks to self-service analytics solutions, which lessens the need for specialist data experts to handle everyday analytics activities. Furthermore, companies may obtain outside support by forming alliances with consultants or data analytics service providers that can give experience and direction in creating and executing successful data analytics plans. Through the implementation of talent development strategies, user-friendly solutions, and external collaborations, businesses may effectively tackle the issue of insufficient help and realize the full potential of their data analytics programs.

2.9 Ambiguity

Ambiguity, which refers to ambiguity or lack of clarity in the data itself as well as in the aims and objectives of the analytics projects, is a significant difficulty in the field of data analytics (Gupta et al., 2018). Because of conflicting definitions, different formats, or confusing labeling, data might be ambiguous, which makes it challenging to draw reliable conclusions. Ambiguity in organizational analytics goals can cause misdirected efforts since various stakeholders will perceive the same goals differently, which will negatively impact the effectiveness of data-driven projects as a whole.

Even if they are aware of the advantages of automation, users may experience anxiety or confusion while transferring from conventional data processing techniques. Nobody like change, particularly if it disturbs their comfort zone or usual routine.

It's critical to demonstrate how adjustments to analytics can simplify the position and make it more purposeful and satisfying in order to solve this HR issue. Employees may spend more time acting on insights by doing away with pointless processes like data collecting and report construction when they have access to complete data analytics.

Data ambiguity is a problem that must be solved by putting strict data governance procedures in place. A key component of ensuring consistency and clarity in the data being analyzed is the establishment of precise data definitions, metadata standards, and data quality measurements. Organizations must also make investments in comprehensive data documentation procedures that capture the context, data sources, and data transformations. Together with making the data easier to grasp, this documentation promotes knowledge sharing among team members.

Working together and communicating effectively become critical when handling ambiguity regarding analytics objectives. It is imperative for organizations to endeavor towards establishing a mutual comprehension among stakeholders about the objectives and anticipated results of data analytics endeavors. Frequent lines of communication, such as training courses, seminars, and feedback loops, can aid in goal clarification and expectation alignment. Organizations may effectively navigate through ambiguous circumstances and ensure that their data analytics activities are meaningful, focused, and in line with company goals by cultivating a culture of clarity and openness.

2.10 Budget

A key component of every data analytics project is budget management, and having insufficient funding may be quite difficult. Projects involving data analytics may have high upfront expenses for technology, infrastructure, hiring qualified staff, and continuing upkeep. The difficulty comes when companies have limited funds, making it difficult for them to invest in the equipment, personnel, and technology needed for efficient data analytics.

Organizations that have budgetary restrictions in data analytics should take a proactive approach to resource allocation. This entails setting investment priorities according to how they could affect business results. Identifying low-cost, high-impact projects can assist businesses in optimizing their resource allocation. For instance, cloud computing services offer an affordable substitute for conventional on-premises infrastructure, enabling businesses to increase resources as needed without having to make substantial upfront commitments.

Optimizing budget usage for data analytics also requires cooperation and cross-functional relationships. Organizations may make sure that financial allocations are in line with strategic objectives by encouraging collaboration across IT, finance, and business departments (*Artificial Intelligence, Machine Learning and Big Data in Finance - OECD,* n.d.). Furthermore, using community-driven resources and open-source technologies can be an affordable way to get access to strong analytics skills without having to make significant financial commitments. In order to optimize the effect of analytics projects within budgetary limits, tackling budget difficulties in data analytics ultimately involves a mix of strategic planning, prioritizing, and cooperative decision-making.

2.11 Talent Shortage

In the field of data analytics, where there is a constant need for qualified individuals but a dearth of supply, the talent gap is a major problem. People having a broad skill set, such as competence in statistical analysis, programming, data visualization, and domain-specific expertise, are needed for the complex nature of data analytics. The lack of people with this set of abilities might make it difficult for firms to use their data to its fullest. A shortage of talent is the reason why some firms have trouble with analysis. This is particularly valid for organizations without official risk departments. Workers can lack the skills or expertise necessary to do in-depth data analysis.

Organizations are investing in workforce development programs and upskilling activities in response to the skills shortage. Partnerships with academic institutions and internal training initiatives may support the development of current staff members and new hires, giving them the tools, they need to succeed in data analytics positions.

Organizations are also reassessing their hiring practices in an effort to find candidates who can provide fresh viewpoints to the sector and who have a wider range of skills or varied experiences.

Specifically addressing, two strategies are used to lessen this challenge: first, analytical ability is addressed throughout the employment process; second, an intuitive analysis system is used. While the second option will make the analytical process easier for everyone, the first alternative makes sure that talents are available. This kind of technology is accessible to all users, regardless of ability level.

PwC suggests the following possible remedies:

- Skill-based hiring as opposed to degree requirements
- Putting money into continuous training initiatives that link education to practical work experience
- Collaborating with other organizations and academic establishments to develop a varied pool of applicants
- Creating mentoring initiatives
- Investigating novel approaches to cultivate current talent, such as MOOCs (Massive Online Open Courses), boot camps, and certificate programs.

Another tactic to address the skills gap is collaboration with outside partners, like as consultants or service providers for data analytics. Through these collaborations, businesses may quickly cover talent gaps and obtain useful insights for particular initiatives by gaining access to specialized knowledge. Moreover, ordinary analytical work may be completed by non-experts by utilizing modern analytics tools with user-friendly interfaces, which lessens the need for a limited number of highly qualified individuals. Through the implementation of a multifaceted approach that includes talent development, strategic recruiting, and external collaborations, firms may effectively address the talent shortage in the data analytics field and cultivate a skilled and diverse workforce.

2.12 Analyzing Data at Scale

When a company expands and the amount of data it collects increases, analytics can be challenging to scale. Information gathering and report creation get more and more complicated. In the field of data analytics, analyzing data at scale is a crucial problem, especially since the amount, velocity, and diversity of data keep growing exponentially. Large datasets are frequently difficult for traditional data processing methods to handle effectively, which causes processing times to increase and performance bottlenecks. To handle this problem, the organization needs a system that can expand with it. Scalable analytics solutions are necessary as firms gather enormous volumes of data from many sources in order to quickly extract actionable insights.

Even though it could take some time to overcome these obstacles, data analysis has several advantages that make the effort worthwhile. Make immediate improvements to your company and think about purchasing a data analytics solution. Organizations are resorting to distributed computing architectures and cutting-edge technology to tackle the problem of large-scale data analysis. Organizations may split data processing operations over numerous nodes or clusters thanks to the scalable and parallel processing capabilities of big data frameworks like Apache Hadoop and Spark. By enabling enterprises to dynamically expand resources in response to demand, cloud-based solutions further improve scalability and guarantee peak analytical workload performance.

Additionally, businesses are looking at how specialist hardware, including Field-Programmable Gate Arrays (FPGAs) and Graphics Processing Units (GPUs), may speed up data analytics processes. By dramatically reducing processing times for intricate analytical algorithms, these hardware accelerators let businesses examine massive information more effectively. Organizations may overcome the difficulties of analyzing data at scale and maintain the agility and responsiveness of data analytics operations to the needs of contemporary, data-intensive settings by adopting scalable technologies and architectures.

2.13 Security

Big Data volumes' sheer scale creates a number of significant security hurdles, such as the requirement for real-time security analytics, data privacy concerns, and the creation of false data. When working with large data sets, tracing the provenance of data becomes challenging without the proper infrastructure. This makes figuring out where a data leak originated extremely difficult.

The application of real-time security analytics is necessary to address security issues in the context of big data. Large data volumes necessitate sophisticated analytics skills that can quickly identify and address security issues. Organizations may continually monitor data streams, spot abnormalities, and proactively mitigate possible security breaches by utilizing machine learning algorithms and artificial intelligence. The capacity to protect sensitive data and preserve the integrity of big datasets is improved by this proactive approach.

Data Privacy Concerns: Given the growing emphasis on data privacy laws,

There are no sources in the current document.businesses need to deal with the difficulties of safeguarding private data in big databases (Sutikno et al., 2014). Strong data encryption techniques should be used to protect data from unwanted access, both while it's in transit and when it's at rest. Organizations must also set up and implement stringent access controls to guarantee that only those with the proper authorization may see and modify sensitive data. To further improve data privacy efforts and make sure security measures stay in line with changing regulatory standards, regular audits and compliance checks can be conducted.

False Data Creation: One particular difficulty in Big Data security is the possibility of creating misleading data. Large datasets may be manipulated or tainted with misleading information by malicious actors, which might compromise decision-making processes and result in erroneous analysis. In order to identify and lessen the effects of erroneous data, data integrity checks and validation procedures must be put in place. By offering a decentralized and impenetrable ledger, blockchain technology may also improve data validity and dependability, giving enterprises confidence in the data they rely for crucial analytics.

Tracing Data Provenance: Large datasets make it more difficult to trace the origins of data, which makes determining the source of a data breach difficult. Putting in place the right architecture for data lineage tracking is essential to comprehending the flow of data across the systems of a business. This entails creating a thorough audit trail, logging data alterations, and gathering metadata. Organizations may improve their capacity to trace data moves, investigate security events, and find possible vulnerabilities more successfully with a well-implemented data provenance system.

Remote keeping: Organizations that use off-site data management services from outside vendors have data control security issues. There is still a chance of security breaches even if these services frequently use high-level security procedures. Organizations should think about installing their own cloud encryption keys to reduce this risk, since this would provide them more control over data access and guarantee an extra degree of security for sensitive data kept offsite.

Inadequate identity management: In the context of Big Data, improper credential management can result in complex audit trails and slow breach discovery. This is a serious security concern. Ensuring that people only have access to the information required for their tasks requires granular access control. By preventing unwanted access to vital data, identity and access management (IAM) systems that are strong can help enterprises enforce appropriate access rules, expedite audit trails, and improve overall security.

Human mistakes: Inaccuracies in implementation that occur while configuring new hardware might lead to vulnerabilities in Big Data security. Because different teams are not equally adept at safeguarding each endpoint, it is imperative to continue funding training and awareness initiatives. Standardized security standards and frequent security audits can boost the overall security posture by assisting in the detection and correction of any human mistakes.

IoT projects: The incorporation of IoT devices expands the possible attack surface with new endpoints and devices, posing new difficulties to Big Data security.

Hackers have several ways to enter the network because to the massive volumes of data produced by IoT devices and sensors. In order to reduce the security threats associated with these networked technologies, it is imperative that IoT devices be equipped with strong security mechanisms, such as device authentication, encryption, and frequent firmware upgrades. The robustness of Big Data security against changing cyber threats is further strengthened by ongoing monitoring and threat detection tailored to IoT contexts.

3. CONCLUSION

Organizations encounter a variety of issues in the ever-changing field of data analytics, many of which call for creative solutions. While real-time analytics demands the use of cutting-edge tools and cooperative methods, handling the volume of data calls for scalable technology and all-encompassing governance systems. Strategic hiring and upskilling programs are key components of attempts to address the skills shortage, while data validation and quality management are essential for guaranteeing the dependability of insights. Budgetary restrictions and ambiguity necessitate priority and clear communication, while security concerns require real-time analytics, strong encryption, and preventative steps against ever-evolving threats. A comprehensive and flexible strategy is essential for helping firms overcome these obstacles and realize the full value of data analytics in the Big Data age.

REFERENCES

Artificial Intelligence, Machine Learning and Big Data in Finance. (n.d.). OECD. https://www.oecd.org/finance/artificial-intelligence-machine-learning-big-data-in-finance.htm

Data Management Study: The Past, Present, and Future of Data. (n.d.). DNB. https://www.dnb.com/perspectives/master-data/data-management-report.html

Elgendy, N., & Elragal, A. (2014). Big data analytics: A literature review paper. Lecture Notes in Computer Science (Including Subseries Lecture Notes in Artificial Intelligence and Lecture Notes in Bioinformatics), 8557 LNAI, (pp. 214–227). Springer. doi:10.1007/978-3-319-08976-8_16

Gupta, A. K., Singhal, S., & Garg, R. R. (2018). Challenges and issues in data analytics. *Proceedings - 2018 8th International Conference on Communication Systems and Network Technologies, CSNT 2018*, (pp. 144–150). IEEE. 10.1109/CSNT.2018.8820251

Hariri, R. H., Fredericks, E. M., & Bowers, K. M. (2019). Uncertainty in big data analytics: Survey, opportunities, and challenges. *Journal of Big Data*, 6(1), 1–16. doi:10.1186/s40537-019-0206-3

Economic Times. (2023). Leadership Challenges in the Digital Age: Navigating Disruption. *The Economic Times*. https://economictimes.indiatimes.com/jobs/c-suite/leadership-challenges-in-the-digital-age-navigating-disruption/articleshow/104625059.cms?from=mdr

Leonard, D. K., Bloom, G., Hanson, K., O'Farrell, J., & Spicer, N. (2013). Institutional Solutions to the Asymmetric Information Problem in Health and Development Services for the Poor. *World Development*, 48, 71–87. doi:10.1016/j.worlddev.2013.04.003

Liu, X., Dastjerdi, A. V., & Buyya, R. (2016). Stream processing in IoT: Foundations, state-of-the-art, and future directions. *Internet of Things: Principles and Paradigms*, 145–161. doi:10.1016/B978-0-12-805395-9.00008-3

Luan, H., Geczy, P., Lai, H., Gobert, J., Yang, S. J. H., Ogata, H., Baltes, J., Guerra, R., Li, P., & Tsai, C. C. (2020). Challenges and Future Directions of Big Data and Artificial Intelligence in Education. *Frontiers in Psychology*, 11, 580820. doi:10.3389/fpsyg.2020.580820 PMID:33192896

Quality data proves critical to business performance. (n.d.). Experianplc. https://www.experianplc.com/newsroom/press-releases/2022/quality-data-proves-critical-to-business-performance

Sarker, I. H. (2021). Machine Learning: Algorithms, Real-World Applications and Research Directions. *SN Computer Science*, 2(3), 1–21. doi:10.1007/s42979-021-00592-x PMID:33778771

Sutikno, T., Stiawan, D., & Subroto, I. M. I. (2014). Fortifying Big Data infrastructures to Face Security and Privacy Issues. [Telecommunication Computing Electronics and Control]. *TELKOMNIKA*, 12(4), 751–752. doi:10.12928/telkomnika.v12i4.957

Tsai, C. W., Lai, C. F., Chao, H. C., & Vasilakos, A. V. (2015). Big data analytics: A survey. *Journal of Big Data*, 2(1), 21. doi:10.1186/s40537-015-0030-3 PMID:26191487

Unveiling The Future Of Big Data: Insights And Innovations. (n.d.). Avenga. https://www.avenga.com/magazine/trends-and-future-forecasts-in-big-data/

V's Of Big Data – CopyAssignment. (n.d.). PathStream. https://copyassignment.com/3-vs-of-big-data/

Chapter 3
Advances in Marine Animal Detection Techniques:
A Comprehensive Review and Analysis

Gypsy Nandi
Assam Don Bosco University, India

Yadika Prasad
Assam Don Bosco University, India

ABSTRACT

Technological advancement has now allowed researchers to overcome barriers that exist in the research of marine animals. While traditional methods provided limited insights and relied heavily on sound signals, the advent of sophisticated image and video- capturing devices has made it possible to collect data on marine animals in their natural habitat. This has allowed research into the detection and classification of marine animals underwater to rapidly rise in the last few decades. Computer vision and deep learning have given unprecedented results in this field in recent years yielding efficient results with low computational power. This chapter discusses the trends in the evolution of techniques used in underwater marine animal detection. This chapter also serves as a valuable resource in the field of marine research for researchers and practitioners alike to better understand the capabilities and limitations of specific areas. It will help in the further enhancement of techniques in the area of marine animal detection.

DOI: 10.4018/979-8-3693-2260-4.ch003

1. INTRODUCTION

Almost 75% of the world is comprised of water which is a major natural resource. The water and ocean ecology plays a vital role in sustaining humans on Earth. The ocean itself is a subject of study to a multitude of disciples. Marine animals play a vital role in the global ecosystem, and the existence of diverse marine life around the globe makes the task of research and automation in this area an arduous one. Several factors pose a challenge in the detection and monitoring of marine animals such as the vastness of the ocean, the underwater environment, the variables of weather and the cryptic nature of marine species. Human activities and the exploitation of water bodies in recent years have affected marine ecology.

With pollution affecting the water bodies over different parts of the world, several marine species remain unaccounted for on the status of their existence. As an important element of world ecology and as a source of food, health, and life for marine animals, a need to protect these natural resources has given rise to several systems and technologies. This need has attracted numerous research from multiple disciples to focus on marine life and its ecology. With the development of machine learning and the introduction of several deep learning algorithms, several technological advances are continuously being made in this area of uncertainty and the unknown, which not only aims at the protection of marine life but also looks into the study of marine data to avoid disasters by detecting anomalies in water bodies by setting up monitoring systems with deep learning capabilities.

This chapter provides a comprehensive overview of the research on marine animal detection, comparing recent techniques used in the detection and monitoring of marine life. It chronologically arranges the various techniques used over time to provide a picture of the progression in this field. While there have been developments with acoustic and eDNA survey methods, this chapter focuses on computer vision and deep learning methods used to detect underwater marine life. It also compares the datasets used for the research.

The chapter begins by discussing the challenges of marine animal detection, which include the vastness of the ocean, the challenging underwater environment, and the cryptic nature of several marine species. It then provides an overview of the different types of marine animal detection methods. The chapter then focuses on computer vision and deep learning methods for marine animal detection. It discusses the advantages of these methods, such as their ability to automatically detect and classify marine animals in underwater images and videos. It also discusses the challenges of using these methods, such as the need for large and well-labeled datasets. The chapter then compares the datasets that are used for marine animal detection research. It discusses the different types of datasets available, such as public datasets and private datasets. It also discusses the challenges of collecting and labeling marine animal datasets.

2. BACKGROUND AND MOTIVATION

Marine life plays an essential role in the ecosystem. It is a very important area of research because it helps in understanding the distribution and abundance of species existing. It helps in understanding the behavior pattern and keeping track of marine species. However, there are several challenges involved in the research of an area that occupies almost 75% of the globe. The vast area itself presents a daunting challenge in the collection of data. It is simply not possible to physically survey all the water bodies, so sampling techniques are used for research. Underwater environment is often challenging as the visibility is poor and currents can be a hindrance in the process of the survey. Special and cryptic species existing in unique habitats are difficult to hear, see and sample, hence there is not sufficient data to research such species.

A variety of methods are used for the detection of marine animals. They can be divided into two categories: direct and indirect methods. Direct methods involve direct observation of animals physically or through underwater cameras. Visual surveys, UAV (Unmanned Automatic Vehicle), underwater cameras, and tagging are some examples of direct methods. Indirect methods usually involve the detection of signs of presence such as tracks, sound signals etc. Acoustic surveys, eDNA surveys, and remote sensing are some examples of indirect methods.

Early research on marine life detection was conducted in the 1900s using SONAR(Sound Navigation and Ranging). Originally developed for military purposes, SONAR uses sound waves underwater to detect objects. It uses the sound signals from animals to detect and identify its species used SONAR to detect schools of fish and other marine animals to study their behavior (Sea Animal Dataset, 2023). Early studies on the detection of marine life that used computer applications started in the 1970s. A computer-based system for detecting and tracking marine mammals that used underwater acoustic reading was developed by a team of scientists at UCSD (Dakhil et al., 2022). This was considered groundbreaking research but was limited by computing power. It could only detect and track a limited number of species of marine life. Several sophisticated advancements have followed ever since. Significant developments were made after the introduction of computer vision and deep learning algorithms.

Marine life is essential in maintaining a balanced ecosystem globally. It is an important area of research as it is a great contributor to the natural balance. It helps in the regulation of food chains and ecosystems. It is also one of the largest sources of food and livelihood around the globe. The development of advanced systems can help to monitor the populations of endangered species and protect them from threats such as habitat destruction and overfishing.

The survey aims to provide a comprehensive overview of the current state of research in the field of marine animal detection. It is a rapidly evolving field with new algorithms being introduced with a focus on computer vision and deep learning algorithms. This chapter further aims to highlight the progression of techniques in this field. Further, this survey will compare the different datasets that are used for marine animal detection, underlining the strengths and weaknesses of each dataset. This survey will be a valuable resource which will help to advance marine animal detection and also help to inform new research and development in the field of marine life detection.

Research on several techniques used in the detection of marine animals has been conducted over the years. Depending on the training data used each technique shows different levels of accuracy. Each technique was developed after modification to some specific algorithms to focus on visual detection. Some of the most common algorithms modified and further enhanced to achieve better results in research are as follows:

2.1 Segmentation

Segmentation is the process of dividing an image into segments where each segment represents an object or a region in the image. Segmentation techniques are used in object detection. There are several segmentation algorithms developed each with its own set of strengths and weaknesses. One widely used segmentation technique is semantic segmentation, which assigns a specific class label to each pixel in an image, allowing for detailed understanding of object boundaries. Another approach is instance segmentation,

which goes a step further by not only labeling pixels with object classes but also distinguishing between individual instances of the same class. These segmentation algorithms play a crucial role in computer vision tasks, such as autonomous driving, medical image analysis, and image understanding, enhancing the capabilities of object detection systems.

2.2 Convolutional Neural Networks

CNNs are neural networks inspired by the visual cortex of the brain, which is responsible for the processing of visual information. These are a category of deep learning algorithms suited for image recognition and classification tasks. CNN is composed of several layers, where each layer is designated a task. Usually, the first layer performs the convolution operation followed by subsequent layers that perform

Figure 1. Process of CNN

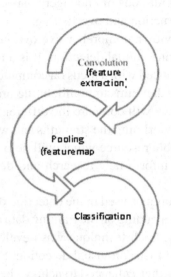

that task of pooling by reducing the feature map extracted in the first stage so that it is not affected by changes. The last layer performs the classification operation. CNNs are robust and can achieve high classification accuracy compared to other neural networks.

Figure 1 depicts the various tasks performed at each layer during the process of CNN. These tasks mainly consist of convolution, pooling and classification. Each of these tasks is briefly described below:

- **Convolution**: In the convolution layer, filters are applied to the input data to extract features and capture spatial relationships. This process helps the network identify patterns such as edges, textures, and shapes within the input.
- **Pooling**: Following convolution, pooling layers reduce the spatial dimensions of the feature maps, helping to decrease computation complexity and retain important features. Common pooling techniques include max pooling, which selects the maximum value from a group of neighbouring pixels, and average pooling, which computes the average.
- **Classification:** In the final classification layer, fully connected neurons use the extracted features to make predictions. This layer transforms the high-level features into class scores, enabling the convolutional neural network (CNN) to categorize input data into different classes based on learned patterns and representations.

2.3 YOLO

YOLO or You Only Look Once is a type of object detection algorithm that divides an image in small cell grids and predicts the presence of an object in the cells. It also predicts the bounding box around the cell and the class of the object. It requires being trained on large image datasets and bounding boxes before they are used to detect live objects. The advantage of this algorithm is that it is very fast and with high rate of accuracy. It is also capable of detecting a variety of objects. Its speed and accuracy have gained in popularity in live monitoring of underwater marine animals (Shankar et al., 2023).

There have been several developments since the first version of YOLO was released with every version achieving faster and better results. The current version YOLOv8 based on EfficientNets is much more accurate and efficient than the predecessors making them effective in real-time monitoring. This continuous evolution in YOLO architecture reflects the ongoing efforts to push the boundaries of efficiency and effectiveness in computer vision applications.

3. RELATED WORK

Research in marine environments can be categorized into several areas. For example, the collection of primary underwater datasets, pre-processing of underwater images and videos using computer vision and machine learning, detection of an underwater object using visual, and sound navigation and machine learning tools, and so on. These research areas collectively contribute to advancements in marine science, underwater exploration, and environmental monitoring.

There are several literatures available on the topic of marine animals. A review conducted on deep learning techniques used in the recognition and detection of marine animals (Li et al., 2023) summarizes the deep learning techniques that are used in the detection of aquatic animals. It also gives a clear classification of the techniques between recognition and detection and highlights the challenges in this area of research. Zhang et al. summarizes the marine datasets and deep learning algorithms used for application scenarios of maritime object detection (Zhang et al, 2021). It highlights the detection application of the YOLO series model and also discusses the limitations of the approach. Verfuss et al. gives details of different ways in which UAVs are used for the detection of marine animals for monitoring purposes (Verfuss et al., 2019). It also categorizes the existing types of monitoring systems and the limitations of such systems.

Among the literature present till now, there are very few studies conducted that focuses on the detection of underwater marine animals using computer vision and deep learning algorithm (Li et al., 2023), which covered research available till July 2021. The research in the area of underwater marine animals is rapidly growing and new advancements are being made (Nanthini et al., 2022). This survey focuses on addressing the issue highlighting progress in underwater detection using deep learning methods.

4. STANDARD APPROACHES USED

The YOLO series model was introduced in 2016 in the area of object detection which was faster and more accurate. Several versions of improvement followed over the years and YOLOv7 was introduced in 2022. Chen et al. proposes a modified version of YOLOv7

where an additional part "NECK" is incorporated in between the initial two-part model of backbone and head (Chen et al., 2023). The algorithm was tested on the URPCC2020 dataset which includes underwater images of 4 categories. The proposed algorithms Underwater-YCC introduces two convolutional layers to improve detection accuracy and the experimental results displayed improved accuracy after comparison with existing algorithms such as Faster-RCNN and later YOLO series.

An improvement over the above work on the same dataset is discussed elsewhere at (Chen et al., 2023). The proposed method is a modification of YOLOv7 to extract features from the backbone while scanning different visual information to improve the detection accuracy of the organisms. The approach DB- UODN is based on dual-branch feature extraction and focuses on problems with underwater images of small objects, blurred objects and images taken from different angles. The experimental results of the given system are superior to the existing networks. However, the dual backbone structure demands a large number of parameters that require high computation capability, which is not suited for low-computation platforms.

The year 2015 was considered to be an early phase in this field of research and the contribution of their work was presented in (Li et al, 2015), in which segmentation techniques are used to isolate and identify salmons. The system proposed was semi-automated and was targeted to be developed in a fully automated environment. This system could identify 125 fish from 60 images, whereas 1125 images were identified manually by the naked eye which gave an 11% success.

Identifying marine animals underwater is a challenging task due to its poor environment. The lack of a large marine animal segmentation (MAS) dataset has limited the development of deeplearning-based MAS techniques (Li et al., 2021). This issue is addressed by the introduction of a large- scale dataset called MAS3K consisting of 3103 images of marine animals in different conditions (Li et al., 2020). The authors also propose a deep-based MAS network called Enhanced Cascade

Decoder Network (ECD-Net) for multi-scale extraction of features. Experimental results show that ECD-Net was better compared to 10 popular object segmentation models.

Böer et al, carried out an investigation of deep learning models on a fish monitoring system with low-light cameras to check and compare their applicability (Böer et al., 2021). In the stated work, two segmentation models DeepLabv3 and PSPNet, following encoder-decoder architecture are used and employ MobileNetV2 for each of the two segmentation networks. The problem addressed in the work is a binary segmentation issue as only the fish and the background are considered. A test set of 1148 images is used in the experiment to assess the model's generalization capability on completely unseen data. The PSPNet outperforms DeepLabv3 in terms of inference speed with a pixel accuracy of 96.8%.

Karnowski et al. analyzed machine learning practices on ocean data, it also gave a comprehensive review of machine learning integrated with acoustic and visual monitoring applications that are used for identification and positioning, ocean biodiversity monitoring, and deep-sea resource monitoring (Karnowski et al., 2015). The integrated machine learning techniques like Support Vector Machines (SVM), Feed forward Neural Networks (FNN), Convolutional Neural Networks (CNN), and Artificial Neural Networks (ANN) were adjusted to give accurate results for a specific purpose. That is, one or more algorithms are adjusted together to obtain the desired result. Karnowski et al. also pointed out that "to be suitable, an optimal solution should be found by constantly adjusting the algorithm, which requires a huge time cost." (Karnowski et al., 2015). This is one of the challenges faced in the marine environment due to its vast diversity of similar-looking species.

The marine habitat is a challenge in the area of underwater animal detection. French et al. proposed a method to overcome such habitat issues to a certain degree (French et al, 2015). In the proposed model, the researchers used max-RGB and shades of grey methods to achieve enhancement of images with poor resolutions followed by a CNN method to resolve the illumination problem of the underwater images to obtain the illumination map (French et al., 2015). Thereafter, a deep CNN method is applied with two schemes.

In the first scheme, a 1*1 convolution kernel is used on the 26 * 26 feature map and then resized to 13 * 13 after adding a down-sampling layer. In the second method, the down- sampling layer is added first and then the convolutional layer is inserted in the network. which is combined to achieve the output. French et al. infers on the comparison that scheme 2 is better at detecting underwater objects (French et al, 2015). A speed of 50FPS and mAP of 90% is achieved. The algorithm is applied to robots for underwater working operations.

Another study was conducted on whale mother-calf groups using an uncrewed aerial vehicle (UAV) for remote detection of marine life. The author used water column correction, contrast enhancement and edge detection to enhance the visibility of whales in UAV images of animals below the water surface, which may be erroneous in manual counts or automated deep learning-based classifications (Jones et al., 2023).

A similar study was conducted with autonomous underwater vehicles to develop a semi- supervised visual tracking of marine animals to collect real-time datasets. The study used 33 video sequences captured by a mobile camera system of marine animals while following them. This dataset was used to train the currently developed applications specific to the underwater domain and deploy it on an AUV for spontaneous detection of marine life underwater in complex visual environments (Cai et al, 2023).

The authors propose a new framework for the recognition of the fish problem in an open- set manner (Akhtarshenas et al, 2022). The framework employs an encoder to filter out unseen and inappropriate images. This is done by training the auto encoder to reconstruct the available species with high accuracy. In the case of unseen species, the reconstruction error will be too high, so the auto encoder will filter them out. Once the unseen images have been filtered out, the remaining images are passed to a classifier based on *EfficientNet* to be classified into specific fish species. The classifier is trained on a large dataset of fish images, so it can learn to recognize a wide variety of fish species. The work was evaluated on the *WildFish* dataset and achieved an accuracy of 93.7% in the open-set scenario. Figure 2 illustrates the *WildFish* dataset used for training in the work discussed.

It is noteworthy that most of the training data used were still clear water images of fishes which may or may not have depicted their exact living habitat. Such datasets usually did not account for the surrounding environment which results in several

Figure 2. WildFish
(Dakhil et al., 2022)

| Macolor Niger | Dascyllus Melanurus | Dascyllus Aruanus |

| Novaculichthys Taeniourus | Abudefduf Bengalensis Abudefduf Sexfasciatus |

Figure 3. Annotated pictures from Brackish MOT
(Brackish Dataset, 2023)

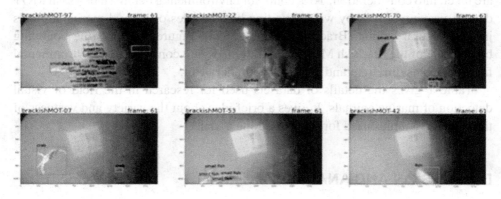

Table 1. List of standard datasets used in given publications

Dataset Name	Details of training data
Underwater Visual Recognition (UVR)	10,000 images of underwater objects and scenes, labelled with 10 different classes, including fish, coral, and invertebrates.
Open Underwater Image Archive (OUIA)	Over 200,000 underwater images, collected from a variety of sources, including research institutions, government agencies, and individuals.
Underwater Object Detection (UOD)	14,000 high-resolution underwater images, labelled with 74,903 objects, and 10 common aquatic categories.
Underwater Image Enhancement (UIE)	950 real-world underwater images, 890 of which have the corresponding reference images.
Fish4Knowledge (F4K)	100,000 images of 1,000 different species of fish. The images were collected over a period of 3 years from 10 different locations around the world.
Underwater Visual Object Tracking Benchmark (UVOT)	10 underwater videos, labelled with the tracking information for the objects of interest.
Underwater Semantic Segmentation Dataset (USSD)	100 underwater images, labelled with the semantic segmentation masks for the objects of interest.
Underwater Marine Animal Detection Dataset (UMADD)	14,674 images of fish, crabs, and other marine animals, collected with a camera mounted 9 meters below the surface on the Limfjords bridge in northern Denmark.
Brackish Dataset	21,924 images of fish, crabs, and other marine animals, collected with a camera mounted 9 meters below the surface on the Limfjords bridge in northern Denmark.
Underwater Fish Image Dataset (UFI)	10,000 images of underwater fish, collected from a variety of sources. The images are labelled with the fish's species.

inaccuracies. With the possibility of sending UAVs for data collection, these issues are taken into consideration. To account for environmental details, a brackish MOT dataset was introduced by with bounding box samples of several marine animals in their natural habitat (Brackish Dataset, 2023). Figure 3 depicts the bounding box sample of the brackish MOT dataset. It takes into consideration environmental factors such as dim light and background underwater.

Table 1 gives the details of datasets used for research in the field of visual detection of marine animals. It gives a brief idea about the variety and vastness of the training samples used for the work done to date.

DISCUSSION AND ANALYSIS

Detection of underwater marine animals is growing rapidly as the technologies advance with a significant focus on computer vision and deep learning. There is progress also being made with remote sensing and image segmentation techniques opening a plethora of opportunities for marine monitoring. (Karnowski et al.; 2015, French et al; 2015, Jones et al;2023, Cai et al; 2023, and Akhtarshenas et al, 2022) focus on using deep learning to improve the detection of marine animals. Karnowski et al. and French et al. propose methods that integrate the acoustic and visual monitoring systems with deep learning to improve upon the system (Karnowski et al. 2015, French et al. 2015). They use multiple algorithms adjusted to give desired or optimal results. However, such approaches do not apply to datasets in an open-set manner.

It may give different results when a different or more complex dataset with multiple species is used. Akhtarshenas et al. uses encoders with CNN to address recognition problems in an open set manner indicating their proposed framework can identify fish not present in the training set (Akhtarshenas et al., 2022). Jones et al. and Cai et al. employ the use of unmanned, unscrewed and autonomous vehicles to efficiently collect more images of marine animals in their natural habitat (Jones et al., 2023, Cai et al, 2023). The usage of autonomous vehicles makes the process less daunting, however, the quality of the images obtained remains an issue which is improved using deep learning algorithms. Both frameworks show significant contributions to the area of detecting. Marine life will help in gaining new insights into their behaviour pattern and ecology.

Figure 4 depicts the distribution of research articles in the domain of marine life detection in the time frame range of 2006 to 2023. Table 2 provides a comprehensive overview of techniques proposed in research publications based on CNN and modifications at several levels for the attainment of better results.

There are several challenges involved in research in the area of marine animals, one of them being the insufficient number of datasets. The available dataset may

Figure 4. Pie-chart of distribution of open access papers in the field of marine life detection from 2006 to 2023
(Source: Google Scholars)

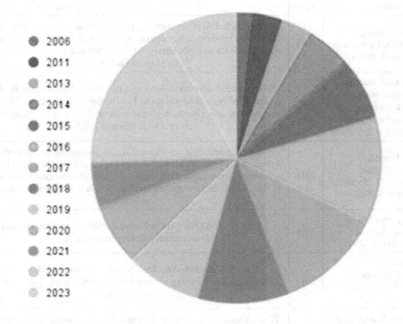

not account for all types of marine life. Due to the quality limitation which is caused by the uncertain and cryptic habitat of the marine animals, a large amount of effort is required in the pre-processing stage preparing the training data. It involves the usage of encoders and decoders for optimization of images. The computational power required to process such training data is very large. However, some works were noted towards research in areas where less computational power can produce the same efficient results.

6. EMERGING TRENDS AND FUTURE DIRECTIONS

Deep Learning is at the forefront in the area of marine animal detection and monitoring. DL can be used to develop new and innovative ways to collect, analyse and interpret data about marine animals in their natural environment. It can used to develop applications for automatic detection and monitoring, which will help develop predictive models. These models will be useful in marine management and the development of effective marine strategies. This can lead to a better understanding of marine life, and keep track of marine population and any future threats that may arise.

Table 2. Notable CNN techniques used in recent publications, specifically between 2014-2016

Authors	Year	Method Used
Xiu Li, Min Shang, HongweiQin, Liansheng Chen (Li et al, 2015)	2015	A pre-trained AlexNet with five convolutional layers and three fully connected layers on a large auxiliary dataset (ILSVRC2012), using the open source Caffe CNN library. The AlexNet is modified in three stages to adapt to Fast-RCNN
Hanguen Kim, Jungmo Koo, Donghoon Kim, Sungwook Jung, Jae- Uk Shin, Serin Lee, Hyun Myung (Kim et al., 2016)	2016	CNN Lenet-5 network is used, and the output dimension of the fully connected layer (F6) was set to 11. The network was trained for 100 epochs by using the back-propagation method. The article does not cover a wide range of jellyfish
Geoffrey French, M. Fisher, Michal Mackiewicz, C. Needle (French et al., 2015)	2015	It uses Segmentation algorithm that uses foreground segmentation to separate fishes with background and other objects. then foreground region are separated into fishes for counting and classification. N4-Fields image transformation algorithm is used for foreground segmentation.
Xin Sun, Junyu Shi, JunyuDong, Xinhua Wang (Sun et al., 2016)	2016	PCANet and Network in Network (NIN) toproduce abstract discriminative features from the Image
J. Karnowski, E. Hutchins,Christine M. Johnson (Karnowski et al., 2015)	2015	Uses RPCA method for background subtraction and detection of dolphins in pool using camera footage. RPCA gives precision when compared to MOG
Xiu Li, Min Shang, Jing Hao,Zhixiong Yang (Li et al., 2016)	2016	ZFnet is used for a pre-trained model. 5 convolutional layers are shared between proposal generation networks RPN and detection networks Fast-RCNN.
David C. Zhang, GiorgosKopanas, C. Desai, S. Chai, M. Piacentino (Zhang et al, 2016)	2016	The proposed algorithm auto-generates large fish samples from detection of flow motion and annotate true-false samples in CNN. Modified non-maximum suppression is applied to find unique region per object.
L. Deng, Dong Yu (Deng et al., 2014)	2014	Provides an overview of the deep learning methods based expertise and application area.

Remote sensing coupled with DL shows promising progress in eliminating some challenging factors in this field. Usage of drones and UAVs to collect data from remote and unapproachable areas will contribute to obtaining better research results. DL integrated with acoustic monitoring may also provide effective results when monitoring of specific or limited distinct species. Satellite imagery and social media data may contribute to research in this field in future. There is a need for a system that effectively detects and classifies marine animals. Such a system can be used for monitoring and overcoming challenges in maintaining the balance of marine life.

7. CONCLUSION

This chapter provides a comprehensive analysis of developments and trends in marine animal detection from 2006 to 2023 open access papers. The chapter discusses the existing and emerging challenges in this area. It emphasizes computer vision and deep learning techniques used to detect and monitor marine life. Different types of datasets are available and research is being conducted on effectively collecting data from the vast expansive water bodies. The developments in these areas can offer predictive models, help in the behaviour study of marine animals and may also help in the discovery of cryptic species that are difficult to detect. However, it is important and emphasize that such developments should done ethically and should bring harm to marine animals or destroy their natural environment.

REFERENCES

Aalborg University. (n.d.). *The Brackish Dataset*. Kaggle. https://www.kaggle.com/aalborguniversity/brackish-dataset

Akhtarshenas, A., & Toosi, R. (2022). An open-set framework for underwater image classification using autoencoders. *SN Applied Sciences*, *4*(8), 229. doi:10.1007/s42452-022-05105-w

Böer, G., Veeramalli, R., & Schramm, H. (2021). Segmentation of Fish in Realistic Underwater Scenes using Lightweight Deep Learning Models. In ROBOVIS (pp. 158- 164). doi:10.5220/0010712700003061

Cai, L., McGuire, N. E., Hanlon, R., Mooney, T. A., & Girdhar, Y. (2023). Semi-supervised Visual Tracking of Marine Animals Using Autonomous Underwater Vehicles. *International Journal of Computer Vision*, *131*(6), 1406–1427. doi:10.1007/s11263-023-01762-5

Chen, X., Yuan, M., Fan, C., Chen, X., Li, Y., & Wang, H. (2023). Research on an Underwater Object Detection Network Based on Dual-Branch Feature Extraction. *Electronics (Basel)*, *12*(16), 3413. doi:10.3390/electronics12163413

Chen, X., Yuan, M., Yang, Q., Yao, H., & Wang, H. (2023). Underwater-YCC: Underwater Target Detection Optimization Algorithm Based on YOLOv7. *Journal of Marine Science and Engineering*, *11*(5), 995. doi:10.3390/jmse11050995

Dakhil, R. A., & Khayeat, A. R. H. (2022). Review On Deep Learning Technique For Underwater Object Detection. *arXiv preprint arXiv:2209.10151*. doi:10.5121/csit.2022.121505

Deng, L., & Yu, D. (2014). Deep Learning: Methods and Applications. *Foundations and Trends in Signal Processing Series.* Research Gate.

French, G., Fisher, M., Mackiewicz, M., & Needle, C. (2015). *Convolutional neural networks for counting fish in fisheries surveillance video.*

Jones, A., Bruce, E., Davies, K. P., & Cato, D. H. (2023). Enhancing UAV images to improve the observation of submerged whales using a water column correction method. *Marine Mammal Science, 39*(2), 696–702. doi:10.1111/mms.12994

Karnowski, J., Hutchins, E., & Johnson, C. (2015, January). Dolphin detection and tracking. In 2015 *IEEE Winter Applications and Computer Vision Workshops* (pp. 51- 56). IEEE.

Kim, H., Koo, J., Kim, D., Jung, S., Shin, J. U., Lee, S., & Myung, H. (2016). Image- based monitoring of jellyfish using deep learning architecture. *IEEE Sensors Journal, 16*(8), 2215–2216. doi:10.1109/JSEN.2016.2517823

Li, J., Xu, W., Deng, L., Xiao, Y., Han, Z., & Zheng, H. (2023). Deep learning for visual recognition and detection of aquatic animals: A review. *Reviews in Aquaculture, 15*(2), 409–433. doi:10.1111/raq.12726

Li, L., Dong, B., Rigall, E., Zhou, T., Dong, J., & Chen, G. (2021). Marine animal segmentation. *IEEE Transactions on Circuits and Systems for Video Technology, 32*(4), 2303–2314. doi:10.1109/TCSVT.2021.3093890

Li, L., Rigall, E., Dong, J., & Chen, G. (2020, November). MAS3K: An open dataset for marine animal segmentation. In *International Symposium on Benchmarking, Measuring and Optimization* (pp. 194-212). Cham: Springer International Publishing.

Li, X., Shang, M., Hao, J., & Yang, Z. (2016, April). Accelerating fish detection and recognition by sharing CNNs with objectness learning. In *OCEANS 2016-Shanghai* (pp. 1–5). IEEE. doi:10.1109/OCEANSAP.2016.7485476

Li, X., Shang, M., Qin, H., & Chen, L. (2015, October). Fast accurate fish detection and recognition of underwater images with fast r-cnn. In *OCEANS 2015-MTS/IEEE Washington* (pp. 1–5). IEEE.

Nanthini, N., Ashiq, A., Aakash, V. S., & Bhuvaneshwaran, M. J. (2022, December). Convolutional Neural Networks (CNN) based Marine Species Identification. In *2022 International Conference on Automation, Computing and Renewable Systems (ICACRS)* (pp. 602-607). IEEE.

Shankar, R., & Muthulakshmi, M. (2023, March). Comparing YOLOV3, YOLOV5 & YOLOV7 Architectures for Underwater Marine Creatures Detection. In *2023 International Conference on Computational Intelligence and Knowledge Economy (ICCIKE)* (pp. 25-30). IEEE.

Sun, X., Shi, J., Dong, J., & Wang, X. (2016, October). Fish recognition from low-resolution underwater images. In *2016 9th International Congress on Image and Signal Processing, BioMedical Engineering and Informatics (CISP-BMEI)* (pp. 471-476). IEEE.

Vencerlanz09. (n.d.). *Sea Animal Dataset*. Kaggle. https://www.kaggle.com/datasets/vencerlanz09/sea-animals-image-dataste

Verfuss, U. K., Aniceto, A. S., Harris, D. V., Gillespie, D., Fielding, S., Jiménez, G., Johnston, P., Sinclair, R. R., Sivertsen, A., Solbø, S. A., Storvold, R., Biuw, M., & Wyatt, R. (2019). A review of unmanned vehicles for the detection and monitoring of marine fauna. *Marine Pollution Bulletin*, *140*, 17–29. doi:10.1016/j.marpolbul.2019.01.009

Zhang, D., Kopanas, G., Desai, C., Chai, S., & Piacentino, M. (2016, March). Unsupervised underwater fish detection fusing flow and objectiveness. In 2016 IEEE Winter Applications of Computer Vision Workshops (WACVW) (pp. 1-7). IEEE. doi:10.1109/WACVW.2016.7470121

Zhang, R., Li, S., Ji, G., Zhao, X., Li, J., & Pan, M. (2021). Survey on deep learning-based marine object detection. *Journal of Advanced Transportation*, *2021*, 1–18. doi:10.1155/2021/8793101

Chapter 4
Analysis of Arima Model for Weather Forecasting in the Assam District

Saurav Bhattacharjee

https://orcid.org/0000-0003-3022-7559
Kamrup Polytechnic, India

Sabiha Raiyesha
Kamrup Polytechnic, India

ABSTRACT

Weather forecasting is a scientific method that involves the prediction of atmospheric conditions at a specific geographic location. The increased volatility over the last decade is owing to an enormous rise in water used for irrigation application throughout agricultural area, much of which evaporates, necessitating accurate forecasting in order to take essential safeguards. In this chapter, an attempt is made to predict the average temperature and maximum temperature through machine learning models. The daily temperature data from 1970 to 2022 were collected from the National Centre of Environmental Information (NCEI). The ARIMA model is used to predict the weather data sets of Tezpur, Assam. Previous conventional models are insufficient to predict forecasting precisely. So statistical models and auto-regressive models are programmed and compared.

DOI: 10.4018/979-8-3693-2260-4.ch004

1. INTRODUCTION

Forecasting weather is the technique of estimating the present condition of the climate for a certain location using an array of meteorological factors. From individual decision-making to large-scale industrial planning, weather forecasting is a vital instrument that supports many aspects of human existence and societal processes. Accurate forecasting has a major impact that extends to the energy industry. It helps in the improvement of power generation and distribution by effectively controlling demand changes. Tezpur is located very near to the Himalayan foothills. The Himalayan range of mountains has the potential to affect local weather patterns (Sharma, et al., 2009). MAPPLS View of Tezpur city and nearby areas affecting the weather formation is shown in Figure 1. Apart from Himalayan influence, the Brahmaputra rivers have the ability to impact humidity levels and play a role in the development of regional weather patterns. Tezpur is located at a modest altitude, and altitude can influence temperature and air conditions.

(Zaw & Naing, 2009) introduced a model for rainfall prediction that utilized multi-variable polynomial regression and then compared the model performance to that of multiple linear regression. Short-term weather forecasting can be conducted using statistical models, which are linear. Weather prediction is possible using statistical forecasting by using historical weather data. (Anusha, et al., 2019) suggested that statistical model called linear regression is used to determine whether dependent and independent variables have a linear relationship. The best-fit line is what the linear regression seeks to identify. A line that covers the greatest number of points with the least amount of error is considered the best-fit line. The algorithm of gradient descent is employed to minimize the error to the greatest extent feasible. Since multiple linear regression involves more than one independent argument, it differs from simple linear regression. (Obeidat, et al., 2020) investigated that there will not be much temperature shift and quantified the error that results from defining a naive prediction that assumes every change will be zero. Similarly for predicting wind speed in the short term, (Yang & Yang, 2020) suggested hybrid Bayesian Ridge Re regression (BRR) - an ensemble empirical mode decomposition (EEMD) approach was presented. Several other methods for weather forecasting have been applied by various researcher to obtain a low forecasting error.

1.1 Research Motivation and Application

Data obtained from global navigation satellite system are uncomplicated and economical methods preferable for low power low tech networks (Guerra, et.al., 2024). In this chapter, an attempt has been made to examine the forecasting techniques used to anticipate seasonal and short-term weather variations in Tezpur, India

Table 1. List of models for numerical weather forecasting

Sl. No	Model	Description	Reference
1	LSTM	RNN model to resolve long term dependency	(Graves, 2012)
2	Hybrid Method	Combination of neural network and grey model	(Zhang, et al.,2019)
3	GRU	Minimise computational cost	(Chung, et al.,2014)
4	FiLM	Amalgamation of Fourier transformation and low rank grid estimation minimises the effect of distortion on time series	(Zhou, et al., 2022)
5	SFA-LSTM	Spatial connection module to record current spatial temporal interaction among numerous metrical information to predict temperature	(Salman, et al.,2015)

which is used to predict the temperature one to three day ahead based on the time series-based structure. In a research article (Schultz, et al., 2020) discussed about the evolving nature of deep learning in which they concluded that end to end deep learning weather application can identify and capitalise on small scale patterns in observational data that are not addressed by the standard Numerical weather prediction. Deep learning may be able to forecast quality requirement of some end users. We have numerically forecasted weather conditions by combining historical weather data from Tezpur city with specific data such as average temperature (Tavg), maximum temperature (Tmax), minimum temperature (Tmin), and precipitation. We also aim to identify which weather parameter are more relevant to forecast as well as the direction of their impact and studied the model list for numerical weather forecasting which is listed in Table 1. This goal can be achieved using time series models which take weather parameter as regressor. Classical tools offer benefits for anticipating difficulties. When multiple solutions provide comparable performance, the Occam's razor concept suggests selecting the simplest option (James, et.al., 2023). The traditional ARIMA (autoregressive integrated moving average) model as investigated by (Box, et.al., 2011) is a viable option for linear data analysis because to its statistical significance, interpretability, and simplicity (Alizadeh & Ma, 2021).

This Chapter uses machine learning methods to improve the region weather forecast accuracy and dependability which will help with resource management in terms of disaster preparedness. It is possible to identify long-term trends and variations in the local climate by analysing historical data sets. More effective and accurate weather forecasting and climate prediction are possible with the progress of machine learning technologies and appropriate methods of data visualization. The main contributions of this study involve the application of machine learning

Figure 1. MAPPLS (Map my India) showing Tezpur (Latitude:26.65 and longitude:92.78) coordinates and its surrounding cities. Brahmaputra river(circled) can contribute the formation of local weather patterns.

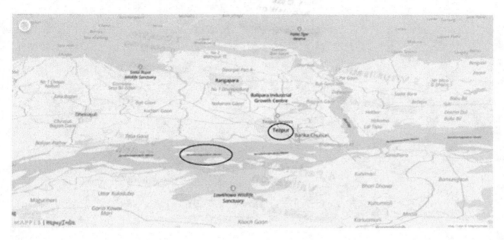

to forecast weather conditions within a short period of time, using computers that require fewer resources.

2. WEATHER FORECASTING STRUCTURE

Massive amounts of useful and useless information exist in unorganized form. After data collection, it is pre-processed to remove unnecessary and inaccurate information and clean it. The data integration method combines data from various sources into a comprehensible storage. Data reduction involves aggregating, deleting features that are not needed, or clustering to minimize data size. The structural layout is described in Figure 2. Data transformation involves normalizing or standardizing data to a format appropriate for processing. Using data transformation techniques can enhance the precision and effectiveness of algorithms while reducing model training time. Pre-processing techniques may function together. The process of choosing and training a model is crucial for any forecasting system.

Weather data from 1970 -2022 for this city has been accessed from the National Centre for Environmental Information. We then train basic machine learning models to predict the weather using combined data (Holmstorm, Dylan, & Christopher, 2016). These simple models work on low-cost, resource-efficient computing platforms, providing accurate forecasts for daily use. Machine learning-based modeling techniques, which include efficient structural and estimation of parameters

Figure 2. Structural layout of weather forecasting

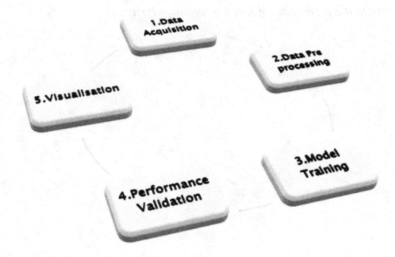

methods, have been considered as a substitute approach for modeling complex and dynamic systems.

The application of statistical machine learning (ML) algorithms to the problems whose solutions require knowledge is challenging to explain. In contrast to traditional techniques for time series analysis and prediction, machine learning models need less data to forecast future time series. The internal network parameters are modified using an appropriate tuning method based on the provided time series. Because machine learning techniques have proven to be successful in modeling dynamic systems in a wide range of scientific and technical applications, it is reasonable to conclude that they are also a viable and efficient method for modeling meteorological processes. When it is not possible to model the entire internal parameter of a weather-related event or a portion of it, machine learning methods of modeling provide an obvious practical and efficient alternative for constructing input–output forecasting models. Despite the demonstrated efficacy of these models, the suitability of machine learning modeling for specific system procedures, such as weather processes, remains uncertain. As a result, an analysis of various machine learning modeling methods is necessary to assess their effectiveness and determine the most optimal approach. An appropriate forecasting model that fits the application region is selected and developed utilizing the training datasets. After training is completed, the model performance is assessed by RMSE (Root mean square error) and lastly, the data can be visualized using suitable graphs and plots such as Scatter Plots.

Figure 3. Classification of weather forecasting models based on methodology and prediction parameters

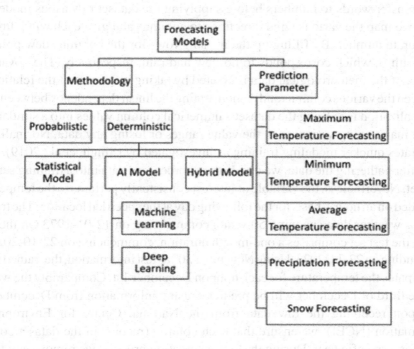

3. CLASSIFICATION OF WEATHER FORECASTING MODELS

Weather forecasting techniques can be classified depending on variables, duration, and the amount of time steps. However, for our study in this chapter we will focus on statistical models classified by technique based on the parameter to be forecasted as described in Figure 3. Popular statistical models include VAR, multiple regression, ARMA, and ARIMA. The ARIMA model is a kind of statistical model that makes predictions based on past observations by analysing time series data. One such statistical model for forecasting time series vectors is vector autoregression.

4. WEATHER DATA PRE-PROCESSING TECHNIQUES

The weather data pre-processing approach is data preparation, which is converting unprocessed data into a format that may be used. There are some missing values in the dataset.

To instruct the model using this dataset, we employed the subsequent methods for preprocessing. Since no real-world dataset is full, we enter in columns and values and transfer words to numbers before supplying the dataset to various models. To start, we map the various wind directions to columns and give each wind direction a separate number. By filling up the missing rows for the columns dew point and rain with 0, which corresponds to no dew and rain, respectively. The covariance matrix of the meteorological data is created by taking into account the relationship between the various columns and demonstrating the linear dependency between them. Normalization is to bring the dataset's numerical column values into a similar scale while maintaining variances in the value ranges or losing any data. Normalization facilitates quicker modeling training as investigated by (Singh, et al., 2019).

After gathering the data, we divide the unprocessed data into a training set and a test set. Nevertheless, the variable of interest consistently pertains to the temperature recorded on an hourly basis for the following day at the specified location. The training set has weather data spanning 50 years, commencing on 12-01-1973. On the other hand, the test set comprises a one-month duration, commencing on 22-10-2023 and concluding on 22-11-2023. Using November 30th as test information, the trained model anticipates the temperature for each hour on December 1st. Comparably the weather on the third of December will be predicted using information from December 2nd.

Upon receiving the raw data from the National Centre for Environmental Information (NCEI), we ensure that each column (record) in the dataset contains data for a specific year. During the dataset creation process, we remove any feature that contains empty or invalid data, before we split the data into training and test sets (Kumar, et al., 2012). This is because the quantity of feature variables required for training and test data is identical. Physical techniques rely on (NWP) and manufacturer power curves to address historical data gaps (Wang et al., 2019). After the separation, there's no assurance that they will both contain all the category values for the appropriate characteristics if we convert them. The number of features for the training set and the test set will differ depending on whether the number of category values in each set is equal or not. As a result, we must do this conversion before partitioning the datasets into sets for training and testing. The square root of the root mean square is calculated. Figure 4 depicts the pre-processing layout structure in programming language as how the data is processed from importing libraries to encoding the variable and splitting the weather data into data sets.

5.RESULT AND ANALYSIS

Using the data collected from the weather stations, we have developed models, and here we evaluate them in detail. An increase in training data improves prediction

Figure 4. Layout of data pre-processing in Python

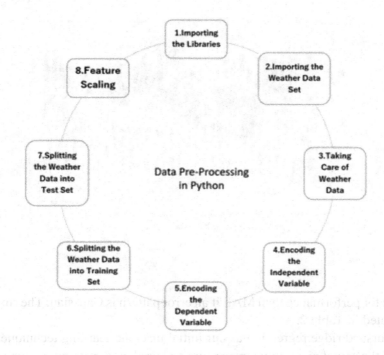

accuracy, as shown in the first set of findings. The inclusion of this data into our model training significantly improved the performance, as shown in the second set of findings.

5.1 Cleaning the Data Set

This step contains the dataset which contains only variables indexes our valid column list and generate columns with no values. The year index is the converted-to-date time index which has the advantage to subset and we can find the values of average monthly temperature and average hourly temperature. From the sample data set in figure 5, we can analyse the maximum and minimum temperature plot-wise.

5.2 Evaluation of Correcting Method

Root-mean-square error (RMSE) indicators are used to get the algorithm's error percentage. Another way to determine performance indicators is MAE (mean absolute error). (Chai & Dexler, 2014) investigated that RMSE is a more accurate

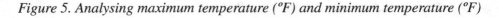

Figure 5. Analysing maximum temperature (°F) and minimum temperature (°F)

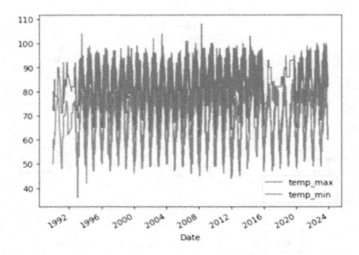

indicator for performance than MAE if an error pattern is Gaussian. The rmse value is illustrated in Table 2.

We pursued ridge regression as our initial machine-learning technique. Figure 6 depicts the actual maximum temperature and predicted maximum temperature in

Figure 6. Actual maximum temperature vs. predicted maximum temperature. Vertical axis represent temperature in degree Fahrenheit.

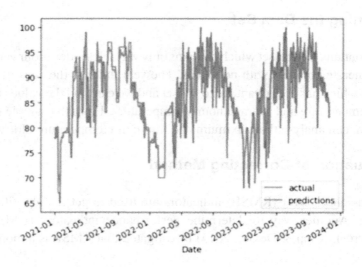

Fahrenheit. The data ranging from January 2021 to January 2024.In this specific regression model, there is a significantly large root mean square error (RMSE) of approximately 0.98% as illustrated in Table 2. Subsequently, we employ the Multi-Layer Perception Regressor (MLPR), a neural network consisting of two layers. Regrettably, the MLPR approach exhibits a large root mean square error (RMSE) in this particular scenario.

5.3 Weather Prediction Using the ARIMA Model

To begin analysing a time series, the initial step is to read the data and create visual representations. We utilize the pd. read_csv function to extract the data, ensuring that Pandas correctly interprets the data as date values rather than string values. Subsequently, we exclude any instances with missing values and display the dimensions of the dataset. The df. head () function displays the initial rows of the dataset. Subsequently, we graphed the data.

Stationarity is a prerequisite for modelling any time-series data. Stationary refers to the condition when the statistical characteristics of a system remain unchanged over time. If the statistical features exhibit temporal variability, we will be unable to make any predictions. The following are the essential characteristics that any stationary model will possess;

1.   Consistent average.
2.   Consistent variance.
3.   There is no occurrence of fluctuations.

We conducted the Augmented Dickey-Fuller Test (ADF) to assess the stationarity. Data is considered stationary if the p-value is less than 0.05, whereas data is considered non-stationary if the p-value is greater than 0.05. ARIMA consists of three components: auto-regression, integration, and moving average. This implies that we are utilizing the past values from the time series to forecast future outcomes. The "pmdarima" library autonomously determines the sequence of the ARIMA model. We provide our data directly to the auto_arima model in python programming. The function uses the AIC score as a metric to evaluate the quality of a specific order model. Its primary objective is to reduce the Akaike Information Criterion (AIC) score. The optimal ARIMA model appears to be one of the following sequences (1, 1, 2) having an optimal AIC value of 23343.616. Before training the model, it is necessary to segregate the data-set in to separate sections for training and testing. After preparing the algorithm, we instructed it to generate forecasts on the test information and evaluate its performance. Additionally, we specify the preferred sequence of the ARIMA model. The ARIMA, which stands for autoregression,

Table 2. SARIMAX results of forecasting

Auto regression and moving average	Coefficient value	Standard error	z	p*>z
ar. L_1	0.66	0.072	9.272	0
ma. L_1	-1.14	0.074	-15.456	0
ma. L_2	0.1780	0.039	4.507	0
ma. L_3	0.045	0.025	1.802	0.072
Sigma (δ_2)	18.226	0.298	61.142	0
Mean Square error (%)	0.98			

integrated, moving average function will thereafter use the chosen order to match a model to the data used for training.

Applying the Box-Jenkins approach allows us to have a better grasp of the distinctions between ARIMA and SARIMA. Furthermore, the benefits of selecting the suitable model will be clearly stated. Auto-co-relation function (ACF) and Partial-auto co-relation function (PACF) graphs assisted in determining optimal values for variables p and q. The approach involves fitting the ARIMA model for several values of p and q and selecting the best value based on parameters like AIC and BIC.AIC (Akaike information criterion) is a statistic that indicates how good a model is.BIC (the Bayesian information criterion) is similar to AIC; thus, a lower value indicates a better model.

Figure 7. Actual maximum temperature versus ARIMA maximum temperature model prediction temperature

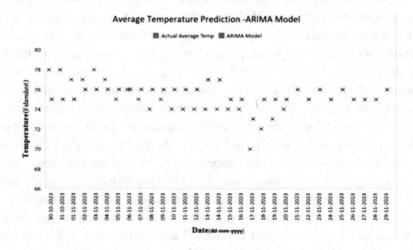

Figure 8. Actual average temperature versus ARIMA model prediction temperature

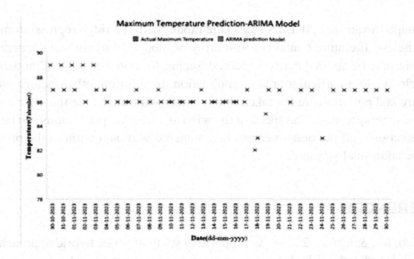

Figure 7 and 8 represent the actual maximum temperate and average temperature versus predicted ARIMA model temperature respectively. The errors in prediction or residuals in the test set, which can be referred to as the deviation between the predicted and actual target values. However, with bigger test forms, it is obvious that learning the model is necessary with data from numerous nearby cities outperforms training with just one city (Jakaria, et al.,2020).

6. CONCLUSION

ARIMA statistical model is used to predict the weather for medium-range prediction. The data-gathering period ranges from the beginning of 1973 to the end of November 2023. For the data, the maximum and average temperatures are determined. ARIMA model outperformed regression analysis for an accurate solution. The autoregressive integral moving average (ARIMA) model may be adopted as a principal source of automated guidance for all time scales except the shortest forecast of a few hours. The ARIMA model outperformed regression models in a 30-day sample dataset, exhibiting a substantial disparity in initial days and a little disparity in later days. Mean square error of 0.98 was found in the ARIMA model. This study suggest that while artificial intelligence algorithms are important ARIMA models can also be affective for short term prediction resulting in lower average root mean square error and fewer adverse effects from missing data.

6.1 Future Scope

This chapter examines ARIMA stochastic model with the ridge regression model. Nevertheless, literature contains a vast array of models, ranging from generalized ones that may be applied across several domains, to more specialized models that are exclusive to a particular area or application. In addition, other factors such as moisture and pollution are not taken into account while analysing the decrease and increase in temperature. The speed of the wind and weather predictions can be used for prediction, and the outcomes can be compared with and without the presence of these additional variables.

REFERENCES

Alizadeh, M., & Ma, J. (2021). A comparitive study of series hybrid approaches to model and predict the Vehicle operating states. *Computers & Industrial Engineering, 162*, 107770. doi:10.1016/j.cie.2021.107770

Anusha, N., Chaitanya, M. S., & Reddy, G. J. (2019). Weather Prediction using Multi Linear Regression algorithm. *Material Science and Engineering. IOP Conference Series.*

Box, G. E., Jenkins, G. M., & Reinsel, G. C. (2011). *Time series analysis:Forecasting and Control*. John Wiley and Sons.

Chai, T., & Dexler, R. R. (2014). Root mean Square error or Mean Absolute Error-Arguements avoiding RMSE in the literature. *Geoscience model devlopment, 7*(3), 1247-1250.

Chung, J., Gulcehre, C., Cho, K., & Bengio, Y. (2014). Empirical evaluation of Gated Recurrent neural network on Sequence Modelling. *arxiv.*

Graves, A. (2012). Long Short time memory. *Supervised sequence Labelling with recurrent neural network*, 37-45.

Guerra, R. R., Vizziello, A., Savazzib, P., Goldoni, E., & Gamba, P. (2024). Forecasting LoRaWAN RSSI using weather parameters:A comparitive study of ARIMA,artificial intelligence and hybrid approaches. *Computer Networks, 243*, 110258. doi:10.1016/j.comnet.2024.110258

Holmstorm, M., Dylan, L., & Christopher, V. (2016). *Machine learning applied to weather forecasting*. Meterological Applied.

Jakaria, A., Hossain, M. M., & Mohammad, A. (2020). Smart Weather Forecasting Using Machine Learning:A Case Study in Tennessee. *Computers & Society*.

James, G., Witten, D., Hastie, T., Tibshirani, R., & Taylor, J. (2023). *An introduction to statistical learning:with application in R*. Springer Nature. doi:10.1007/978-3-031-38747-0

Kumar, A., Singh, M. P., Ghosh, S., & Anand, A. (2012). Weather forecasting model using artificial neural network. *Procedia Technology*, 311–318.

Obeidat, F. A., Spencer, B., & Alfandi, O. (2020). Consistently accurate forecasts of temperature within buildings from sensor data using lasso and ridge regression. *Future Generation Computer Systems*, *110*, 382–392. doi:10.1016/j.future.2018.02.035

Salman, A. G., Kanigoro, B., & Heryadi, Y. (2015). Weather Forecasting using deep learning techniques. *International conference on Advanced computer science and information system*, (pp. 281-285). Research Gate.

Schultz, M. G., Betancourt, C., Gong, B., Kleinert, F., Langguth, M., Leufan, L. H., & Standtler, S. (2020). Can deep learning beat numerical weather prediction'. The Royal Society Publishing, 379.

Sharma, E., Chettri, N., Tse-ring, K., Jing, A. B., Mool, F., & Eriksson, M. (2009). *Climate change Impacts and Vulnerability in the Eastern Himalayas*. International centre for integrated Mountain devlopment Kathmandu Nepal.

Wang, H., Han, S., Liu, Y., Yan, J., & Li, L. (2019). Sequence transfer correction algorithm for numerical weather prediction wind speed and its application in a wind power forecasting system. *Applied Energy*, *237*, 1–10. doi:10.1016/j.apenergy.2018.12.076

Yang, Y., & Yang, Y. (2020). *Hybrid prediction method for wind speed combining ensemble empirical mode decomposition and bayesian ridge regression*. IEEE. doi:10.1109/ACCESS.2020.2984020

Zaw, W. T., & Naing, T. T. (2009). *Modelling of Rainfall Prediction Over Mynamar Using Polynomial Regression*. *International Conference on Computer Engineering and Technology*, Singapore.

Zhang, Y., Sun, H., & Guo, Y. (2019). Wind power prediction based on PSO-SVR and grey combination model. *IEEE Access : Practical Innovations, Open Solutions*, *7*, 136254–136267. doi:10.1109/ACCESS.2019.2942012

Zhou, T., Ziging, M., Wen, Q., Sun, L., Yao, T., Yin, W., & Jin, R. (2022). FiLm:Frequency improved legendre memory model for long time series forecasting. *Advances in Neural Information Processing Systems*, 12677–12690.

Chapter 5

Critical Approaches to Data Engineering Systems Innovation and Industry Application Using IoT

Naren Kathirvel
Anand Institute of Higher Technology, India

Kathirvel Ayyaswamy
iD https://orcid.org/0000-0002-5347-9110
Department of Computer Science and Engineering, Panimalar Engineering College, India

B. Santhoshi
St. Anne's Arts and Science College, India

ABSTRACT

The IoT influence presents new design and implementation challenges in a variety of fields, including seamless platform integration, context-based cognitive network integration, new mobile sensor/actuator network paradigms, architectural domains for smart farming, infrastructure, healthcare, agriculture, business, and commerce. Applications for automation in the internet of robotic things (IoRT) are numerous and are developing quickly. IoRT blends the strength of robots and the internet of things (IoT), resulting in creative solutions for a range of sectors. While ensuring the authenticity of the content in this introduction, the authors shall investigate the wide range of IoRT automation applications. IoRT automation refers to a broad range of endeavors that use connected gadgets, sensors, and autonomous machinery to improve production, efficiency, and safety across a variety of industries. These regions are general categories into which these programs can be placed: Industry 4.0 and manufacturing

DOI: 10.4018/979-8-3693-2260-4.ch005

1 INTERNET OF ROBOTIC THINGS AUTOMATION

1.1 Artificial Intelligence

The realm of IoT and autonomous operations has shown great potential with the emergence of IoRT technology. Communication-centered robots that connect to wireless sensors and other network resources are becoming increasingly popular in the world of robotics. These robots can easily integrate with wired or IoT networks, allowing for the seamless utilization of IoRT's autonomous functions in this field. The IoRT technology has shown promising results in the domains of IoT and autonomous operations. The latest trend in robotics is centered around communication-oriented robots that can connect with sensors and other network resources wirelessly. These robots can integrate with either wired or IoT networks, and the self-sufficient operations of the IoRT technology can be seamlessly leveraged in this industry. The incorporation of cutting-edge sensing, actuating, communication, and computing technologies elevates the original concept of IoT to new heights. This results in enhanced operational efficiency, enables businesses to uncover fresh prospects, and empowers them to predict potential hazards. These advancements present unprecedented opportunities for both consumers and providers of IoT and robotics solutions.

The Technical Committee on Networked Robots of the IEEE Robotics and Automation Society defines two types of networked robots:

- **Remote -operated robots,**

Networked systems make it simple for human managers to issue directives and get feedback, boosting the availability of crucial resources for study, instruction, and public awareness.This connectivity between robots and humans has a significant impact on shared responsibilities, including teleoperation and human-robot interaction. Additionally, the ability to reprogram and adapt robots on the network is affected. These technologies are now widely available for remote meeting assistance and telepresence medical equipment. Cloud robotic systems allow robots to exchange knowledge and learn from each other, while cloud infrastructure provides elastic resources to help robots overcome limitations in networked robotics.

- **Automated robots**

In highly advanced systems, robots and sensors are able to communicate with one another with minimal human intervention. This network of sensors expands the robots' sensing abilities, enabling them to interact over long distances and plan their actions accordingly. To prolong the lifespan and usefulness of the sensor network, robots can deploy, repair, and maintain it. However, a significant challenge in networked robots is establishing a scientific foundation that connects communication in order to control and enable new capabilities. Updating functionality and operations, whether remotely or locally, typically require specialized knowledge and longer maintenance periods in closed systems without open interfaces or communication channels.

By utilizing open interfaces, security and efficiency can be guaranteed through this approach. For networked robots to share information among themselves and with powerful workstations used for intensive offline processing, wireless networks are essential. These technologies encounter a number of technological obstacles, including installation, inspection, safety, the localization of operations sensor and actuators fusion, networking noise, trustworthiness, congestion, latency, stability, and range and power constraints.

The Internet of Robotic Things is a complex field that requires careful consideration of these issues. Fortunately, new hardware, software, and communication standards are emerging, providing new capabilities and possibilities.

IoT technologies and applications are fundamentally changing people's and society's perspectives on technology and business. It is vital to incorporate new IoT concepts, designs, and techniques into the conception and creation of open IoT platforms in order to support future advancements where IoT services and infrastructure will collide with artificial and autonomous system technologies. New apps, increased functionality, new business models, and investment opportunities will all be made possible by this (Vermesan et al., 2022).

Figure 1. Artificial intelligence project

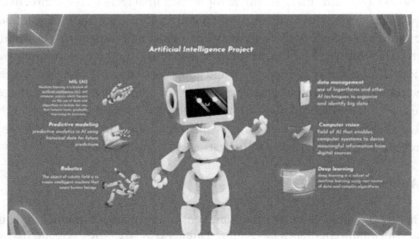

1.2 Converging Sensing/Actuating Information Network

There exists a wide variety of products that differ in their level of intricacy, sensing and acting capabilities, communication, processing power, intelligence, mobility, and platform compatibility. When we use the term "robotic," we are referring to a specific subset of these products that are highly advanced, intelligent, and self-governing. These robotic devices rely on both edge computing and cloud IoT platforms, and incorporate cutting-edge robotics and artificial intelligence techniques to function.

In order to provide specialized solutions for certain jobs, the Internet of Robotic Things (IoRT) is a sophisticated network of devices that uses path and motion planning as well as motion control. This autonomous system architecture is integrated into the larger IoT architecture, and is defined by six fundamental characteristics.

- **Sensing-** In the realm of IoT and robotics, the term "sensing" is frequently utilized to describe the capacity of devices or "Things" to communicate with other IoT devices and individuals. This communication is typically unidirectional, from the device to the human, which empowers people to participate in the IoT ecosystem based on their own IoT concept or service paradigm. Thanks to extensive research into the flexibility of this feature, "Sensing-as-a-Service" has been integrated into numerous IoT solutions.
- **Actuating-** While it is widely recognized that actuating based on a comprehensive approach is a valuable aspect of IoT verticals, it has yet to be made available in the open market. This feature empowers devices to take action in response to physical and/or virtual activities. To ensure that actuating is both reliable and secure, services must be established to support the open, multi-vendor development, deployment, and operation of IoT applications. Through extensive research, the concept of "Actuation has emerged as a new prototype for IoT, providing a user-friendly experience that encourages acceptance and engagement for managed IoT devices. Innovative installations are necessary to enable actuating and bring this technology to life.
- **Control-** This is a structured set of activities, mainly at the application layer, that operates in a loop or series of loops, referred to as Control Loops, which define the functions and services. To ensure proper sequencing mechanisms, the architecture's comprehensive security concepts must be reflected in the interface definitions. These interfaces are crafted to grant access to sensing data and control mechanisms. Within the control loop, various entities such as applications and cloud services can be integrated.
- **Planning-** The orchestration feature plays a crucial role in streamlining the logic that interconnects various internal components of the platform, enabling seamless completion of service requests. It guarantees that high-quality

standards are upheld throughout the entire life-cycle of the IoT application. To ensure that service requirements are in accordance with processed data and knowledge entities as well as platform-specific representation, the planning process employs a robotic sequence engine based on logic. The recording of user-defined representations of data and resources by the orchestration logic facilitates the server definition process.

- **Perception-** The interdisciplinary field of robotics involves integrating sensor data with knowledge modeling for enhanced functionality. Robots use a variety of techniques, including human-interface layout, software development, cloud-based architectures, analytics of data, multiple-agent systems, machine sensing systems, and occasionally artificial intelligence, to build seamless contact between themselves and people. Robots may identify and understand their surroundings through perception, freeing people to perform specialized activities.

- **Cognition-** This feature equips the robot with monitoring and sensing capabilities, allowing it to gather sensor data from various sources and utilize both local and distributed intelligence. This demonstrates the device's impressive capabilities, as it can analyze data from observed events, often employing edge or fog computing. These foundational elements support the device's third capability, which involves autonomous decision-making for actions such as physical manipulation or control in the real world. The device can navigate and operate in its designated physical environment, as well as notify or alert based on physical event analysis. The following subsections offer an overview of the IoRT technologies utilized in creating, utilizing, and deploying IoRT applications (Vermesan et al., 2022).

1.2.1 Sensors and Actuators

IoT and robotics rely on two fundamental technologies: sensors and actuators. These components are crucial for IoRT systems to function properly, as they provide essential functionalities and well-defined interfaces for identification and reaction. In contrast to IoT, the practical functionality of IoRT building blocks is based on sensors and actuators. Robotic Interaction Services (RoIS) define HRI functions and the usage of external building blocks, as well as abstracting the hardware in service robots. HRI functions, such as facial recognition and wheel control, rely on sensors and actuators like radar, lidar, cameras, and microphones. These components are physically implemented on the robot or in the environment, enabling logical functional aspects such as person detection and identification. This standard allows for the development of HRI apps that can be used on both devices and gateways. Actuation is a crucial aspect of robotics that enables the manipulation of items, movement of people and products, and even the functioning of automated doors. Numerous actuation approaches, including automated strategy and execution by multiple robots, have been developed in the field of robotics.

1.2.2 Emerging IoRT Technologies

Cost effective a solid-state semiconductors (CMOS) photographic sensors with proactive illumination are needed for IoRT applications to operate correctly in a variety of weather situations, including sunlight, darkness, rain, fog, and dust. These sensors must have high accuracy and resolution for both vertical object identification and horizontal road surface scanning. Most sensors now only provide 2D sensing data, therefore sensor fusion is primarily concerned with 2D representation. However, more height data, 3D visualization, and the combining of actuators and sensors are needed to better future IoRT activities. Robotic objects require a customized environment model that utilizes existing and new sensor technology in order to generate an ideal 3D environmental model that balances resource consumption and maximized performance. LIDAR systems, which use a revolving, scanning mirror to provide a complete picture, give autonomous robotic objects and cars 360-degree vision. For self-driving, autonomous robotic things, LIDAR systems provide precise 3D data on the immediate surroundings that can be utilized for obstacle avoidance, motion vector

Figure 2. Yearly shift from non-IoT to IoT devices

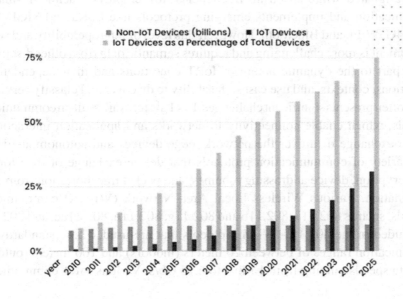

analysis, object recognition, and collision prediction. However, LIDAR systems are ineffective for close-range control, so radars must be added to autonomous robotic objects and vehicles. The 76-81 GHz frequency range is typically used for radar because of its RF propagation characteristics and necessary resolution. The radar equipment is small, emits less power, and has a lower risk of mutual interference, making it an effective method for collision avoidance in conditions such as smoke, dust, or other weather conditions.

IoT devices around the world are taking over non IoT devices. The US, China, as well as the developed countries in the European Union and the Asia Pacific region, are leading IoT markets. The region is predicted to lead in expenditure and uptake in the worldwide market, in line with other APAC-related trends. According to market predictions, China will account for two-thirds of the industrial IoT market in the APAC region by 2025 (Finance online 2023).

1.2.3 Communication Technologies

The communication infrastructure of IoRT necessitates novel methods in order to allow virtualization of operations on current computing engines and facilitate the usage of such infrastructures in diverse fields. These strategies should make it possible to exchange data streams (important for 3D-awareness and imaging systems), communicate internally, and use edge computing. Time-critical communication is essential for collision avoidance, which significantly lowers accidents and collisions. IoRT commonly operates local robots using networking technology and remote robots using designated white spectrum frequencies. IoT employs machine-to-machine communication and implements emerging protocols like LoRa and SIGFOX, as well as 4G, WiFi, and Bluetooth. However, this level of interoperability and service development is more challenging and requires semantic data from other disciplines. Due in part to the dynamic nature of IoRT conditions and their dependence on applications, contexts, and use cases, the ability to discover and classify services of objects often presents significant challenges. IoRT systems are built on communication protocols, which enable connectivity to networks and application interaction. In order to exchange data over the network, edge devices and autonomous devices use a variety of communication protocols that define exchange of data formats, data encryption, device addressing schemes, and packet transportation from origin to destination. Various Wireless Local Area Network (WLAN) communication standards, such as 802.11a, 802.11b and 802.11g, 802.11n, 802.11ac, and 802.11ad, are included in the 802.11 - Wi-Fi protocols that are used. These standards offer communication ranges of between 20 meters (indoors) and 100 meters (outdoors) with data speeds ranging from 1 Mb/s to 6.75 Gb/s. Various IoRT communication techniques can be used to achieve shared real-time computation, data exchange, and internal communication (Vermesan et al., 2022).

1.2.4 Voice Recognition, Voice Control

Nowadays, chatbots and devices with microphones are commonly used for communication. As the IoRT advances, more endpoints are created for people and robots to interact. This leads to the emergence of a new digital experience where robotic objects and humans collaborate, resulting in IoRT mesh development through mutual contact between robotic entities.

People should be able to communicate with robot fleets in more natural ways for IoRT applications that include tour-guiding, elder care, recovery, search and rescue, monitoring, education, general support in everyday settings, and in workplaces, factories, and homes. When creating IoRT applications, multimodal interfaces that deal with detection of movement, auditory localization, people monitoring, users (or fellow person/robot) localization, along with the merging of different modalities are essential. Using knowledge of the robot's movements and postures, powerful noise-reduction techniques can be used for speech recognition and voice control.

To reduce background noise, the microphone's quality is crucial for automatic speech recognition. A speech recognition automation system for robots can accurately identify voices from adults as well as kids in crowded spaces thanks to the reduction of reverberation, disruption, and noise in a portable multiple channels of communication technique with an outlier-robust broader side-lobe canceller method and a feature-space noise reduction criterion (Vermesan et al., 2022).

1.2.5 Machine Learning as Enabler for Adaptive

The Internet of Things (IoT) community recognizes the significance of incorporating Machine Learning (ML) techniques into IoT devices for effective management of the vast and diverse sensory data generated by network nodes. This integration enables IoRT solutions to adjust to different environments, while IoRT apps can learn from their surroundings and experiences. The ML service needs to be intelligent and distributed enough to encompass every IoRT node, including those at the network's edge. By performing early data fusion and predictive analyses, this distributed and embedded intelligence can generate high-level aggregated information from the device/sensor's low-level data. These forecasts might be used as inputs for an innovative method of learning on an alternative network node, which would then carry out additional forecasts and data fusion operations. This would result in the development of a smart network of machine learning algorithms that would carry out progressive compilations of the sensed data (Vermesan et al., 2022).

1.3 Marketplace for an IoRT Ecosystem

Mechanisms for the monetization of service components and data are required to encourage participation and the development of an IoRT ecosystem. A market place must be established as the center of an IoRT ecosystem. A marketplace facilitates registration and the discovery of offerings, as well as the data or attributes that services provide. These services may act on robots or objects directly or as separate components accessible through IoRT platforms. Selling and buying of products and services take place in the marketplace, which acts as a central location for transactions.

- Offering authentication, where a supplier of an offering can provide a metadata description for the marketplace to ingest and index to help with discovery.
- Offering discovery, where a customer searches for offerings using a marketplace search interface. To facilitate data registration and discovery, common ontologies for the semantic description of data must be established.
- Role and privileges management could be used to secure access to the market. Authentication and authorization can also be used to secure access to the marketplace.
- Reputation management, which involves consumer evaluations of suppliers and their goods; these evaluations may be taken into consideration when selecting search outcomes and during investigation. Auditing and accounting, wherein a customer's use of a service is monitored and providers can make a fee for this usage at their discretion. This function is crucial for making IoRT monetization possible and giving the ecosystem's growth drive. The management of different data-providing licenses is closely related to it (Vermesan et al., 2022).

1.3.1 Orchestration

Supporting with providing composition generation, instantiation, maintenance, and dissemination. This feature of an online marketplace fosters the reuse of enrolled offers since it permits their use in other processes, even if it is not required. Due to orchestration, a customised manufacturing procedure might be represented as a cooperation of numerous robotic item functions, for instance (Vermesan et al., 2022).

1.3.4 The Applications in Warehouse and E-Commerce

IoRT was developed in reaction to the growth of e-commerce, where human warehouse workers and autonomous robots coexist. Collaborative robots can help logistics organizations by alleviating some staffing shortages and the demanding nature of the work. One typical use for IoRT is the delivery of goods by fleets of autonomous robots within a range of between three and five kilometers, carrying loads as large as ten kilos, at speeds in the range of eight to ten kilometers per hour. Robots may be controlled and monitored remotely if they encounter circumstances that prevent them from traveling autonomously (Verseman et al., 2022).

1.4 IoRT Practical Applications in Commerce

Amazon has assembled a team to examine possible uses for autonomous technology inside its expanding logistics network. The company won't be building self-driving cars; instead, it will act as a think tank to help the biggest online retailer in the world incorporate automation into its logistical plan. By further automating administrative tasks, Amazon may reduce delivery costs, giving them a vital competitive edge.

Automated forklifts, for example, might save labor costs in the company's operations; the Kiva robots have demonstrated 20% lower operational costs.

1.4.1 Both Amusement and Wellbeing

By fusing communication technologies with robot sensing abilities, telepresence robotics enables more complex human-robot interaction. It enables people to virtually roam and gaze around distant areas, participate in business meetings, and keep a watch on patients or elderly individuals at residence or in medical institutions. Cinemas, theaters, and retail environments all provide creative and exciting venues to integrate modern technologies. Since the ability to move around and live in social and natural surroundings is necessary for a normal lifestyle, communal and open spaces will get more attention as locations for technology in the future. Service robots are employed in a range of social tasks, such as grocery shopping, outdoor cleaning, and visiting historical sites (Vermesan et al., 2022).

1.4.2 Coordination

To achieve the IoRT's collective optimization goals, robot collaboration must be correctly taken into consideration. When these problems develop in multimodal robot networks that are outfitted with a range of actuators, sensors, and on-board computing systems, etc. to effectively accomplish the required tasks, both the implementation and the design of MRS synchronization pose substantial hurdles. The difficulty of the assigned job must be considered when estimating the complexity of the assignments the collaborative MRS must develop, which leads to an estimate of a reasonable number of robots to carry out that assigned task. Another alternative is to divide the task up among several robot subgroups.

1.5 Health-Care Robotics Process Automation Paradigm

Any country's medical industry generates a considerable amount of employment and cash. It consists of things like medical insurance, clinical research, and hospital supplies. It could be challenging to compile and assess data, such as information on pharmacological qualities, that is scattered across several organizational factors against the backdrop of the healthcare business. tests, laboratory tools for technological developments, outside routes, health portals, scanning diagnostics administration, sequence-dependent arranging programs, Preservation offers, and improvements in human resource utilization. Health care organizations must rely on people to complete conventional challenging tasks that need a lot of concentrated work since interoperability across various systems can occasionally be challenging.

In the healthcare sector, the three main participants are patients, doctors, and health insurance. Creating a far more accurate and efficient internal process is essential to maintaining the balance between the rising patient demand and the records needed for surveillance, insurance demands, etc. Alternatives to computerized testing that are based on modern science and technology, like automated robotic processes, could assist clinicians in managing details such as doctor licenses, documenting and patient incentives healthcare provider schedules, programming, statements of billing and claim management, patient information, Medicare payment and adherence, and supplemental insurance policies to increase utility, reduce costs, and set limits on care. The benefit of robotic process automation is that it guarantees that its applications and tools have excellent visual designs that improve user experience (UX) for patients. The objective is to provide a simple framework that almost anyone with a fundamental understanding of modern technology may use. In order to satisfy the requirements of the final consumers, it must also be thoroughly modified. It is stated that science of computation and mechanical engineering are combined in modern robot technology. It is also extending its area of influence and communicating wisely with others. Three significant uses of automation in medicine are robotic assistants, rehabilitation tools, and medical automation. By providing better findings, more precise availability, and higher efficacy, robots are offering medical institutions an economic edge over their rivals. To make it easier for physicians to carry out their duties and deliver patients with exceptional medical treatment, several large firms and mega-specialty organizations have started up and investing in robots (Subeesh et al., 2021).

1.6 Operative Robotics

With the use of robotic surgery, physicians can perform complex surgeries with fewer incisions. Surgery is arguably the most well-known use of robots in the healthcare sector. It made it possible for doctors to do accurate punctures and encouraged the creation of fresh non-invasive methods (Subeesh et al., 2021).

1.6.1 Radiographer Robotics

Radiologists will receive training in sophisticated diagnostic imaging interpretation. In addition to earlier scans, doctors will consider a patient's complete medical history. Robotic surgeons won't tire out from doing constant surgeries all year (Subeesh et al., 2021).

1.6.2 Rehabilitating Robotics

Lightweight, portable digital exoskeletons provide solutions for flexible appendages. After chemotherapy and more procedures, a variety of robotic wheelchairs may aid with the brain's ability to reconstruct suitable connections between neurons. Robots that replicate human movement are now being researched in an effort to trick the brain into reacting (Subeesh et al., 2021).

1.6.3 Software in Smooth Robots and Prosthetics

1.6.3.1 Smooth Grippers

Thinking about the inherent flexibility and compliance of DEA synthetic muscle tissues, growing gentle grippers based on DEA synthetic muscular tissues provides a brand new way to grasp objects with one-of-a-kind shapes and brands. Various soft grippers evolved based on DEA synthetic muscle groups.

1.7 Vibrotactile Stimulation

Recent studies have used vibrating sleeves, pressure points in prosthetic sockets, and friction modulation on touch screen surfaces as examples of vibrotactile feedback. The pair's ability to collaborate is improved by vibrotactile stimuli and haptic signals, which without hindering task flow, can considerably increase the information the machine provides to the user. As was explained throughout the study, one-way intent transmission—from the person to the robot—has made task-specific robotic assistance conceivable. We discussed how most research conducted at pHRI treats the autonomous device as a passive spectator of human conduct and, at most, enables the robot to offer feedback on its present condition and/or intended use. Evidence that reciprocal signaling between an automated device and a person significantly enhances interaction was covered. These contacts, however bidirectional, have so far allowed for task negotiating or the progressive development of mutual comprehension and alignment. Through bidirectional discourse, which depends on both the psychological well-being of the person interacting and the dialogue history, more adaptable cooperation may be made feasible. As a result, the robot would be able to provide feedback on its current state and/or intended function.

1.8 Estimated Usage and Success Rate of Robotics in Health- Care

.In the healthcare industry and other connected companies, the usage of robotics and automated technologies has increased. The market for health care robots is anticipated to expand quickly over the following decades, hitting 9 trillion dollars by 2024, according the forecast of the Global Association of Robots. Robotics also helps healthcare professionals like healthcare professionals complete complex and exacting tasks more quickly and accurately, enhancing the efficiency of the entire medical sector.

Robot-assisted therapy may allow for therapeutic procedures that are more efficient, available, and enjoyable than conventional therapy. So far, there have been conflicting findings regarding how clinical outcome markers are impacted by robot-assisted training. Customized robot-assisted training has been demonstrated in some trials to be superior to conventional therapy, while no statistically significant differences in clinical outcomes have been found in other investigations. However, there is solid proof that patients who actively engage in therapy benefit from it. These optimistic findings spur research that reliably identifies intent and provides real-time accomplishment and effort metrics in order to promote patient engagement.

Significance of Robotic process automation in health-care sector

- By employing machine artificial neural networks to quickly gain and incorporate clinical data from lab technologies, third-party entry points, health insurance pathways screening imaging equipment, sequence-dependent set up, as well as additional multiple systems, we aim to lessen the difficulties faced by medical professionals when coping with the complicated layout of procedures and a volume of patient and health care facility statistical analysis.
- Learning more about robots to improve patient care is the aim of automation in the medical sector. In order to accomplish that, it also becomes essential to build the appropriate automated machinery and work with experts to make it. To completely understand the importance of the uses of machine learning in healthcare, additional study is necessary.
- • Since people's potential for compassion is linked to either their humanity or chaotic structure, further research is still needed to determine whether or

not medical professionals can substitute people. Empathy may be shown by robots and machine learning toward people, and it can also be shown through preprogrammed actions.

1.9 IoT in Transportation

In addition to making it easier to get from one place to another, IoT in transportation also increases safety and appropriateness. For instance, a smart car may do multiple functions at once, including communication, pleasure, navigation, and more reliable, efficient transportation. Travelers may stay connected to all kinds of transportation at all times thanks to IoT. Several wireless technologies, including Wi-Fi, Bluetooth 3G, 4G, smart transportation systems, and even other vehicles, connect the car to the internet. A more sophisticated version of geo-fencing has been developed in this sector. It records the coordinates of a given location along with the position of an object or device (Perwej et al., 2019).

1.10 Applications of IoT and AI in Agriculture Automation

By integrating better programs, an IoT environment powered by AI has a surprising ability to increase the control and specificity of farming operations. The potential of these most recent technological developments in farm operations is limitless because they might automate difficult tasks with little manual labor.

1.10.1 Smart Farm

Today's farmers use a range of farm machinery and equipment to complete a number of agricultural jobs. Tractors are included in them and are regarded as the most important and indispensable farm energy source. Tractor performance monitors gather data, take measurements, and help with remote process observation. The variables that are frequently taken into consideration include power, consumption of fuel, draught, and wheel slip.

DGPS, or the Global Positioning System with Difference. The GPS system is a crucial part of the system that provides spatial values. As a result, the tractor-implement system may be evaluated, documented, and monitored in terms of how it is functioning in relation to the position. Given that the soil texture and land slope have an influence on how well a tractor-implement system operates, this mapping technique is highly useful for estimating the costs of crop production inside the field limits.

Robotic harvesters, rice cultivators have adopted that function with efficiency that is nearly equivalent to that of a human. The image collecting module was the primary element of the robotic fruits harvester prototype. This was followed by an image editing module mounted on a motorised carriage. The information was utilized to determine which fruits and vegetables might be gathered using an object identification method based on computer vision.

1.10.2 UAV or Drones

Drones were first utilized for military operations, but they have increasingly been modified for use in agriculture. Another development in agriculture is the automation of numerous agricultural operations using drones, including pesticide application and land monitoring. Unmanned aerial vehicles (UAVs), which are characterized as airplane without a human pilot on board, include agricultural drones in their category. A central processor unit, a GPS receiver, a laser, a radar, a camera, a gyroscope, an accelerometer, a compass, and other sensors are all included in the drone gadget. Actuators and motors are also included for carrying out necessary activities. The remote control is used to interact with this via wireless communication. UAVs' integrated thermal and multi-spectral detectors allow them to survey hectares of fields in a single flight (Subeesh et al., 2021).

1.10.3 Irrigation

The "per drop more crop" strategy has been developed to ensure proper use of the limited supplies of water, which is necessary to meet our future food demands. The sensors' usage of data-transmission protocols like MQTT makes real-time monitoring possible. Data is made available to subjects in MQTT, and people who are enrolled to such topics are the only ones who may read the data. MQTT has the advantage of being small and simple for the network to control. The processing unit of the module is equipped with a relay and a motor and is ready to accept commands from the outside. A MQTT dashboard may be used to view the data (Subeesh et al., 2021).

1.10.4 Fertilizers Application

Businesses now push farmers to embrace technology-enabled agricultural practices and digital farming approaches. Using IoT technologies can make fertilizer application more sophisticated. An NPK sensor can be used to monitor the concentrations of nitrogen, phosphorus, and potassium (K). This sensor can be made using resistors, LEDs, and light-dependent resistors. The concepts of colorimetry and the photoconductivity are the foundation of the sensor's operation. An on-chip processing unit receives data from the NPK sensors directly. The use of edge computing or cloud computing is used to conduct further research. The low-cost

SPAD was developed for the field-based indirect evaluation of crop leaf chlorophyll content (Subeesh et al., 2021).

1.10.5 Weed and Pest Control

Application of herbicides is still challenging due to its unfavorable impacts, which include harm to the environment and human health. Additionally, conventional weeding methods uniformly spray pesticides throughout the whole field whether or not there are weeds, which raises the price of herbicides and boosts greenhouse gas emissions. Incorporating robots, the Internet of Things, and innovative image processing techniques into a site-specific system is one effective way to address all of these problems. Weeds in a field can be found using both RGB and the infrared imaging sensors (IR).

With the use of a sprayer, imaging devices, sensors, and system-on-chips like the Raspberry Pi, systems created utilizing the Internet of Things may manage weeds by dousing them in herbicide. The critical aspect of managing weeds is handled by an AI-based categorization method (Subeesh et al., 2021).

1.10.6 Storage of Farm Products

A helpful instrument for monitoring the quality of agricultural products maintained in storage containers are wireless sensor nodes. Moisture and temperature detectors can be used to make sure that the storage room is kept at the ideal temperature and humidity levels. The values in the time series of sensor readings could vary slightly. In order to evaluate both humidity and temperature fluctuations in the storage system, cumulative data are acquired from this. Each of these thresholds is determined with respect to the crop kept in the storage facility. Data aggregation is done at the remote databases server, which acts as a gateway to connect sensor nodes to the World Wide Web. Coupling the data findings to the local farmers' ongoing surveillance of the storage conditions on a local level (Subeesh et al., 2021).

1.11 Sustainable Agriculture

Sustainable agricultural practices are anticipated to provide a number of advantages, including enhanced soil fertility, environmental protection, and a greater supply of the planet's natural resources. By following a variety of goals, sustainable agriculture seeks to increase productive agricultural revenue. Promote effective environmental management (Uprety et al., 2023).

For agriculture to be sustainable, data must be easily accessible. Smart farming enables both cost-effective and sustainable agriculture through the use of earth observation data and navigation satellites, making it easier for farmers to make informed agricultural decisions. The main types of sustainability are three.

Figure 3. Agricultural applications of IOT

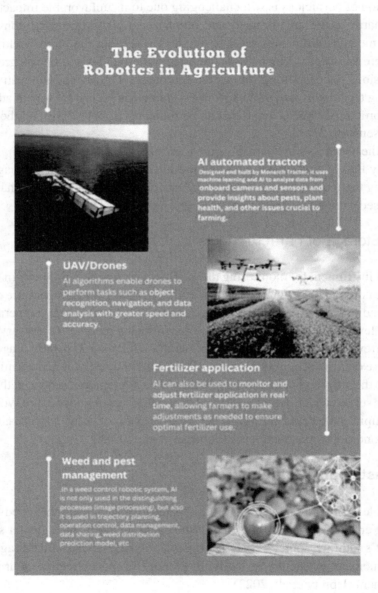

- Environmental Sustainability Sustainability assures that nature may be used regularly and without interference from various variables at the ecological level, preventing it from being used as an infinite supply of resources. A focus in renewable energy sources, outdoor safety, and water conservation are a few examples of realistic adaptation.
- Social Sustainability: At the social level, sustainability may plant the seeds for the development of individuals, groups, and societies to provide realistic and really isolated personal enjoyment, healthcare, and education throughout the globe.
- Economic sustainability: Business activities and the related flow of capital will support various pillars of viability for an all-around improvement (Uprety et al., 2023).

1.12 Machine Intelligence

The development of IoRT is greatly affected by the field of AI. Specific robotic devices are becoming more capable thanks to AI algorithms.

The sensor fusion capacities of IoRT devices are enhanced by artificial intelligence (AI) technologies, such as lenses for detecting sight, chemical detectors for distinguishing smell and taste, microphone for listening, pressure detectors for feeling touch/pressure, etc.

In order to deliver analytics and insights, as well as to improve the capabilities of one's robotic toys and their cooperative behaviors as a fleet, AI techniques and approaches are applied in all kinds of IoRT platforms. Convolutional artificial neural networks (CNNs), a type of deep neural network, are used to evaluate and extract visual properties from images. The techniques are designed to divide and de-noise monitored signals in order to achieve substantial variation or potential defect detection rates, which will enhance the efficacy of the recognition function.

In order to deliver analytics and insights, as well as to improve the capabilities of the individual automated machinery and their collaborative behaviors as a fleet, the various levels of IoRT platforms utilize AI approaches and methodology. Convolutional neural networks (CNNs), for example, are neural networks with deep connections that are used to analyze images and extract their visual characteristics. To enhance the effectiveness of the acknowledgment function by obtaining extraordinary variation or prospective defect detection rates, the procedures are made to partition and de-noise monitored signals. IoRT applications may now manage very big data sets as a result of the transition from central compute to edge/fog nodes. This strategy, which fuses effective production inspection technologies with edge processing, is also applied. Technologies for production inspection are also. By adapting a CNNs

Figure 4. Machine intelligence

engine to the cloud computing environment, this strategy significantly increases the computational effectiveness of a verification model that can determine the type and severity of faults. Robotic machines collect video, compress video data, pre-process video images, and segment video using perception tools like cameras. Utilizing perceptual technologies, such as cameras, images are first processed and segmented. It might be possible to increase the accuracy of item recognition by working together to create an environment and scenery-aware adaption model utilizing data from different video capture equipment. IoRT equipment, servers at the edge, and the cloud must all share the same amount of DL compute, hence a suitable offloading method must be developed.

When assessing network health, video encoded data, information rates/usage, power consumption, processing delay, framing rate, and the computational correctness of analytics, significant trade-offs must be taken into account. The potential exists for multiple distributed edge autonomous gadgets to collaborate at the edge to provide better services. Condensing the DL frameworks at the outer layer can enhance system performance through computing edge collaboration and the distribution of capabilities (Vermesan et al., 2020).

1.13 Virtual and Augmented Reality

Immersive technology (such VR and AR) may now be incorporated into interfaces for users of automated machines as well as for robotic tools that communicate with the interface of IoRT platform systems. This is possible because IoRT applications are becoming more cognitively capable at the edge. For IoRT systems to be more dependable, end-to-end security, electronic identities, and mobile data/knowledge security all need to be enhanced. This criteria is based on cognitive skills based on emerging AI algorithms. Future distributed IoRT architectures will require concepts like adaptability, end-to-end reliability, privacy, and intelligent connectivity in order to move away from existing centralized IoRT systems. A fluid data flow and expertise exchanging across IoRT applications/services executing at the edge or in the cloud is required to support the utilization of computing at the edges, software that uses cloud computing of operations, and rule-driven policy execution while maintaining the integrity and privacy of data. Applications for the Internet of Things (IoRT) may use VR/AR for learning, maneuvering, and support functions. While the technology known as augmented reality (AR) supersedes information generated by computers over the actual world to retain time and space coherence and enable in-the-moment communication, virtual reality (VR) replicates occurrences (Vermesan et al., 2020).

1.14 Integration of Digital Twins With IOT

Digital Twins (DT) is a brilliant concept that has recently emerged. It involves creating a digital replica of a real system, seen from the perspective of Cyber Physical Systems (CPS). This virtual replica mimics the actual performance of the system. Throughout the entire development lifecycle, information from the virtual system, combined with that of the real system, characterizes the data from the physical system. By combining the digital and real counterparts, a more effective way of handling, controlling, and improving coordination when the system is operating is achieved.

Digital twins refer to virtual models of physical objects or systems used for real-time monitoring and management. Meanwhile, IoT is a network of interconnected devices capable of data sharing and communication. When integrated, digital twins and IoT can produce intelligent systems that optimize performance and anticipate potential problems. By analyzing data collected from digital twins and IoT devices, artificial intelligence (AI) can identify patterns and offer predictions.

It is effectively incorporated into a variety of applications, including medicinal systems, industry, the aviation industry, the agricultural sector, urban planning, and weather prediction (Hemdan et al., 2023).

1.15 Biomedical Application

The industry that has profited the most from applying digital twin ideas is biomedical healthcare. Digital twin applications in biomedical fields have been made possible by new IoT, fitness, and e-health technologies. In the healthcare sector, DTs technologies are used to analyze and propose medications, identify lifestyle changes, improve hospital operations, do remote surgery, and help policymakers with providing healthcare to patients. In vitro methods for forecasting how the actual organ will function in either stated scenario will be developed with the help of a DT virtualized biological approach by physicians as they look into how the development of digital twins in the medical field impacts treatment, diagnosis, and overall health.

1.16 Smart Cities

Smarter features for smart cities are now being presented via digital twin advancements. Research on this topic has evolved along with (IoT) and communications, which has boosted interest in the digitization of our lives. A framework for creating smart medical amenities for people in smart cities using digital twins is described and to use a knowledge-based approach with artificial intelligence to provide categorization and decision-making methods for managing mobility and power in a major city. Digital twins are used to control energy in smart cities (Talaat et al., 2023).

1.17 Energy Management

With the ever growing demand for energy supply energy management is becoming a pivotal part of our life. A benchmark based on the analysis of data from smart meters is created in to create a daily suggestion for energy building. The framework will examine how these procedures may assist in power control that is as near to actual as possible and will ascertain the differences between what is new from traditional and yearly energy assessment techniques. The paradigm is built by combining digital twins with information and communication technology to provide a strong promise for improving the effectiveness of catastrophe management measures (Perwej et al., 2019).

1.18 Intelligent Connectivity

Depending on the application, the intelligent connectivity infrastructure must operate as a continuous and compatible network to support heterogeneous devices with a range of intelligence competencies and connectivity requirements. This is because strong, resilient, and dependable connection networks are necessary for IoRT applications. The connection infrastructure must be flexible enough to respond to changing environmental conditions, as well as to expected and unanticipated events and circumstances. The intelligent infrastructure for connectivity must function as a continuous and interoperable network in order to serve heterogeneous devices with varied intelligence features and connectivity needs, depending on the application. This is because robust, resilient, and dependable connectivity networks are necessary for IoRT applications. The linkage infrastructure must be flexible enough to respond to changing environmental conditions, as well as to expected and unanticipated events and circumstances. In order to meet operational requirements and "the economic viability of the vehicular networks," artificial intelligence (AI) methods like machine learning (ML) are employed as useful tools to address the difficulties faced in 5G technology wireless technology (such as cached data, processing, and communication operations).

To support new connectivity, which has developed into the enabler for the future IoRT intelligent services, wireless and cellular networks utilized for telecommunications must offer predictable/guaranteed latency.

Peer-to-peer and/or broadcast communication techniques are available for direct communication and data sharing on IoRT devices. The forthcoming 5G wireless technology will have an average latency performance ranging from 1-10 ms in contrast to the current 4G mobile technology's latency efficiency of 80-100 ms, thanks to the use of SDN (software-defined networking) and the virtualization of network functions (NFV). Applications for dispersed networks are supported in order to meet the stringent energy efficiency standards required to cover large outdoor regions, deep indoor or underground locations, or mobile objects moving quickly. These applications are built for the edge and the cloud. The architecture and additional functions of the 5G network are designed to fulfill the Latency, reliability, and throughput are requirements for IoRT applications that are both mission- and safety-critical. Future directions in physical human-robot interaction for embodied communication

It consists of multimodal communication, assistance for emergent, unforeseen behavior, and communication during collaboration (safe operation guaranteed by autonomy while allowing continual adaptation). These goals take into consideration how individuals and their surroundings alter over time, enabling a process of coadaptation between humans and automated systems However, they also have one thing in common: there are currently no standardized algorithmic tools available. We shall discuss this in more detail below. Therefore, datasets are needed for comparing and evaluating the features of the current pHRI, testing algorithmic tools relevant to the pHRI, and certifying algorithms prior to use with people.(kalinowska et al., 2023)

1.19 Continual Adaptation With Safety Guarantees

pHRI may provide a safety risk due to the immediate mechanical contact and power exchange. As a result, enabling pHRI has placed a high priority on safety. However, it is unclear how to ensure safety without restricting robot motion parameters (such as torque or velocity) and performance limits. Due to the lack of reliable alternatives, the ISO standards from 2016 point to quantifiable biomechanical restrictions, such as acceptable threshold forces or pressures for certain body regions, as a requirement for collaborative robots.

These initiatives provide a step toward offering standardized safety assurances for data-driven autonomous machines (given acceptable assumptions). Notably, only a small number of research have taken continuous or long-term adaptation into account. Most work has concentrated on learning within a constrained period following initial engagement. One explanation for this is because, although evaluating the effectiveness and safety of data-driven approaches is difficult, doing so for systems that are constantly evolving is considerably more difficult. The development of methods for long-term learning facilitation and data-driven safety verification should be the main areas of research to come. While giving specifications that are adequate for nonstationary simulations and take into account variation in humans and adaptation, we should try to give safety assurances that, at the very least, retain states within safe sets and adhere to temporal logic criteria (Kalinowska et al., 2023).

1.20 Multimodal Dialogue

Similar to how we try to deduce pertinent assessment signals from an individual for the robot, the robot should try to provide the individual with data signals. The mobility of the robot is often used in human-robot systems to provide implicit feedback to the human partner. In certain pieces, anthropomorphic cues or exaggerated robot movements are used to strengthen the connection.

As a result of making robotic behaviors more predictable, intentional communication motion has been proven to increase engagement since it enables users to foresee the robot's motions and modify their own behavior accordingly (Kalinowska et al., 2023).

1.21 Industrial IOT

The expansion and use of the internet of things (IoT) in industrial applications and sectors is referred to as the "industrial internet of things" (IIoT) more credibility because to its substantial focus on big data, machine-to-machine connectivity, and machine learning. The Industrial Internet of Things is made up of numerous devices that are linked together through communications software. Without the need for human involvement, the outcomes networks, are able to rapidly respond on information after exchanging, analyzing, monitoring, and collecting it in order to modify their behavior or their surroundings (Perwej et al., 2019).

1.22 IOT Fire Forcast Detectors

To detect fires early, scientists and engineers have created vision-based fire detectors (VFDs) as well as sound-, flame-, temperature-, gas-, and solid-sensitive fire sensors. Smoke's chemical properties are detected by sensors, which activates an alarm. The YOLOv8 detection model, used by the (Smart fire detection) SFDS approach, provides quick and accurate object identification without the requirement for a regional proposal network. The system is improved to need fewer parameters for detection, increasing its effectiveness. The SFDS utilize computer vision to automatically detect fires in photo and video feeds (Talaat et al., 2023).

1.23 IOT Based Greenhouse Management

To achieve high-efficiency monitoring of environmental data, an IoT monitoring management device for a greenhouse is developed. Organizational framework of the Internet of Things system for managing and monitoring the environment in greenhouses. The system's main parts are a remote web server and a smart gateway running an Android operating system. Using a data collecting device, the gateway gathers greenhouse environmental data, which is then stored in a SQLite database. In the meanwhile, the gateway is used to send the greenhouse's environmental data to the server. The greenhouse's equipment, including the windows, fans, and heating units, is under the supervision of the control node. Output from the gateway is received by and managed by the server system (Subeesh et al., 2021).

1.24 IOT Architecture Domain

Smart, linked houses may be divided into two basic architectural types: distributed and centralized.

1.24.1 Centralized Smart Home Architecture

A computer system that is responsible for controlling the control system is used in a centralized smarthome design for collecting information from sensors, interacting with users, implementing control algorithms, and instructing actuators. In addition to performing the control function, it is responsible for connecting the smarthome to the outside world through the Internet and offering services to its inhabitants.

1.34.2 Distributed Smart Home Architecture

The software for the control system is envisioned and developed as a distributed computing system in a distributed smarthome architecture. The distributed design takes advantage of the processing power of intelligent objects to integrate software modules into the smart home network's nodes (Perwej et al., 2019).

1.25 Emergent Interfaces

The communication agent (human or robot) must have a correct mental representation of the communication rules in order for the signaling model outlined above to work, and this hypothesis that the mental representation is correct is frequently static. New symbolic languages will be the foundation for communication if we are to move toward active nonverbal interaction between humans and technology.

We can connect with assistive technology using our kinematic, muscular, and cognitive null space—excess degree of freedom—while avoiding major increases in cognitive burden. The developer chooses a group of vectors in the neural null space, and the operator, who is a human being, is trained to read and create them. As a starting point, languages can be specified and programmed in the robot. There is an apparent way to symbolize the connection of the continuous 2D regulated space onto the corresponding 2D action space of the robotic machine, making the language simple to learn, if we are mapping joystick signals to the action space of a motorized wheelchair (Kalinowska et al., 2023).

REFERENCES

Hemdan, E. E. D., El-Shafai, W., & Sayed, A. (2023). Integrating Digital Twins with IoT-Based Blockchain: Concept, Architecture, Challenges, and Future Scope. *Wireless Personal Communications, 131*(3), 1–24. doi:10.1007/s11277-023-10538-6 PMID:37360142

Kalinowska, A., Pilarski, P. M., & Murphey, T. D. (2023). Embodied Communication: How Robots and People Communicate Through Physical Interaction. *Annual Review of Control, Robotics, and Autonomous Systems, 6*(1), 205–232. doi:10.1146/annurev-control-070122-102501

Kaur, J. (2023). Robotic Process Automation in Healthcare Sector. In *E3S Web of Conferences* (Vol. 391, p. 01008). EDP Sciences.

Perwej, Y., Haq, K., Parwej, F., Mumdouh, M., & Hassan, M. (2019). The internet of things (IoT) and its application domains. *International Journal of Computer Applications*, *975*(8887), 182. doi:10.5120/ijca2019918763

Subeesh, A., & Mehta, C. R. (2021). Automation and digitization of agriculture using artificial intelligence and internet of things. *Artificial Intelligence in Agriculture*, *5*, 278–291. doi:10.1016/j.aiia.2021.11.004

Talaat, F. M., & ZainEldin, H. (2023). An improved fire detection approach based on YOLO-v8 for smart cities. *Neural Computing & Applications*, *35*(28), 1–16. doi:10.1007/s00521-023-08809-1 PMID:37362562

Uprety, D., Banarjee, D., Kumar, N., & Dhiman, A. (2023). *Smart Sustainable Farming Using IOT, Cloud Computing and Big Data* (No. 10814). EasyChair.

Vermesan, O., Bahr, R., Ottella, M., Serrano, M., Karlsen, T., Wahlstrøm, T., Sand, H. E., Ashwathnarayan, M., & Gamba, M. T. (2020). Internet of robotic things intelligent connectivity and platforms. *Frontiers in Robotics and AI*, *7*, 104. doi:10.3389/frobt.2020.00104 PMID:33501271

Vermesan, O., Bröring, A., Tragos, E., Serrano, M., Bacciu, D., Chessa, S., & Bahr, R. (2022). Internet of robotic things–converging sensing/actuating, hyperconnectivity, artificial intelligence and IoT platforms. In *Cognitive Hyperconnected Digital Transformation* (pp. 97–155). River Publishers. doi:10.1201/9781003337584-4

Chapter 6
Data Insight Unveiled:
Navigating Critical Approaches and Challenges in Diverse Domains Through Advanced Data Analysis

K. Sudha
RMD Engineering College, India

B. Yamini
SRM Institute of Science and Technology, India

C. Balakrishnan
S.A. Engineering College, India

R. Siva Subramanian
 https://orcid.org/0000-0002-7509-9223
RMK College of Engineering and Technology, India

T. P. Anish
RMK College of Engineering and Technology, India

T. Nithya
Rajalakshmi Institute of Technology, India

M. Nalini
S.A. Engineering College, India

ABSTRACT

Data engineering solutions have become important in our quickly evolving technological world for handling and analysing the massive volumes of data generated every day. The chapter examines data engineering systems exponential expansion and data analysis's growing importance across businesses. It highlights data-driven healthcare's transformational influence on patient care and treatment advances, while noting privacy and ethical issues. The research analyses data categorisation techniques, focusing on machine learning and deep learning for healthcare and agricultural decision support systems. The story expects AI and blockchain integration in emerging decision support systems. Data analysis in clinical trials, precision healthcare decision-making, and agricultural applications are also covered. The conclusion is that data analytics improves weather prediction accuracy and gives useful insights for scholars and practitioners navigating the complex world of data analysis.

DOI: 10.4018/979-8-3693-2260-4.ch006

1. INTRODUCTION

1.1 Background

Technology continues to evolve and one of the fast-rising systems in that domain has been the software behind data engineering. Data engineering systems are advancing quickly, and an exponential increase in the volume, velocity diverse of data being created worldwide is feeding into this backdrop for a variety of reasons (Brunton et al 2022). This development is not linear but rather rapid owing to the proliferation of linked devices and other factors such as advancements in processing power and storage capacity. The widespread use of technologies related to data engineering has transformed organisational operations, making it possible for organisations to gain formerly inaccessible insights from massive databases. Another background aspect is the expanding relevance of data analysis, which is directly related to the expansion of data engineering systems (Nguyen et al., 2018). As businesses deal with huge datasets, the ability to extract relevant insights from this vast sea of data becomes more important. Data analysis is critical in converting raw information into usable forms that can be used to make educated decisions across sectors. Its significance extends beyond economic areas to agriculture, health, and experimental sciences, where it may transform procedures and results.

1.1.1 Rapid Growth of Data Engineering Systems

Data engineering systems are widely used, which emphasises how the digital revolution has changed many economic sectors. Major corporations are investing in advanced data management systems and using technology like cloud computing and massive volume records processing in order to efficiently handle and use enormous amounts of data. Governments, educational institutions, and non-profit organisations are all making significant investments in data infrastructure to keep up with the growing market demand. This trend is not only seen in the commercial sector. This evolution is further accelerated by the emergence of the Internet of Things (IoT), since linked devices continually provide a steady supply of data. Robust data engineering solutions that can handle the dynamic nature of IoT-generated data are essential in this networked environment.

1.1.2 Increasing Significance of Data Analysis

While data engineering systems are more and more often used, the process of analysis becomes even more vital, which is what enables these not only to become some sort if libraries but priceless resources. The better an organisation is able to sort through massive information and find patterns, trends, or correlations the easier it will be for them regarding decision-making processes And standardisation of operations. In industries that naturally involve complicated decision-making such as healthcare, data analysis has gained prominence to the point of being indispensable in improving patient care and treatment protocols. Precision farming techniques in agriculture are based on data analysis to achieve the best use of crop production and resources. Advancement in a variety of fields, from weather forecasting to experimental sets is driven by data analysis.

1.2 Purpose of the Survey

1.2.1 Overview of Critical Approaches to Data Engineering Systems

The study's main goal is to provide a thorough summary of the major strategies for creating data engineering systems. Methods and frameworks to effectively organise, analyse, and store this enormous quantity of data are urgently needed due to the exponential rise of data. This study looks at these foundational approaches to find the most recent developments in the development and use of data engineering systems. It looks at cutting edge technologies like cloud computing, distributed computing, and scalable storage that are designed to handle massive datasets. In order to improve data analytics, accessibility, and integration, new ideas like data lakes and data warehouses are being investigated. In addition, the research examines technological difficulties and important procedures including data governance, quality assurance, and security best practices. Companies are finding it difficult to protect important and sensitive data assets, which emphasises how crucial it is to maintain data integrity, privacy, and compliance. In order to successfully meet changing demands and issues, data infrastructure designers and optimizers must possess proficiency in several domains.

1.2.2 Exploration of Data Analysis in Various Industries

The survey's second purpose is sector-wide data analysis. Understanding that data analysis crosses industry borders, the research analyses how data-driven insights are employed across industries. Every industry has various data analysis opportunities and challenges, and the survey will explain them. The study will involve healthcare, agriculture, decision support systems, and experiments. It will show each setting's applications, methods, and trends. Data analysis approaches are flexible and adaptable, as shown by this study. By optimising processes, making decisions, and inspiring innovation, data analytics may transform an industry. By comparing applications in diverse domains, the research hopes to identify correlations and trends that may effect other businesses. Investigating data analysis across industries aims to give a comprehensive picture of data-driven approaches' practical ramifications. Decision-makers who want to strategically enhance their firms using data analysis and researchers who wish to contribute may utilise this material. The survey provides a comprehensive understanding of critical approaches to data engineering systems, illuminates data analysis applications across industries, and adds to the body of knowledge and promotes informed decision-making in a data-centric world.

2. HEALTHCARE DATA ANALYSIS

The healthcare industry is at the forefront of using data analysis to improve treatment approaches, patient care, and overall operational effectiveness. This section explores the prospects and developments in data analysis integration into healthcare systems, along with the corresponding risks and difficulties.

2.1 Opportunities and Advancements

The most obvious sign of the change in paradigm is that data analysis techniques are becoming increasingly integrated into healthcare systems, providing more and better results for patients (Guo, C., & Chen, J. 2023). On one hand, healthcare practitioners can derive a wealth of information from Electronic Health Records EHRs and various health data sources; on the other hand, by using tools for data analysis, they can uncover insightful information. This integration allows for a comprehensive understanding of the health of the patient, which in turn enables proactive disease management, tailored treatment regimens, and more precise diagnoses. Machine learning algorithms and other advanced analytics technologies can be used in healthcare systems to identify patterns and trends that would not be obvious with more standard methods. Predictive analytics assists preventive healthcare programmes by identifying individuals at risk, optimizing resource allocation, and forecasting disease outbreaks. Effect on Patient Care and Treatment: Patient care and treatment is highly influenced by data analysis (M. Ambigavathi and D. Sridharan 2019). By analysing the past patient data, healthcare professionals could identify treatment regimens, best practices as well as potential areas of improvement. Fast real-time data processing accelerates emergency response thus shortens the process of diagnosis and supports prompt decision-making. In addition, treatment strategies personalised according to a patient's genetic makeup and unique health history are enabled by personalised medicine driven by acquisition data. As a result, treatments are more focused and achieve success. Data-driven insights are not only important to clinical research and medication development, but they also significantly shorten the search for new medicines and treatments. By having a good understanding of the different patient groups and how they respond to various therapies, healthcare practitioners can improve treatment methods as well as reduce side effects.

2.2 Threats and Challenges

Privacy and Security Issues with Healthcare Data: Issues of privacy and security are numerous when integrating data analysis into healthcare systems. Sensitive patient data is comprised of medical and personal information pertaining to the individual (K. Sharma and K. M. Balamurugan, 2021). Confidentiality and the integrity of this data must be ensured to maintain patient confidence and meet legal requirements. Healthcare organizations are constantly vulnerable to cyber-attacks, illegal access and data breaches. Medical record security is governed by regulations such as the Health Insurance Portability and Accountability Act (HIPAA) in the United States. To safeguard patient data while it is being processed, health care systems need to have strong encryption, access controls, and auditing procedures in place. To protect patient privacy and the security of patient data, compliance with these standards is essential. Maintaining openness, eliminating possible biases in algorithms, and exercising proper control over the use of patient data are only a few of the many aspects of health data analysis that ethical issues include. There are new difficulties when using AI and machine learning to analyse healthcare data, including making sure accountability, interpretability, and algorithmic fairness are met. Achieving the proper balance between protecting individual privacy rights and utilising data to improve medical care requires a lot of ethical thought. Healthcare workers and data analysts must consider how their evaluation could impact marginalized groups in order to avoid biased outcomes and foster an open environment concerning the use of data (J. Ranjith and K. Mahantesh, 2019). It takes significant ethical consideration to strike a balance between protecting individual privacy rights and using data to improve medical care. Healthcare workers and data analysts need to think about how their analysis could affect marginalised groups in order to prevent biassed results and promote an open culture around data use.

3. DATA ANALYSIS CLASSIFICATION METHODS

Data analysis relies on classification algorithms to classify and label data for predictive modelling and decision-making. This section covers machine learning algorithms and deep learning classification methods and their applications in healthcare and agriculture.

Figure 1. Data analysis classification methods

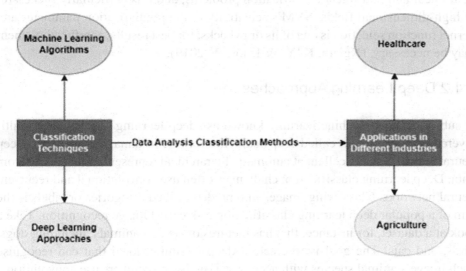

3.1 Classification Techniques

3.1.1 Machine Learning Algorithms

Machine learning algorithms identify data patterns and correlations through statistical and computational techniques, which serve as the foundation of categorisation systems. Supervised Learning trains models to predict or categorise unknown data based on labelled datasets. Common machine learning classification methods include Naive Bayes, Random Forests, SVMs and Decision Trees (Sen et al 2020). Decision trees are flexible models that work well for problems involving regression and classification. They function by dividing the input space into areas recursively, each of which is associated with a distinct class or value. conclusion trees are straightforward and simple to understand because of their tree-like representation, in which each branch denotes a conclusion based on a certain attribute of the input data. Decision trees may also handle categorical and numerical data, which extends their applicability to a broad variety of issues. On the other hand, if decision trees are very complicated, they may overfit and perform poorly when applied to new data. Strong supervised learning models that are often utilised for classification problems are support vector machines (Yamini, B et al 2023). SVM operates by maximising the margin the distance between the hyperplane and the closest data points while identifying the ideal hyperplane that divides the input data into distinct classes (support vectors). With the application of various kernel functions, SVM can handle both linear and non-linear classification problems, and it is particularly successful in high-dimensional fields. SVM's sensitivity to the regularisation parameter and kernel function selection is one of its drawbacks; for best results, careful adjustment may be necessary. (Ngiam, K. Y., & Khor, W. 2019).

3.1.2 Deep Learning Approaches

A sub-domain of machine learning known as "deep learning" investigates multi-layered neural networks called deep neural networks (Prasanna, V et al 2023). Deep neural networks are excellent at automatic hierarchical representation leaning from data. Deep learning classification challenges often use convolutional and recurrent neural networks. Classifying images into predetermined categories or labels is the aim of a popular deep learning classification task called image recognition. Take a look at a dataset, for instance, that has pictures of several animals, including dogs, birds, and cats. The goal is to create a deep learning model that can recognise each image's animal species with accuracy. Usually, researchers use convolutional neural networks (CNNs) to address this problem. Because CNNs can automatically learn features at multiple levels of abstraction from the raw pixel data, they are well-suited for image classification applications. For example, the CNN may learn to identify basic characteristics like edges and textures in the upper layers of the network, and more intricate patterns like forms and objects in the lower levels. In the training phase, labelled pictures are input into the CNN, and it uses a technique known as backpropagation to modify its internal parameters in order to minimise the discrepancy between the actual and predicted labels. The model may be taught and then used to accurately categorise fresh, unseen pictures. Overall, deep neural networks' ability to automatically build hierarchical representations from data to handle challenging classification problems is shown by deep learning classification difficulties like image recognition. (Liu, H., & Lang, B. 2019).

3.2 Applications in Different Industries

3.2.1 Healthcare

Classification aids patient care, treatment planning, and diagnosis. Medical imaging images may be categorised by machine learning algorithms to detect abnormalities or malignancy. CNNs are very useful in image-based diagnostics, generating automated and exact assessments. Predictive analytics classification methods may identify people at risk of specific diseases for preventative treatment. By predicting readmission or identifying high-risk patients, healthcare providers may better allocate resources and improve patient outcomes (Sathya et al 2020).

Figure 2. The function of DSS in data analysis

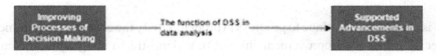

3.2.2 Agriculture

Agriculture uses classification for disease detection, crop management, and precision farming. Remote sensing data may be categorised by machine learning algorithms to assess crop health, identify insect infestations, and predict agricultural productivity. Farmers may utilise this data to boost productivity, make data-driven decisions, and optimise resource usage. CNN-based deep learning approaches have been effective in crop categorisation using satellite data. By distinguishing crop types or identifying problem areas, farmers may improve agricultural production with targeted actions (Benos et al 2021). In conclusion, classification approaches, whether based on deep learning or machine learning algorithms, are used in many fields. Both versatile and effective, they help solve complex agricultural and healthcare concerns, improving resource optimisation, decision-making, and diagnosis.

4. DECISION SUPPORT SYSTEMS (DSS) AND FUTURE PROSPECTS

4.1 The Function of DSS in Data Analysis

4.1.1 Improving Processes of Decision-Making

Decision Support Systems (DSS) are essential to data analysis because they provide information and tools that help decision-makers make well-informed, strategic decisions. DSS uses data analysis to provide decision-makers pertinent facts, trends, and projections, enabling a thorough grasp of the business environment. Decision Support Systems (DSS) improve decision-making processes by lowering uncertainty and encouraging evidence-based decisions by combining data from several sources and using analytical models.

4.1.2 Supported Advancements in DSS

DSS is expected to continue to progress in order to satisfy the changing requirements of decision-makers. Improvements in real-time data stream integration, increased visualisation methods, and predictive analytics are among the anticipated advances. It is anticipated that DSS would become more approachable, guaranteeing accessibility for decision-makers at different organisational levels. Furthermore, improvements in machine learning algorithms can make it possible for DSS to provide more precise and customised insights, enhancing decision-making skills even more.

4.2 Integration With Emerging Technologies

4.2.1. Intelligent AI for Decision Assistance

Decision Support Systems (DSS) utilising machine learning algorithms may adapt and improve over time, giving decision-makers more accurate a nd timely data (Stone et al 2020). Several strategies exist for these algorithms to evolve: 1. Continuous Learning: As fresh data becomes available, machine learning algorithms may learn. Online learning or incremental learning lets the model adapt to data patterns and trends. As more data is added, the algorithm may enhance its prediction and insight accuracy. 2. Algorithm Optimisation: Researchers are always creating new methods and algorithms to enhance machine learning models. These improvements may entail improving algorithms, training methods, or neuroscience and cognitive science discoveries. With these optimisations in DSS, decision-makers may get improved forecasts and assistance. 3. New Data Source Integration: Machine learning algorithms may be upgraded to analyse new data sources. DSS may combine data from IoT devices, social media, and other databases to better understand decision-making elements. Machine learning algorithms may provide decision-makers with more complete and actionable insights by using additional data sources. 4. Feedback Loops: Machine learning algorithms may improve with user and stakeholder input. These algorithms may improve their decision-making by analysing prior choices and modifying their techniques. This cyclical feedback loop helps DSS adapt and evolve, improving user decision support.

4.2.2 DSS and Blockchain

Blockchain's decentralisation, immutability, transparency, and cryptographic security assure data integrity and secure information sharing in Decision Support Systems (DSS).

1. Decentralisation: Blockchain is a decentralised network of nodes with no central authority. Instead, each node stores a copy of the blockchain ledger. Decentralisation eliminates a single point of failure, limiting data modification and unauthorised access. 2. Immutability: After being recorded on the blockchain, data cannot be changed retrospectively. Each blockchain block includes a cryptographic hash of the preceding block, establishing an immutable chain. This immutability guarantees the blockchain's data's integrity. 3. Transparency: Blockchain technology lets all network members see the whole transaction history, making transactions transparent and auditable. Blockchain transactions are visible and verifiable, offering a data audit trail. Transparency builds stakeholder confidence and data management responsibility. 4. Cryptographic Security: Blockchain secures data transfers and sensitive data using cryptography. Cryptographically signed and validated blockchain transactions restrict data access and modification to authorised parties. Blockchain networks confirm transactions and prevent data manipulation using consensus algorithms like PoW or PoS.

5. METHODS FOR CLINICAL TRIAL AND ANALYSIS

5.1 Importance of Data Analysis in Clinical Trials

5.1.1. Accelerating Drug Discovery

Rapid drug discovery in clinical trials is made possible in large part by data analysis(Lin et al 2020). Researchers are able to forecast effectiveness, assess safety profiles, and find possible drug candidates by analysing large datasets created during preclinical and clinical stages. Drug development takes less time and money when promising compounds are prioritised with the use of advanced analytics. Researchers may find patterns and connections by using data analysis, which helps them make better judgements as they look for new and efficient therapies.

5.1.2. Maintaining Trial Precision

For regulatory approval and later patient treatment, clinical trial results must be accurate. Through close examination of patient data, the identification of anomalies, and the reduction of biases, data analysis guarantees the accuracy and consistency of trial outcomes. Advanced analytics and statistical techniques support the validity of trial results by offering a thorough comprehension of treatment effects. For treatments to be shown safe and effective and to inspire trust in the scientific community, regulatory agencies, and medical professionals, accurate data analysis is essential.

5.2 Difficulties and New Approaches

5.2.1. Clinical Trial Big Data

Big data in clinical trials is bringing with it both potential and difficulties. On the one hand, the abundance of data enables more thorough analysis, which may reveal patient subgroups and minor therapy effects. Large dataset management, processing, and analysis, however, present difficulties. To effectively handle big data, emerging technologies include cloud computing, machine learning algorithms, and sophisticated data management systems. With the help of these technologies, data processing may be streamlined and valuable insights can be extracted by researchers without sacrificing the accuracy of their study.

5.2.2. Intelligent Data Tracking

Finding adverse events or protocol violations in clinical trials may take longer when using traditional techniques of frequent data review. This problem is solved by real-time data monitoring, which is made possible by advanced analytics and data visualisation technologies. Constant observation improves the capacity to identify problems early, protecting participant safety and data integrity. Real-time analysis-driven adaptive trial designs enable researchers to make well-informed choices during the trial, possibly reducing trial durations and optimising study results.

6. DATA ANALYSIS FOR PRECISION DECISION MAKING

6.1 Precision Medicine and Data Analytics

6.1.1. Customized Treatment Approaches

Precision medicine is made possible by data analytics, which is essential in customising medical treatments to each patient's specific needs (McPadden et al 2019). Precision medicine uses massive databases including genetic data, clinical notes, and lifestyle variables to uncover particular biomarkers and molecular fingerprints linked to various illnesses. With this degree of detail, medical professionals may create personalised treatment plans that maximise therapeutic results. Data analytics finds patterns and connections using complex algorithms and machine learning models, which help medical personnel choose the best courses of action for each patient. By going beyond the conventional one-size-fits-all model, this customised strategy promotes focused therapies that take patient groups' diversity into account. Data

Figure 3. Agri-Farming industries methodology

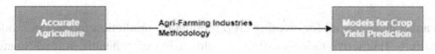

analytics-enabled precision decision-making maximises therapeutic effectiveness, reduces side effects, and optimises overall patient outcomes.

6.1.2. Implications for Ethics in Precise Decision Making

Although precision decision-making has great potential, there are ethical issues that need to be carefully considered. Sensitive genetic and health data integration raises questions about patient privacy, permission, and possible information exploitation. The advantages of precision medicine should be available to a wide range of people, preventing inequities in the delivery of healthcare, therefore concerns of fairness and access are also ethically relevant. In precision medicine, it is essential to ensure that patients are aware of the consequences of sharing their data for individualised treatment plans and that they provide their informed permission. Additionally, there's a need for ethical frameworks that govern the appropriate use of data, addressing issues about discrimination, stigmatisation, and unexpected repercussions. Establishing a delicate equilibrium between the possible advantages and moral dilemmas is crucial for promoting confidence in accurate decision-making procedures.

7. AGRICULTURAL DATA ANALYSIS

7.1 Agri-Farming Industries Methodology

7.1.1. Accurate Agriculture

Data analysis technologies have made precision agriculture a new discipline in agri-farming. Modern technology like sensors, GPS, and data analytics optimises many agricultural processes. Accurate data collection and analysis allow farmers to tailor pest control, fertilisation, and irrigation to each field area. This targeted approach boosts agricultural yield and quality while reducing environmental impact and resource consumption.

7.1.2. Models for Crop Yield Prediction

Data analysis is crucial for creating crop production prediction models in modern agriculture. Predictive models estimate yields using crop health, soil parameters, and meteorological data (Van Klompenburg et al., 2020). These models guide farmers' market strategy, crop management, and harvest timing choices. Accurate crop production projections enable proactive strategies to optimise yield, decrease risks, and ensure sustainable farming.

7.2 Agricultural Data Analysis Software Modules

7.2.1. IoT Integration in Agriculture

IoT integration in agriculture involves installing sensors and networked devices. These devices monitor temperature, humidity, soil moisture, and other things. Farmers may update their land information using data analysis. IoT in agriculture helps farmers identify plant illnesses, adjust irrigation schedules based on data, and effectively allocate resources.

7.2.2. Remote Sensing and Data Analytics

Remote sensing and data analytics are powerful tools for agricultural landscape analysis. Satellite and drone photos provide crop health, growth, and stress factors. This large picture volume is handled by data analytics to instruct farmers. This technology lets farmers monitor large areas, spot crop illnesses and nutrient deficiencies, and make educated decisions to boost productivity.

8. WEB-BASED DATA VALIDATION SYSTEMS

8.1 Importance of Data Validation

8.1.1. Ensuring Data Accuracy

Data validation is crucial because it guarantees the dependability and correctness of the information included in datasets. Data that is inconsistent or inaccurate might result in faulty analysis, poor decisions, and jeopardised company procedures. The methodical process of examining and confirming data for quality, consistency, and completeness is known as data validation. It guarantees that information entering

Figure 4. Web-Based data validation systems

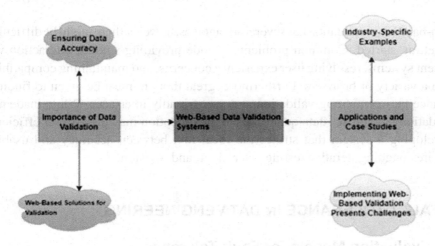

a system or database satisfies certain criteria, improving the general calibre and reliability of the data utilised for a range of applications.

8.1.2. Web-Based Solutions for Validation

The validation process is made more accessible and efficient by web-based data validation systems. These technologies lower the possibility of mistakes at the data entering stage by implementing real-time validation checks using the web's capabilities. Web forms may have validation rules, which provide users immediate feedback. Examples of these rules include necessary fields, data format requirements, and range checks. Web-based validation's instantaneous nature helps to keep reliable data throughout its lifespan in a proactive manner.

8.2 Applications and Case Studies

8.2.1. Industry-Specific Examples

These examples highlight the many uses for web-based data validation. Web-based validation, for example, minimises mistakes that might have major financial ramifications by ensuring proper entry of financial transactions in the banking industry. Validation checks are performed on patient data submitted via online interfaces in the healthcare industry to ensure the accuracy of medical records. These illustrations highlight how important web-based data validation is to the industry as a whole for guaranteeing data accuracy and adherence to industry standards.

8.2.2. Implementing Web-Based Validation Presents Challenges

Web-based data validation has several advantages, however there might be difficulties in getting started. Common problems include providing smooth interaction with current systems, resolving user experience concerns, and maintaining compatibility with a variety of browsers. Furthermore, great thought must be given to finding a balance between strong validation and user-friendly interfaces. While inadequate validation jeopardises data quality, too tight validation may impair user efficiency. Developing a system that strikes the ideal mix between accuracy and usability requires ongoing iterative testing, user input, and revision.

9. FAULT TOLERANCE IN DATA ENGINEERING

9.1 Evaluation Models for Fault Tolerance

9.1.1. Reliability Metrics

Reliability metrics are used in data engineering fault tolerance to evaluate and improve system resilience. Reliability measures quantify how long a system can function without experiencing any problems. Mean Time to Recovery (MTTR) and Mean Time Between Failures (MTBF) are examples of common metrics. Whereas MTTR gauges the typical amount of time needed to return a system to normal function after a breakdown, MTBF evaluates the average amount of time a system runs before a failure occurs. These metrics provide standards for recovery and dependability, which help engineers create fault-tolerant systems.

9.1.2. Strategies for Redundancy

One of the most important aspects of fault tolerance is redundancy. They include making duplicates of essential system parts in case of a failure to guarantee system continuation. There are many ways to create redundancy: network redundancy (ensuring multiple network channels), software redundancy (using backup software systems), and hardware redundancy (duplication of physical components). The particular needs and system criticality of the data engineering rely on the redundancy solutions used. Redundancy that is properly established reduces the effect of failures and ensures smooth operation even when components encounter problems.

9.2 Utilisation in Various Sectors

9.2.1. Systems of Healthcare

Fault tolerance is essential in healthcare systems because system availability and data quality are critical. Ensuring patient care requires consistent access to treatment plans, diagnostic tools, and patient records. The flawless operation of healthcare systems is guaranteed by fault-tolerant data engineering, even in the event of hardware malfunctions or network problems. Reliability in measurements and redundancy in crucial components help healthcare data systems be resilient, reducing downtime and preserving patient data integrity.

9.2.2. Electricity Production

Data engineering systems play a critical role in the power generating industry's monitoring and management of energy output. In order to provide a steady and uninterrupted power supply and avoid downtime, fault tolerance is essential. Power generation engineers use evaluation models, such reliability metrics, to evaluate the effectiveness of predictive maintenance tools and control systems. Redundancy techniques protect against malfunctions that might cause power outages, especially in control and communication systems. Fault-tolerant data engineering guarantees the dependable functioning of important infrastructure in the power generating industry, where real-time data is essential for grid stability.

10. HEURISTIC DATA ANALYSIS TECHNIQUES FOR RECORD MANAGEMENT

10.1 Overview of Heuristic Approaches

10.1.1. Enhancing Record Management Efficiency

The goal of heuristic approaches in data analysis for record management is to increase productivity via the use of intuitive, rule-based techniques. These strategies include the creation of heuristic algorithms, which give certain rules or patterns precedence over laborious computing techniques. Heuristic methods simplify the process of categorising, retrieving, and organising data in record administration. Heuristic techniques may efficiently and rapidly classify records by using domain-specific knowledge and presumptions, hence maximising the overall effectiveness of record management systems.

10.1.2. Cognitive Record Ordering Techniques

A subclass of heuristic techniques called intelligent record sorting algorithms seeks to dynamically arrange records according to user behaviour, patterns, or significance. These algorithms anticipate how records should be arranged for certain users or situations by adapting and learning from past use patterns. These heuristics enhance user experience by adding intelligence to the sorting process, enabling more personalised and intuitive record retrieval.

10.2 Case Studies and Difficulties in Implementation

10.2.1. Real-World Applications

Heuristic data analysis methods have practical uses in a range of fields. Intelligent record sorting algorithms in customer relationship management (CRM) systems may rank leads according to engagement metrics or past conversions. Heuristics may be used in document management systems to automatically identify and classify documents, making retrieval easier. The adaptability of heuristic techniques in tackling particular record management difficulties across sectors is shown by real-world applications.

10.2.2. Tackling Restrictions and Enhancing Heuristic Methods

Heuristic approaches have advantages, but their scalability and flexibility are limited. Implementations and case studies provide information on how to deal with these constraints. It is crucial to continuously improve heuristic algorithms based on user input and changing data trends. Continuous optimisation is necessary to address issues like underfitting or overfitting, particularly in dynamic contexts. Additionally, resolving the trade-off between computing efficiency and accuracy is vital to guarantee that heuristic strategies remain successful and scalable in handling huge datasets.

11. DATA ANALYSIS MODEL FOR EXPERIMENTAL SETUP AND ANALYSIS

11.1 Importance of Data Analysis in Experimental Design

11.1.1. Optimizing Experimental Parameters

For the purpose of optimising parameters and guaranteeing the efficacy and efficiency of trials, data analysis is essential to experimental design. Researchers may fine-tune experimental settings by identifying the most important elements influencing results using statistical analysis and modelling. By concentrating on important variables, this optimisation approach improves the accuracy and dependability of studies while conserving resources and time. Scientific studies are made more successful when researchers are able to make well-informed judgements on the parameters of their experiments thanks to data analysis.

11.1.2. Assuring the Reproducibility of Data

Reproducibility of experimental outcomes is largely dependent on data processing. The dependability and consistency of data across studies may be evaluated by researchers by using rigors statistical tools and validation approaches. In order to increase trust in scientific discoveries and make it easier for other researchers to verify experimental results, reproducibility is essential. Strong data analysis enhances accountability and openness in research, which raises the legitimacy of scientific findings.

11.2 Future Trends in the Analysis of Experimental Data

11.2.1. AI and Machine Learning Integration

More artificial intelligence (AI) and machine learning (ML) approaches will be integrated into experimental data analysis in the future (Rajendran et al 2023). These technologies are capable of handling complicated information, seeing patterns, and producing insights that conventional analytical techniques would find difficult to provide. Predictive modelling, automatic pattern recognition, and the identification of new links in experimental data are all made possible by AI and ML. The efficiency and depth of data analysis are improved by this integration, giving researchers important information for better experimental design decision-making (Kumar et al., 2023).

11.2.2. Collaborative Data Sharing Platforms

Platforms for collaboration are becoming essential for analysing experimental data. These systems enable smooth data exchange between researchers, promoting cooperation and quickening the advancement of science. Cross-validation of results, investigation of many viewpoints, and integration of data from several trials are made possible via shared datasets. The scientific community is made more transparent and linked via collaborative platforms, which also allow researchers to use a larger data set for in-depth analysis.

12. DATA ANALYSIS FOR SOLAR PV POWER GENERATION

12.1 Estimation of Unknown Parameters in Solar PV Systems

12.1.1. Modeling Solar Panel Behaviour

Estimating unknown parameters is a crucial aspect of data analysis in solar PV power production, especially when modelling the behaviour of solar panels. Optimising energy output requires an understanding of how solar panels react to changing environmental factors, such as temperature and sunshine intensity. Data-driven models forecast how various factors affect solar panel efficiency by analysing previous performance data. With the use of this modelling, the behaviour of solar panels may be accurately represented, improving system design and performance optimisation.

12.1.2. Estimating Output Power

Predicting the electricity production of solar PV systems is another use of parameter estimation. In order to forecast the anticipated electricity production, data analysis approaches, such as machine learning algorithms, make use of historical data, weather trends, and solar panel properties. This predictive capacity is necessary for grid integration, energy planning, and guaranteeing a steady supply of electricity. Stakeholders may make educated choices regarding energy distribution, storage, and system maintenance with the help of accurate forecasts.

12.2 Applications in Maximum Power Point Tracking (MPPT) and Efficiency Improvement

12.2.1. Difficulties in Partial Shading Situations

Dealing with partial shade situations, in which certain solar panel sections get less sunlight owing to impediments or environmental variables, is one difficulty for solar PV systems. In order to detect and lessen the effects of partial shading on electricity production, data analysis is essential. Algorithms examine shade patterns and past data to use efficient tactics, including system reconfiguration or individual panel operation adjustments, to maximise power production under difficult circumstances.

12.2.2. Data-Driven Solutions for Increased Efficiency

Data analysis offers data-driven solutions to raise solar photovoltaic systems' efficiency. Through the constant monitoring and analysis of performance data, algorithms are able to detect abnormalities, trends, and possible problems in real time. With this proactive approach, maintenance requirements can be swiftly addressed, efficiency can be maximised, and the overall performance of the solar power production system may be optimised. Solar PV systems can adjust to changing climatic circumstances using data-driven solutions, which guarantees maximum energy production and system lifespan.

13. DATA ANALYSIS FOR WEATHER FORECASTING

13.1 Significance of Data Analytics in Weather Prediction

13.1.1. Improving Accuracy of Forecast Models

A key factor in improving the precision of weather forecasting models is data analytics. Meteorologists are able to improve and calibrate forecasting models via the examination of large datasets that include historical weather patterns, atmospheric conditions, and real-time observations. Complex patterns are identified by sophisticated statistical approaches and machine learning algorithms, which help to provide forecasts that are more accurate. The value of data analytics is found in its capacity to identify patterns and linkages that more conventional approaches would miss, which eventually leads to ongoing improvements in weather prediction accuracy.

13.1.2. Real-Time Data Integration

Accurate and timely weather forecasts depend on real-time data integration. The integration of current information from several sources, such as satellites, weather stations, and distant sensors, is made possible via data analytics. Integrating real-time data helps forecast models to dynamically alter, offering more accurate and current forecasts. Predictions for short-term and immediate weather occurrences are more reliable when real-time data analysis and incorporation guarantee that weather forecasts reflect the most recent atmospheric conditions.

13.2 Difficulties and Emerging Technologies

13.2.1. Meteorological Big Data

Big data's introduction to meteorology brings with it both benefits and problems. Advanced data processing and storage capabilities are needed due to the sheer amount and diversity of data provided by sensors, satellites, and other sources. Big data analytics in meteorology, on the other hand, makes it possible to extract insightful information that makes more precise and nuanced weather forecasts. Meteorologists may better understand meteorological events by modelling complicated atmospheric interactions via the handling of huge datasets.

13.2.2. Machine Learning for Identifying Weather Patterns

Machine learning ML is becoming more and more popular in the weather pattern detection field, because it is a powerful method of finding complicated patterns in the meteorological data. Machine learning algorithms may help to forecast weather phenomena more accurately by analyzing trends in atmospheric variables. Machine learning makes the understanding of complex relationships better by training models to learn based on past data, which in turn helps meteorologist identify and predict weather trends more precisely. Incorporating machine learning in weather forecasting is a viable method to improve prediction skills and understand the nuances of climate systems. In general, data analytics is the cornerstone of weather forecasting because it enables real-time integration and the analysis of massive data sets, which has the effect of increasing the accuracy of predictions. Innovative analytics of issues such as big data and the process of machine learning as well as other emerging technologies in the study of weather patterns is leading us into a new age of more detailed and more knowledgeable weather forecasts (Gracious et al., 2023).

14. CONCLUSION

The Impact of Data Analysis in Healthcare: The use of data analysis in healthcare has produced major breakthroughs and possibilities that have enhanced patient care and treatment approaches. But there are obstacles to overcome, including ethical and privacy issues, which must be carefully considered. Techniques of Classification: Examining categorisation techniques in general, and machine learning and deep learning in particular, showed how widely used they are in healthcare and agriculture, where they are essential for predictive modelling and decision assistance. Systems for Decision Support (DSS): The function of DSS in data analysis, together with its expected advancements and incorporation with cutting-edge technologies like blockchain and artificial intelligence, highlights its growing importance in improving decision-making procedures in a variety of sectors. Analysis of Clinical Trial Data: The significance of data analysis in clinical trials was underlined, removing obstacles and opening the door to more effective drug development and trial accuracy, particularly with big data integration and real-time monitoring. Medical Decision Making with Precision: Healthcare is changing as a result of the combination of data analytics and precision medicine, which offers individualised treatment plans. Precision decision-making has ethical ramifications that emphasise the need of responsible application. Agricultural Data Analysis: The study examined techniques used by the agri-farming sectors, with a focus on crop yield prediction models, precision agriculture, and the use of IoT and remote sensing for data analytics. Web-Based Systems for Validating Data: In addition to highlighting the significance of data validation, the study examined web-based solutions, provided examples relevant to certain industries, and addressed implementation issues. Fault Tolerance in Data Engineering: Evaluation models were covered, with applicability in a variety of sectors including power generation and healthcare systems. These models included reliability measures and redundancy techniques. Record Management Using Heuristic Data Analysis: We looked at heuristic methods to record management, which increase productivity by using intelligent record sorting algorithms. We also discussed practical applications and areas for further development. Model for Experimental Data Analysis: It was emphasised how crucial data analysis is to the design of experiments, parameter optimisation, and data repeatability. Future developments were explored, such as AI integration and cooperative platforms for data exchange. Meteorological and Solar PV Data Analysis: It was investigated how data analysis may be used to generate solar PV electricity, particularly for estimating unknown parameters and handling problems when there is partial shade. The importance of data analytics in weather forecasting was also explained, with an emphasis on enhancing accuracy and using cutting-edge technologies like big data and machine learning.

In addition to offering a broad overview of the existing situation, the survey points forth potential future study areas and objectives. The integration of artificial intelligence (AI), machine learning, and collaboration platforms across many areas presents significant opportunities to enhance data analysis skills as technology progresses. Exciting directions for future study include addressing ethical issues, improving heuristic techniques, and solving difficulties with fault tolerance and experimental data processing. Examining the long-term effects of precision medicine and using data analytics to support personalised treatment opens up new avenues in the field of healthcare. Research is still being done on how to best integrate IoT and use remote sensing for more sustainable and productive farming methods. There is much to learn about the ongoing development of web-based validation systems and the investigation of fault tolerance in many sectors. Interdisciplinary cooperation, using cutting-edge technology, and tackling the changing problems brought on by large and complicated datasets are key components of the data analysis of the future. It is recommended that scholars, professionals, and decision-makers use these chances to promote creativity and further the continuous progress of data analysis in many fields.

REFERENCES

Ambigavathi, M., & Sridharan, D. (2018). Big Data Analytics in Healthcare. *2018 Tenth International Conference on Advanced Computing (ICoAC)*, Chennai, India. 10.1109/ICoAC44903.2018.8939061

Benos, L., Tagarakis, A. C., Dolias, G., Berruto, R., Kateris, D., & Bochtis, D. (2021). Machine learning in agriculture: A comprehensive updated review. *Sensors (Basel)*, *21*(11), 3758. doi:10.3390/s21113758 PMID:34071553

Brunton, S. L., Nathan Kutz, J., Manohar, K., Aravkin, A. Y., Morgansen, K., Klemisch, J., Goebel, N., Buttrick, J., Poskin, J., Blom-Schieber, A. W., Hogan, T., & McDonald, D. (2021). Data-driven aerospace engineering: Reframing the industry with machine learning. *AIAA Journal*, *59*(8), 2820–2847. doi:10.2514/1.J060131

Gracious, L. A., Jasmine, R. M., Pooja, E., Anish, T. P., Johncy, G., & Subramanian, R. S. (2023, October). Machine Learning and Deep Learning Transforming Healthcare: An Extensive Exploration of Applications, Algorithms, and Prospects. In *2023 4th IEEE Global Conference for Advancement in Technology (GCAT)* (pp. 1-6). IEEE.

Guo, C., & Chen, J. (2023). Big data analytics in healthcare. In *Knowledge Technology and Systems: Toward Establishing Knowledge Systems Science* (pp. 27–70). Springer Nature Singapore. doi:10.1007/978-981-99-1075-5_2

Kumar, V. N., Gayathri, S., Deepa, S., Varun, C. M., & Subramanian, R. S. (2023, August). A comprehensive survey of machine learning: Advancements, applications, and challenges. In *2023 Second International Conference on Augmented Intelligence and Sustainable Systems (ICAISS)* (pp. 354-361). IEEE.

Lin, X., Li, X., & Lin, X. (2020). A review on applications of computational methods in drug screening and design. *Molecules (Basel, Switzerland), 25*(6), 1375. doi:10.3390/molecules25061375 PMID:32197324

Liu, H., & Lang, B. (2019). Machine learning and deep learning methods for intrusion detection systems: A survey. *applied sciences, 9*(20), 4396.

McPadden, J., Durant, T. J., Bunch, D. R., Coppi, A., Price, N., Rodgerson, K., Torre, C. J. Jr, Byron, W., Hsiao, A. L., Krumholz, H. M., & Schulz, W. L. (2019). Health care and precision medicine research: Analysis of a scalable data science platform. *Journal of Medical Internet Research, 21*(4), e13043. doi:10.2196/13043 PMID:30964441

Ngiam, K. Y., & Khor, W. (2019). Big data and machine learning algorithms for health-care delivery. *The Lancet. Oncology, 20*(5), e262–e273. doi:10.1016/S1470-2045(19)30149-4 PMID:31044724

Nguyen, T., Li, Z. H. O. U., Spiegler, V., Ieromonachou, P., & Lin, Y. (2018). Big data analytics in supply chain management: A state-of-the-art literature review. *Computers & Operations Research, 98*, 254–264. doi:10.1016/j.cor.2017.07.004

Prasanna, V., & Ambhika, C. (2023). A Comprehensive Survey of Deep Learning: Advancements, Applications, and Challenges. *International Journal on Recent and Innovation Trends in Computing and Communication, 11*(8s), 445–453. doi:10.17762/ijritcc.v11i8s.7225

Rajendran, T., Rajathi, S. A., Balakrishnan, C., Aswini, J., Prakash, R. B., & Subramanian, R. S. (2023, December). Risk Prediction Modeling for Breast Cancer using Supervised Machine Learning Approaches. In *2023 2nd International Conference on Automation, Computing and Renewable Systems (ICACRS)* (pp. 702-708). IEEE. 10.1109/ICACRS58579.2023.10404482

Ranjith, J., & Mahantesh, K. (2019). *Privacy and Security issues in Smart Health Care*. 2019 4th International Conference on Electrical, Electronics, Communication, Computer Technologies and Optimization Techniques (ICEECCOT), Mysuru, India. 10.1109/ICEECCOT46775.2019.9114681

Sathya, D., Sudha, V., & Jagadeesan, D. (2020). Application of machine learning techniques in healthcare. In *Handbook of Research on Applications and Implementations of Machine Learning Techniques* (pp. 289–304). IGI Global. doi:10.4018/978-1-5225-9902-9.ch015

Sen, P. C., Hajra, M., & Ghosh, M. (2020). Supervised classification algorithms in machine learning: A survey and review. In *Emerging Technology in Modelling and Graphics: Proceedings of IEM Graph 2018* (pp. 99-111). Springer Singapore. 10.1007/978-981-13-7403-6_11

Sharma, K., & Baalamurugan, K. M. (2021). *A review on Big Data Privacy and Security Techniques for the Healthcare Records*. 2021 3rd International Conference on Advances in Computing, Communication Control and Networking (ICAC3N), Greater Noida, India. 10.1109/ICAC3N53548.2021.9725455

Stone, M., Aravopoulou, E., Ekinci, Y., Evans, G., Hobbs, M., Labib, A., Laughlin, P., Machtynger, J., & Machtynger, L. (2020). Artificial intelligence (AI) in strategic marketing decision-making: A research agenda. *The Bottom Line (New York, N.Y.)*, *33*(2), 183–200. doi:10.1108/BL-03-2020-0022

Van Klompenburg, T., Kassahun, A., & Catal, C. (2020). Crop yield prediction using machine learning: A systematic literature review. *Computers and Electronics in Agriculture*, *177*, 105709. doi:10.1016/j.compag.2020.105709

Yamini, B., Kaneti, V. R., & Nalini, M. (2023). Machine Learning-driven PCOS prediction for early detection and tailored interventions. *SSRG International Journal of Electrical and Electronics Engineering*, *10*(9), 61–75. doi:10.14445/23488379/IJEEE-V10I9P106

Chapter 7
Design and Economic Analysis of Grid–Connected PV System in Kamrup Polytechnic

Sabiha Raiyesha
Assam Don Bosco University, India

Papul Changmai
Assam Don Bosco University, India

ABSTRACT

Educational institutes have ample potential and good scope to generate solar energy. As these institutes function during daytime, the generated energy can be used in order to meet the electricity requirements of the campus. It can both be designed to work as grid-connected and off-grid mode using the unused rooftops of these institutes. In this study, a 90 kWp grid connected solar photovoltaic system for Kamrup Polytechnic in Baihata Chariali has been designed at the proposed rooftop. It simulated using PVsyst version7.0.9 simulation tool. The annual energy generation from simulation for the 90 kWp grid connected 12675 kWh with a performance ratio of 73.1%. Economic analysis of these PV systems has also been performed to determine the annual levelised cost of energy production which is found to range from about Rs 3.170/kWp for 90 kWp PV system. This work summarizes the estimation of electrical load in Kamrup polytechnic, the design of PV system, the simulation results, performance analysis, as well as economic analysis for grid connected PVsystem.

DOI: 10.4018/979-8-3693-2260-4.ch007

1. INTRODUCTION

The most ample and plentiful energy source on Earth is solar energy. A renewable resource, solar energy has great potential for our future in clean energy. Each photon of sunlight that reaches Earth carries energy that powers several processes on our planet, such as weather patterns and energy sources, in addition to giving light during the day. The amount of solar radiation that reaches the surface of the Earth in only one hour could hypothetically provide all of the world's energy demands for over a year. By using solar thermal or photovoltaic collectors, we can capture this energy and transform it into useful energy. The exponential rise of solar energy places it among the most affordable and rapidly expanding power sources globally. Improvements in solar panel technology are driving its progress, which has positive effects on the environment as well as the economy. Nonetheless, it's important to take into account difficulties like the requirement for smooth interaction with current energy networks and energy storage for sporadic availability. Since solar irradiance varies by area globally, customisation is required for optimal solar energy consumption. The efficiency and accessibility of solar technology are being shaped by continuous study and innovation in the pursuit of greener energy.

1.1 Photovoltaic System

In photovoltaics, light is directly converted at the atomic level into electrical power. Photoelectric materials, which absorb light photons and release electrons as a result, are necessary for this process. These freed electrons produce an electric current that may be used to create power when they are collected. When certain materials were exposed to light in 1839, French physicist Edmund Becquerel noticed that they might produce a little electric current. This observation led to the discovery of the photoelectric effect. Albert Einstein won the Nobel Prize in physics in 1905 for his explanations of the nature of light and the photoelectric effect, which established the groundwork for photovoltaic technology. Bell Laboratories produced the first solar battery in 1954, which marked the beginning of the development of useful photovoltaic modules. Photovoltaic technology gained popularity as a practical power source for non-space applications during the 1970s energy crisis.

1.2 Types of Photovoltaic Systems

The photovoltaic (PV) effect is used by solar panels to convert solar radiation or sunlight into direct current (DC) electricity. This direct current (DC) electricity may be converted to alternating current (AC) power using a solar converter, or it can be stored in a battery. Appliances in the home can then be powered by this AC electricity. Any extra solar energy may be stored using different battery storage systems or fed into the electrical grid to earn revenue. A photovoltaic system may be classified into three primary groups based on how it is set up: stand-alone, grid-connected, and hybrid PV systems. Despite these variations, the essential ideas and elements of a fundamental PV systems don't change. These systems' adaptability originates from their capacity to meet certain requirements by adjusting the type and quantity of the essential components.

Standalone PV system: In a stand-alone PV system, a bank of batteries is charged by the solar panels without being linked to the grid. The power generated by the solar panels is stored in these batteries, which are subsequently used to supply electricity to the electrical loads. For a very long time, stand-alone solar power systems have been utilized in places without access to a public grid. A standalone photovoltaic system is a group of linked electrical parts that we may use to harness solar energy to create electricity and meet our daily energy needs without having to worry about periods of time when there might not be enough sunshine (Dobos, 2013). This kind of system is only beneficial when a load has to run at night or in another moment when there isn't any sunshine for a while. One solar PV array, two charge controllers, three inverters, four batteries, five cables, and six protection devices make up such a system. The system's component requirements will depend on the location's radiation intensity and load requirements.

Grid-connected PV system: A solar PV power system that generates energy and is connected to the utility grid is known as a grid-connected photovoltaic system, or grid-connected PV system. Solar panels, one or more inverters, a power conditioning unit, and apparatus to connect to the grid make up a grid-connected photovoltaic system. The scale of these systems varies, from modest rooftop installations for homes and businesses to huge utility-scale solar power plants. Grid-connected designs, in contrast to stand-alone power systems, usually do not feature an integrated battery solution because of their comparatively high cost. When everything is working well, the grid-connected PV system feeds back excess electricity to the utility grid, which is more than what the connected load can use (Gupta and Sisodia, 2013).

PV hybrid system: These days, hybrid systems come in a variety of shapes and sizes and integrate solar and battery storage into one unit. Even currently operating grid-connected devices can now benefit from the integration of battery storage due to the declining cost of battery storage. This development makes it possible to store solar energy produced during the day for usage at night. The grid provides consumers with the best of both worlds by acting as a dependable backup once the stored energy is used up. Hybrid systems may also use cheap off-peak power, which is frequently available from midnight until six in the morning, to charge batteries. Here's a breakdown of how a hybrid system operates (N. Manoj Kumar, K. Sudhakar, M. Samykano, 2014).

(i) Battery Bank: In a hybrid system, the battery bank receives any solar power surplus over what your property's appliances require. The battery bank stops receiving electricity from the solar system after it is fully charged. You may then use the energy that is stored in the batteries to power your house, generally in the evening when electricity prices are at their greatest.

(ii) Electricity Grid and Meter: The amount of excess solar electricity that is not utilized by your appliances may be exported through your meter and sent into the grid, depending on how your hybrid system is set up and the regulations of your utility provider. When your batteries run out of useable power and your solar system isn't working, your appliances will start using electricity from the grid

2. LITERATURE SURVEY

Numerous and extensive studies have been examined with various approaches to the design and performance evaluation of PV systems. Due in large part to their significant cost decrease, a large body of research has highlighted the revolutionary potential of PV systems in the energy environment. The body of research continually highlights how powerful solar PV systems are at enabling countries to become energy sovereign and independent. The best solar energy is captured during the sun's zenith, which is usually about noon, and this results in increased power production. On the other hand, cloud cover reduces the efficiency with which sunlight is absorbed since clouds reflect sunlight, which lowers panel absorption. During hot summer days with high temperatures and rapid heat buildup, solar power output might decrease by 10% to 25 percent. This decrease can be attributed to increased heat producing increased semiconductor conductivity, which upsets charge balance and weakens the electric field. Humidity seeping into solar panel frames can also impair panel performance, thus reducing power production and perhaps leading to long-term performance deterioration.

A number of factors, such as wind speed, ambient temperature, and sun irradiation, affect how well PV systems operate. It is difficult to maintain constant sun insolation levels, which affects PV array performance. PV system performance can significantly decline in situations of non-uniform insolation, such as partial shading of cells caused by transient clouds, shadows from surrounding structures, and distant shadowing.

Kumar et al. looked at the viability of building a 1 MW grid-connected solar plant on several University Malaysia Pahang (UMP) campuses. The commercial and domain properties of the PV plant were assessed using standard criteria using the software tools PVGIS and PV Watt.

Psomopoulos et al. provided information on the performance of Greece's current PV parks, which include a 105.6 kWp PV plant, a 9.6 kWp roof-integrated PV array, and an installation with a 98.4 kWp 2-axis tracking mechanism. The quantity of power produced by the existing PV parks is measured and quantified using the modeling tools PVGIS, PV Watt, and RET Screen. The software outputs were verified using real-time figures that demonstrated the advantages of each software product.

Baitule et al. examined the feasibility of building a 100% solar PV base on a MANIT campus in Bhopal, by A 5 MWp PV plant is suggested to be installed on the campus's open space and rooftop area. The Solar Advisory Model (SAM) and PV Syst software tools are used to assess the solar PV plant's technological and financial viability.

Abbood et al. summarized a PV system design of a 1 MW grid-connected under the Iraq climate condition. Since the city has considerably high solar radiation it has a high potential to build PV systems on large scales. In the first year, an estimated 1757.8 MWh of energy were produced, resulting in a total life cycle production of 40,445 MWh, with an average capacity factor of 19.83% and a performance ratio that ranges from 86.4% to 73%.

Shukla et al. employed SolarGIS PV planner software to analyze the output of a 110 kWp rooftop solar PV plant. Four distinct module types are simulated in order to calculate the energy yield and performance ratio. The authors came to the conclusion that energy yields are observed in the range of 2.67 kWh/kWp to 3.36 kWh/kWp, and the performance ratio runs from 70 to 80%.

Malvoni et al. carried out research that looked at a 960 kWp photovoltaic (PV) system's performance in southern Italy over the course of 43 months. Evaluating energy yields, losses, and overall efficiency was the main objective. The study also included a performance comparison of this system with comparable photovoltaic installations located in different climates, with an emphasis on deterioration rates. In order to do this, the research rates. SAM and PV Syst, two widely used PV modeling tools, were utilized in the study to accomplish this. These techniques were used to contrast the predicted results with the examined PV system's actual performance. According to the findings, PV Syst understated the average yearly energy delivered into the grid by almost 3.3%, while SAM underestimated it by about 3.0%. PV Syst performed better overall than the SAM approach in spite of these differences.

Kumar et al. suggested a machine-learning approach to predict the sun irradiation for the next three years. The paper emphasizes how this algorithm may be used to predict future energy potentials and rates of deterioration in order to increase the capacity of power projects. Kumar et al. used the PV Syst tool to forecast how a 200 kWp rooftop solar power plant on a complex will run. 292,954 MWh of energy can be generated annually with a 77.27% energy loss and a −26.5% PR loss.

3. OBJECTIVES

The sun emits an ample quantity of energy into Earth, enough to meet the planet's energy needs for a whole year. Photovoltaic cells, as these panels are called, are found on a variety of surfaces, including computers, roofs, and spaceships. These solar cells, which are made of semiconductor materials like to those in computer chips, work by releasing electrons from atoms when exposed to sunlight. As the electrons go through the cell, electricity is produced by their movement.

Moreover, a battery can be included which functions as a power source by recycling water to produce electricity. A typical solar panel may generate 200 watts or more of power on average. It takes around 25 solar panels, or a five-kilowatt-hour array, to power a building the size of a bank. About 1,000 watts of sunshine are absorbed by these solar panels per square meter of surface area. A higher facility, such as a high school, requires a capacity of 6.25 megawatts, or 24 solar panels.

The project is carried out undertaking three objectives –

(i)   To estimate the electrical load demand of Kamrup Polytechnic: The load demand comprises of the existing electrical loads of the three building namely Administrative Building, Academic Building and the Workshop. The total electrical demand of the different type of loads like - lighting, appliances, data processing, laboratory and workshop loads of Kamrup Polytechnic is calculated

(ii) To design the grid connected solar photovoltaic system for the Kamrup Polytechnic: Depending upon the load, a grid connected PV plant of that capacity is designed to meet the electrical demand of Kamrup Polytechnic. Open rooftop area of the buildings are accounted as per required by the design of the PV plant for the arrangement of the panels.

(iii) To estimate the cost of electricity generation from the solar power system: The potential and cost effectiveness from the designed solar PV power plant is to be analyzed

4. METHODOLOGY

In order to match the rated power output, the photovoltaic array's size is decided by the PV system's overall capacity. This entails using module specs to fulfill the needs of the system. However, evaluating the proposed system's viability and modeling it in the desired site are crucial steps before implementation. Several software systems are available for doing this examination. The reports produced by these simulations help in evaluating and choosing the best model to use in practice. Here, the system specs and geographical information are crucial.

There are several simulation tools available for evaluating the performance of PV systems. Here are a few of them:

(i)   PV*SOL: This program helps with the design and modeling of solar PV systems that are site-specific. It needs input for things like location coordinates, weather information, and system and auxiliary device specs.

(ii) SolarGIS: An online modeling program that uses satellite maps as assistance, it helps with designing and optimizing solar PV systems, comparing energy outputs from various PV technologies, and prospecting sites. Data on PV technology, local coordinates, AC/DC losses, load demand, and cable size are required.

(iii) PVGIS: This open-source research tool helps with EU policy-making and makes it easier to evaluate the effectiveness of PV technology in certain geographical areas. It needs information on the mounting position, monthly values of the atmospheric condition, and total irradiance.

(iv) SISIFO: An open web service program for simulating photovoltaic systems that requires data on the location of the system, solar resource statistics, technical specs of the system, and, optionally, financial factors.

(v)   PVsyst: This program offers a complete database of PV panels, inverters, and meteorological data, and it facilitates the construction of whole PV systems that are linked to the grid. It computes the cost analysis of the system's installation and electricity generation.

Precise measurements of the rooftop areas of the two existing buildings at the project site are necessary for system installation. For an accurate evaluation and analysis, meteorological information for the area—such as temperature, solar radiation, and other pertinent factors—will also be required.

4.1 Simulation Software

A software program called PVsyst was created at the University of Geneva with the express purpose of being used as an energy modeling tool for photovoltaic (PV) system research, simulation, and design. PVsyst is a modeling program that, in its 7.0.9 edition, primarily focuses on carefully examining, sizing, and analyzing data for whole solar systems. PV systems of all kinds, including grid-connected, standalone, pumping, and DC-grid topologies, are covered by this program. It is noteworthy for providing large databases with meteorological information and parts related to PV systems, in addition to more general tools for solar energy research. The program is divided into four main sections:

(i)   Initial Design: This phase allows for a quick assessment of a project's possibilities and potential drawbacks in a particular setting. It functions as the first stage of sizing. In this mode, real system components do not need to be specified because the program evaluates system yields in monthly increments fast and with just a few generic system features or parameters. It also offers a ballpark estimate of the system cost. Although this degree of precision is especially useful for grid-connected systems and architects, it is not meant for in-depth reporting.

(ii) Project Design: This section, which forms the software's core, is essential for a full project analysis. It entails choosing meteorological data, planning the system, carrying out research on shade, calculating losses, and assessing financial factors. The simulation provides a comprehensive report and additional data, covering an entire year in hourly stages. These outcomes are arranged in a "project" framework that include meteorological and geographic information. Users can carry out parameter analysis and optimizations using different simulation runs, or variations. Users choose certain system components and set things like plane orientation (including tracking planes and shed mounting choices). The program helps with PV array design by figuring out how many PV modules to put in series and parallel using the selected inverter model for a grid-connected.

(iii) Parameter Analysis: Users may now select more complex parameters and see more detailed impacts, including mismatch, thermal behavior, wiring, module quality, incidence angle losses, horizon shading, and partial shading from objects nearby that affect the PV array. Numerous simulation variables are included in the findings, which may be exported to other applications and shown in monthly, daily, or hourly figures. The Loss Diagram function is especially helpful in locating flaws in the system architecture. Every simulation run produces a report with the main findings and all of the simulation's parameters. It also makes a thorough economic analysis possible with real component pricing, additional expenses, and investment requirements. The program also determines the quantity of CO_2 emissions that are prevented.

(iv) Databases: This section is devoted to database management for PV components and meteorological data. It includes activities including setting up and maintaining geographic locations, producing and displaying hourly meteorological data, and importing meteorological data from custom ASCII files or preset sources. Databases of manufacturers and parts used in PV installations, such as PV modules, inverters, batteries, and other parts, are also kept in this section.

(v) Tools: It is used for quickly predicting and visualizing a PV installation's behavior are provided in this section. It also provides specific tools that are helpful for maintaining solar energy installations. Tables and graphs showing solar geometry parameters or climatic data, irradiation simulations under a clear day model, evaluations of PV array performance under partial shade or module mismatch (Baruah, Boruah and Prasanth, 2017).

4.1.1 Meteorological Data in PVSyst

The simulation process requires the following meteorological data –

1) Global horizontal irradiation
2) Ambient temperature
3) Diffuse horizontal irradiation

4.1.2 Terminologies in PVSyst

In the simulation, a set of terms with specific meanings is utilized:

(i) Albedo: The percentage of incoming solar radiation that the ground reflects back toward a plane that is inclined is known as albedo. As the surface is horizontal, its value is 0; as the tilt angle varies, it rises.

(ii) Plane Orientation: In order to customize the plane's orientation during simulations, PVsyst provides a number of options, such as monitoring tilt axis, seasonal tilt adjustment, multi orientations, and fixed tilted plane. A fixed tilted plane orientation is used for this project.

(iii) Tilt Angle: The angle formed by the PV module's plane and the horizontal plane is called the tilt angle. A location's ideal tilt angle must be selected in order to maximize solar radiation collection and increase energy production.

(iv) Nominal Power (Pnom): Pnom, as defined by the PV module manufacturer, is the installed output power of the photovoltaic array under Standard Test Conditions (STC), which include 1000 W/m², 25°C, and AM 1.5. This amount is expressed in kWp.

(v) Reference Yield (Yr): Yr is the optimal array yield (i.e., no losses) determined by Pnom. It shows the expected energy production in kWh for every occurrence that occurs over the course of an hour.

(vi) Array Yield (Ya): Ya determines the daily energy output of the PV array, which is expressed in terms of kWh per kWp per day.

(vii) System Yield or Final Yield (Yf): Yf represents the daily usable energy output of the entire system, which is expressed as kWh per kWp per day. This value denotes the total AC energy generated by the PV system within a specific time frame (daily, monthly, or yearly).

(viii) Collection Loss or Capture Loss (Lc): Thermal, wiring, module quality, mismatch, incidence angle losses, shading, dirt, Maximum Power Point (MPP) tracking, regulatory losses, and other inefficiencies are all included in Lc, which includes array losses. In mathematics, Lc is determined by deducting Ya from Yr.

(ix) System Loss (Ls): Ls is the total losses of the PV system, which includes inverter losses for systems that are linked to the grid. To compute this number, take Yf and subtract it from Yr.

(x) Unused Energy Loss (Lu): Lu is the potential energy at the array output that is not used because of system saturation in a DC-grid system, which can be brought on by a full battery or a constrained load. Lc is subtracted from Yr to determine Lu.

(xi) Performance Ratio (PR):PR is the final yield (Yf) divided by the reference yield (Yr). Regarding the nominal installed power of the PV system, it offers insights into the system's overall efficiency.

4.1.3 Array and System Losses in PVsyst

Array losses in the context of PV systems refer to elements that reduce a PV array's energy output relative to the nominal power of PV modules under Standard Test Conditions (STC), as defined by manufacturers. The following forms of losses that impact PV arrays or systems are taken into account by the software:

(i) Incidence Angle (IAM) Loss: As the angle of incidence increases, optical reflections become more intense, resulting in a decrease in the amount of light that reaches PV cell surfaces. When the irradiance that reaches the cells is lower than it would be at normal incidence, this impact happens.

(ii) Soiling Loss: The buildup of dirt and its impact on system functionality lead to soiling loss. This unpredictability is influenced by variables like precipitation and environmental conditions. The accumulation of dust, Dust retention is made worse and partial shadowing of lower cells is introduced by lichens and moss growing along module frames. Monthly soiling loss factor specifications expressed as percentages of STC values are supported by PVsyst. This loss is accounted for during simulation as a decrease in irradiation.

(iii) Thermal Losses: Module temperatures that are higher than the typical test settings (25°C) result in thermal losses. At Maximum Power Point (MPP), crystalline silicon cells, for example, lose around 0.4 percent of their temperature. The array's thermal behavior, which has a big impact on electrical performance, is determined by the equilibrium between cell heating from incoming irradiance and ambient temperature.

(iv) LID Losses: The term "Light-Induced Degradation" (LID) describes the decrease in performance that crystal modules show within the first few hours of exposure to sunshine. This phenomena, which usually ranges from 1% to 3%, is related to the quality of wafer production. Performance is lost while using LID as opposed to STC, especially if modules are arranged according to the findings of the factory's final flash test in order to calculate nominal power.

(v) Module Quality Loss: Loss of Module Quality indicates the decline in module performance as measured against manufacturer standards. PVsyst uses efficient specification parameters to determine the fundamental properties of a PV array. The program interprets this number as half the inferior tolerance by default, meaning that the average power of the provided module sample falls between the nominal value and the lower tolerance.

(vi) Mismatch Loss: Variations in I-V characteristics between modules or solar cells within a string cause mismatch loss. This mismatch has an impact on overall performance since the string's current is determined by its lowest current. Based on user input, PVsyst calculates the mismatch loss parameter, which stays constant during in-depth simulations.

(vii) Ohmic wiring Loss: Between the power of the module and the power of the terminal array, ohmic wire resistance causes losses (I^2R). For the whole array, PVsyst uses a global resistance parameter R to specify these losses. For STC circumstances resistance, the program recommends a baseline global wiring loss percentage of 3%. Furthermore, PVsyst suggests setting

125

the default value for iron loss to 0.1% of nominal power. During simulation, the ohmic loss is calculated as R*I2, guaranteeing that the annual resistive loss % stays lower than the nominal loss at STC.

5. DESIGN AND SIMULATION OF 90KWP ROOFTOP PVSYSTEM

For determining the capacity of grid connected PV System to be installed we need to find out the electrical load demand of Kamrup Polytechnic.The total load of the institute is distributed among administrative building, academic building and workshop. As we will be needing open rooftops for PVplant, the administrative building of the Institute Campus will be considered for this project used. By considering the light loads, fan loads, socket etc the total load demand is estimated.

Table 1. Estimated Demand Load of Kamrup Polytechnic

Sl.No.	BUILDING	PARAMETERS	
		Open Rooftop Area	Load Demand
1.	Administrative Building	756m²	15700W
2.	Academic Building	403 m²	57660W
3.	Workshop	---	16640W
	TOTAL		90000W

Figure 1. Aerial view of Kamrup Polytechnic
(Source-GoogleMaps)

Figure 2. Open rooftop area of administrative building

5.1 Simulation of 90KWp PV Plant

PVsyst simulation to build a 90 kWp grid-connected photovoltaic system. Additionally, this part calculates the PV system's energy generating cost. In order to showcase the technologies of grid-connected solar PV systems, Kamrup Polytechnic plans to build a 90kWp solar PV plant to supply the electricity required for its campus project. As input data, PVsyst uses the worldwide horizontal solar radiation and the monthly average ambient temperature that are retrieved from the PVGIS system database. To achieve maximum global incidence irradiance on the module plane, the simulation takes into account PV modules inclined at an angle relative to the region's latitude. The 90 kWp PV's monthly energy output systems, their performance ratios, and the many losses that transpire within the systems are contrasted, with the outcomes being shown.

Table 2. Site meteorological data for grid-connected 90 kWp PV system design

PARAMETERS	INPUT
Site Location	Kamrup Polytechnic, Baihata Chariali, Assam
Latitude	26.33 °N
Longitude	91.73 °N
Time Zone	+ 0530 Hrs from GMT
Altitude	50 meter from Mean Sea Level

For designing the 90kWp PV system in PVsyst 7.0.9 software, the monthly meteorological data for Baihata Chariali i.e. horizontal global and diffuse irradiation, ambient temperature and wind velocity are imported from the PVGIS system database in PVsyst by defining the geographical co-ordinates (latitude, longitude and altitude) of Baihata Chariali. This is the first step of simulation.

In the second step, PV system is grid-connected with fixed tilted plane and a tilt angle of 26^0 is considered for design which gives a transposition factor of 1.12 and -0.2% loss with respect to the optimum orientation. Moreover, an azimuth angle of 0^0 is considered in this design. Next the system is defined under the system configuration of the PVsyst software. 7.0.9.The PV system components are selected which include module type with specific watt power rating and the inverter, including number of inverters.

5.1.1 Sizing of PV System

The size and configuration of the PV array are optimized to obtain the maximum energy yield by the system for Baihata Chariali location. The sizing of the PV system is carried out in PVsyst either through the planned power or through the available area, which helps in calculating the rated capacity of the system to be installed.

Determination of a PV system: The whole capacity of the PV system that must be placed in the Kamrup Polytechnic Administrative Building's accessible rooftop space is pre-sized in PVsyst with the PV module rated at 250 Wp nominal power output in mind. A total of 90kWp of installed capacity is needed for the systems, and 360 modules are needed.

PV array sizing: The solar array is able to be sized in accordance with the manufacturer's specified module dimensions to satisfy the system's rated power output at a certain DC output voltage. PV modules are joined in parallel and series to create an array. To achieve the nominal voltage of the PV system, the modules are linked in series, often known as strings. The strings are then connected in parallel to generate the entire current needed to match the array output with the inverter input terminals.

Size of inverters: In a photovoltaic system, an inverter transforms the DC power output from the array into AC power that may be sent into the grid with the utility grid's voltage and frequency levels. For the PV system to run efficiently close to its maximum power point, the overload capability and efficiency characteristic of a grid-connected inverter should be considered when designing it to work with an array.

Table 3. PV module parameters used for design purpose in PVsyst

PARAMETERS	INPUT
Maximum Power	250 Wp
VOC	37.50 V
Vmp	30.50 V
ISC	8.70 A
Imp	8.20 A
Tolerance	+ / - 3%
Module Efficiency	15%
Technology	Mono-crystalline Si
No of Cells	60 in series

Table 4. Inverter parameters used for design purpose in PVsyst

PARAMETERS	INPUT
AC nominal output	30000 W
Max AC current	52 A
Max PV current	106 A
Minimum MPP voltage	300 V
Nominal MPP voltage	450 V
Input Maximum Voltage	650 V
MPP Voltage range	300 - 600 V
Frequency range	50 / 60 Hz
No of phases	3 phase

Table 5. Solar array design for grid-connected 90 kWp PV system

PARAMETERS	INPUT
Power rating of each PV module	250 Wp
No of module per string	15
No of strings in parallel	24
Total no of modules	360
Array Power output	90 kWp

5.1.2 Simulation of 90KWp PVSystem

According to the meteo data in PVsyst, the global horizontal and diffuse Irradiation for Baihata Chariali is observed to be 1736.4 kWh/m2/year based on the meteo data in PVsyst, with an annual average ambient temperature of 24.23 ⁰C. At a tilt angle of 26°, the collecting plane's yearly global irradiation incidence is 1826.6 kWh/m2. Optical losses such as IAM, transposition, and shading loss factors for the tilted module are taken into account when calculating the global effective irradiation. The predicted energy generation for the grid-connected rooftop 90 kWp PV system in Kamrup Polytechnic's administrative building is displayed in Table 6.

5.1.3 Performance analysis of 90KWp Grid connected PV System

(i) Energy Generated: The 90 kWp grid-connected rooftop photovoltaic system in the Kamrup Polytechnic, Baihata Chariali administrative building is estimated to generate 12675 kWh of electricity per year through simulation, with a worldwide effective irradiation of 1826.6 kWh/m2/year falling on the surface

Table 6. Simulated results of grid-connected rooftop PV system

Month	Tilted at 0⁰	Tilted at 26⁰ (south facing)	Ambient Temperature (⁰C)	Energy injected into grid (kWh)
	Global horizontal irradiation (kWh/m²/month)	Global effective irradiation (kWh/m²/month)		
Jan	128.6	166.8	17.94	12270
Feb	112.2	127.4	21.41	9270
Mar	174.8	187.9	25.14	13190
Apr	168.1	162.4	25.33	10470
May	184.5	164.6	26.92	11560
Jun	120.8	104.3	27.40	7440
Jul	159.1	139.7	28.36	9880
Aug	143.6	133.1	27.90	9430
Sep	156.3	159.3	27.85	9840
Oct	147.0	167.9	25.75	10660
Nov	124.6	157.6	22.99	11360
Dec	116.8	155.5	19.87	11380
Total	1736.4	1826.6	24.23	12675

Figure 3. Variation of monthly energy generation with global effective irradiation

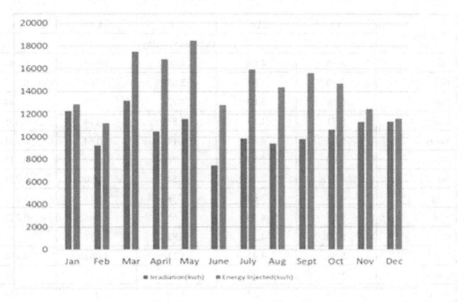

of the array at a 26° tilt angle. The monthly energy generation fluctuation for a 90 kWp photovoltaic system in Baihata Chariali with respect to global effective irradiance is depicted in Figure 3. The slanted PV modules' monthly average solar radiation fluctuation shows that solar radiation peaks in March (187.9 kWh/m2) and less in June (104.3 kWh/m2). March had the greatest energy generation, coing in at 13190kWh. Conversely, June has the lowest energy generation of any month at just 7440 kWh.

(ii) Normalised Energy Production: Table 7 displays the normalized performance coefficients for a 90 kWp photovoltaic system. The coefficients are as follows: Yr stands for reference yield, Ya for array yield, Yf for final yield, Lc for array capture loss, Ls for system loss, and PR for performance ratio. From a lower value of 2.97 kWh/kWp/day in June to a maximum value of 5.02 kWh/kWp/day in March the array yield of PV modules fluctuates. From 3.70 kWh/kWp/day in June to 6.38 kWh/kWp/day in March, the reference yield changes. The ultimate yield indicates the amount of AC energy output generated by the inverter that can be sent into the grid. From a minimum of 2.97 kWh/kWp/day in June to a maximum of 4.73 kWh/kWp/day in March, the monthly final output fluctuates.

Table 7. Normalized performance co-efficient

Month	Yr	Ya	Yf	Lc	Ls
	(kWh/kWp/day)				
Jan	5.66	4.66	4.40	1.004	0.263
Feb	4.80	3.91	3.68	0.883	0.237
Mar	6.38	5.02	4.73	1.355	0.294
Apr	5.71	4.53	3.88	1.174	0.655
May	5.62	4.44	4.14	1.184	0.291
Jun	3.70	2.97	2.76	0.732	0.213
Jul	4.77	3.79	3.54	0.980	0.251
Aug	4.54	3.63	3.38	0.915	0.245
Sep	5.59	4.43	3.65	1.165	0.783
Oct	5.70	4.55	3.82	1.151	0.731
Nov	5.53	4.47	4.21	1.061	0.264
Dec	5.28	4.33	4.08	0.954	0.253
Average	5.28	4.23	3.86	1.048	0.373

Figure 4. Comparison of array yield and final yield of PVsystem with reference yield

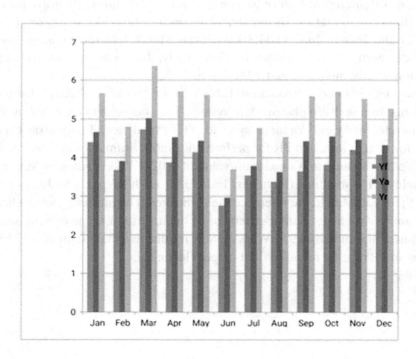

Figure 5. Normalized productions (per Installed kWp) for PV system

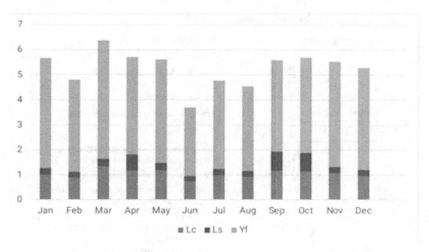

Figures 5 and 6 display the normalized capture losses Lc and system losses Ls for a PV system with nominal power of 90 kWp for each month throughout a year with regard to the normalized system production Yf. The system losses vary from 0.213 kWh/kWp/day in June to 0.783 kWh/kWp/day in September, whereas the monthly average capture losses range from 0.732 kWh/kWp/day in June to 1.355 kWh/kWp/day in March.

The yearly average capture losses and system losses for the 90 kWp PV system with an average normalized energy production of 3.86 kWh/kWp/day are 1.048 kWh/kWp/day and 0.373 kWh/kWp/day, respectively. . In March, when the energy generation in is the highest (13190 kWh), the final yield is 4.73 kWh/kWp/day with capture loss of 1.355 kWh/kWp/day and system loss of 0.294 kWh/kWp/day. In June, when the energy generation is the lowest (7440 kWh), the final yield is 2.76 kWh/kWp/day with capture loss of 0.732 kWh/kWp/day and system loss of 0.213 kWh/kWp/day

(iii) Loss Analysis Of 90Kwp Pv System: The loss diagram obtained in PVsyst simulation for the 90 kWp capacity photovoltaic systems is shown in Figure 6. The maximum loss in the system is due to the temperature which around 8.9% . The simulated losses for the 90 kWp capacity PV systems in Kamrup Polytechnic, Baihata Chariali are summarized in Table 8.

Figure 6. Loss diagram of 90KWp PVsystem in kamrup polytechnic

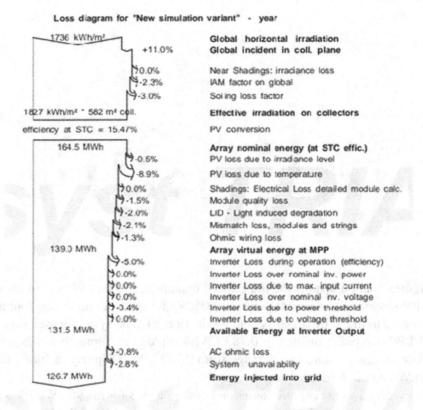

Table 8. Different system losses in 90 kWp PV system

Losses	Fraction (%)
Loss due to temperature	8.9
Array soiling loss	3
Module quality loss	1.5
Light induced degradation loss	2
Module array mismatch loss	2
Ohmic wiring loss	1.5
Inverter loss during operation	5
AC Ohmic Loss	0.8
Unavailibility of the system	2

Table 9. Month wise performance ratio for 90 kWp PV system

Month	PR Value
Jan	0.776
Feb	0.767
Mar	0.741
Apr	0.680
May	0.737
Jun	0.745
Jul	0.742
Aug	0.745
Sep	0.652
Oct	0.670
Nov	0.761
Dec	0.772
Average	0.731

Figure 7. Month-wise performance ratio for 90 kWp PV system

Figure 8. Variation of monthly performance ratio with ambient temperature

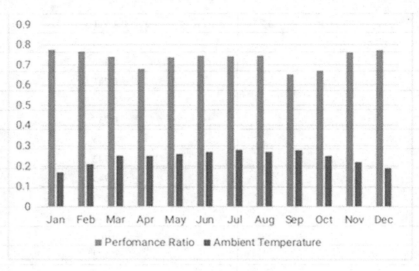

Table 10. Month-wise system efficiencies for 90 kWp PV system

Month	System Efficiency (%)
Jan	13.63
Feb	13.46
Mar	13.01
Apr	11.93
May	12.95
June	13.07
July	13.03
Aug	13.07
Sept	11.44
Oct	11.76
Nov	13.35
Dec	13.54
Annual Average Sys Efficiency	12.83

(iv) Perfomance Ratio (PR) Of the PV System:The PR of the PV system depends on both the PV module and inverter performance, both of which are strongly influenced by the operating temperature. Figure 7 and Figure 8 depicts the month wise performance ratio for 90 kWp PV system and its variation of monthy performance ratio vs ambient temperature respectively.The PR is maximum at the month of January(0.776) and minimum at the month of September(0.652) .

(v) System (Sys) Efficiency Of PV System:Solar power efficiency depends on variety of factors including proper installation and assessment of the structure.The efficiency of a PV system is the measurement of how much of the available solar energy a solar cell converts. Table 10. and Figure 9. shows month wise system efficiencies for 90 Kwp PV system. The annual average system efficiency for the 90 kWp PV systems is found to be 12.83%.

Table 11. Economic analysis of 90 kWp PV system

Input Parameters	Value
Numbers of PV module	360
Cost of each module (Rs)	20,000.00
Total cost of PV modules (Rs.)	7,200,000.00
Inverter cost (Rs)	1,60,000.00
Number of Inverters	3
Total cost of inverters (Rs)	4,80,000.00
Mounting structures (Rs)	1,08,000.00
Installation charges (Rs)	2,70,000.00
Taxes, Duties and Overheads (Rs)	60,000.00
Life of PV System (yr)	20
Life of Inverter (yr)	10
Life of Auxiliaries (yr)	10
Annual Electricity generation (kWh)	127000
Maintenance and others (Rs)	290000.00
Total Operating Costs (Rs)	350,000.00
Total Installation Costs(Rs)	8,058,000.00
LCOE (Rs/kWh)	3.170
Payback Period	4.2 yrs

5.1.4 Economic Analysis of 90KWp Grid Connected PV System

During procurement of the 90 kWp solar PV systems at Administrative building of Kamrup Polytechnic, the solar module cost is approximately Rs 80/Wp. The levelized cost of energy was calculated at Rs 3.170 per kWh.

6. CONCLUSION

Estimation, design and simulation has been carried out using PVsyst 7.0.9 simulation tool for assessment of energy generation on grid connected solar PV system is done .The estimated electrical load of Kamrup Polytechnic, Baihata Chariali is 90 kWp .The annual energy generation for the 90 kWp grid connected 127000 kWh (approximately) from the simulation. The PVsyst tool provides the detailed analysis of all types of losses.

The performance ratio for 90 kWp grid connected PV systems are found out to be 73.1%, with normalized production of 3.86 kWh/kWp/day. The performance of the PV systems depends on site meteorological conditions and module technology. The month wise system efficiency is found out having average system effiency of 12.83%

The levelised cost of energy for 90 kWp grid connected PV systems are Rs 3.170/kWh.

The cost of PV systems is sharply reducing in the last five years and it will reduce more due to wide spread large scale plant along with improved technologies, higher efficiency and lower cost of modules. This will also make the cost of generation from PV systems close to the conventional energy sources. Moreover, PV system has the advantages of no CO_2 emissions the saved CO_2 emmisions is 2909.567 tons with no moving parts and least maintenance of the system. Increasing environmental hazards and with slowly exhausting of conventional energy sources the need of PV technology is in high demand Hence, PV technology is considered to be one of the most feasible renewable energy for electricity generation.

REFERENCES

Abbood, A. A., Salih, M. A., & Mohammed, A. Y. (2018). Modeling and simulation of 1 MW grid connected photovoltaic system in Karbala city. *International Journal of Energy and Environment, 9*(2), 153–168.

Baitule, A. S., & Sudhakar, K. (2017). Solar powered green campus: A simulation study. *The International Journal of Low Carbon Technologies, 12*(4), 400–410. doi:10.1093/ijlct/ctx011

Barua, S., Prasath, R. A., & Boruah, D. (2017, February). Rooftop Solar Photovoltaic System Design and Assessment for the Academic Campus Using PVsyst Software. *International Journal of Electronics and Electrical Engineering, 5*(1), 76–83. doi:10.18178/ijeee.5.1.76-83

Huld, T. (2017). PV MAPS: Software tools and data for the estimation of solar radiation and photovoltaic module performance over large geographical areas. *Solar Energy, 142*, 171–181. doi:10.1016/j.solener.2016.12.014

Kumar, N. M., & Subathra, M. S. P. (2019). Three years ahead solar irradiance forecasting to quantify degradation influenced energy potentials from thin film (a-Si) photovoltaic system. *Results in Physics, 12*, 701–703. doi:10.1016/j.rinp.2018.12.027

Kumi, E. N., & Brew-Hammond, A. (2013). *Design and Analysis of a 1 MW Grid-Connected Solar PV System in Ghana.* ATPS (African Technology Policy Studies Network).

Malvoni, M., Leggieri, A., Maggiotto, G., Congedo, P. M., & De Giorgi, M. G. (2017). Long term performance, losses and efficiency analysis of a 960 kWP photovoltaic system in the Mediterranean climate. *Energy Conversion and Management, 145*, 169–181. doi:10.1016/j.enconman.2017.04.075

Manoj Kumar, N., Sudhakar, K., & Samykano, M. (2019). Techno-economic analysis of 1 MWp grid connected solar PV plant in Malaysia. *Int. J. Ambient Energy, 40*(4), 434–443. doi:10.1080/01430750.2017.1410226

Psomopoulos, C. S., Loannidis, G. C., & Kaminaris, S. D. (2015). A Comparative Evaluation of Photovoltaic Electricity Production Assessment Software (PVGIS, PV Watts and RETScreen*). Environmental Processes, 2*(S1), 175–189. doi:10.1007/s40710-015-0092-4

Sharma, R., & Goel, S. (2017). Performance analysis of a 11.2 kWp roof top grid-connected PV system in Eastern India. *Energy Reports*, *3*, 76–84. doi:10.1016/j.egyr.2017.05.001

Shukla, A. K., Sudhakar, K., & Baredar, P. (2016). Simulation and performance analysis of 110 kWp grid- connected photovoltaic system for residential building in India: A comparative analysis of various PV technology. *Energy Reports*, *2*, 82–88. doi:10.1016/j.egyr.2016.04.001

Sisodia, D., & Gupta, M. K. (2013, September). Modeling And Control Of A Grid Connected Photovoltaic System Using Matlab, *International Journal of Latest Technology in Engineering, Management &. Applied Sciences (Basel, Switzerland)*, *II*(IX), 69–74.

APPENDIX

Figure 9. PV module specification, array inverter sizing conditions for 90 kWp system in PV

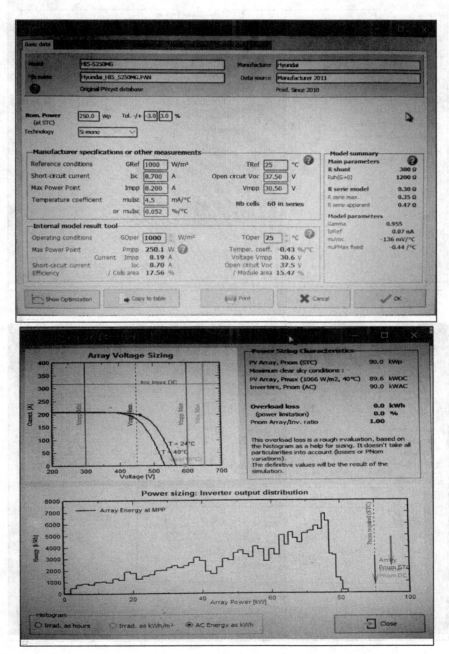

Figure 10. Inverter specification and efficiency curve for 90 kWp grid connected system in PV Syst

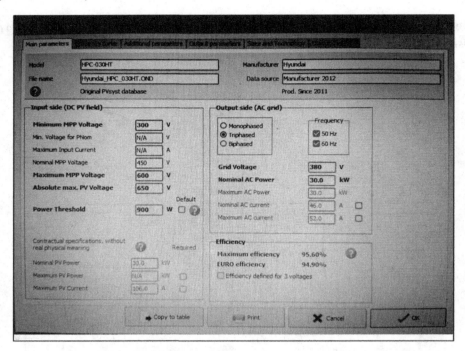

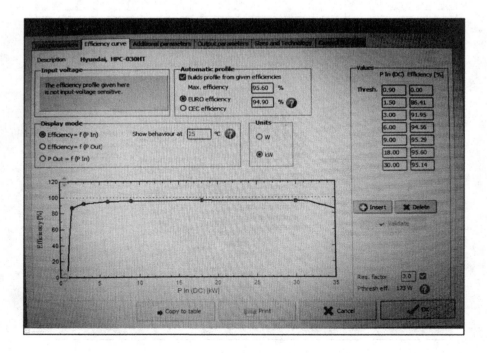

Chapter 8
Diabetes Prediction Using Novel Machine Learning Methods

Sagar Saikia

ⓘ https://orcid.org/0000-0002-7984-9618
National Institute of Technology, Meghalaya, India

Jonti Deuri
Assam Don Bosco University, India

Riya Deka
NERIM Group of Institutions, India

Rituparna Nath
NERIM Group of Institutions, India

ABSTRACT

Diabetes is a prevalent and chronic health condition affecting millions globally. Diabetes is caused by a combination of many factors including obesity, excessive blood glucose levels, abnormal cholesterol levels, family history, physical inactivity, bad food habits, and other causes. Frequent urination, increased thirst, increased hunger, and loss of weight are the common symptoms of diabetes. A person having diabetes has heavy risks of heart disease, kidney disease, nerve damage, diabetic retinopathy, brain stroke, foot ulcer, etc. These risks factors can be reduced by early detections of disease. The big challenge for the health care industries nowadays is to give a more precise result which could easily predict whether a patient is having or diagnosed with such disease.

DOI: 10.4018/979-8-3693-2260-4.ch008

1. INTRODUCTION

Diabetes is a chronic, metabolic disease characterized by elevated levels of blood glucose (or blood sugar), which leads over time to serious damage to the heart, blood vessels, eyes, kidneys and nerves. The most common is type 2 diabetes, usually in adults, which occurs when the body becomes resistant to insulin or doesn't make enough insulin. In the past 3 decades the prevalence of type 2 diabetes has raised dramatically in countries of all income levels. Type 1 diabetes, once known as juvenile diabetes or insulin-dependent diabetes, is a chronic condition in which the pancreas produces little or no insulin by itself. For people living with diabetes, access to affordable treatment, including insulin, is critical to their survival.

In recent years, the integration of Machine Learning (ML) techniques has shown promising results in various medical applications, including disease prediction. This study aims to explore the application of ML algorithms for diabetes prediction using readily available clinical and demographic data. In existing method, the classification and prediction accuracy is not so high. This research showcases the potential of ML techniques in accurately predicting diabetes using clinical and demographic data. The interpretability of these models contributes to their clinical utility and facilitates their integration into healthcare systems for improved diabetes management.

2. LITERATURE REVIEW

Tasin et al.(2022) proposed automatic diabetes prediction system employing XGBoost machine learning framework with ADASYN. Later deployed the model into a website and Android smartphone application. Data used in this model predicting diabetes based on PIMA Indian Dataset for female.

Bhavya et al. (2020) developed a system using machine learning that predicts diabetes using old patients data. The proposed system used one of the popular machine learning algorithms KNN and obtained higher accuracy. And later an interface was designed for Admin and members.

Tejas N.Joshi and Prof. Pramila M. Chawan (2018) presented a system Diabetes Prediction Using Machine Learning by applying three algorithms including Artificial Neural Network (ANN), Support Vector Machine (SVM), and Logistic Regression. This project proposed earlier detection of diabetes in an effective way.

Priya Gandhi and Dr. Gayatri S Pandi(2022) developed a system Diabetes Prediction using Machine Learning Techniques based on PIMA Indian Diabetes Dataset for female patients. Machine learning algorithm used in this system are Naïve Bayes Classifier, Decision Tree, SVM, and KNN. SVM obtained highest accuracy of 90.23%.

Swapna et al. (2018) used Deep Learning model for prediction of diabetes by applying Deep Learning networks such as Recurrent Neural Network (RNN), Long Short Term Memory (LSTM), Convolutional Neural Network (CNN), Hybrid Network (CNN-LSTM), SVM. Deep Learning is a subset of Machine Learning. Unlike Machine Learning, in Deep Learning feature extraction, data visualization, classifications are not done [4]. Result achieved applying Deep Learning gives optimal accuracy than other techniques.

Rahul et al. (2020) proposed a system of predicting diabetes using KNN algorithm. The proposed system can predict accurately if a patient has diabetes or not.

Leon et al. (2020) presented a system of prediction diabetes using machine learning applying ensemble learning technique such as RMSE, RF, LightGBM, Glmnet, XGBoost and got higher accuracy.

Mitesh et al. (2019) used four machine learning algorithms such as Naïve Bayes, Decision Tree, SVM, KNN. Above all models, Naïve Bayes classifier can predict more accurately whether a patients has chance of diabetes or not than other model.

KM Jyoti Rani (2020) proposed a system Diabetes Prediction Using Machine Learning by five algorithms such as KNN, Logistic Regression, Decision Tree, Random Forest, SVM. Among the models, Decision Tree algorithm obtained highest training and testing accuracy of 98% and 99%.

Olta Llaha and Amarildo Rista(2021) proposed a system Prediction and Detection of Diabetes using Machine Learning algorithms Naïve Bayes, SVM, Decision Tree(C4.5), ANN. Decision Tree(C4.5) got highest accuracy of 79.3%.

EVWIEPAEFE A E. and ABDULKADIR NAFISAT used KNN, Decision Tree, ANN for diabetes prediction and ANN obtained highest accuracy of 97%. The proposed model gives one of the best result using Neural Network.

G & Research department of computer science St. Joseph College, principal investigator Dr. L. Arockiam (July 2017-June 2019) developed a system by collecting real patients data in the state Tamil Nadu. The study included total 15344 participants of both male and female of age above 18 years. In this project, three diabetes predictive models are developed using BigML tool. and later the model was developed using web interface.

A.K. Jaggi et al. (2021) proposed a model of diabetes prediction using Artificial Neural Network (ANN) consists of six dense layers. The model obtained accuracy of 77% and later an online web application was developed where user can enter data and check whether the person is diabetic or not.

Chaitali et al. (2023) describes a model of prediction of diabetes by applying machine learning algorithm SVM, ANN, Logistic Regression, Decision Tree and Random Forest. The proposed model used the dataset from UCI machine learning repository and got an accuracy of more than 85.

Viswanatha et al. (2023) proposed a model of predicting diabetes using two datasets, one is PIMA Indians Diabetes dataset another one is from Vanderbilt, based on a study of rural African Americans in Virginia, US. Dataset 1 obtained higher accuracy 78% by using aggregation technique Maximum Voting and dataset obtained higher accuracy 93% by using combined technique maximum polling and stacking.

Himanshu Nadda and Piyush Thakur designed a system of diabetes prediction using machine learning algorithms Logistic Regression, Random Forest Classifier, Naïve Bayes, Decision Tree, SVM, ANN. ANN obtained highest accuracy of 80%.

Abnoosian et al. (2023) proposed an innovative pipeline-based multi-classification framework to predict diabetes using imbalanced Iraqi Patient Dataset of Diabetes. The proposed model uses different types of algorithm such as KNN, SVM, DT, RF, AdaBoost, GNB. Since the model has imbalanced data, k-fold cross-validation technique is used. The combination of KNN, AB, DT and RF gives the highest accuracy of predicting diabetes.[20]

B.S.A. et al. (2022) designed a model for diabetes prediction using machine learning algorithms LGBM, GB, RF, XGB, DT, NB, SVM. Proposed model used two datasets, one is Pima Indian Dataset from UCI repository and another one is DMS(Diabetes Mellitus Survey). LGBM gives highest accuracy for both datasets.

Shahid et al. proposed machine learning developed a machine learning model for predicting diabetes based on PIMA Indian Dataset for female obtained from UCI machine learning repository. Algorithms used in the proposed system are XGBoost, CatBoost, LightGBM, AdaBoost and Gradient Boosting. Among these algorithms, Gradient Boosting scores highest accuracy of 96%.

H.El Massari et al. proposed a machine learning model for prediction of diabetes based on PIMA Indians dataset. Proposed method used following algorithms such as SVM, KNN, ANN, LR, NB, DT and ontology classifier. Among these algorithms, ontology classifier got highest accuracy of 77.5%.

3. PROPOSED SYSTEM

This project aims to develop a predictive model for diabetes using Machine Learning techniques. The proposed system utilizes a dataset containing relevant medical information to train and validate the models accuracy in predicting the likelihood of diabetes in individuals. The project focuses on enhancing early detection and prevention of diabetes through data driven insights.

4. OBJECTIVES

- Develop a machine learning model for diabetes prediction.
- Improve accuracy to aid in early intervention.

5. METHODOLOGY

5.1 Dataset Description

The dataset used in the system is from Kaggle.This dataset is originally from the National Institute of Diabetes and Digestive and Kidney Diseases. The objective of the dataset is to diagnostically predict whether or not a patient has diabetes, based on certain diagnostic measurements included in the dataset. Several constraints were placed on the selection of these instances from a larger database. In particular, all patients here are females at least 21 years old of Pima Indian heritage.

5.2 Contents of Dataset

The datasets consists of several medical predictor variables and one target variable, Outcome. Predictor variables include the number of pregnancies the patient has had, their BMI, insulin level, age, and so on.
Dataset has data related to 768 female patients with 9 attributes:

- Pregnancy: several times the patient has been pregnant.
- Glucose: plasma glucose concentration over two hours orally glucose tolerance tests.
- Blood pressure: diastolic blood pressure (mm Hg).
- Skin thickness: Triceps skin fold thickness (mm).
- Insulin: two-hour serum insulin (mu U/ml).
- BMI: body mass index (weight in kg/ (height in meters)^2).
- Diabetes Pedigree Function/DPF: A function that calculates the probability diabetes based on family history.
- Age: in years.
- Outcome: Categorical variable (0 if not diabetic, 1 if diabetic). it is target variable.

Each attributes represents different aspects of a person's health and medical history. By analyzing these attributes, machine learning models can identify the patterns and relationships that contribute an individual's risk of developing diabetes.

Figure 1. First five rows of dataset

```
In [4]: df.head()

Out[4]:
        Pregnancies Glucose BloodPressure SkinThickness Insulin BMI DiabetesPedigreeFunction Age Outcome
    0        6        148         72            35          0   33.6           0.627            50     1
    1        1         85         66            29          0   26.6           0.351            31     0
    2        8        183         64             0          0   23.3           0.672            32     1
    3        1         89         66            23         94   28.1           0.167            21     0
    4        0        137         40            35        168   43.1           2.288            33     1
```

Since the dataset has data related to female patients, one of the important attribute is number of pregnancies. Pregnancy is associated with significant hormonal changes, including increased insulin resistance. This hormonal change can affect glucose metabolism and increase the risk of gestational diabetes during pregnancy. Hence, number of pregnancies can be relevant factor risk of developing diabetes.

5.4 Data Pre-Processing

Data preprocessing is the process of generating raw data for machine learning models. This is the first step in creating a machine-learning model. This is the most complex and time-consuming aspect of data science. Data preprocessing is required in machine learning algorithms to reduce its complexities.

Data in the real world can have many problems. It can miss some elements or pieces of information. While incomplete or missing data is completely useless, adjusting and refining the data to make it valuable is the primary objective of data preprocessing.

This process includes following steps: handling missing data, dealing with duplicate data, splitting data to train and test split, importing necessary libraries for example pandas, numpy, matplotlib and seaborn etc.

5.5 Exploratory Data Analysis

Exploratory Data Analysis (EDA) is a crucial step in the process of understanding and analyzing a dataset in machine learning and data science. The primary goal of EDA is to summarize the main characteristics of the data, gain insights into its structure, and identify patterns, relationships, and potential outliers. Data visualization is a part of exploratory data analysis. Data visualization techniques used in this project is histogram, scatterplot, pairplot, heatmap.

Figure 2. System architecture

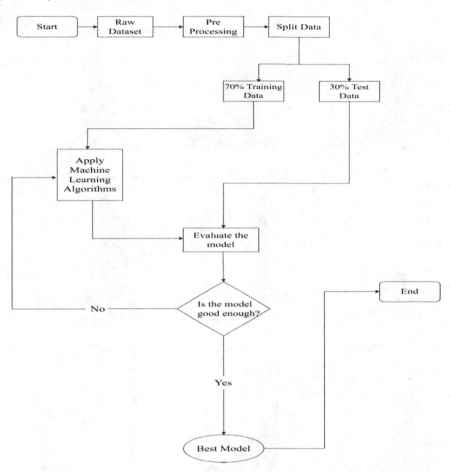

6. MODELS

KNN: The K-Nearest Neighbors (KNN) algorithm is a robust machine learning method employed to tackle classification and regression problems. By capitalizing on the concept of similarity, KNN predicts the label or value of a new data point by considering its K closest neighbors in the training dataset. The K-NN algorithm works by finding the K nearest neighbors to a given data point based on a distance metric, such as Euclidean distance, Manhattan distance, Minkowski Distance. The class or value of the data point is then determined by the majority vote or average of the K neighbors. This approach allows the algorithm to adapt to different patterns and make predictions based on the local structure of the data. KNN often called

Figure 3. Histogram

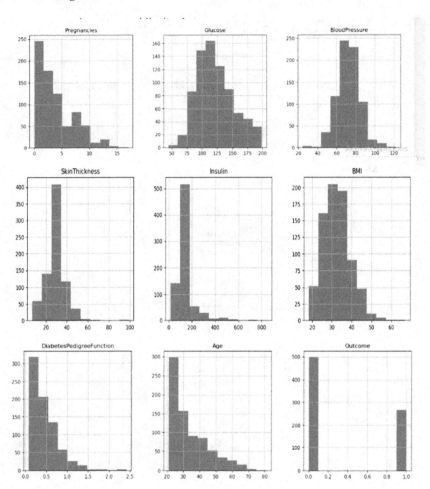

lazy learner because does not learn during training phase, instead it memorize the entire training dataset and makes predictions by comparing new instances to the stored example.

6.1 Euclidean Distance

$$d(x, y) = \sqrt{\sum_{i=1}^{n} (x_i - y_i)^2}$$

Figure 4. Scatterplot

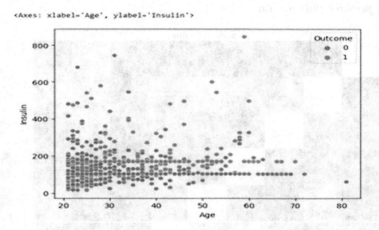

Figure 5. Pairplot

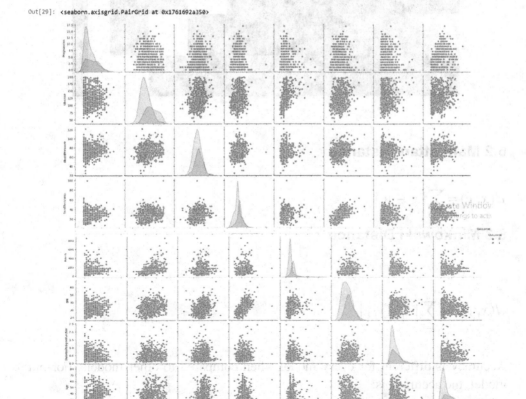

Figure 6. Heatmap: Dark shades represent negative correlation while lighter shades represent positive correlation

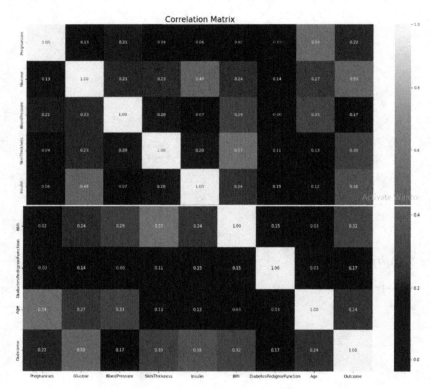

6.2 Manhattan Distance

$$d(x, y) = \sum_{i=1}^{n} | x_i - y_i |$$

6.3 Minkowski Distance

$$d(x, y) = \left(\sum_{i=1}^{n} | x_i - y_i | \right)^{\frac{1}{c}}$$

Accuracy is different for every model when compared to other models. For our model, the accuracy is:

Table 1. Accuracy

Model	Training Accuracy	Test Accuracy
KNN	0.86	0.83

6.4 Logistic Regression

Logistic regression, despite its name, is a classification model rather than regression model. Logistic regression is a simple and more efficient method for binary and linear classification problems. It is a classification model, which is very easy to realize and achieves very good performance with linearly separable classes. It is an extensively employed algorithm for classification in industry. The logistic regression model is a statistical method for binary classification that can be generalized to multiclass classification.

Figure 7. Sigmoid curve of logistic regression

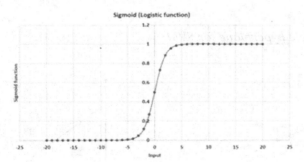

Table 2. Accuracy of our model for logistic regression

Model	Training Accuracy	Test Accuracy
Logistic Regression	0.84	0.88

6.5 SVM

A support vector machine (SVM) is a type of algorithm used in machine learning to solve classification and regression tasks; SVMs are particularly good at solving binary classification problems, which require classifying the elements of a data set into two groups.

The aim of a support vector machine algorithm is to find the best possible line, or decision boundary, that separates the data points of different data classes. This boundary is called a hyperplane when working in high-dimensional feature spaces. The idea is to maximize the margin, which is the distance between the hyperplane and the closest data points of each category, thus making it easy to distinguish data classes.

6.6 Decision Tree Classifier

Decision Tree is a Supervised learning technique that can be used for both classification and Regression problems, but mostly it is preferred for solving Classification problems. It is a tree-structured classifier, where internal nodes represent the features of a dataset, branches represent the decision rules and each leaf node represents the outcome.

Figure 8. Possible hyperplane for SVM

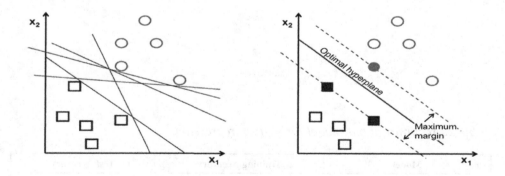

Table 3. Accuracy of our model for SVM

Model	Training Accuracy	Test Accuracy
SVM	0.89	0.84

Figure 9. Decision tree

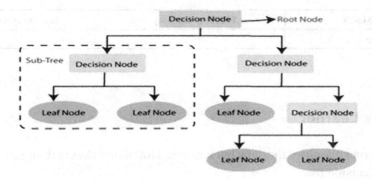

In a Decision tree, there are two nodes, which are the Decision Node and Leaf Node. Decision nodes are used to make any decision and have multiple branches, whereas Leaf nodes are the output of those decisions and do not contain any further branches.

In a decision tree, for predicting the class of the given dataset, the algorithm starts from the root node of the tree. This algorithm compares the values of root attribute with the record (real dataset) attribute and, based on the comparison, follows the branch and jumps to the next node.

For the next node, the algorithm again compares the attribute value with the other sub-nodes and move further. It continues the process until it reaches the leaf node of the tree.

In our model, the accuracy of Decision Tree Algorithm (Hyper parameter Tuned):

6.7 Gradient Boosting

Boosting is a special type of Ensemble Learning technique that works by combining several weak learners (predictors with poor accuracy typically decision tree) into a strong learner (a model with strong accuracy). This works by each model paying attention to its predecessor's mistakes. One of the most popular boosting technique is Gradient Boosting.

Gradient Boosting consists of three parts:

6.8 Loss Function

The loss function's purpose is to calculate how well the model predicts, given the available data. Depending on the particular issue at hand, this may change.

Table 4. Accuracy of decision tree algorithm

Model	Training Accuracy	Test Accuracy
Decision Tree	0.86	0.81

6.9 Weak Learner

A weak learner classifies the data, but it makes a lot of mistakes in doing so. Usually, these are decision trees.

6.10 Additive Model

This is how the trees are added incrementally, iteratively, and sequentially. You should be getting closer to your final model with each iteration.

For our model, accuracy of Gradient Boosting:

6.11 XGB

XGBoost is an optimized distributed gradient boosting library designed for efficient and scalable training of machine learning models. It is an ensemble learning method that combines the predictions of multiple weak models to produce a stronger prediction. XGBoost stands for "Extreme Gradient Boosting" and it has become one of the most popular and widely used machine learning algorithms due to its ability to handle large datasets and its ability to achieve state-of-the-art performance in many machine learning tasks such as classification and regression.

One of the key features of XGBoost is its efficient handling of missing values, which allows it to handle real-world data with missing values without requiring significant pre-processing. Additionally, XGB has built-in support for parallel processing, making it possible to train models on large datasets in a reasonable amount of time.

For our model, accuracy of XGB is:

Table 5. Accuracy of gradient boosting

Model	Training Accuracy	Test Accuracy
Gradient Boosting	1	0.89

Figure 10. Architecture of XGB

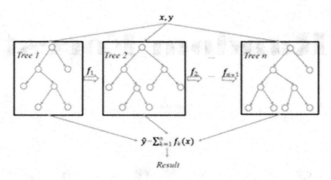

Table 6. Accuracy of XGB

Model	Training Accuracy	Test Accuracy
XGB	0.98	0.86

6.12 Random Forest

The random forest algorithm is an extension of the bagging method as it utilizes both bagging and feature randomness to create an uncorrelated forest of decision trees. Feature randomness generates a random subset of features, which ensures low correlation among decision trees.

Random forest algorithms have three main hyperparameters, which need to be set before training. These include node size, the number of trees, and the number of features sampled. From there, the random forest classifier can be used to solve for regression or classification problems.

The random forest algorithm is made up of a collection of decision trees, and each tree in the ensemble is comprised of a data sample drawn from a training set with replacement, called the bootstrap sample. Of that training sample, one-third of it is set aside as test data, known as the out-of-bag (oob) sample. Another instance of randomness is then injected through feature bagging, adding more diversity to the dataset and reducing the correlation among decision trees. Depending on the type of problem, the determination of the prediction will vary. For a regression task, the individual decision trees will be averaged, and for a classification task, a majority vote- i.e. the most frequent categorical variable-will yield the predicted class. Finally, the oob sample is then used for cross-validation, finalizing that prediction.

For our model, accuracy of Random Forest is:

Figure 11. Random forest

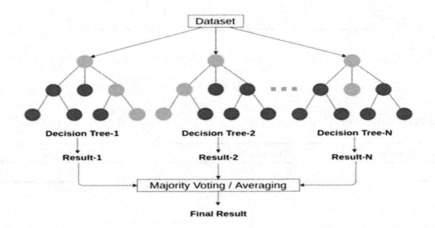

Table 7. Accuracy of random forest

Model	Training Accuracy	Test Accuracy
Random Forest	0.98	0.92

6.13 Confusion Matrix

Confusion Matrix is a performance measurement for machine learning classification. When assessing a classification model's performance, a confusion matrix is essential. It offers a thorough analysis of true positive (TP), true negative (TN), false positive (FP), and false negative (FN) predictions, facilitating a more profound comprehension of a model's recall, accuracy, precision, and overall effectiveness in class distinction.

6.14 Confusion Matrix Metrics

Accuracy: It is the summation of all true value divided by total values.

$$\text{Accuracy} = \frac{TP + TN}{TP + TN + FP + FN}$$

Precision: True positives divided by the total number of predicted positive values.

$$\text{Precision} = \frac{TP}{TP + FP}$$

Recall: True positive is divided by true positive and false negative.

$$\text{Recall} = \frac{TP}{TP + FN}$$

F-1 Score: It is the harmonic mean of Recall and Precision.

$$\text{F1-Score} = \frac{2 * \text{Precision} * \text{Recall}}{\text{Precision} + \text{Recall}}$$

Confusion matrix for KNN and Random Forest:
Result:
After training and evaluation, here is final accuracy score of all the models.
We can see that Random Forest Classifier has highest accuracy, i.e. 92%. So it will be considered as final and best model.

7. CONCLUSION

In conclusion, our machine learning-based diabetes prediction project has successfully demonstrated the effectiveness of employing advanced algorithms to forecast the likelihood of diabetes onset. Through the utilization of a diverse dataset and feature engineering techniques, our model achieved commendable accuracy, sensitivity, and specificity in predicting diabetes.

This project opens avenues for future research in the broader field of predictive healthcare analytics. As technology continues to evolve, the potential impact on public health becomes even more significant. By staying at the forefront of these advancements, we can contribute to a future where diseases are not only treated but predicted and prevented with precision.

Figure 12. Confusion matrix for KNN

```
In [73]:  # confusion matrix

          print(confusion_matrix(y_test, y_pred))

          [[135  12]
           [ 31  50]]

In [74]:  # classification report

          print(classification_report(y_test, y_pred))

                        precision    recall  f1-score   support

                     0       0.81      0.92      0.86       147
                     1       0.81      0.62      0.70        81

              accuracy                           0.81       228
```

Figure 13. Confusion matrix for random forest

```
In [99]:   # confusion matrix

           print(confusion_matrix(y_test, y_pred))

           [[139   8]
            [ 10  71]]

In [100]:  # classification report

           print(classification_report(y_test, y_pred))

                         precision    recall  f1-score   support

                      0       0.93      0.95      0.94       147
                      1       0.90      0.88      0.89        81

               accuracy                           0.92       228
              macro avg       0.92      0.91      0.91       228
           weighted avg       0.92      0.92      0.92       228
```

Figure 14. Output

```
Out[114]:
                                         Model   Score
            4         Random Forest Classifier   92.11
            5    Gradient Boosting Classifier    89.04
            0              Logistic Regression   88.16
            6                         XgBoost    86.84
            2                            SVM    84.21
            1                            KNN    83.33
            3        Decision Tree Classifier    81.58
```

8. FUTURE SCOPE

The future scope of diabetes prediction using machine learning is promising. Advancement may include improved model accuracy through more extensive datasets, integration with wearable devices for real-time monitoring, and personalized treatment recommendations. Ethical considerations and regulatory frameworks will likely evolve to ensure responsible implementation in healthcare. Collaboration between data scientists, healthcare professionals, and policymakers will be key for unlocking the full potential of this technology in managing and preventing diabetes.

REFERENCES

Abnoosian, K., Farnoosh, R., & Behzadi, M. H. (2023). Prediction of diabetes disease using an ensemble of machine learning multi-classifier models. *BMC Bioinformatics*, *24*(1), 337. doi:10.1186/s12859-023-05465-z PMID:37697283

Ahmed, N., Ahammed, R., Islam, M. M., Uddin, M. A., Akhter, A., Talukder, M. A., & Paul, B. K. (2021). Md. Manowarul Islam, Md. Ashraf Uddin, Arnisha Akhter, Md. Alamin Talukder, Bikash Kumar Paul, Machine learning based diabetes prediction and development of smart web application. *International Journal of Cognitive Computing in Engineering*, *2*(June), 229–241. doi:10.1016/j.ijcce.2021.12.001

Bhavya, M. R., Sanjay, H. C., Suraj, S. K., Savant, A., & Sanjay, M. (2020). Diabetes Prediction using Machine Learning. *IJARCCE, 9*.

El Massari, H., Sabouri, Z., Mhammedi S., & Gherabi, N. (2022). Diabetes Prediction Using Machine Learning Algorithms and Ontology. *Journal of ICT Standardization,* *10*(2), 319–338. doi:10.13052/jicts2245-800X.10212

Evwiekpaefe, A E. & Abdulkadir, N. (2021). *A Predictive Model For Diabetes Using Machine Learning Techniques (A Case Studyof Some Selected Hospitals In Kaduna Metropolis)*. [Master of Science in Computer Science Theses, Kennesaw State University].

Gandhi, P. (2022). Diabetes Prediction using Machine Learning Techniques. *IJRPR, 3*(2), 77-82.

Jaggi, A. K., Sharma, A., Sharma, N., Singh, R., & Chakraborty, P. S. (2021). Diabetes Prediction Using Machine Learning. Intelligent Systems. ResearchGate. doi:10.1007/978-981-33-6081-5_34

Jyoti, R. (2020), Diabetes Prediction Using Machine Learning. IJSRCSEIT, 6(4).

Kopitar, L., Kocbek, P., Cilar, L., Sheikh, A., & Stiglic, G. (2020). Early detection of type 2 diabetes mellitus using machine learning based prediction models. *Scientific Reports*, *10*(1), 11981. doi:10.1038/s41598-020-68771-z PMID:32686721

Mahjan, C., Marathe, S. N., & Choudhari, S. (2023), Diabetes Prediction Using Machine Learning Approach. *IRJMETS, 05*(2).

Olta, L. (2021). *Prediction and Detection of Diabetes using Machine Learning*. RTA-CSIT 2021, Tirana, Albania.

Shahid, M. (2023). *An ensemble learning approach for diabetes prediction using boosting techniques*. Front. Genet. . doi:10.3389/fgene.2023.1252159

Shamreen Ahamed, B., & Meenakshi, S. (2022). Diabetes Mellitus Disease Prediction Using Machine Learning Classifiers with Oversampling and Feature Augmentation. Advances in Human-Computer Interaction. doi:10.1155/2022/9220560

Swapna, G., Vinayakumar, R., & Soman, K. P. (2018, December). Diabetes detection using deep learning algorithms (2018). *ICT Express*, *4*(4), 243–246. doi:10.1016/j.icte.2018.10.005

Tasin, I., Nabil, T., Islam, S., & Khan, R. (2022). Diabetes prediction using machine learning and explainable AI techniques. *Healthc Technol Lett. 2023 Feb-Apr; 10*(1-2). doi: : PMC10107388PMID: 37077883 doi:10.1049/htl2.12039PMCID

Viswanatha, V., Ramachandra, A.C., & Dhanush, M. (2023). Diabetes Prediction Using Machine Learning Approach. *Strad Research, 10*(8).

Warke, M., Kumar, V., Tarale, S., & Galgat, P. (2019). Diabetes Diagnosis using Machine Learning Algorithms. *IRJET, 06*(3).

Wee, B. F., Sivakumar, S., & Lim, K. H. (2023). *Diabetes detection based on machine learning and deep learning approaches*. Multimed Tools Appl. doi:10.1007/s11042-023-16407-5

Chapter 9
Harvesting Insights:
A Comprehensive Data Analysis Methodology for Sustainable Agri Farming Practices

Jonti Deuri
Assam Don Bosco University, India

Dhanjit Gogoi
Assam Secratariate, India

Sagar Saikia
National Institute of Technology, Meghalaya, India

ABSTRACT

The agricultural sector is undergoing frequent transformation and the inclusion of data analysis techniques have the potential to revolutionize the traditional farming practices. In recent years, use of data analysis methodologies with farming has become very important, as it can make farming more sustainable and efficient in the future. The main objective of this chapter is to explore and establish a comprehensive data analysis methodology for sustainable farming. The relationship between data-driven approaches and the advancement of commercially and environmentally sound and economically viable agricultural practices are explored. By combining computer science and engineering with farming knowledge, this new method aims to change how farming can be done in an advanced way and wants to use resources better, grow more crops, and encourage sustainable farming.

DOI: 10.4018/979-8-3693-2260-4.ch009

1. INTRODUCTION

In the dynamic landscape of agriculture, the convergence of technology and sustainable practices has emerged as a pivotal focus for ensuring global food security, environmental conservation, and economic viability (Lobell et al., 2009). As the world's population is increasing, there's a high demand for effective and economical cultivating strategies, compelling the farming segment to grasp data-driven approaches for sophisticated decision-making (Saravanan et al., 2014). In the early days, farmers used their experience and instincts to deal with problems caused by changing weather, limited resources, and market changes. With new technology and sensors on farms, data analysis is now very important for making crops grow better, causing less harm to the environment, and making sure farms can keep going strong (Mulla, 2013).

The aim of this chapter is to give a thorough review of the data analysis techniques that enable practitioners of Agri-farming to make decisions based on the best available information (De Baets et al., 2019). Today's farmers have access to a wide range of tools, much like the crops they grow: from satellite photography and machine learning algorithms to precision farming and Internet of Things devices. Farmers may use data to their advantage by using it to acquire useful insights about crop performance, weather patterns, insect dynamics, and soil health. This allows them to implement proactive and adaptive tactics that increase productivity while reducing negative environmental effects (Haghverdi et al., 2019).

A new era of greater data availability essential for crop planning, management, and decision-making has been brought about by the integration of digital technology in agriculture (Lobell et al., 2009). This inflow of data comes from a variety of sources, including digital imagery from remote sensing platforms like satellites, fixed-wing aircraft, handheld devices, tractor-mounted equipment, and Unmanned Aerial Systems (UAS), as well as sensors like GPS, yield, weather, and soil sensors (Mulla, 2013). Based on light sources, active and passive sensors are used in remote sensing—information gathering without physical contact. Active sensors like ground sensors make their own radiation, while passive sensors like remote sensing technology use natural sources like sunlight. Ground sensing is a widely used technology that is now being made in large quantities for use in farming. On the other hand, remote sensing technology is still trying to figure out how well new technologies like UAS can work for agriculture.

The rest of this chapter is organised as follows: section 2 mentions about the numerous data collection and Integration processes; section 3 describes the Data preprocessing, which involves cleaning and transforming raw data to improve its quality and applicability for later analyses, an essential stage in agricultural data analysis; section 4 describes different analytical Models and Algorithms; section 5 is explaining the Basic Principles of Sustainable Agriculture; section 6 talks about the Decision Support Systems, section 7 elaborates the challenges and section 8 shows the future directions followed by section 10 that conclude the chapter with discussing future directions and challenges.

2. DATA COLLECTION AND INTEGRATION

Numerous data sources are used in agriculture to support decision-making procedures, optimize resource distribution, and raise total productivity. These include a wide range of important data sources, such as satellite imaging and precision agricultural sensors, all of which are crucial for providing information for strategic and operational decisions made in the agricultural sector. The different areas of data sources are as follows:

2.1 Agricultural Sensors

Agricultural sensors are essential to contemporary farming methods because they offer actionable insights and real-time data that maximize farm efficiency, resource management, and crop management. These sensors allow farmers to monitor critical characteristics like soil moisture, temperature, humidity, and nutrient levels with unprecedented precision. They are outfitted with a variety of technologies, including GPS, the Internet of Things, and powerful data analytics. Using this information, farmers may improve crop yields and sustainability by making well-informed decisions about fertilization, irrigation, and pest management. A study by Surya and Mandal (2020) claims that productivity and resource management have significantly improved with the integration of agricultural sensors, which has eventually advanced precision agriculture. Agricultural sensors are predicted to become more widely used as technology advances, disrupting conventional farming methods and promoting sustainable agricultural development. The figure 1 and figure 2 shows the soil sensor and crop sensor respectively.

2.1.1 Soil Sensors

With the ability to precisely measure soil conditions and provide real-time monitoring to improve farming methods, soil sensors have become indispensable instruments in contemporary agriculture. These sensors offer important insights into characteristics like temperature, nutrient levels, and soil moisture. They are outfitted with a variety of technologies, including IoT and advanced data analytics. Soil sensors allow farmers to make well-informed decisions on crop management, fertilization, and

Figure 1. Soil sensor

irrigation through continuous monitoring. This leads to increased resource efficiency and sustainable agricultural practices. The importance of infrared thermometry for stomatal conductance estimation is highlighted by (Jones, 2013), demonstrating the various uses of soil sensors in water usage optimization. (Tagarakis et al., 2020) have demonstrated that the incorporation of these sensors into precision agriculture improves both production and environmental sustainability, underscoring their crucial function in contemporary agriculture. These sensors track temperature, fertilizer levels, and soil moisture. Farmers can maximize their use of fertilizer and irrigation by using this knowledge.

2.1.2 Crop Sensors

Crop sensors, sometimes referred to as vegetation or plant sensors, are now essential parts of contemporary precision agriculture, giving farmers access to vital data that helps them maximize crop management and raises overall farm productivity. Data-driven decision-making is made possible by these sensors, which measure a variety of indicators pertaining to environmental factors and plant health. Chlorophyll content is frequently measured by crop sensors, which enables farmers to spot nutrient shortages or insect infestations early on. According to Gitelson et al. (2009), chlorophyll meters, like the SPAD meter, measure the amount of chlorophyll in

Figure 2. Crop sensor

the leaf by measuring its greenness. This helps identify nutrient deficits and stress conditions (Raza, Irfan, et al., (2023)). A popular index, NDVI, is produced using crop sensors, especially those attached to drones or satellites. For evaluating plant health, identifying *illnesses*, and tracking agricultural growth phases, NDVI is useful as it represents the amount of living plants (Tucker, 1979). Crop monitoring equipment uses infrared sensors to measure canopy temperature.

When temperatures deviate from ideal ranges, stress conditions may be indicated, allowing for prompt irrigation or pest management (Jones, 2004). Hand-operated portable sensors, such chlorophyll meters, enable farmers to rapidly evaluate particular sections of a field. For quick decision-making, these sensors offer real-time information (Gitelson et al., 2009). Crop sensors can be installed on tractors and other agricultural gear to provide continuous, on-the-spot data while the machinery traverses the field. These sensors work well for gathering a lot of data. Large-scale, high-resolution data is collected via sensors mounted on satellites and drones. The utilization of remote sensing technology, such as multispectral and hyperspectral sensors, aids in precision agriculture by offering comprehensive data on crop health and variability (Thenkabail et al., 2019).

On the farm, a variety of sensors can be installed to keep an eye on things like cattle status and water and air quality. Data on fuel consumption, equipment

Figure 3. RGB and NDVI satellite imagery

RGB Image   NDVI Image

performance, and operational efficiency are frequently collected by sensors built into contemporary agricultural gear.

2.2 Satellite Imagery

With its ability to provide farmers with an aerial perspective of their fields and vital information regarding crop management, resource efficiency, and sustainable practices, satellite imaging has emerged as an invaluable tool in modern agriculture. With the use of pertinent citations and references, this investigation explores the uses of satellite imaging in agriculture, including important satellite types, data analysis methods, and the revolutionary effects of this technology on farming operations. Crop health can be continuously monitored thanks to satellite imaging, which collects spectrum data in several bands. Sentinel-2 and other high-resolution optical satellites make it easier to identify illnesses, nutritional deficits, and anomalies (Thenkabail et al., 2019). Precision agriculture benefits from the extensive information that satellite data provides on soil conditions, crop growth phases, and variability within fields. This helps farmers maximize inputs for greater efficiency, including water, fertilizer, and insecticides (Wang et al., 2018). Accurate yield estimation is made possible by the application of machine learning algorithms and advanced data analytics to satellite photography. Forecasting crop yield is aided by predictive modelling, which is made possible by combining historical imagery and meteorological data (Inoue et al., 2017). Consider the application of satellite photography to extensive

Figure 4. Satellite imagery

agricultural monitoring. Talk about how precision agriculture is made possible by remote sensing technologies, which enable farmers to make data-driven decisions about planting, irrigation, and pest management. Crop rotation plans and land-use planning are supported by satellite photography. Making educated judgments about sustainable land management techniques is made easier for farmers and policymakers when they can track changes in the land cover over time (Thenkabail et al., 2016). Water management greatly benefits from the use of satellite photography, which determines soil moisture content and directs irrigation techniques. This promotes sustainable agricultural water usage, reduces over-irrigation, and conserves water resources (Bastiaanssen et al., 2015). Figure 4 show the Satellite Imagery devices.

Crop monitoring can benefit from high-resolution optical imagery provided by the Sentinel satellites of the European Space Agency, especially Sentinel-2. According to Drusch et al. (2012), these satellites provide frequent revisits together with a spectrum of spectral bands essential for vegetation study. Long-term agricultural landscape monitoring is aided by Landsat satellites, such as Landsat-8. Their multispectral images with a modest resolution help with the classification of land cover and the identification of changes (Roy et al., 2014).

Every day, NASA's Terra and Aqua satellites offer lower-resolution worldwide coverage using MODIS (Moderate Resolution Imaging Spectroradiometer) as shown in figure 5. For extensive evaluations of vegetation indices and climate trends, it is

Figure 5. MODIS

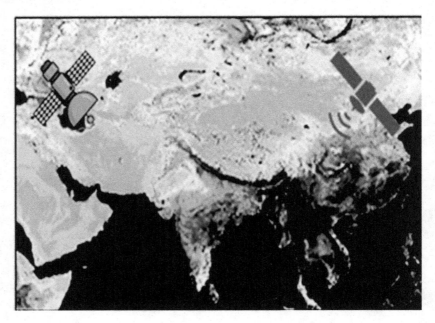

useful (Justice et al., 1998). Even with all of the advantages, there are still issues with cloud coverage, spatial resolution, and data accessibility. By deploying next-generation satellites, enhancing data exchange protocols, and pushing the boundaries of data analytics, satellite imagery in agriculture will be able to overcome these obstacles in the future. A revolutionary force in agriculture, satellite photography provides farmers with previously unattainable information for precision and sustainable farming. The agricultural landscape is expected to undergo a further transformation through the integration of satellite data with other technologies, such as machine learning and the Internet of Things, which will promote efficiency and resilience as technology develops. An all-encompassing perspective of agricultural landscapes is offered by satellite imaging. It can be used to track the health of crops, evaluate the amount of vegetation, and pinpoint pest- or disease-affected areas.

2.3 Farm Management Systems

In order to build a cohesive system that enables thorough analysis, emphasize how important it is for various data sources to work together. Farm Management Systems (FMS) comprise a collection of integrated technologies intended to optimize farming operations by giving farmers access to real-time information and analytical instruments for informed decision-making. These solutions improve farm productivity overall, sustainability, and resource optimization. Farm Management Systems (FMS), which provide comprehensive solutions to optimize farming operations, improve decision-making, and encourage sustainable practices, have emerged as indispensable instruments in contemporary agriculture. Farm management software allows farmers to incorporate data from multiple sources. These platforms make it possible to analyze data and produce insights that may be put to use in improving crop rotation, irrigation strategies, and planting timetables.

For data collection, FMS use a variety of sensors, including as GPS units, weather stations, and soil sensors. The basis for well-informed decision-making is the real-time data these sensors provide on climate, soil conditions, and the placement of machinery (Lowenberg-DeBoer, 2012). The farm's systems and devices can communicate with each other effortlessly thanks to IoT integration. This promotes a connected and cohesive farming environment by facilitating data sharing and communication between sensors, machinery, and the FMS platform (Pathan et al., 2015).

- *Cloud Computing:*

Large datasets may be stored and analyzed more easily with the help of cloud-based FMS platforms. This enables farmers to work with stakeholders, obtain information from anywhere, and take advantage of cutting-edge data analytics technologies for improved decision support (Nassar et al., 2018).

- *Decision Support Systems:*

FMS includes decision support systems that analyze gathered information and offer useful insights. These systems' machine learning algorithms improve forecasts and suggestions' accuracy, helping farmers adjust their tactics (Khaki et al., 2019).

- *GIS, or geographic information system:*

With the use of GIS technology, spatial data may be overlaid and analyzed to reveal details about the topography, soil properties, and other geographic elements that affect crop development.

- *Blockchain Technology:*

More and more research is being done on blockchain to enable traceability in the supply chain for agricultural products. Transparency and authenticity are ensured by recording and confirming each stage of the production process, from the farm to the consumer.

Table 1. Applications of precision agriculture technologies with environmental impact assessment

S. No	Application	Description	Technology Used	Environmental Impact
1	Precision Nutrient Management	Crop sensors offer real-time data to optimize fertilizer application, ensuring efficient nutrient utilization and minimizing environmental impact.	Crop Sensors, IoT	Reduced Environmental Impact
2	Irrigation Management	Canopy temperature and other indicators monitored by crop sensors aid in assessing crop water stress, facilitating informed irrigation scheduling for optimal water use efficiency.	Crop Sensors, Remote Sensing	Enhanced Water Use Efficiency
3	Disease and Pest Detection	NDVI data obtained from crop sensors enables early detection of diseases and pest infestations, enabling timely and targeted interventions by farmers.	Crop Sensors, Remote Sensing	Timely Pest Manage
4	Crop health monitoring	Aerial perspective for crop management, resource efficiency, and sustainability. Continuous crop health monitoring and precision agriculture. Accurate yield estimation with machine learning. Water management through soil moisture assessment. Monitor land cover changes. Enhance precision agriculture for efficient resource use.	Satellite Imagery: - Sentinel-2, Landsat-8, NASA's Terra, Aqua, MODIS, ML, IoT.	Assess irrigation impact on water resources. Potential for positive impact on sustainability practices.
5	Farm Management Systems	Comprehensive solutions for farming optimization and sustainability. Integrates real-time data and analytical tools. Uses sensors for climate and soil data. IoT integration for seamless communication. Blockchain for supply chain traceability. Real-time data for decision-making and sustainable practices.	Sensors: GPS, weather stations, soil sensors. IoT, cloud computing, ML, GIS technology, Blockchain.	Transparent supply chains. Collective data pooling for improved information sharing.

- **Crowdsourced Data:**

Using certain systems, farmers can pool their data to access and share information about insect outbreaks, best practices, and regional trends.

Farmers and other agricultural professionals can maximize resource utilization, improve overall output, and minimize environmental effects by integrating and analyzing data from these various sources. Farm Management Systems are revolutionary instruments that bring in a new era of efficiency, sustainability, and data-driven decision-making in agriculture. The adoption of FMS in farming practices promises to make a substantial contribution to the resilience and prosperity of the agricultural industry as technology advances. The table1 shows the Precision Agriculture Applications and Comprehensive Overview.

3. DATA PREPROCESSING

Data preprocessing, which involves cleaning and transforming raw data to improve its quality and applicability for later analyses, is an essential stage in agricultural data analysis.

3.1 Cleaning and Quality Assurance

Talk about approaches to deal with flaws and inconsistencies in data to guarantee the dependability and correctness of gathered information. Emphasize the need of a thorough data cleaning procedure for preserving the accuracy of ensuing analysis.

3.1.1 Missing Data Imputation

Sensor failures and human error are two typical causes of missing data in agricultural datasets. Imputation techniques assist in estimating missing values based on available data. These techniques include mean imputation, regression imputation, and more sophisticated approaches like k-nearest neighbours. Handling missing data correctly prevents biased results by ensuring that studies are performed on a complete and representative dataset (Little, R. J., & Rubin, D. B. (2019).

3.1.2 Outlier Identification and Elimination

Agricultural data may contain anomalies resulting from measurement errors or severe weather circumstances. Strong statistical approaches or visualization strategies, like z-scores or box plots, aid in the detection and possible elimination of outliers. Handling outliers guarantees that statistical evaluations are not excessively impacted by extreme figures, offering more precise perceptions into the general patterns in agricultural data (Hodge and Austin, 2004).

3.1.3 Standardization and Normalization

The process of standardization entails reducing the mean and standard deviation of numerical features to 0, 1, and 1. Features are normalized to a range, usually between 0 and 1. These methods guarantee that variables with varying scales make equal contributions to the study. Standardization and normalization help machine learning models perform better by preventing certain traits from predominating over others and enabling fair comparisons (Hastie et al., 2009).

3.1.4 Data Quality Assurance

Ensuring that the data meets predetermined criteria is achieved by the implementation of quality checks and validation rules during preparation. Finding errors and inconsistencies as well as comparing data to expected patterns are all part of this process. According to (Redman, 1996), quality assurance protects against incomplete or untrustworthy data, enhancing the validity of later studies and judgments.

3.2 Feature Engineering

Examine methods for deriving significant characteristics from unprocessed data, clarifying how to determine the most important variables to analyse. Show how good feature engineering makes the following analytical models work better.

3.2.1 Feature Engineering

Feature engineering involves creating new variables or transforming existing ones to extract more meaningful information. For example, converting categorical variables into numerical representations or creating derived features that better capture agricultural patterns.

Well-engineered features enhance the interpretability and performance of models, capturing essential information that might be overlooked in raw data (Guyon et al., 2006).

3.2.2 Temporal Aggregation and Smoothing

Temporal data in agriculture often exhibit variability that can be challenging to analyze directly. Aggregation and smoothing techniques, such as moving averages, help reduce noise and reveal underlying trends. Temporal aggregation and smoothing enable a clearer understanding of long-term patterns, supporting more accurate predictions and decision-making in agriculture (Montgomery et al., 2015).

3.2.3 Data Integration

Agricultural datasets often come from diverse sources, including weather stations, sensors, and satellite imagery. Data integration involves merging these heterogeneous datasets into a unified format for comprehensive analysis. Integration allows for a holistic understanding of agricultural systems, leveraging information from various sources to derive meaningful insights (Saravanan et al., 2014).

3.2.4 Data Transformation for Geographic Information Systems (GIS)

Agricultural data often includes spatial information. GIS-based transformations involve converting raw spatial data into usable formats, performing spatial queries, and overlaying different layers for comprehensive analysis. GIS-based transformations enable the exploration of spatial relationships, assisting in precision agriculture and land management (O'Sullivan and Unwin, 2003). In agricultural data analysis, data preparation is essential because it lays the groundwork for precise and trustworthy conclusions. Through the implementation of these techniques, scholars and professionals may guarantee that agricultural datasets are well-refined, representative, and prepared for comprehensive studies that support efficient and sustainable farming methods.

4. ANALYTICAL MODELS AND ALGORITHMS

Agri-farming is undergoing a transformation obligation to analytical models and algorithms, which offer sophisticated instruments for data analysis, forecasting, and decision-making. These computational methods use data to improve agricultural output, make the most use of available resources, and solve issues related to population increase and climate change. This investigation explores the intricacies of analytical models and algorithms in agri-farming, emphasizing their uses, importance, and potential for productive and sustainable agriculture.

4.1 Precision Agriculture and Predictive Modelling

Precision agriculture relies heavily on predictive modelling, using analytical algorithms to forecast crop yields, optimize input usage, and enhance overall farm management. These models consider various factors, including climate conditions, soil health, and crop characteristics. Precision agriculture, enabled by predictive modelling, allows farmers to tailor their practices to specific field conditions, resulting in increased efficiency and reduced environmental impact (Lobell et al., 2009).

4.2 Machine Learning Algorithms for Crop Monitoring

Machine learning algorithms, including supervised and unsupervised learning techniques, are employed for crop monitoring based on data from various sources such as sensors, drones, and satellites. These algorithms analyze patterns in the data to identify crop health, detect diseases, and assess overall growth.

Machine learning facilitates real-time monitoring, enabling early detection of issues and targeted interventions, ultimately improving crop yields and minimizing losses (Mulla, 2013).

4.3 Decision Support Systems (DSS) in Agriculture

Decision Support Systems integrate analytical models and algorithms to assist farmers in making informed decisions. These systems often include modules for crop selection, resource allocation, and risk management, incorporating data from multiple sources. DSS enhance decision-making by providing actionable insights, helping farmers navigate uncertainties and optimize their strategies for improved outcomes (De Baets et al., 2019).

4.4 Geographic Information Systems (GIS) and Spatial Analysis

GIS and spatial analysis models in Agri-farming involve the use of geographical data to analyze and visualize spatial relationships. This includes mapping soil variations, land use patterns, and topography to inform decision-making. Spatial analysis supports precision agriculture by aiding in site-specific management practices, optimizing resource use, and promoting sustainable land use (Saravanan et al., 2014).

4.5 IoT-Based Monitoring Systems

Internet of Things (IoT) technologies integrate with analytical models to create smart farming systems. Sensors collect real-time data on soil moisture, weather conditions, and equipment status. Algorithms process this data to generate actionable insights.

IoT-based monitoring systems provide a comprehensive view of farm operations, allowing farmers to respond proactively to changing conditions and optimize resource usage (Pathan et al., 2015).

4.6 Genetic Algorithms for Crop Breeding

Genetic algorithms are employed in crop breeding programs to optimize the selection of desirable traits. These algorithms simulate natural selection processes to evolve and enhance crop varieties. Genetic algorithms accelerate the crop breeding process, leading to the development of more resilient and high-yielding crop varieties (Jain et al., 2018).

4.7 Automated Irrigation Systems with Data Analytics

Analytical models are applied to data from soil moisture sensors, weather forecasts, and crop water requirements to optimize irrigation practices. Algorithms determine when and how much water is needed, reducing water wastage.

Automated irrigation systems enhance water use efficiency, conserve resources, and contribute to sustainable water management in agriculture (Haghverdi et al., 2019).

4.8 Data-Driven Pest and Disease Management

Analytical models analyze historical data on pest and disease occurrences, weather patterns, and crop susceptibility. These models help predict and manage pest outbreaks through targeted interventions.

Data-driven pest and disease management reduce the reliance on broad-spectrum pesticides, minimizing environmental impact and ensuring healthier crops (Kumar et al., 2016).

4.9 Time Series Analysis for Climate Prediction

Time series analysis, utilizing algorithms like ARIMA or machine learning-based approaches, is employed for climate prediction. These models analyze historical weather data to forecast future conditions.

Accurate climate predictions assist farmers in planning planting and harvesting schedules, adapting to changing weather patterns, and mitigating climate-related risks (Sharma et al., 2021).

4.10 Predictive Modelling

Examine the implementation of machine learning algorithms for yield prediction, considering factors influencing crop growth and harvest. Discuss the potential of predictive modelling in providing actionable insights for farmers. Predictive analytics models utilize historical financial data and market trends to forecast crop prices, input costs, and overall farm profitability. These models aid farmers in making informed financial decisions. Financial predictive analytics support farmers in budgeting, risk management, and long-term planning, contributing to the economic sustainability of agricultural operations.

4.11 Anomaly Detection

Explore the role of anomaly detection in identifying irregularities in crop health. Illustrate how early detection enables farmers to take pre-emptive measures, preventing potential issues and optimizing resource utilization. Analytical models and algorithms are integral to the modernization of agri-farming practices. By leveraging data-driven insights, farmers can enhance productivity, optimize resource utilization, and contribute to sustainable and efficient agriculture. The integration

Table 2. Components of precision agriculture and illustrative examples

Component	Illustration	Technology Used	Environmental Impact	Application Area
Data Integration	A centralized platform consolidates data from sensors, satellites, and weather stations.	• Sensors, • Satellites, • Weather Stations	• Improved decision-making, • Reduced resource wastage	Farm Management
Analytical Models	Machine learning algorithms predict optimal planting times based on historical data.	• ML Algorithms	• Enhanced crop planning, • Disease management	Crop Management
Real-time Sensor Networks	Soil moisture sensors transmit real-time data, enabling timely irrigation decisions.	• Soil Moisture Sensors, • Temperature Sensors	• Efficient water usage, • Timely irrigation	Irrigation Management
Decision Support Systems	A DSS processes data on pest occurrences and weather forecasts for targeted pest control.	• Analytical Models, • Real-time Data	• Timely and targeted pest control, • Reduced crop damage risk	Pest Management
Automation	Automated tractors adjust planting depth and spacing based on real-time soil data.	• Automated Tractors, • Drones	• Precision in farming operations, • Efficient resource utilization	Farm Operations
Variable Rate Technology (VRT)	VRT maps guide fertilizer application, optimizing nutrient distribution and reducing environmental impact.	• Variable Rate Technology	• Optimal resource application, • Reduced environmental impact	Input Application Rates

of these technologies marks a transformative era in which agri-farming becomes increasingly intelligent, adaptive, and resilient to the challenges of a dynamic agricultural landscape.

5. BASIC PRINCIPLES OF SUSTAINABLE AGRICULTURE

Sustainable agriculture minimizes environmental impact by promoting practices that enhance soil health, water quality, and biodiversity while preventing resource depletion and pollution. It prioritizes economic viability for farmers through efficient resource use and market exploration. Additionally, it advocates for fair labor practices, social equity, and community engagement, aiming to meet the needs of present and future generations. Key principles include conservation of resources, biodiversity preservation, soil health maintenance, integrated pest management, climate resilience, and social responsibility.

Firstly, resource efficiency is a central tenet, emphasizing the judicious use of resources such as water, energy, and nutrients. Precision agriculture, crop rotation, and integrated pest management are among the practices employed to optimize resource utilization. Resilience and adaptability constitute another crucial aspect of sustainable agriculture. The aim is to build farming systems that can withstand and adapt to changing environmental conditions, including climate variability. Diverse cropping systems and agroecological approaches contribute significantly to enhancing resilience. The conservation of biodiversity is a fundamental consideration in sustainable farming. Recognizing the importance of biodiversity for ecosystem health, practices such as polyculture, agroforestry, and habitat preservation are implemented to contribute to the conservation of diverse plant and animal species. Finally, the maintenance and improvement of soil health and fertility are paramount in sustainable agriculture. Practices such as cover cropping, organic matter incorporation, and reduced tillage play a pivotal role in enhancing soil fertility and structure. In summary, sustainable agriculture is a holistic approach that not only seeks to minimize environmental impact but also aims to ensure economic viability, promote community well-being, and uphold the principles of resource efficiency, resilience, biodiversity conservation, and soil health.

Data analysis, incorporating satellite imagery, sensors, and GIS technology, plays a pivotal role in enabling farmers to precisely manage inputs such as water, fertilizers, and pesticides. This optimization not only reduces waste but also minimizes environmental impact while enhancing overall resource efficiency. Within this paradigm, several key applications of data analysis in sustainable agriculture emerge.

1.   Predictive Analytics for Crop Management:

Utilizing advanced data analytics, farmers gain insights into crop health, yield predictions, and pest/disease risks. This information empowers informed decision-making regarding planting schedules, pest control strategies, and overall crop management.

2.   IoT Devices for Monitoring and Control:

Internet of Things (IoT) devices, such as sensors and smart farming equipment, generate real-time data on soil moisture, temperature, and crop conditions. This data facilitates timely decision-making, ensuring efficient resource use and effective crop management.

3.   Decision Support Systems for Sustainable Practices:

Data-driven decision support systems provide farmers with recommendations for sustainable practices, considering factors like soil health, climate conditions, and crop rotations. This aids in aligning farming practices with sustainable agriculture principles.

4.   Traceability and Certification:

Blockchain technology and data analytics establish traceability in the agricultural supply chain, ensuring transparency for consumers to make informed choices about sustainably produced products. Certification processes also benefit from data verification.

5.   Climate Data for Adaptation Strategies:

Analysis of historical and real-time climate data assists farmers in adapting to changing weather patterns. Understanding climate trends enables adjustments in planting times, the selection of climate-resilient crops, and the implementation of practices enhancing overall resilience.

6.   Monitoring Ecosystem Health:

Data analysis contributes to monitoring and assessing the health of ecosystems around farms. This involves analyzing biodiversity trends, evaluating the impact of farming practices on local ecosystems, and implementing strategies to enhance biodiversity conservation.

7.   Community Engagement and Data Sharing:

Data analysis facilitates collaboration among farmers, researchers, and communities. This collective approach fosters the development and dissemination of sustainable agricultural practices benefiting the entire farming community.

By leveraging data analysis tools and technologies, farmers can make informed decisions aligned with the principles of sustainable agriculture. This not only improves farm productivity but also contributes to environmental conservation and the overall well-being of agricultural communities.

6. ROLE OF TECHNOLOGY AND DATA IN AGRICULTURAL PRACTICES

In the contemporary landscape of sustainable agriculture, farmers are strategically integrating a range of technological solutions to address key facets such as soil health promotion, water conservation, and biodiversity enhancement.

6.1 Promoting Soil Health

Soil Sensors and Monitoring Systems: Real-time data on moisture levels, temperature, and nutrient content aids informed decisions on irrigation, fertilization, and soil management. Continuous monitoring prevents overuse of inputs and promotes sustainable soil management.

Precision Agriculture: Data analytics-driven technologies enable precise application of inputs, reducing soil compaction, minimizing overuse of fertilizers and pesticides, and promoting optimal soil structure. Tailoring farming practices to specific areas within a field enhances overall soil health.

Digital Soil Mapping: Utilizing data from satellite imagery and ground-based measurements, detailed soil maps are created. This aids farmers in understanding soil property variability across fields, guiding site-specific soil management practices for improved health and fertility.

Cover Cropping and Crop Rotation Planning: Data analysis informs planning of cover cropping and crop rotation strategies based on historical and real-time soil condition data. Optimized planting sequences contribute to improved soil health, erosion reduction, and enhanced nutrient cycling.

IoT and Smart Farming: Integration of IoT devices into smart farming practices facilitates continuous monitoring of soil conditions. Timely data on moisture, temperature, and other parameters allows for proactive soil management, ensuring optimal health throughout the growing season.

6.2 Water Conservation

Satellite Imagery for Irrigation Management: Satellite-based data provides insights into crop water requirements and field-level variability, enabling optimized irrigation schedules and minimizing water wastage.

Drip and Precision Irrigation Systems: Technologies like drip and precision irrigation, supported by data analysis, ensure precise water delivery to crops. This minimizes water use, reduces evaporation, and enhances water-use efficiency.

Weather Data for Water Planning: Real-time and historical weather data anticipate rainfall patterns, guiding informed decisions on when and how much to irrigate. This prevents over-irrigation and ensures efficient water use in agriculture.

Soil Moisture Sensors: Integrated with data analytics, soil moisture sensors provide accurate information about moisture levels, optimizing irrigation schedules and preventing both water stress and excess water application.

Water Quality Monitoring: Real-time monitoring of water quality in irrigation systems helps identify and address issues promptly, contributing to sustainable irrigation practices and overall water conservation.

6.3 Biodiversity Conservation

GIS and Landscape Analysis: GIS technology, coupled with data analysis, supports landscape-level planning for biodiversity conservation. Farmers can identify areas of high biodiversity significance and implement practices that preserve natural habitats.

Agroforestry and Biodiversity-Friendly Practices: Technology assists in designing and implementing agroforestry systems and biodiversity-friendly practices. Data analysis helps farmers select tree species, plan buffer zones, and manage agricultural landscapes to enhance biodiversity.

Monitoring Wildlife Movements: Advanced technologies like GPS tracking and camera traps provide data on wildlife movements within agricultural landscapes. Farmers can plan farming practices to coexist harmoniously with wildlife, contributing to biodiversity conservation and ecosystem balance.

Precision Pest Management: Data-driven precision pest management targets specific areas affected by pests, minimizing the use of broad-spectrum pesticides. This targeted approach helps preserve natural predators and reduces the overall environmental impact of pest control practices.

Crop Diversification Strategies: Data analysis supports the planning of crop diversification strategies that promote biodiversity. Understanding interactions between different crops and their impact on local ecosystems enables farmers to make choices that enhance biodiversity on their farms.

Figure 6. Tech-Driven agri: Sustainable solutions for soil, water, and biodiversity

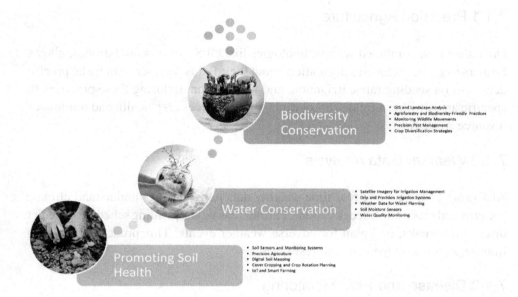

The integration of technology and data-driven approaches is playing a crucial role in promoting soil health, conserving water, and enhancing biodiversity in agriculture. By leveraging these tools, farmers can make informed, precise, and sustainable decisions, thereby contributing to the overall resilience and health of agricultural ecosystems. Figure 3 shows the graphical representation provides a visual overview of how technology and data contribute to sustainable agricultural practices across different aspects such as soil health, water conservation, and biodiversity enhancement.

7. IMPLEMENTING DATA-DRIVEN DECISION MAKING

Data analytics has played a crucial role in transforming agriculture by providing valuable insights that drive informed decision-making in crop management, resource allocation, and yield optimization. Here's how data analytics has impacted these aspects of modern agriculture:

7.1 Crop Management

7.1.1 Precision Agriculture

Data analytics, combined with technologies like GPS, sensors, and drones, allows farmers to gather detailed information about their fields. Farmers can make precise decisions on seeding rates, irrigation, and fertilization, tailoring these practices to specific areas within a field. This optimization enhances crop health and minimizes resource wastage.

7.1.2 Weather Data Analysis

Analyzing historical and real-time weather data helps farmers understand climate patterns and make informed decisions. Farmers can adjust planting schedules, predict disease outbreaks, and plan for adverse weather events. This proactive approach improves crop management and resilience.

7.1.3 Disease and Pest Monitoring

Data analytics is used to monitor and analyze data related to crop diseases and pest infestations.

Early detection allows farmers to implement timely and targeted interventions, reducing the use of pesticides and minimizing crop damage.

7.1.4 Remote Sensing and NDVI Analysis

Satellite and drone imagery, along with Normalized Difference Vegetation Index (NDVI) analysis, provide insights into crop health. Farmers can identify stressed areas, nutrient deficiencies, or water stress early on. This allows for targeted corrective actions, optimizing crop yields.

7.2 Resource Allocation

7.2.1 Irrigation Management

Soil moisture sensors, combined with data analytics, enable precise irrigation management. Farmers can optimize water use by irrigating based on actual soil moisture levels. This reduces water wastage, improves water-use efficiency, and contributes to sustainable farming practices.

7.2.2 Fertilizer Optimization

Data analytics helps farmers analyze soil nutrient levels and predict crop nutrient requirements. Precision application of fertilizers based on data-driven insights minimizes overuse, reduces environmental impact, and improves cost-effectiveness.

7.2.3 Machinery Efficiency

Telematics and sensor data from agricultural machinery are analyzed to optimize field operations. Farmers can monitor and improve the efficiency of machinery, reduce fuel consumption, and minimize soil compaction, contributing to sustainable resource use.

7.2.4 Supply Chain Optimization

Data analytics is used to optimize the supply chain, reducing waste and improving resource efficiency. Efficient logistics and distribution based on data-driven insights enhance resource allocation, reducing losses and ensuring timely delivery of products to markets.

7.3 Yield Optimization

7.3.1 Predictive Analytics

Historical data, combined with predictive analytics, helps forecast potential yields based on various factors. Farmers can make informed decisions on planting, harvesting, and storage, optimizing yield predictions and improving overall production efficiency.

7.3.2 Data-Driven Decision Support Systems

Decision support systems analyze diverse data sets to provide actionable insights. Farmers receive recommendations on optimal planting times, crop varieties, and management practices, contributing to higher yields and improved profitability.

7.3.3 Market Intelligence

Data analytics provides market intelligence, helping farmers understand consumer demand and market trends. Farmers can make informed decisions on crop selection and production volume, aligning their yield with market demand and maximizing profitability.

7.4.4 Varietal Selection

Analyzing historical performance data helps farmers choose crop varieties that perform well in specific conditions. Selecting the right crop varieties based on data-driven insights improves yield potential and resilience to environmental challenges.

Data analytics has revolutionized agriculture by empowering farmers with information that guides informed decision-making in crop management, resource allocation, and yield optimization. The figure 4 provides a visual summary of the key points covered in the content, highlighting the implementation of data-driven decision making in various aspects of agriculture such as crop management, resource allocation, and yield optimization.

Figure 7. Data-Driven agriculture: Optimizing crop management, resource allocation, and yield enhancement

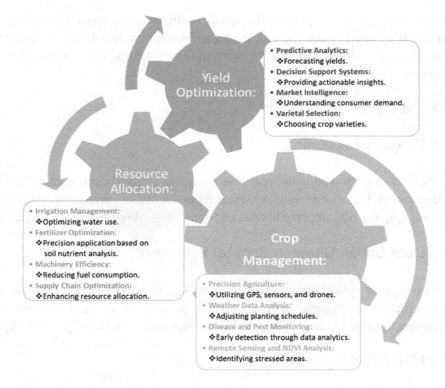

8. CHALLENGES AND OPPORTUNITIES

The integration of an extensive array of technologies in agricultural practices, ranging from crop and soil sensors to blockchain, cloud computing, real-time satellite imagery, NDVI-based sensor networks, precision nutrient and irrigation management, disease and pest detection, decision support systems, crowd-sourced data, weather stations, GIS, and crop breeding, presents a multifaceted landscape of challenges and opportunities. Challenges include the complexity of managing and integrating such a diverse technological ecosystem, which demands significant investments in infrastructure, training, and data management. Ensuring interoperability among these technologies is crucial to harness their full potential. Moreover, issues related to data security and privacy, especially with the incorporation of blockchain, require careful consideration.

On the upside, the opportunities are extensive. These technologies collectively offer unprecedented capabilities for real-time monitoring, data-driven decision-

Table 3. Tech integration in agriculture: Challenges and opportunities

Challenges	Opportunities
1. Complexity of managing diverse technologies	1. Real-time monitoring and data-driven decision-making
2. Significant investment requirements	2. Precision management of resources
3. Ensuring interoperability	3. Disease and pest detection for minimal environmental impact
4. Data security and privacy concerns	4. Enhanced predictive capabilities through satellite imagery
5. Complexity of implementing sensor networks	5. Comprehensive data analytics and GIS integration for valuable insights
6. Difficulties in adopting new technologies	6. Crowd-sourced data for collaborative problem-solving
7. Risk of over-reliance on technology	7. Potential for smart, sustainable, and resilient agriculture
8. Digital divide in technology access	8. Improved productivity and profitability through optimized practices
9. Regulatory challenges	9. Environmental sustainability by reducing resource wastage
10. Environmental impact of technology	10. Empowerment of farmers with access to advanced technologies and information
11. Ethical considerations	11. Innovation and development of new technologies for agricultural challenges
12. Challenges in scaling up adoption	12. Increased resilience to climate change and external factors through adaptation

making, and sustainable agricultural practices. Precision management of nutrients and irrigation, coupled with disease and pest detection through advanced sensor networks, can optimize resource use and minimize environmental impact. The use of real-time satellite imagery and weather stations enhances predictive capabilities, contributing to more resilient and adaptive farming practices. The comprehensive data analytics and GIS integration further empower farmers with valuable insights, while crowd-sourced data fosters a collaborative approach to problem-solving. Agri-tech startups in developing economies face challenges like technology adoption barriers, funding constraints, and regulatory hurdles, while also encountering opportunities for innovation and market expansion. Case studies illustrate how these startups navigate obstacles and leverage opportunities. Policy, investment, and entrepreneurial initiatives can support their growth, fostering sustainable agriculture, economic resilience, and environmental sustainability (Bethi S.K and Deshmukh S.S., 2023).

Overall, the amalgamation of these technologies has the potential to usher in a new era of smart, sustainable, and resilient agriculture, though not without its accompanying set of challenges.

This table presents a clear overview of the issues and opportunities associated with the integration of technology in agriculture.

9. FUTURE DIRECTIONS

In the ongoing evolution of agricultural harvesting practices, this chapter advocates for the exploration of advanced technologies to enhance efficiency, precision, and sustainability. Our focal points include the integration of cutting-edge solutions that are aimed at fortifying security and traceability. The potential impact on harvesting lies in the capacity for immediate, precision-enhancing adjustments based on localized data. Real-time analysis of harvesting data on pre-defined parameters is a must to optimize efficiency and accuracy throughout the harvesting process. Moreover, blockchain technology is identified as a critical component in the future landscape of agricultural harvesting. It guarantees traceability and accountability throughout the agricultural supply chain, fortifying the integrity of harvested data.

Collectively, the integration of soil sensors, crop sensors, blockchain technology, NDVI platforms, with up-to-date satellite imagery, cloud computing and a robust decision support system heralds a transformative era in agricultural harvesting. The envisioned outcome is a technologically advanced and environmentally conscious agricultural sector, marked by heightened efficiency, precision, and sustainability.

10. CONCLUSION

The chapter concludes by summarizing the key findings and insights derived from the exploration of data analysis methodologies in sustainable agriculture. It emphasizes the transformative potential of "harvesting insights" and underscores the imperative for continued research and innovation in marrying data analytics with Agri-farming practices for a sustainable future. The data analysis methodology outlined in this article underscores the transformative potential of integrating IoT, machine learning, and remote sensing in sustainable agriculture. By providing farmers with actionable insights, these methodologies aim to pave the way for a more resilient and environmentally conscious farming future.

Looking forward, our chapter contributes to the broader discourse on the transformative potential of modern technologies in shaping the agricultural landscape. The future envisioned is a technologically advanced and environmentally conscious sector for a sustainable future in agricultural harvesting. As we continue to delve into these innovations, we anticipate further collaboration and interdisciplinary efforts to bring these advancements to fruition, ensuring a more resilient and efficient agricultural ecosystem for generations to come.

REFERENCES

Bastiaanssen, W. G. M. (2015). A new satellite-based methodology for assessing and mapping the impact of floods on rice agriculture. *Agricultural Water Management*, *149*, 38–53.

Bethi, S. K., & Deshmukh, S. S. (2023) Challenges and Opportunities for Agri-Tech Startups in Developing Economies. *International Journal of AgricultureSciences*, *15(9)*, 12661-12666

De Baets, S. (2019). Decision Support Systems in Agriculture: A Systematic Review. *Computers and Electronics in Agriculture*, *157*, 112–125.

De Baets, S. (2019). Decision Support Systems in Agriculture: A Systematic Review. *Computers and Electronics in Agriculture*, *157*, 112–125.

Drusch, M., Del Bello, U., Carlier, S., Colin, O., Fernandez, V., Gascon, F., Hoersch, B., Isola, C., Laberinti, P., Martimort, P., Meygret, A., Spoto, F., Sy, O., Marchese, F., & Bargellini, P. (2012). Sentinel-2: ESA's Optical High-Resolution Mission for GMES Operational Services. *Remote Sensing of Environment*, *120*, 25–36. doi:10.1016/j.rse.2011.11.026

Gitelson, A. A., Chivkunova, O. B., & Merzlyak, M. N. (2009). Nondestructive estimation of anthocyanins and chlorophylls in anthocyanic leaves. *American Journal of Botany*, *96*(10), 1861–1868. doi:10.3732/ajb.0800395 PMID:21622307

Guyon, I. (2006). *Feature Extraction: Foundations and Applications*. Springer. doi:10.1007/978-3-540-35488-8

Haghverdi, A. (2019). Precision Agriculture Irrigation Management Using Machine Learning Algorithms. *Computers and Electronics in Agriculture*, *161*, 280–294.

Haghverdi, A. (2019). Precision Agriculture Irrigation Management Using Machine Learning Algorithms. *Computers and Electronics in Agriculture*, *161*, 280–294.

Hastie, T., Tibshirani, R., & Friedman, J. (2009). *The Elements of Statistical Learning: Data Mining, Inference, and Prediction*. Springer. doi:10.1007/978-0-387-84858-7

Hodge, V. J., & Austin, J. (2004). A Survey of Outlier Detection Methodologies. *Artificial Intelligence Review*, *22*(2), 85–126. doi:10.1023/B:AIRE.0000045502.10941.a9

Inoue, Y. (2017). Monitoring Rice Growth for Yield Prediction Based on UAV-SfM 3D Modeling and High-Resolution Satellite Multispectral Imagery. *Remote Sensing*, *9*(1), 53.

Jain, A. (2018). A Comprehensive Review on Genetic Algorithm: Past, Present, and Future. *Applied Intelligence*, *48*(12), 4333–4370.

Jones, H. G. (2004). Irrigation scheduling: Advantages and pitfalls of plant-based methods. *Journal of Experimental Botany*, *55*(407), 2427–2436. doi:10.1093/jxb/erh213 PMID:15286143

Jones, H. G. (2013). Use of infrared thermometry for estimation of stomatal conductance as a possible aid to irrigation scheduling. *Agricultural and Forest Meteorology*, *177*, 129–139. doi:10.1016/j.agrformet.2013.04.031

Justice, C. O., Vermote, E., Townshend, J. R. G., Defries, R., Roy, D. P., Hall, D. K., Salomonson, V. V., Privette, J. L., Riggs, G., Strahler, A., Lucht, W., Myneni, R. B., Knyazikhin, Y., Running, S. W., Nemani, R. R., Zhengming Wan, Huete, A. R., van Leeuwen, W., Wolfe, R. E., & Barnsley, M. J. (1998). The Moderate Resolution Imaging Spectroradiometer (MODIS): Land remote sensing for global change research. *IEEE Transactions on Geoscience and Remote Sensing*, *36*(4), 1228–1249. doi:10.1109/36.701075

Khaki, S. (2019). A Comprehensive Review on Decision Support Systems for Sustainable Agriculture: A Food-Energy-Water Nexus Perspective. *Sustainability*, *11*(13), 3532.

Kumar, P. (2016). Applications of Artificial Intelligence Techniques in Agriculture. *Annals of Agricultural Science*, *61*(1), 31–41.

Little, R. J., & Rubin, D. B. (2019). *Statistical analysis with missing data* (Vol. 793). John Wiley & Sons.

Lobell, D. B., Hammer, G. L., McLean, G., Messina, C., Roberts, M. J., & Schlenker, W. (2009). The Critical Role of Extreme Heat for Maize Production in the United States. *Nature Climate Change*, *3*(5), 497–501. doi:10.1038/nclimate1832

Lobell, D. B., Hammer, G. L., McLean, G., Messina, C., Roberts, M. J., & Schlenker, W. (2009). The Critical Role of Extreme Heat for Maize Production in the United States. *Nature Climate Change*, *3*(5), 497–501. doi:10.1038/nclimate1832

Lowenberg-DeBoer, J. (2012). Precision Agriculture for Grain Crops in the US Midwest. *Plant Science*, *18*, 484–491.

Montgomery, D. C. (2015). *Introduction to Time Series Analysis and Forecasting*. John Wiley & Sons.

Mulla, D. J. (2013). Twenty-Five Years of Remote Sensing in Precision Agriculture: Key Advances and Remaining Knowledge Gaps. *Biosystems Engineering*, *114*(4), 358–371. doi:10.1016/j.biosystemseng.2012.08.009

Mulla, D. J. (2013). Twenty-Five Years of Remote Sensing in Precision Agriculture: Key Advances and Remaining Knowledge Gaps. *Biosystems Engineering*, *114*(4), 358–371. doi:10.1016/j.biosystemseng.2012.08.009

Nassar, A. K. (2018). Cloud-Based Farm Management Systems: An Overview and Comparison. *Computers and Electronics in Agriculture*, *144*, 291–307.

O'Sullivan, D., & Unwin, D. (2003). *Geographic Information Analysis*. John Wiley & Sons.

Pathan, S. K. (2015). Internet of Things: Architectures, Protocols, and Applications. *Journal of Industrial Information Integration*, *1*, 3–13.

Pathan, S. K. (2015). Internet of Things: Architectures, Protocols, and Applications. *Journal of Industrial Information Integration*, *1*, 3–13.

Raza, I. (2023). Precision Nutrient Application Techniques to Improve Soil Fertility and Crop Yield: A Review with Future Prospect. *International Research Journal of Education and Technology*, *5*(08), 109–123.

Redman, T. C. (1996). *Data Quality for the Information Age*.

Roy, D. P. (2014). Landsat-8: Science and product vision for terrestrial global change research. *Remote Sensing of Environment*, *145*, 154–172. doi:10.1016/j. rse.2014.02.001

Saravanan, N. (2014). Spatial Data Integration for Precision Agriculture: A Review. *Computers and Electronics in Agriculture*, *110*, 1–12.

Saravanan, N. (2014). Spatial data integration for precision agriculture: A review. *Computers and Electronics in Agriculture*, *110*, 1–12.

Sharma, N. (2021). Crop Yield Prediction Using Machine Learning Algorithms: A Comprehensive Review. *Computers and Electronics in Agriculture*, *180*, 106034.

Surya, S., & Mandal, P. (2020). Role of IoT in agriculture: A comprehensive review. *Journal of King Saud University. Computer and Information Sciences*. doi:10.1016/j. jksuci.2020.01.042

Tagarakis, A. C. (2020). Smart agriculture: A review of technologies in precision farming. *Agricultural Systems*, *182*, 102896. doi:10.1016/j.agsy.2020.102896

ThenkabailP. S. (2016). Global Food Security Support Analysis Data (GFSAD) Cropland Extent 2015 Africa 30 m. doi:10.3334/ORNLDAAC/1346

Thenkabail, P. S. (2019). Remote Sensing of Crop Types for Agricultural Supply Management. *Agronomy Journal*, *111*(3), 1009–1028.

Tucker, C. J. (1979). Red and photographic infrared linear combinations for monitoring vegetation. *Remote Sensing of Environment*, *8*(2), 127–150. doi:10.1016/0034-4257(79)90013-0

Wang, Y. (2018). Remote Sensing for Precision Agriculture: Recent Advances and Future Prospects. *Yaogan Xuebao*, *22*(1), 3–23.

Chapter 10
Machine Learning Algorithms Used for Iris Flower Classification

Rituparna Nath
NERIM Group of Institutions, India

Arunima Devi
NERIM Group of Institutions, India

ABSTRACT

Classification is a supervised machine learning technique which is used to predict group membership for data instances. For simplification of classification, one may use scikit-learn tool kit. This chapter mainly focuses on the classification of Iris dataset using scikit-learn. It concerns the recognition of Iris flower species (setosa, versicolor, and verginica) on the basis of the measurements of length and width of sepal and petal of the flower. One can generate classification models by using various machine learning algorithms through training the iris flower dataset, and can choose the model with highest accuracy to predict the species of iris flower more precisely. Classification of Iris dataset would be detecting patterns from examining sepal and petal size of the Iris flower and how the prediction was made from analyzing the pattern to form the class of Iris flower. By using this pattern and classification, in future upcoming years the unseen data can be predicted more precisely. The goal here is to gain insights to model the probabilities of class membership, conditioned on the flower features. The proposed chapter mainly focuses on how one can train their model with data using machine learning algorithms to predict the species of Iris flower by input of the unseen data using what it has learnt from the trained data.

DOI: 10.4018/979-8-3693-2260-4.ch010

1. INTRODUCTION

Machine learning is a process of feeding a machine enough data to train and predict a possible outcome using the algorithms. The more the processed or useful data is fed to the machine the more efficient the machine will become. It has tools and technology that we can utilize to answer questions with our data. Machine Learning can work on two values viz., discrete and continuous. The use and applications of Machine Learning has wide area like Weather forecast, Image Recognition, Spam detection, Traffic Prediction, Speech Recognition, Automatic Language Translation, Biometric attendance, Product Recommendations, Computer vision, Stock Market Trading, Medical Diagnosis and many more (Shukla A., Pant H., Agarwal A. & Mishra P., 2020).

The learning methods of Machine Learning are of three types viz., supervised, unsupervised and reinforcement learning. Supervised learning contains instances of a training data set which is composed of different input attributes and an expected output. Classification which is the sub part of supervised learning where the computer program learns from the input given to it and uses this learning to classify new observation. There are various types of classification techniques; these are Decision Trees, Bayes Classifier, Nearest Neighbor, Support Vector Machine, Neural Networks and many more (Shukla A., Pant H., Agarwal A. & Mishra P., 2020).

The iris flower classification problem provides a hands-on introduction to machine learning, enabling practitioners to grasp essential concepts, data preprocessing, model training, evaluation, and deployment. It's a stepping stone toward more complex classification tasks and a foundation for understanding various machine learning algorithms. Iris flower classification using machine learning serves as an educational tool for understanding fundamental concepts in machine learning and classification. It has real-world applications in botany, agriculture, and environmental sciences for automating the classification of iris species based on their features. Furthermore, the iris flower classification problem serves as a benchmark for testing and comparing the performance of different machine learning models, fostering a deeper comprehension of algorithmic strengths and weaknesses. Its simplicity makes it an ideal starting point for beginners while providing a robust foundation for more advanced studies. The knowledge gained from this exercise goes beyond iris classification, providing transferable skills that can be applied to many fields. As machine learning continues to evolve, iris datasets remain a timeless resource for understanding and understanding the interactions between data and algorithms in distributed operations (Suchitra G., 2023).

This research work mainly focuses on the exploratory data analysis and classification of Iris Flower dataset using supervised machine learning. The problem concerns with getting insights and discovering the underlying structure of the dataset alongwih detecting outliers and anomalies. Further, the problem concerns with the recognition of Iris flower species (setosa, versicolor and verginica) on the basis of the measurements of length and width of sepal and petal of the flower. We can generate classification model by using various machine learning algorithms through training the Iris Flower dataset and can choose the model with highest accuracy to predict the species of iris flower more precisely. The programming language used in this project was Python. Moreover, a typical and simple machine learning algorithm called KNN is introduced to achieve the highest accuracy. The case study of Iris recognition will show how to implement machine learning by using Scikit-learn software. In this project we will train our model with data using machine learning to predict the species of iris flower by input of the unseen data using what it has learnt from the trained data.

1.1 K-Nearest Neighbor (KNN) Algorithm

K-Nearest Neighbors is one of the most basic yet essential classification algorithms in Machine Learning. It belongs to the supervised learning domain and finds intense application in pattern recognition, datamining, and intrusion detection. KNN algorithm stores all the available data and classifies a new data point based on the similarity. This means when new data appears then it can be easily classified into a well suite category by using KNN algorithm. KNN algorithm can be used for Regression as well as for Classification but mostly it is used for the Classification problems. KNN is a non-parametric algorithm, which means it does not make any assumption on underlying data. It is also called a lazy learner algorithm because it does not learn from the training set immediately instead it stores the dataset and at the time of classification, it performs an action on the dataset. The K-Nearest Neighbors (KNN) algorithm is a robust and intuitive machine learning method employed to tackle classification and regression problems. By capitalizing on the concept of similarity, KNN predicts the label or value of a new data point by considering its K closest neighbors in the training dataset.

KNN stores the whole preparing dataset which it utilizes as its representation. KNN does not get familiar with any model. KNN makes expectations without a moment to spare by computing the comparability between a material test and each preparation case. There are numerous partition measures to look over to coordinate the structure of your information. That it is a shrewd idea to rescale your information, for example, utilizing standardization, when utilizing KNN (Naik G., Birari D., Sonavane B. & Bhagat N., 2019).

1.2 Distance Metrics Used in KNN Algorithm

When KNN has unseen observation, then similarity is determine by distance metric between two data points (Shukla A., Pant H., Agarwal A. & Mishra P., 2020). As we know that the KNN algorithm helps us identify the nearest points or the groups for a query point. But to determine the closest groups or the nearest points for a query point we need some metric. For this purpose, we use below distance metrics:

1.2.1 Euclidean Distance

This is nothing but the Cartesian distance between the two points which are in the plane/hyperplane. Euclidean distance can also be visualized as the length of the straight line that joins the two points which are into consideration. This metric helps us calculate the net displacement done between the two states of an object.

$$d(x,y) = \sqrt{\sum_{i=1}^{n}(x_i - y_i)^2}$$

1.2.2 Manhattan Distance

Manhattan Distance metric is generally used when we are interested in the total distance traveled by the object instead of the displacement. This metric is calculated by summing the absolute difference between the coordinates of the points in n-dimensions.

$$d(x,y) = \sum_{i=1}^{n}|x_i - y_i|$$

1.2.3 Minkowski Distance

We can say that the Euclidean, as well as the Manhattan distance, are special cases of the Minkowski distance.

$$D(X,Y) = \left(\sum_{i=1}^{n}|x_i - y_i|^p\right)^{1/p}$$

From the formula above we can say that when $p = 2$ then it is the same as the formula for the Euclidean distance and when $p = 1$ then we obtain the formula for the Manhattan distance.

1.3 Working of KNN Algorithm

The working of KNN can be explained on the basis of the below algorithm:

Step-1: Select the number K of the neighbors
Step-2: Calculate the Euclidean distance of K number of neighbors
Step-3: Take the K nearest neighbors as per the calculated Euclidean distance.
Step-4: Among these k neighbors, count the number of the data points in each category.
Step-5: Assign the new data points to that category for which the number of the neighbor is maximum.
Step-6: Our model is ready.

1.4 Flowchart of KNN Algorithm

Figure 1 shows a flowchart of the KNN algorithm.

1.5 Defining K in KNN Algorithm

The value of K in the KNN algorithm defines how many neighbors will be checked to determine the classification of a specific query point. For example, if K=1, the instance will be assigned to the same class as its single nearest neighbor. Defining K can be a balancing act as different values can lead to overfitting or underfitting. Lower values of K can have high variance, but low bias, and larger values of K may lead to high bias and lower variance. The choice of K will largely depend on the input data as data with more outliers or noise will likely perform better with higher values of K. Overall, it is recommended to have an odd number for K to avoid ties in classification, and cross-validation tactics can help one choose the optimal K for their dataset.

1.6 Naïve Bayes Algorithm

Naïve Bayes algorithm is a supervised learning algorithm, which is based on **Bayes theorem** and used for solving classification problems. The Naïve Bayes algorithm is comprised of two words Naïve and Bayes, which can be described as:

Figure 1. KNN algorithm flowchart
(Mahdiani R. M., Khamehchi E., Hajirezaie S. & Sarapardeh H. M., 2020)

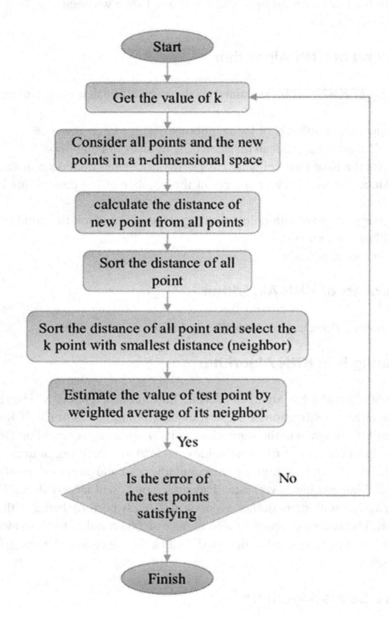

Naïve: It is called Naïve because it assumes that the occurrence of a certain feature is independent of the occurrence of other features. The classifier assumes that the features used to describe an observation are conditionally independent, given the class label. Such as if the fruit is identified on the bases of color, shape, and taste, then red, spherical, and sweet fruit is recognized as an apple. Hence each feature individually contributes to identify that it is an apple without depending on each other.

Bayes: The "Bayes" part of the name refers to Reverend Thomas Bayes, an 18th-century statistician and theologian who formulated Bayes' theorem.

Naïve Bayes Classifier is one of the simple and most effective Classification algorithms which help in building the fast machine learning models that can make quick predictions. It is a probabilistic classifier, which means it predicts on the basis of the probability of an object. It is mainly used in text classification that includes a high-dimensional training dataset. In spite of their apparently over-simplified assumptions, naive Bayes classifiers have worked quite well in many real-world situations, famously document classification and spam filtering. They require a small amount of training data to estimate the necessary parameters.

Naive Bayes learners and classifiers can be extremely fast compared to more sophisticated methods. The decoupling of the class conditional feature distributions means that each distribution can be independently estimated as a one dimensional distribution. This in turn helps to alleviate problems stemming from the curse of dimensionality.

1.7 Bayes Theorem

Bayes' theorem is also known as **Bayes' Rule** or **Bayes' law**, which is used to determine the probability of a hypothesis with prior knowledge. It depends on the conditional probability. The formula for Bayes' theorem is given as:

$$P(A \mid B) = \frac{P(B \mid A)P(A)}{P(B)}$$

where,

P(A|B) is Posterior probability: Probability of hypothesis A on the observed event B.

P(B|A) is Likelihood probability: Probability of the evidence given that the probability of a hypothesis is true.

P(A) is Prior Probability: Probability of hypothesis before observing the evidence.

P(B) is Marginal Probability: Probability of Evidence.

Bayesian Probability allows to calculate the conditional probabilities. It enables to use of partial knowledge for calculating the probability of the occurrence of a specific event. This algorithm is used for developing models for prediction and classification problems like Naive Bayes.

The Bayesian Rule is used in probability theory for computing - conditional probabilities. What is important is that one cannot discover just how the evidence will impact the probability of an event occurring, but one can find the exact probability.

There are training data to train a model and make it functional. Then it is needed to validate the data for evaluating the model and making new predictions. Finally, it is needed to call the input attributes "evidence" and label them "outputs" in the training data. Using conditional probability denoted by P(E|O), one can calculate the probability of the evidence from the given outputs. The ultimate goal is to compute P(O|E) - the probability of output based on the current attributes. When the problem has two outputs, one can calculate the probability of every outcome and say which one wins. Whereas if one has various input attributes, then the Naïve Bayesian Algorithm will be needed.

1.8 Types of Naïve Bayes Model

There are three types of Naive Bayes Model, which are given below:

- **Gaussian**: The Gaussian model assumes that features follow a normal distribution. This means if predictors take continuous values instead of discrete, then the model assumes that these values are sampled from the Gaussian distribution. A Gaussian distribution is also called Normal distribution When plotted, it gives a bell shaped curve which is symmetric about the mean of the feature values shown in Figure 2.
- **Multinomial**: The Multinomial Naïve Bayes classifier is used when the data is multinomial distributed. Feature vectors represent the frequencies with which certain events have been generated by a multinomial distribution. It is primarily used for document classification problems; it means a particular document belongs to which category such as Sports, Politics, education, etc. The classifier uses the frequency of words for the predictors.
- **Bernoulli**: The Bernoulli classifier works similar to the Multinomial classifier, but the predictor variables are the independent Booleans variables. Such as if a particular word is present or not in a document. Like the multinomial model, this model is popular for document classification tasks, where binary term occurrence (i.e. a word occurs in a document or not) features are used rather than term frequencies (i.e. frequency of a word in the document).
- **Optimal**: Optimal Naïve Bayes selects the class that has the greatest posterior probability of happenings. As per the name, it is optimal. But it will go through all the possibilities, which is very slow and time-consuming.

Figure 2. Gaussian model of normal distribution

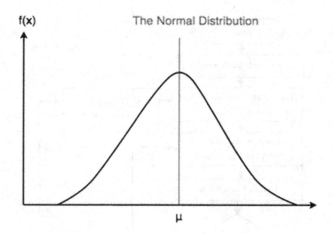

1.9 Working of Naïve Bayes Algorithm in Python

A classification model can be built that uses Sklearn to see how the Naïve Bayes Classifier works. Sklearn is also known as Scikit-Learn. It is an open-source machine-learning library that is written in Python. The working of the Naïve Bayes Algorithm can be understood by following the below steps:

Step 1	- Import basic libraries
Step 2	- Importing the dataset
Step 3	- Data preprocessing
Step 4	- Training the model
Step 5	- Testing and evaluation of the model
Step 6	- Visualizing the model

1.10 Flowchart of Naïve Bayes Algorithm

Figure 3 shows a flowchart of the Naïve Bayes algorithm.

1.11 Decision Tree Algorithm

Decision Tree is a supervised learning technique that can be used for both classification and Regression problems, but mostly it is preferred for solving Classification problems. It is a tree-structured classifier, where internal nodes represent the features of a dataset, branches represent the decision rules and each leaf node represents the outcome. In a Decision tree, there are two nodes, which are the Decision Node and Leaf Node.

Figure 3. Naïve Bayes algorithm flowchart
(Sneha N. & Gangil T., 2019)

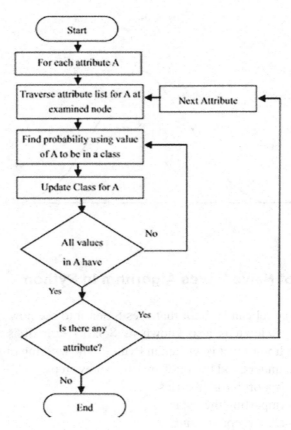

Decision nodes are used to make any decision and have multiple branches, whereas Leaf nodes are the output of those decisions and do not contain any further branches. The decisions or the test are performed on the basis of features of the given dataset. It is a graphical representation for getting all the possible solutions to a problem/ decision based on given conditions. It is called a decision tree because, similar to a tree, it starts with the root node, which expands on further branches and constructs a tree-like structure. In order to build a tree, we use the CART algorithm, which stands for Classification and Regression Tree algorithm. A decision tree simply asks a question, and based on the answer (Yes/No), it further split the tree into subtrees.

Figure 4 explains the general structure of a decision tree:

Figure 4. Structure of decision tree

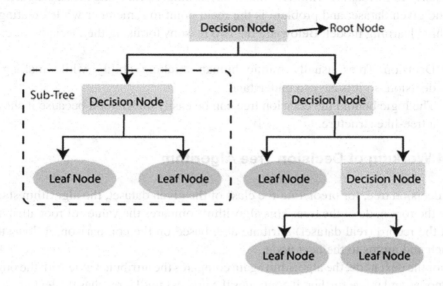

1.12 Formation of a Decision Tree

The process of forming a decision tree involves recursively partitioning the data based on the values of different attributes. The algorithm selects the best attribute to split the data at each internal node, based on certain criteria such as information gain or Gini impurity. This splitting process continues until a stopping criterion is met, such as reaching a maximum depth or having a minimum number of instances in a leaf node.

1.13 Decision Tree in Machine Learning

Decision trees are widely used in machine learning for a number of reasons. Decision trees are so versatile in simulating intricate decision-making processes, because of their interpretability and versatility. Their portrayal of complex choice scenarios that take into account a variety of causes and outcomes is made possible by their hierarchical structure. They provide comprehensible insights into the decision logic, decision trees are especially helpful for tasks involving categorization and regression. They are proficient with both numerical and categorical data, and they can easily adapt to a variety of datasets thanks to their autonomous feature selection capability. Decision trees also provide simple visualization, which helps to comprehend and elucidate the underlying decision processes in a model.

There are various algorithms in Machine learning, so choosing the best algorithm for the given dataset and problem is the main point to remember while creating a machine learning model. Below are the two reasons for using the Decision tree:

- Decision Trees usually mimic human thinking ability while making a decision, so it is easy to understand.
- The logic behind the decision tree can be easily understood because it shows a tree-like structure.

1.14 Working of Decision Tree Algorithm

In a decision tree, for predicting the class of the given dataset, the algorithm starts from the root node of the tree. This algorithm compares the values of root attribute with the record (real dataset) attribute and, based on the comparison, follows the branch and jumps to the next node.

For the next node, the algorithm again compares the attribute value with the other sub-nodes and move further. It continues the process until it reaches the leaf node of the tree. The complete process can be better understood using the below algorithm:

Step-1: Begin the tree with the root node, says S, which contains the complete dataset.

Step-2: Find the best attribute in the dataset using **Attribute Selection Measure (ASM).**

Step-3: Divide the S into subsets that contains possible values for the best attributes.

Step-4: Generate the decision tree node, which contains the best attribute.

Step-5: Recursively make new decision trees using the subsets of the dataset created in step -3. Continue this process until a stage is reached where you cannot further classify the nodes and called the final node as a leaf node.

1.15 Flowchart of Decision Tree Algorithm

Figure 5 shows a flowchart of the decision tree algorithm.

1.16 Attribute Selection Measures

While implementing a Decision tree, the main issue arises that how to select the best attribute for the root node and for sub-nodes. So, to solve such problems there is a technique which is called as Attribute selection measure or ASM. By this measurement, we can easily select the best attribute for the nodes of the tree. There are two popular techniques for ASM, which are:

Figure 5. Decision Tree Algorithm Flowchart
(Fu Y., Yin Z., Su M., Wu Y. & Liu G., 2020)

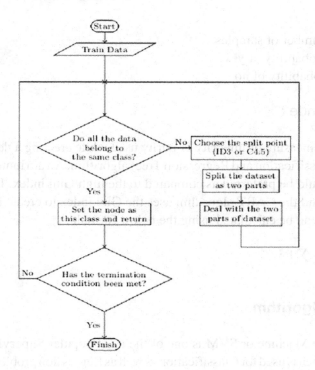

- Information Gain
- Gini Index

1.16.1 Information Gain

Information gain is the measurement of changes in entropy after the segmentation of a dataset based on an attribute. It calculates how much information a feature provides us about a class. According to the value of information gain, we split the node and build the decision tree. A decision tree algorithm always tries to maximize the value of information gain, and a node/attribute having the highest information gain is split first. It can be calculated using the below formula:

Information Gain = Entropy(S)- [(Weighted Avg) *Entropy(each feature)

Entropy: Entropy is a metric to measure the impurity in a given attribute. It specifies randomness in data. Entropy can be calculated as:

Entropy(s) = -P(yes)log2 P(yes)- P(no) log2 P(no)

where,
S= Total number of samples
P(yes) = probability of yes
P(no) = probability of no

1.16.2 Gini Index

Gini index is a measure of impurity or purity used while creating a decision tree in the CART (Classification and Regression Tree) algorithm. An attribute with the low Gini index should be preferred as compared to the high Gini index. It only creates binary splits, and the CART algorithm uses the Gini index to create binary splits.

Gini index can be calculated using the below formula:

Gini Index= 1- $\sum_j P_j^2$

1.17 SVM Algorithm

Support Vector Machine or SVM is one of the most popular Supervised Learning algorithms, which is used for Classification as well as Regression problems. However, primarily, it is used for Classification problems in Machine Learning. The goal of the SVM algorithm is to create the best line or decision boundary that can segregate n-dimensional space into classes so that we can easily put the new data point in the correct category in the future. This best decision boundary is called a hyperplane. SVM chooses the extreme points or vectors that help in creating the hyperplane. These extreme cases are called as support vectors, and hence algorithm is termed as Support Vector Machine.

In SVM dimensionality reduction techniques like Principal Component Analysis (PCA) and Scallers are used to classify dataset expeditiously. The first step towards implementation of SVM is data exploration. The initial configuration of hyper parameters like degree of polynomial or type of kernel are done by data exploration .Here we use two variables x and y, where x and y represent the features matrix and the target vector respectively. Dimensionality reduction is used to reduce the number of features in dataset which further reduces the computations. Iris dataset have four dimensions, with the help of dimensionality reduction it will be projected into a 3 dimensions space where the number of features is 3. We split the transformed data into two part, these are 80% of training set and 20% of test set (Shukla A., Pant H., Agarwal A. & Mishra P., 2020).

Figure 6. SVM algorithm view

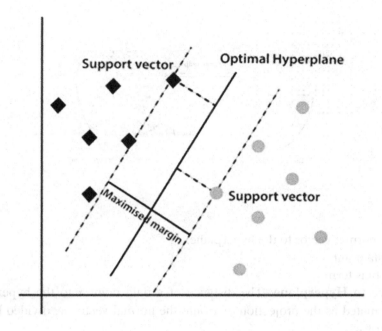

1.18 Mathematical Intuition

The mathematical intuition of SVM revolves around finding the best hyperplane that separates the data with the largest margin, while support vectors dictate the position of the hyperplane. The optimization problem ensures that the hyperplane has the maximum margin and correctly classifies the data points. This intuition can be explained through the geometry and linear algebra involved in the SVM algorithm.

Step-by-step mathematical intuition of SVM is as follows:

Geometry of Hyperplane: In a binary classification problem, consider two classes of data points in a multi-dimensional feature space. A hyperplane is a flat affine subspace that divides the space into two halves, each containing data points of one class.

Maximizing Margin: SVM aims to find the hyperplane that maximizes the margin between the closest data points of the two classes. The closest data points, known as support vectors, lie on the margins and determine the position of the hyperplane.

Equation of Hyperplane: The equation of a hyperplane in a feature space can be represented as:

$$w^T x + b = 0$$

Figure 7. Mathematical intuition of SVM

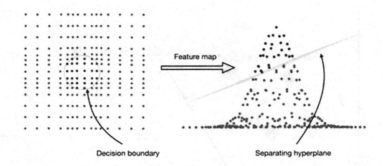

where,

w is the normal vector to the hyperplane.

x is a data point.

b is the bias term.

Distance to Hyperplane: The distance of a data point x to the hyperplane can be calculated as the projection of x onto the normal vector w, divided by the magnitude of w:

$$d = \frac{|w^T x + b|}{|w|}$$

Margin Calculation: The margin is the distance between the two parallel hyperplanes that pass through the support vectors of the two classes. It can be calculated as the difference between the distances of the two support vectors to the hyperplane.

Optimization Problem: The goal is to find the optimal w and b that define the hyperplane while satisfying certain constraints. The margin should be maximized, which means minimizing w's magnitude.

Solving the Optimization Problem: The optimization problem can be formulated as a convex quadratic programming problem. Various optimization algorithms can be used to find the optimal w and b that satisfy the constraints and maximize the margin.

Kernel Trick for Non-Linearity: If the data is not linearly separable, the kernel trick is used to implicitly map the data into a higher-dimensional space. The inner products in the higher-dimensional space correspond to evaluations of a kernel function. This enables SVM to separate data that might not be linearly separable in the original feature space.

1.19 SVM Implementation in Python

Step-1: Import the libraries.
Step-2: Load the dataset.
Step-3: Split dataset into x and y.
Step-4: Split the X and Y dataset into the training set and test set.
Step-5: Perform Feature Scaling.
Step-6: Fit SVM to the training set.
Step-7: Predict the test set results.
Step8: Make the Confusion Matrix.
Step-9: Visualize the test set results.

1.20 Flowchart of SVM Algorithm

Figure 8 shows a flowchart of the SVM algorithm.

2. IMPLEMENTATION ON IRIS DATASET USING PYTHON

Different datasets of Iris Flower are assembled. There are absolutely 150 datasets having a place with three unique types of Iris Flower that is Setosa, Versicolor and Virginca. The gathered Iris Datasets are stacked into the Machine Learning Model. Scikit-learn accompanies a couple of standard datasets, for example the Iris dataset for order (Naik G., Birari D., Sonavane B. & Bhagat N., 2019).

3. RESEARCH APPROACH

The paper employs that the iris classification task was performed using four different learning algorithms: K-Nearest Neighbor (KNN) algorithm, Naïve Bayes algorithm, Decision Tree and Support Vector Machine (SVM).

The KNN algorithm implemented in Python turned out to be the most successful among the training examples with 100% accuracy using 9 neighbors. There are three different groups of iris data (setosa, versicolor and virginica) and as the basis of this study, the KNN algorithm has been cleverly used to model the data.

The code in Figure 9 describes the implementation of **KNN Algorithm** on Iris Flower Dataset.

Let us now try to scale the dataset (Figure 10).

The next task is to find the optimal number of neighbors for best results (Figure 11).

Figure 8. SVM algorithm flowchart
(Muzzammel R. & Raza A., 2020)

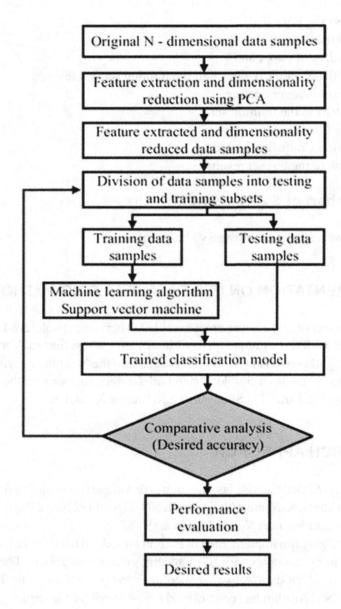

An accuracy of 100% can be obtained on K = 9, 11, 13, 17 and 19. So, 9 numbers of neighbors are chosen to fit into the model (Figure 12).

Figure 9. KNN algorithm on iris flower dataset

```
In [50]: model = KNeighborsClassifier() #creating the model

In [51]: model.fit(X_train,y_train) #training the model

Out[51]: ▸ KNeighborsClassifier
         KNeighborsClassifier()

In [52]: ypred = model.predict(X_test) #evaluating the model

In [53]: ypred

Out[53]: array(['Iris-versicolor', 'Iris-versicolor', 'Iris-virginica',
                'Iris-setosa', 'Iris-virginica', 'Iris-versicolor',
                'Iris-versicolor', 'Iris-setosa', 'Iris-virginica',
                'Iris-virginica', 'Iris-setosa', 'Iris-setosa', 'Iris-setosa',
                'Iris-virginica', 'Iris-virginica', 'Iris-setosa',
                'Iris-versicolor', 'Iris-setosa', 'Iris-virginica', 'Iris-setosa',
                'Iris-versicolor', 'Iris-virginica', 'Iris-setosa', 'Iris-setosa',
                'Iris-setosa', 'Iris-versicolor', 'Iris-virginica',
                'Iris-virginica', 'Iris-virginica', 'Iris-versicolor'],
               dtype=object)

In [54]: from sklearn.metrics import accuracy_score

In [55]: accuracy_score(y_test,ypred) #checking the accuracy

Out[55]: 0.9666666666666667
```

Figure 10. Scale of the dataset

```
In [56]: #scaling the data
         from sklearn.preprocessing import StandardScaler

In [57]: scalar = StandardScaler()

In [58]: X_train_scaled = scalar.fit_transform(X_train)
         X_test_scaled = scalar.transform(X_test)

In [59]: model_1 = KNeighborsClassifier() # n = 5
         model_1.fit(X_train_scaled,y_train)
         ypred_1 = model_1.predict(X_test_scaled)

In [60]: ypred_1

Out[60]: array(['Iris-versicolor', 'Iris-virginica', 'Iris-virginica',
                'Iris-setosa', 'Iris-virginica', 'Iris-versicolor',
                'Iris-versicolor', 'Iris-setosa', 'Iris-versicolor',
                'Iris-virginica', 'Iris-setosa', 'Iris-setosa', 'Iris-setosa',
                'Iris-virginica', 'Iris-virginica', 'Iris-setosa',
                'Iris-versicolor', 'Iris-setosa', 'Iris-virginica', 'Iris-setosa',
                'Iris-versicolor', 'Iris-versicolor', 'Iris-setosa', 'Iris-setosa',
                'Iris-versicolor', 'Iris-versicolor', 'Iris-virginica',
                'Iris-virginica', 'Iris-virginica', 'Iris-versicolor'],
               dtype=object)

In [61]: accuracy_score(y_test,ypred_1)

Out[61]: 0.8666666666666667
```

Figure 11. Best results

```
In [62]: for i in range(3,30,2):
             model_i = KNeighborsClassifier(n_neighbors=i)
             model_i.fit(X_train_scaled, y_train)
             ypred_i = model_i.predict(X_test_scaled)
             a = accuracy_score(y_test, ypred_i)
             print (f" (For k = {i}, the accuracy is {a})")

         (For k = 3, the accuracy is 0.8666666666666667)
         (For k = 5, the accuracy is 0.8666666666666667)
         (For k = 7, the accuracy is 0.9333333333333333)
         (For k = 9, the accuracy is 1.0)
         (For k = 11, the accuracy is 1.0)
         (For k = 13, the accuracy is 1.0)
         (For k = 15, the accuracy is 0.9666666666666667)
         (For k = 17, the accuracy is 1.0)
         (For k = 19, the accuracy is 1.0)
         (For k = 21, the accuracy is 0.9333333333333333)
         (For k = 23, the accuracy is 0.9333333333333333)
         (For k = 25, the accuracy is 0.9333333333333333)
         (For k = 27, the accuracy is 0.9)
         (For k = 29, the accuracy is 0.9)
```

Figure 12. Accuracy of 100% can be obtained on K = 9, 11, 13, 17 and 19

```
In [63]: model_final = KNeighborsClassifier(n_neighbors = 9)

In [64]: model_final.fit(X_train_scaled,y_train)

Out[64]:  ▾        KNeighborsClassifier
         KNeighborsClassifier(n_neighbors=9)

In [65]: ypred_final = model_final.predict(X_test_scaled)

In [66]: accuracy_score(y_test,ypred_final)

Out[66]: 1.0
```

The code in Figure 13 describes the implementation of **Naïve Bayes Algorithm** on Iris Flower Dataset.

The code in Figure 14 describes the implementation of **Decision Tree Algorithm** on Iris Flower Dataset.

The code in Figure 15 describes the implementation of **SVM Algorithm** on Iris Flower Dataset.

Scaling of the dataset can be seen from Figure 16.

Iris dataset contains three different iris types to test the performance of machine learning classifiers. With the successful application of KNN, Naïve Bayes, Decision Tree and SVM algorithms, this study not only demonstrates their performance in iris classification but also demonstrates the importance of various method benchmarks in evaluating the effectiveness of such models.

Figure 13. Naïve Bayes algorithm on iris flower dataset

```
In [73]: from sklearn.naive_bayes import GaussianNB

In [74]: gb = GaussianNB()

In [75]: gb.fit(X_train,y_train)

Out[75]: ▾ GaussianNB
         GaussianNB()

In [76]: ypred2 = gb.predict(X_test)

In [77]: ypred2

Out[77]: array(['Iris-versicolor', 'Iris-versicolor', 'Iris-virginica',
                'Iris-setosa', 'Iris-virginica', 'Iris-versicolor',
                'Iris-virginica', 'Iris-setosa', 'Iris-virginica',
                'Iris-virginica', 'Iris-setosa', 'Iris-setosa', 'Iris-setosa',
                'Iris-virginica', 'Iris-virginica', 'Iris-setosa',
                'Iris-versicolor', 'Iris-setosa', 'Iris-virginica', 'Iris-setosa',
                'Iris-versicolor', 'Iris-versicolor', 'Iris-setosa', 'Iris-setosa',
                'Iris-versicolor', 'Iris-versicolor', 'Iris-virginica',
                'Iris-virginica', 'Iris-virginica', 'Iris-versicolor'],
               dtype='<U15')

In [79]: scalar2 = StandardScaler()

In [80]: X_train_scaled2 = scalar2.fit_transform(X_train)
         X_test_scaled2 = scalar2.transform(X_test)

In [81]: model_2 = GaussianNB()

In [82]: model_2.fit(X_train_scaled2,y_train)


Out[82]: ▾ GaussianNB
         GaussianNB()

In [83]: ypred_2 = model_2.predict(X_test_scaled2)

In [84]: ypred_2

Out[84]: array(['Iris-versicolor', 'Iris-versicolor', 'Iris-virginica',
                'Iris-setosa', 'Iris-virginica', 'Iris-versicolor',
                'Iris-virginica', 'Iris-setosa', 'Iris-virginica',
                'Iris-virginica', 'Iris-setosa', 'Iris-setosa', 'Iris-setosa',
                'Iris-virginica', 'Iris-virginica',
                'Iris-versicolor', 'Iris-setosa', 'Iris-virginica', 'Iris-setosa',
                'Iris-versicolor', 'Iris-versicolor', 'Iris-setosa', 'Iris-setosa',
                'Iris-versicolor', 'Iris-versicolor', 'Iris-virginica',
                'Iris-virginica', 'Iris-virginica', 'Iris-versicolor'],
               dtype='<U15')

In [85]: accuracy_score(y_test,ypred_2)

Out[85]: 0.9
```

4. RESULT

After the implementation of all the four algorithms, it is the time to actually test the model by providing it with some unseen data. For that purpose we provide the

Figure 14. Decision tree algorithm on iris flower dataset

```
In [91]:  from sklearn.tree import DecisionTreeClassifier

In [92]:  dtree = DecisionTreeClassifier()

In [93]:  dtree.fit(X_train,y_train)

Out[93]:  · DecisionTreeClassifier
          DecisionTreeClassifier()

In [94]:  ypred3 = dtree.predict(X_test)

In [95]:  ypred3

Out[95]:  array(['Iris-versicolor', 'Iris-versicolor', 'Iris-virginica',
                 'Iris-setosa', 'Iris-virginica', 'Iris-versicolor',
                 'Iris-versicolor', 'Iris-setosa', 'Iris-virginica',
                 'Iris-virginica', 'Iris-setosa', 'Iris-setosa', 'Iris-setosa',
                 'Iris-virginica', 'Iris-virginica', 'Iris-setosa',
                 'Iris-versicolor', 'Iris-setosa', 'Iris-virginica', 'Iris-setosa',
                 'Iris-virginica', 'Iris-virginica', 'Iris-setosa', 'Iris-setosa',
                 'Iris-versicolor', 'Iris-versicolor', 'Iris-virginica',
                 'Iris-virginica', 'Iris-virginica', 'Iris-versicolor'],
                dtype=object)

In [97]:  scalar3 = StandardScaler()

In [98]:  X_train_scaled3 = scalar3.fit_transform(X_train)
          X_test_scaled3 = scalar3.transform(X_test)

In [99]:  model_3 = DecisionTreeClassifier()

In [100]: model_3.fit(X_train_scaled3,y_train)

Out[100]: · DecisionTreeClassifier
          DecisionTreeClassifier()

In [101]: ypred_3 = model_3.predict(X_test_scaled3)

In [102]: ypred_3

Out[102]: array(['Iris-versicolor', 'Iris-versicolor', 'Iris-virginica',
                 'Iris-setosa', 'Iris-virginica', 'Iris-versicolor',
                 'Iris-versicolor', 'Iris-setosa', 'Iris-virginica',
                 'Iris-virginica', 'Iris-setosa', 'Iris-setosa', 'Iris-setosa',
                 'Iris-virginica', 'Iris-virginica', 'Iris-setosa',
                 'Iris-versicolor', 'Iris-setosa', 'Iris-virginica', 'Iris-setosa',
                 'Iris-virginica', 'Iris-virginica', 'Iris-setosa', 'Iris-setosa',
                 'Iris-versicolor', 'Iris-versicolor', 'Iris-virginica',
                 'Iris-virginica', 'Iris-virginica', 'Iris-versicolor'],
                dtype=object)

In [103]: accuracy_score(y_test,ypred_3)

Out[103]: 0.9333333333333333
```

model with new sepal length, sepal width, petal length and petal width. Figure 17 is the implementation of the code.

The above prediction shows that the new iris flower belongs to the Iris-verginica species.

Figure 15. SVM algorithm on iris flower dataset

```
In [109.  from sklearn.svm import SVC

In [110.  svm = SVC()

In [111   svm.fit(X_train,y_train)

Out[111]:  ▾ SVC
           SVC()


In [112.  ypred4 = svm.predict(X_test)

In [113.  ypred4

Out[113]:  array(['Iris-versicolor', 'Iris-versicolor', 'Iris-virginica',
                  'Iris-setosa', 'Iris-virginica', 'Iris-versicolor',
                  'Iris-versicolor', 'Iris-setosa', 'Iris-virginica',
                  'Iris-virginica', 'Iris-setosa', 'Iris-setosa', 'Iris-setosa',
                  'Iris-virginica', 'Iris-virginica', 'Iris-setosa',
                  'Iris-versicolor', 'Iris-setosa', 'Iris-virginica', 'Iris-setosa',
                  'Iris-versicolor', 'Iris-virginica', 'Iris-setosa', 'Iris-setosa',
                  'Iris-versicolor', 'Iris-versicolor', 'Iris-virginica',
                  'Iris-virginica', 'Iris-virginica', 'Iris-versicolor'],
                 dtype=object)
```

Figure 16. Scaling of the dataset

```
In [115.  scalar4 = StandardScaler()

In [116.  X_train_scaled4 = scalar4.fit_transform(X_train)
          X_test_scaled4 = scalar4.transform(X_test)

In [117.  model_4 = SVC()

In [118.  model_4.fit(X_train_scaled4,y_train)

Out[118]:  ▾ SVC
           SVC()


In [119.  ypred_4 = model_4.predict(X_test_scaled4)

In [120.  ypred_4

Out[120]:  array(['Iris-versicolor', 'Iris-versicolor', 'Iris-virginica',
                  'Iris-setosa', 'Iris-virginica', 'Iris-versicolor',
                  'Iris-versicolor', 'Iris-setosa', 'Iris-virginica',
                  'Iris-virginica', 'Iris-setosa', 'Iris-setosa', 'Iris-setosa',
                  'Iris-virginica', 'Iris-virginica', 'Iris-setosa',
                  'Iris-versicolor', 'Iris-setosa', 'Iris-virginica', 'Iris-setosa',
                  'Iris-versicolor', 'Iris-virginica', 'Iris-setosa', 'Iris-setosa',
                  'Iris-versicolor', 'Iris-versicolor', 'Iris-virginica',
                  'Iris-virginica', 'Iris-virginica', 'Iris-versicolor'],
                 dtype=object)

In [121.  accuracy_score(y_test,ypred_4)

Out[121]:  0.9666666666666667
```

Figure 17. Results

```
In [127.  #predicting unseen data
          x_new = np.array([[6.1,3,4.6,1.4]])
          x_new = scalar.transform(x_new)
          prediction = model_final.predict(x_new)
          print(f"The species of the iris flower is {prediction}")

          The species of the iris flower is ['Iris-versicolor']
```

5. CONCLUSION

In summary, it is a valuable learning experience for new operators when solving iris classification problems through machine learning. This exercise provides a way to master the fundamentals of machine learning, including preprocessing, model training, evaluation, and even deployment. The simplicity and ease of use of the Iris dataset make it an excellent starting point for students to expertly interpret data and understand the nuances of various machine learning algorithms. Apart from its important teaching, the iris classification model is also a simple task for further classification as the basis for responding to complex challenges in many fields. Moreover, the practical use of iris classification is remote. Automation of iris type identification in botany, agriculture and environmental science streamlines the research process and leads to deeper understanding of plant biodiversity, precision agriculture and ecological studies. This utility demonstrates the suitability and suitability of the model in solving today's problems in this area. More importantly, using machine learning to classify iris not only provides a better understanding of the underlying concepts, but also allows doctors to apply their skills to real situations. It shows the relationship between learning and practical application and demonstrates the difference of machine learning in understanding and solving complex problems in different domains.

In this chapter, we learn to train our own supervised machine learning model using Iris Flower Classification Project with machine learning. The work also shows how to use SciKit-learn software to learn machine learning. The deployed model allows users to input sepal and petal measurements and receive predictions of the Iris flower species.

REFERENCES

Mahdiani, R. M., Khamehchi, E., Hajirezaie, S., & Sarapardeh, H. M. (2020). Modeling viscosity of crude oil using k-nearest neighbor algorithm. *Advances in Geo-Energy Research*, 4(4), 435–447. doi:10.46690/ager.2020.04.08

Muzzammel, R., & Raza, A. (2020). *A Support Vector Machine Learning-Based Protection Technique for MT-HVDC Systems.* MDPI energies. Fu Y., Yin Z., Su M., Wu Y. & Liu G. (2020). *Construction and Reasoning Approach of Belief Rule-Base for Classification Base on Decision Tree. IEEE Access : Practical Innovations, Open Solutions.*

Naik G., Birari D., Sonavane, B., & Bhagat, N. (2019). Classification of Iris Flower Species Using Machine Learning. *International Journal for Research in Engineering Application & Management.*

Shukla, A., Pant, H., Agarwal, A., & Mishra, P. (2020, May). Flower Classification using Supervised Learning. *International Journal of Engineering Research & Technology (IJERT), 9*(05).

Sneha, N., & Gangil, T. (2019). Analysis of diabetes mellitus for early prediction using optimal features selection. *Journal of Big Data, 6*(1), 13. doi:10.1186/s40537-019-0175-6

Suchitra, G. (2023, December). Iris Classification Using Machine Learning. *International Journal of Research Publication and Reviews, 4*(12), 4129–4131.

Chapter 11
Microservices Architecture for Data Analytics in IoT Applications

Arunjyoti Das

 https://orcid.org/0009-0005-0701-2850
National Informatics Centre, India

Abhijit Bora

 https://orcid.org/0000-0002-7754-639X
Assam Don Bosco University, India

ABSTRACT

The internet of things (IoT) is a network of physical objects with sensors, software, and network connectivity built in to enable data collection and sharing. It has led to an exponential increase in data generation, necessitating the development of effective statistical analysis for a range of IoT applications. Predictive analytics is an essential procedure that converts unprocessed data into meaningful insights. To improve decision-making and enhance IoT application performance, it is crucial to create innovative data processing methods and predictive analytical models that can handle the volume and complexity of IoT data. Microservices-based strategies can be implemented to create scalable, reusable, and effective IoT-based analytics solutions.

DOI: 10.4018/979-8-3693-2260-4.ch011

1. INTRODUCTION

A network of physical objects with sensors, software, and network connectivity built in to enable data collection and sharing is known as the Internet of Things, or IoT. IoT has emerged as one of the 21st century's most significant technologies in the last few years. Now that everyday objects like vehicles, baby monitors, thermostats, and kitchen appliances can be connected to the internet through embedded devices, communication between people, processes, and things may happen seamlessly.

The widespread adoption of IoT and cloud computing has been accompanied with an exponential increase in data generation, necessitating the development of effective statistical analysis for a range of IoT applications. Because typical methods for processing data cannot handle massive volumes of data, IoT big data analytics has become an important area of study (Acharjya et al., 2016).

Predictive analytics is an essential procedure that converts unprocessed data into meaningful insights. It has been extensively utilized in several fields, such as social networking analysis, medical care, management of energy, and smart homes (Saggi et al., 2018). For improved decision-making and enhanced IoT application performance, it is crucial to create innovative data processing methods and predictive analytical models which can handle the volume and complexity of IoT data.

Numerous issues have arisen as a result of the increasing amount of data generated by Internet of Things devices and the demand for effective, scalable, and efficient analytics solutions (Tariq et al., 2019). Overcoming the shortcomings of monolithic service delivery approaches is a significant problem, in addition to other ones like the growing volume of raw data and the variety of data types and forms that need to be analyzed. The limitations of monolithic architectures can be solved and the creation of scalable, reusable, and effective IoT-based analytics solutions can be possible by implementing a microservices-based strategy. It will enhance the effectiveness of the IoT-based applications. In this chapter, we are about to study various aspects, strategy and effectiveness of the Microservice architecture for Data Analysis in IoT applications.

2. BACKGROUND AND RELATED STUDY

There is limited study available for architecture with IoT and microservices –based architecture with IoT. Hence a comprehensive study on this topic is not yet done. There are a few noted architectural difficulties with the internet of things (Maney et al., 2017; Shahid et al., 2017; Jacob et al., 2018; Oquendo et al., 2017). We have figured out some quality attributes of IoT (Kim, 2016). Other issues with the internet of things have been noted, such as scalability and interoperability.

Issues with implementation, competency, security, privacy, data volume, mobility, interoperability, and scalability have all been brought up in relation to IoT (Ninikrishna et al., 2017; Patra et al., 2017; Breivold at al., 2015).

As far as we are aware, no research on Microservice Architecture (MSA) for Internet of Things systems specifically addresses the application of Microservices architecture for IoT systems. We, aim to propose an Architecture for IoT applications that uses the Cloud Technology to deliver scalable robust and loosely coupled interconnected Micro Services based approach for Data Analytics.

2.1 Hardware

Smart devices, which are made up of sensors and actuators, play a critical role in the hardware level of IoT architecture by capturing and processing signals. Actuators transform electrical signals into physical movements or actions, whereas sensors are in charge of gathering data produced by the environment around them. Sensors facilitate the connectivity of physical equipment and digital networks by gathering data in real-time.

2.2 Communication

Within the IoT ecosystem, hardware-level data collection is typically kept in the cloud for later research and analysis. Yet in order to do this, data transfer from sensors to storage and analytics applications must be dependable and effective. Middleware for communication and networking are useful in this situation.

Their main responsibility is to ensure that data is securely and seamlessly moved from sensors to the cloud. Depending on the needs of the application, several middleware technologies are employed, including Ethernet, RFID, and WiFi.

2.3 Data Storage and Analysis

It is essential to store and analyze the data produced by IoT devices in order to get valuable insights that can guide decision-making (Ahmed et al., 2017). With the use of descriptive analytics, historical context is provided by summarizing and describing previous data and events. In order to produce well-informed forecasts about future events, predictive analytics uses machine learning (ML) techniques and statistical models to find trends and patterns in historical data. Prescriptive analytics goes beyond analysis and offers suggestions on how to proceed in order to accomplish a goal.

2.4 IoT Architecture

The business layer, application layer, processing layer, network layer, and perception layer make up the five layers of the widely used Internet of Things architectural stack. Every layer plays an important role in the entire operation of the Internet of Things system, from data collection and processing to insightful analysis and appropriate response. An outline of the duties of these many tiers can be found in the points shown in Figure 1 (Li et al, 2015).

Figure 1. 5 Layers of IoT architecture

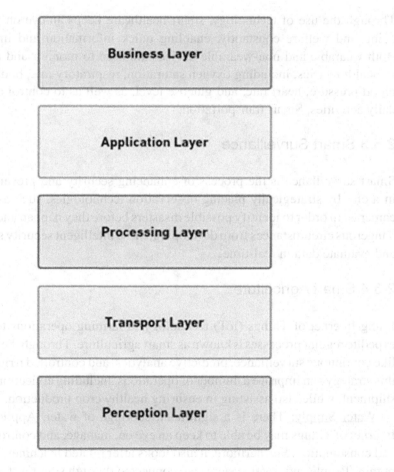

2.5 Applications of IoT

Some of the major applications of IoT in real time applications are mentioned below-

2.5.1 Smart Homes

Internet-connected appliances like lights, TVs, and refrigerators that communicate with one another and with people make up smart homes. Improving device control and achieving optimal energy usage are the main objectives of smart home implementation.

2.5.2 Smart Healthcare

Through the use of technology, smart healthcare keeps an eye on patients' well-being and welfare constantly, enabling quick information and improving care. Both wearable and non-wearable devices are used to monitor and record a range of health metrics, including oxygen saturation, respiratory rate, body temperature, blood pressure, heart rate, and glucose level, as well as to control an individual's daily activities. Smart transportation:

2.5.3 Smart Surveillance

Smart surveillance is the process of enhancing security and preventing incidents in a city by strategically placing observation technologies, such as sophisticated cameras. In order to identify possible disasters before they happen and assist prevent dangerous circumstances from developing, these intelligent security systems collect and evaluate data in real-time.

2.5.4 Smart Agriculture

Using Internet of Things (IoT) technology in farming operations to improve and expedite regular processes is known as smart agriculture. Through the use of services like continuous surveillance, predictive analytics, and controlled irrigation systems, this strategy can improve a number of operations, including collection, packing, and shipment, while also assisting in ensuring healthy crop production.

Water Supply: There is a significant shortage of water. Applications for the Internet of Things may be able to keep an eye on, manage, and control water quality and consumption. Furthermore, it also looks after related machinery like pipes and pumps. People and water systems are connected through smart water technologies.

2.6 Microservices Architecture

Big data analytics and the Internet of Things are now prominent research topics. However, a considerable disparity persists between the IoT's capacity to collect environmental data and the analytical skills needed to evaluate it. This poses a number of difficulties, making the use of data analytics in Internet of Things systems difficult. Managing heterogeneous IoT data, analyzing obtained data quickly, and developing and maintaining adaptive functions that can be used in a variety of contexts and applications are some of the trickiest problems. The greatest solution to these problems is not a monolithic system but rather one that is flexible and scalable. The microservices-based architecture has been the method of choice for developing IoT applications in this context in a number of recent research projects.

The creation of flexible and distributed applications has become popular thanks to the microservices architecture, which has revolutionized software application development. In a microservices-based architecture, every service is built independently, utilizing low-cost communication methods and standards that are customized to satisfy particular business needs. This approach is particularly beneficial in resource-constrained environments such as the Internet of Things, where various analytical tasks require a modular framework. With this design, specific analytic features are managed by a group of independent services that may be developed, grown, and run independently of other services.

2.7 Microservices Advantages for IoT Data Analytics

In IoT systems, the microservices architecture is becoming more and more popular because of its many benefits. The following are some of this development style's primary advantages.

Availability: The microservices design offers software systems with reduced downtime due to the autonomous nature of the services, which significantly improves and increases overall performance. In actuality, a failure affects only the impacted entities and has no effect on the system as a whole. These entities might be replaced by using dedicated payment processes.

Modularity: Programs can benefit from microservices' strong encapsulation, clear linkages, and well-defined interactions. Any design that provides an established connection for extra services can be used to create a microservice. Internal to the service, its implementation specifics are modifiable without impacting or synchronizing the remaining components of the system. Because microservice dependencies are specified by coordination for choreography principles, they are explicit.

223

Scalability: Software development teams can utilize multiple technologies and languages of programming every each service without worrying about incompatibilities thanks to the microservices architecture. This implies that teams can update specific services without affecting the system as a whole and select the optimal tech stack for each module. Furthermore, it is possible to introduce components without requiring re-deployment or downtime. Moreover, the deployment of services across numerous servers can mitigate the effect of resource-intensive elements on the overall performance of the system.

Resilience: Because separate service deployment improves fault separation, performance problems are simpler to find and address with a microservices design. Because only the particular service is impacted in the event of a failure, developers can more easily roll back updates or make modifications to the service while having an impact on the program as a whole. This lessens the chance of any downtime.

2.8 IoT Data Analytics Approaches Based on Microservices Architecture

In a monolithic architecture, all the services are developed on a unique repository which is being updated by several developers. In this scenario, when a new feature is to be added or dropped then we must try to ascertain that other services should continue working in the same way that they were working earlier. This is not guaranteed in Monolithic Architecture. On the other hand, when an updated version is ready for deployment in the production environment, then and all services have to be restarted to be effective with the new update. Here comes one major problem, that when one part fails, then all of the services goes down (Villamizar et al., 2015).

Such a structure is inappropriate for the Internet of Things, as it integrates numerous technologies (Vresk et al., 2016). To address these problems, novel architectural patterns have been created. Scalability and reusability are two of these solutions, and the microservices pattern is one of them (Drimtry at al., 2014). The dispersion of the applications into a collection of services, each of which is independent of the others, is suggested by the microservice-based architecture.

With this method, it is possible to grow, update, and evolve without affecting other services. Multiple instances of a microservice can be deployed, and distinct services can be hosted on the same server. Communication between these services can be established using APIs.

2.9 Proposed Approach Architecture

A server-less method is another paradigm that is employed in the suggested IoT platform (Baldini et al., 2017). Generally speaking, the term "server-less" refers to the computing architecture where the provider permits us to run "functions," or short bursts of code, without having to worry about the infrastructure. Under this model, the provider sets a set of guidelines for processing, determines a payment plan for the usage of the resources, and offers them transparently. It also automatically scales the resources if demand increases and releases them when they are not needed. Application designs known as server-less architectures integrate third-party Backend as a Service (BaaS) and/or allow bespoke code to run in managed and ephemeral containers offered by Functions as a Service (FaaS) platforms. BaaS: refers to the incorporation of third-party services and applications to manage the logic and status of an application. They are usually applications that use databases in the cloud or third-party services, such as authentication.

- **BaaS**: It describes the use of outside programs and services to control an application's logic and state. Typically, these are apps that make use of third-party services like authentication or cloud-based databases.
- **FaaS**: it permits the execution of any bespoke code without the need for managing or provisioning servers.

These kinds of designs' primary advantages are their decreased complexity, operating costs, and development time. It is also regarded as a sustainable computing option. Similar to microservices, they enhance the system's horizontal scalability (Lowery, 2016).

Figure 2. Proposed microservices based architecture for IoT enabled applications

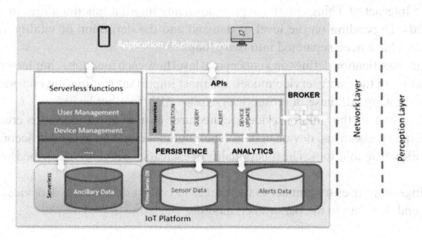

225

Some examples of server-less applications are Amazon Web Services with Lambda, S3 and DynamoDB (storage) or Google Cloud with Cloud Functions, Cloud Firestore (storage) and Cloud Pub/Sub (messaging).

This architecture is divided into two scopes: *Physical* and *Cyber*.

From a hardware standpoint, IoT devices are represented by the Physical scope, which is located on the right side of the dashed line in Figure 2. This section comprises the network and perception layers. These two levels encompass the Internet of Things (IoT) devices and how each device can connect to either Capture or Act, based on its capabilities.

On the left side of the figure, is the *Cyber* scope. In the Cloud and Client environments, two levels are displayed. The IoT platform itself is the initial layer in this context. The most crucial component of the architecture is the Internet of Things platform, which is also essential for enabling other crucial functions like device administration, interoperability, security, reusability, and massive data management.

The various parts that make up the Internet of Things platform can be divided into two main layers: services and data. First, we draw the boundaries of the service layer. A broker is one way to access the IoT platform. This component enables the use of numerous protocols to establish connections with various IoT devices. This component improves data-level interoperability, scalability, and flexibility (Naik N., 2017). It can support some well-known protocols, like Advanced Message Queuing Protocol (AMQP), Message Queue Telemetry Transport (MQTT) and Simple (or Streaming) Text-Oriented Message Protocol (STOMP). The IoT platform-logic and IoT devices are connected via this broker. The two sides are connected twice, and it has the ability to send and receive data with the edge devices.

The message queuing system is provided by the broker. Among its advantages are interface decoupling, redundancy, scalability, flexibility, and delivery sequence and guarantee.

The Internet of Things platform provides many internal functionalities to meet all needs. Depending on the level of demand and the definition of vitality, these capacities have been separated into two groups.

This classification defines on a conceptual level how each function is implemented. In addition to the microservice model, the most important features are considered, e.g. swallowing All these microservices expose APIs to other layers.

According to this microservice architecture, four microservices are created: intake, query, alarm and device update. Their number could be expanded according to more specific solutions. The functionality of each microservice is described below.

- Ingestion: tries to connect to the broker to collect data from IoT devices and send that data to the persistence module.

- Query: provides various functions for retrieving historical data from an IoT device.
- Alert: is responsible for collecting alerts and sending them to the clients.
- Devices: the goal is to connect to IoT devices to send them over-the-air updates and ensure the integrity of the IoT device network.

For the most common IoT platform functions, such as user and device management, where the implementation does not need to be managed at a low level and the function is not critical in terms of volume, speed and variability, the server-less paradigm is used.

In this way, two capabilities are defined using this approach:

- User management is used to manage the registration, removal, discovery & authentication of system users.
- Device management is used to manage the registration, removal, discovery & authentication of IoT devices.

The other two parts or modules of the service level are Persistence and Analytics. Some microservices like ingest or query use the first module Persistence. The main purpose of this module is to store persistent information about the observation layer and other generated data. This data is stored for analytical retrieval or implementation. The analytics module uses analytics to trigger specific events/alerts or detect specific activity.

The second layer of the platform is called Data, and as the name suggests, it stores all the information produced by the system. This data is divided into two categories: data used by microservices and data used by server-less operations. The first data category is further divided into two groups: observation data and alarm data. The first group consists of all the information provided by the perception layer of IoT devices and the triggered alarm log. The second group, server-less data, contains auxiliary data needed to perform server-less operations.

The IoT platform layer connects to the business layer and applications at the top of the figure. Applications to investigate all of the IoT platform's functionalities and how to combine and apply them to provide an end-user with a productive and helpful view will be found in this final layer.

SUMMARY

We have provided a thorough architectural design in this work to oversee the entire Internet of Things lifecycle. The lifecycle comprises four stages, as previously mentioned: capture, communicate, analyze, and act (C2A2). Based on these layers, a generic architecture that aligns with the phases of the Internet of Things lifecycle has been defined. This architecture is approved to meet the primary specifications for Internet of Things solutions.

Different challenges need to be addressed by IoT solutions. The fact that IoT devices are diverse is among the most important of these. These devices are energy-constrained and have limited computational power. IoT devices are deployed in challenging conditions, and occasionally they must use batteries that use energy-saving methods when there is no access to electricity. It is imperative that the IoT platform can address every issue and requirement mentioned and abstract them so that other parties can use them with ease.

The suggested IoT platform is functionally capable of managing and locating IoT for simple use and connectivity. A few server-less functions for managing devices and users are defined in order to accomplish that goal. Data management is another prerequisite. Influxdb and Kapacitor, which manage the collection, processing, storing, and analysis of data, can be employed to address this. An event management system is supported by capacitor. In addition to supporting various notification delivery methods like email, Slack, and HTTP, it provides a full notification system.

In terms of scalability, adding more IoT devices is ensured by the broker and the microservices architecture. The thorough analysis of performance performed on a single server guarantees the scalability and stability of the system in other complex deployments with larger capacities.

Future Scope of Study: We may analyse the IoT platform in two aspects:

- **Scalability**. Time-sensitive applications should benefit from the IoT platform's ability to manage thousands of IoT devices publishing observations with the least amount of latency. Metrics like throughput and response time can provide useful insights into the maintenance of scalability. Excellent performance is indicated by a high throughput rate, which should increase linearly with the number of devices. The quantity of messages that an IoT platform receives and processes in a second is known as throughput. Fast platform processing and response are indicative of a low response time.
- **Stability.** A number of metrics, including CPU and active memory usage, are used to measure the system's stability. The average OS core utilization of all CPU physical cores indicates CPU usage. The amount of Megabytes (MB) in memory at test time, as of the end of the experiment, is shown in active memory.

Such performance testing in proper environment may provide acceptability of the proposed architecture which may be considered for future cope of study.

REFERENCES

Acharjya, D. P., & Ahmed, K. (2016). A survey on big data analytics: Challenges, open research issues and tools. *International Journal of Advanced Computer Science and Applications*, 7(2), 511–518.

Ahmed, E., Yaqoob, I., Hashem, I. A. T., Khan, I., Ahmed, A. I. A., Imran, M., & Vasilakos, A. V. (2017). The role of big data analytics in internet of things. *Computer Networks*, 129, 459–471. doi:10.1016/j.comnet.2017.06.013

Baldini, I., Castro, P., Chang, K., Cheng, P., Fink, S., Ishakian, V., Mitchell, N., Muthusamy, V., Rabbah, R., & Slominski, A. (2017). Research Advances in Cloud Computing. Springer; Berlin/Heidelberg.

Breivold, H., & Sandstrom, K. (2015). Internet of Things for Industrial Automation — Challenges and Technical Solutions. *2015 IEEE International Conference on Data Science and Data Intensive Systems*. IEEE. 10.1109/DSDIS.2015.11

Chen, S., Xu, H., Liu, D., Hu, B., & Wang, H. (2014). A Vision of IoT: Applications, Challenges, and Opportunities With China Perspective. *IEEE Internet of Things Journal*, 1(4), 349–359. doi:10.1109/JIOT.2014.2337336

del Rio, J., Toma, D. M., Martinez, E., O'Reilly, T. C., Delory, E., Pearlman, J. S., Waldmann, C., & Jirka, S. (2018). A Sensor Web Architecture For Integrating Smart Oceanographic Sensors Into The Semantic Sensor Web [Institute Of Electrical And Electronics Engineers] [IEEE]. *IEEE Journal of Oceanic Engineering*, 43(4), 830–842. doi:10.1109/JOE.2017.2768178

Dmitry, N., & Manfred, S. S. (2014). On micro-services architecture. *International Journal of Open Information Technologies, 2*(9).

Farhan, L. (2018). A Concise Review On Internet Of Things (Iot) -Problems, Challenges And Opportunities. *2018 11th International Symposium On Communication Systems, Networks & Digital Signal Processing (CSNDSP)*. IEEE 10.1109/CSNDSP.2018.8471762

Galletta, A. (2018). A Microservices-Based Platform For Efficiently Managing Oceanographic Data. 2018 4Th International Conference On Big Data Innovations And Applications (Innovate-Data). IEEE. 10.1109/Innovate-Data.2018.00011

Jacob, P., & Mani, P. (2018). Software architecture pattern selection model for Internet of Things based systems. *IET Software*, 12(5), 390–396. doi:10.1049/iet-sen.2017.0206

Jacob, P., & Mani, P. (2018). Software architecture pattern selection model for Internet of Things based systems. IET Software, 12. doi:10.1049/iet-sen.2017.0206

Kim, M. (2016). A Quality Model for Evaluating IoT Applications. *International Journal of Computer and Electric al Engineering*, *8*(1), 66–76. doi:10.17706/IJCEE.2016.8.1.66-76

Li, S., Xu, L. D., & Zhao, S. (2015). The internet of things: A survey. *Information Systems Frontiers*, *17*(2), 243–259. doi:10.1007/s10796-014-9492-7

Lowery, C. (2016). *Emerging Technology Analysis: Serverless Computing and Function Platform as a Service*. Gartner Research.

Manev, D., & Dimov, A. (2017). Facilitation of IoT software maintenance via code analysis and generation. *The 2nd International Multidisciplinary Conference on Computer and Energy Science (SpliTech)*, (pp. 1-6). IEEE.

Naik, N. (2017). Choice of effective messaging protocols for IoT systems: MQTT, CoAP, AMQP and HTTP. *Proceedings of the 2017 IEEE International Systems Engineering Symposium (ISSE)*; Vienna, Austria. 10.1109/SysEng.2017.8088251

Ninikrishna, T., Sarkar, S., Tengshe, R., Jha, M., Sharma, L., Daliya, V., & Routray, S. (2017). Software defined IoT: Issues and challenges. *2017 International Conference on Computing Methodologies and Communication (ICCMC)*. IEEE. 10.1109/ICCMC.2017.8282560

Oquendo, F. (2017). Software architecture of self-organizing systems-of-systems for the Internet-of-Things with SosADL. *The 12th System of Systems Engineering Conference (SoSE)*, (pp. 1-6). IEEE. 10.1109/SYSOSE.2017.7994959

Patra, L., & Rao, U. (2016). Internet of Things — Archit ecture, applications, security and other major challenges. *3rd International Conference on Computing for Sustainable Global Development (INDIACom)*. IEEE.

Saggi, M. K., & Jain, S. (2018). A survey towards an integration of big data analytics to big insights for value-creation. *Information Processing & Management*, *54*(5), 758–790. doi:10.1016/j.ipm.2018.01.010

Shahid, N., & Aneja, S. (2017). Internet of Things: Vision, application areas and research challenges. *International Conference on I-SMAC (IoT in Social, Mobile, Analytics and Cloud) (I-SMAC)*, (pp. 583-587). IEEE. 10.1109/I-SMAC.2017.8058246

Tariq, N., Asim, M., Al-Obeidat, F., Zubair Farooqi, M., Baker, T., Hammoudeh, M., & Ghafir, I. (2019). The security of big data in fog enabled IoT applications including block chain: A survey. *Sensors (Basel)*, *19*(8), 1788. doi:10.3390/s19081788 PMID:31013993

Villamizar, M., Garcés, O., Castro, H., Verano, M., Salamanca, L., Casallas, R., & Gil, S. (2015). *Evaluating the monolithic and the microservice architecture pattern to deploy web applications in the cloud.* Proceedings of the 2015 10th Computing Colombian Conference (10CCC); Bogota, Colombia. 10.1109/ColumbianCC.2015.7333476

Vresk, T., & Čavrak, I. (2016). *Architecture of an interoperable IoT platform based on microservices.* Proceedings of the 2016 39th International Convention on Information and Communication Technology, Electronics and Microelectronics (MIPRO); Opatija, Croatia. 10.1109/MIPRO.2016.7522321

Chapter 12
NEOTracker:
Near–Earth Object Detection and Analysis

Lianmuansang Samte
ⓘ https://orcid.org/0009-0004-8130-482X
Assam Don Bosco University, India

Bhargav Kalpa Hazarika
ⓘ https://orcid.org/0009-0005-7195-7023
Assam Don Bosco University, India

Aditya Kumar Rabha
ⓘ https://orcid.org/0009-0001-4605-4384
Assam Don Bosco University, India

Gypsy Nandi
Assam Don Bosco University, India

ABSTRACT

Near-Earth objects (NEOs) are asteroids or comets that have their orbits in close proximity with Earth. Some objects amongst these are known to be potentially hazardous and pose a risk of collision. This chapter developed four supervised machine learning algorithms, namely, logistic regression, random forest, support vector machine, and XGBoost, for the detection and classification of hazardous near-earth objects. Two datasets were utilised, the first taken from the Kaggle website, and the second generated from NASA's JPL Small-Body database. Feature importance analysis of these datasets was done by analysing the Shapley values of the individual features in both datasets. This chapter concludes by finding all models to have performed sufficiently well, with XGBoost found to be the best and most consistent performing across both datasets. Additionally, both min and max diameter, and the absolute magnitude features for the Kaggle dataset, and the H and moid features for the JPL dataset were found to be the most impactful features for classifying hazardous near-earth objects.

DOI: 10.4018/979-8-3693-2260-4.ch012

1. INTRODUCTION

Near-Earth Objects (NEOs) are asteroids or comets that have orbits that bring them into close proximity with Earth. NEOs can be defined as small bodies that have a perihelion distance of less than 1.3 Astronomical Units (AU), where 1 AU is the average distance between the Earth and the Sun (NASA, n.d.). These objects are largely composed of ice and rock, originating as remnants from the formation of the solar system. The discovery of NEOs can be said to be relatively recent in scientific history, with the first NEO, 433 Eros, being discovered in 1898. NEOs are categorised into four orbit classes, namely, Atira, Aten, Apollo, and Amor, based on their semi-major axis, perihelion distance, and aphelion distance (NASA, n.d).

This chapter seeks to develop machine learning models that will be able to accurately identify and assess whether these NEOs are hazardous to Earth. This will be done by selecting four machine learning algorithms, training and testing the chosen algorithms based on two selected datasets, and assessing the performance of these algorithms. Secondly, this chapter also aims to identify the features that are impactful in identifying hazardous NEOs by analysing the Shapley values of each individual feature in both datasets.

The next section of this chapter discusses the background and motivations behind this chapter, which will provide details on the background information regarding this topic, as well as addressing the relevance and motivations for conducting research on this particular topic. Following that section, a study on the related works in, or similar to, the field of detecting and classifying potentially hazardous NEOs using machine learning techniques shall be conducted. This will be followed by the standard approaches, wherein the chapter will highlight the standard approaches and methodologies to be utilised for the purpose of classifying potentially hazardous NEOs. The discussion and analysis section will follow, which will include detailed discussions on the performances of the chosen algorithms, analysing findings and their implications as well as analysing the most important features for hazardous NEO classification. Finally, the conclusion section of this chapter will include the final concluding remarks for this research, where the key findings of this chapter will be highlighted and discussed.

2. BACKGROUND AND MOTIVATION

Studies show that an asteroid approximately 66 million years ago, now known as the Chicxulub asteroid, was responsible for the mass extinction of about 3/4th of plant and animal life on Earth. A massive crater can be seen today in Chicxulub, Mexico as evidence of the destruction it caused, and the potential threat of NEOs similar to it.

The Tunguska Event can be taken as an example of a more recent asteroid impact, which took place in 1908. It is the largest impact on Earth in recorded history, causing widespread destruction around the Podkamennaya Tunguska River. The possible damage and loss of life it would have caused had it occurred near civilisation can only be speculated. However, events such as these serve as a reminder of how important it is to be able to detect potential impacts in the future and undertake necessary safeguards.

Thus, monitoring and detecting these NEOs is of crucial importance to understand potential impact threats, as well as allowing sufficient time for the development of mitigation strategies. Regardless of whether they are larger or smaller in diameter than the Chicxulub asteroid, this increasing concern regarding potential NEO impacts necessitates the development of early detection and identification techniques. The application of machine learning models in this field can help automate the process of classification of hazardous NEOs, which would provide consistent and reliable results if the correct machine learning algorithms were to be used.

The research currently available in this field, discussed in detail in the next section, provide relevant insight into how classification of hazardous NEOs can be accomplished. However, these papers written operated on only one dataset each. Thus, the use of multiple datasets, which this chapter seeks to do, in order to compare and analyse the performance of these machine learning algorithms could provide a different and perhaps a more in-depth perspective in this field. The advantage of doing so is that it takes into account feature and data variability by using datasets that have features varying from one another, allowing for a more robust and generalised analysis of the results found.

In addition, to the best knowledge of the authors, there does not currently exist any elaborate and in-depth analysis specifically addressing the impactful or important features that contribute to the classification of potentially hazardous NEOs. This chapter serves to bridge that gap in research and provide a detailed analysis in that regard.

2.1 Related Work

Wang (2023) used seven algorithms, namely, Logistic Regression, K-Nearest Neighbour, Random Forest, Decision Tree, Naïve Bayes, Gradient Boosting, and Voting Classifier, to predict hazardous asteroids. The dataset used consists of 90,837 rows and 9 columns. The author found that combined/ensemble models displayed the best results in predicting hazardous asteroids, and in addition, an algorithm such as Gradient Boosting would be the preferred choice as it resulted in the lowest number of false predictions, and would therefore pose the lowest risk.

In a paper by Upender *et al*. (2022), the authors generated a dataset with certain handpicked parameters from NASA's Jet Propulsion Laboratory small-body database in order to predict potentially hazardous asteroids. They built several well-performing models in this regard, and found that the XGBoost Classifier model provided the best accuracy and F1-score, with an F1-score of 1.00 and 0.98 on non-hazardous and potentially hazardous asteroids respectively.

McLemore (2022) trained four models to classify hazardous and non-hazardous asteroids. A dataset consisting of 3749 rows and 40 columns was used. The author used correlation plot to compare the features, and tested different parameters to solve the problem of an imbalanced dataset. It was found that XGBoost had the most significant improvements among all the models. Furthermore, the author stated that although precision is an important metric, in the case of data such as these, having a high recall is much more important, due to the fact that a low recall means that the model is misidentifying hazardous asteroids as non-hazardous, which would be very dangerous.

Bagane *et al*. (2023) built an intelligent system for the prediction of potentially hazardous near-earth objects using Random Forest, Support Vector Machine, and Logistic Regression algorithms, with a maximum accuracy score of 91.68 for Random Forest. They also provided valuable insight into the relevance of certain features over others for the process of such classifications.

Bahel *et al*. (2021) used Logistic Regression, K-Nearest Neighbour, Decision Tree, and Random Forest models to classify hazardous asteroids. They found that Random Forest, in comparison to the other models, resulted in greater overall performance. The authors observed that the accuracy metric alone is not sufficient to provide a representation of a model's performance, especially due to imbalanced data points present in classification problems. Further, they stated that probabilistic prediction models tend to develop a bias towards the class with higher data points, whereas this problem does not exist for tree structures.

Chhibber *et al*. (2022) utilised the Azure Machine Learning Studio in order to compare the efficacy of various machine learning models for classifying potentially hazardous asteroids. They sourced their dataset from the NeoWs web service, and utilised a wide variety of algorithms in order to perform this classification. Ultimately, the authors found that Random Forest, which they referred to as Decision Forest, was the most appropriate model for undertaking this task as it resulted in the highest AUC score of 0.999, with Boosted Decision Forest and Neural Network performing almost as optimally with an AUC score of 0.998 each.

Reddy *et al*. (2023) built six machine learning models to predict hazardous asteroids. Among these models, Logistic Regression, Random Forest, and Decision Tree were found to be the most individually accurate. Thus, these three models were selected and the Majority Voting Technique was applied. The authors found that the combined result from this technique resulted in an accuracy of 100%, while the highest among that of the individual models was 99.86%.

Si (2020) trained several models to classify hazardous and non-hazardous asteroids. The author used a dataset consisting of 4,688 rows and 40 columns. From the dataset, 15 features were selected. The author stated that the Random Forest algorithm with tree number 15 was found to be the most optimal model for classifying hazardous asteroids. Furthermore, the XGBoost model was found to be equally as accurate as Random Forest, with the latter performing slightly better due to its faster training time.

Babu Rao *et al.* (2023) developed six machine learning models to predict hazardous asteroids, namely, Naïve Bayes, Logistic Regression, Random Forest, Decision Tree, K-Nearest Neighbour, and Support Vector Machine. Their testing found that all six models performed sufficiently well, with Random Forest resulting in the highest accuracy at 0.999, and K-Nearest Neighbour performing relatively the worst in comparison, with an accuracy of 0.899.

Reddy *et al.* (2021) used XGBoost, Random Forest, and Support Vector Machine algorithms and employed XGBClassifier to all three algorithms in order to enhance prediction of hazardous asteroids. The authors used Mutual Information method for feature selection. The authors found that there were significant and substantial improvements in performance of the three algorithms when they were implemented with XGBClassifier.

Pasko (2018) trained a Support Vector Machine model with an RBF kernel along with the DBSCAN algorithm to predict the orbital patterns of undiscovered potentially hazardous asteroids. The author was able to identify the boundaries of potentially hazardous asteroids in 2-D and 3-D regions, with the model providing an accuracy of 91% in that regard.

In a paper written by Bhavsar *et al.* (2023), the authors attempted to classify potentially hazardous asteroids using quantum machine learning. The authors described the limitations of contemporary machine learning classifiers, stating that their dependence on the volume and integrity of the training dataset could lead to overfitting if those training datasets were insufficient or poor-quality. This exemplified itself during their research when the four machine learning algorithms they chose were subject to the aforementioned overfitting issues.

Basu (2019) was able to predict the diameter of an asteroid using a multi-layer perceptron regressor. The author commented on the importance of an asteroid's diameter in assessing its hazardous nature. The performance of the perceptron regressor was compared with other models such as gradient boosting regressor, XGBoost regressor, etc. but was found to be the best performing.

Ranaweera and Fernando (2022) used deep learning to predict potentially hazardous asteroids. They defined potentially hazardous asteroids as asteroids having an Earth Minimum Orbit Intersection Distance (MOID) of 0.05 AU or less, and an absolute magnitude (H) of 22.0 or less. The authors used SVM models with four different kernels, Logistic Regression, K-Near Neighbour, and Multi-Layer Perceptron algorithms for their prediction, and found that the SVM model with the RBF kernel had the highest precision score.

In a paper written by Jain *et al.* (2021), the authors were able to detect and assess the risk of asteroids using a convolutional neural network object detection algorithm known as YOLO. The authors were able to calculate the distance, velocity, size, and time taken to reach earth based on the images processed by the model. The authors were then able to use these findings to assess the risk factor of these asteroids.

2.2 Standard Approaches

This chapter seeks to classify NEOs that are potentially hazardous to earth, and identify which features are impactful and provide significant contributions to this classification. As stated in the introductory section of this chapter, this will be accomplished by implementing four machine learning algorithms, namely, Logistic Regression, Random Forest, Support Vector Machine (SVM), and XGBoost. These specific algorithms were chosen as they were found to be consistently the best performing after conducting a study of other research papers written in the field of hazardous NEO classification (see, e.g., McLemore, 2022; Ranaweera et al., 2022; Si, 2020; Upender et al., 2022).

These algorithms will be trained and tested on two datasets, the first being a dataset sourced from and publicly available on the Kaggle website ('Kaggle dataset'), and the second dataset generated using NASA's Jet Propulsion Laboratory Small-Body Database Search Engine ('JPL dataset').

The primary objective will be to evaluate the performance of each algorithm based on five metrics: Accuracy, Precision, Recall, F1-Score, and ROC-AUC Score. Among these metrics, special emphasis must be given to the recall metric, as it is a measure of the proportion of correctly identified true positives relative to the total number of actual positive instances (true positives + false negatives) in a given dataset. In the case of hazardous NEO classification, it is of the utmost importance to reduce the number of false negatives as much as possible in order to minimise the threat of hazardous NEOs being misclassified (McLemore, 2022). Therefore, an important consideration to keep in mind when analysing the algorithms is that they each must result in sufficiently high recall scores.

This chapter will now discuss the two datasets in detail and outline the steps taken to preprocess both datasets, along with correlation matrices for both datasets.

Table 1. Kaggle dataset column names and their descriptions

Column Name	Column Description
id	Unique identifier for each asteroid
name	Name given by NASA
est_diameter_min	Minimum Estimated Diameter in kilometres
est_diameter_max	Maximum Estimated Diameter in kilometres
relative_velocity	Velocity of object relative to Earth
miss_distance	Distance in kilometres object missed Earth
Column Name	Column Description
orbiting_body	Planet that the asteroid orbits
Column Name	Column Description
sentry_object	Whether included in sentry - an automated collision monitoring system
absolute_magnitude	Describes intrinsic luminosity
hazardous	Boolean feature that shows whether asteroid is harmful or not

2.2.1 Kaggle Dataset

This dataset contains NASA certified asteroids classified as NEOs compiled by Sameep Vani (2022) and made available for the public domain on Kaggle. The original dataset contains 90,836 rows and 10 columns. Details regarding the column names and their descriptions are provided below in Table 1.

The target variable for this dataset is the 'hazardous' column, which contains string values of 'true' representing hazardous NEOs, or 'false' representing non-hazardous NEOs. Binary encoding was performed to convert these string values into integer values, with 0 representing non-hazardous, and 1 representing hazardous. This was done for the sake of convenience and to maintain consistency across the analysis to be done for this chapter. Figure 1 provided below depicts the distribution of true and false values present in the dataset.

The columns 'name', 'orbiting_body', and 'sentry_object' were dropped due to the fact that the 'name' column in itself does not provide any significant insight for binary classification. The 'id' column is sufficient enough to provide a way of identifying each individual NEO in the dataset. However, the year of discovery of the NEO was extracted from the values of the 'name' column, to create a new 'year' column as the year of discovery of an NEO is significant to note. It depicts the rapid increase in frequency of NEOs discovered in more recent years with the advancements in technology as compared to the first few discoveries.

Figure 1. Distribution of true and false values of the 'hazardous' feature in the Kaggle dataset

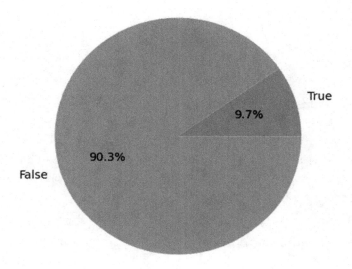

Distribution of 'hazardous' feature

Further, the 'orbiting_body' and 'sentry_object' columns both contain the same values of 'Earth' and 'false' respectively for all rows in the dataset, and thus useful information cannot be extracted from these columns for this chapter. Provided below in Figure 2 is the distribution of the remaining columns before preprocessing.

A novel column labelled as 'proximity_velocity_ratio' was created, and was computed by dividing the 'miss_distance' value by the 'relative_velocity' value for a given row. This column is a ratio of the distance of an object's closest approach to Earth, i.e, its 'miss_distance' value, divided by that object's velocity relative to Earth, i.e, its 'relative_velocity' value. This column is significant as it may provide insights into the potential severity of NEO encounters, with higher values indicating a closer and faster approach.

Additionally, all rows with missing values were dropped. Outliers present in the features that exhibited highly right skewed distributions were removed. In the case of est_diameter_min, all records greater than 1.5 were removed, and natural log transformation was performed. Further outliers were removed by using the Z-Score technique. For est_diameter_max, all values greater than 2.5 were removed. In the case of relative_velocity, outliers were detected and removed using the Z-score technique. The miss_distance and absolute_magnitude features did not contain

Figure 2. Distribution of features in the Kaggle dataset before preprocessing

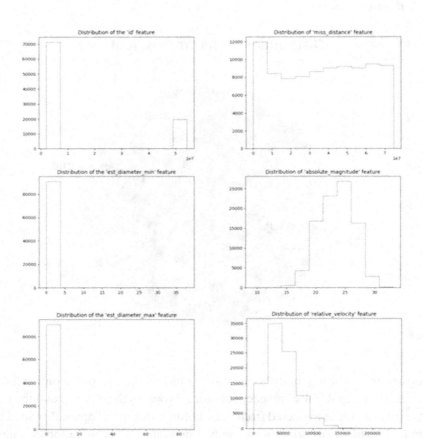

any outliers, which was verified using the Z-Score technique. Finally, outliers for the proximity_velocity_value feature were detected using the Interquartile Range technique, and all values greater than 12,500 were removed.

Standardisation was also performed on all features except 'year.' Finally, the dataset was balanced via random undersampling of a 50:50 ratio, consisting of a total of 16,170 rows. Provided below in Figure 3 is an illustration of the features after all preprocessing were accomplished.

Provided above in Figure 4 is a visualisation that depicts the increase in frequency of NEOs that were discovered in recent years. This can be attributed to the improvements made in technology capable of detecting these NEOs.

Figure 3. Distribution of features in the Kaggle dataset after preprocessing

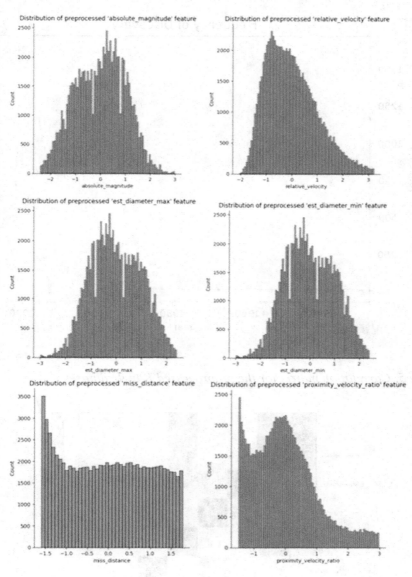

2.2.2 Correlation Matrix

There are several points to take note of from the correlation matrix provided above in Figure 5. Firstly, it can be seen that the minimum and maximum estimated diameter features have a perfect positive correlation of 1.00 with each other. Thus, we can

Figure 4. Distribution of the 'year' feature in the Kaggle dataset after preprocessing

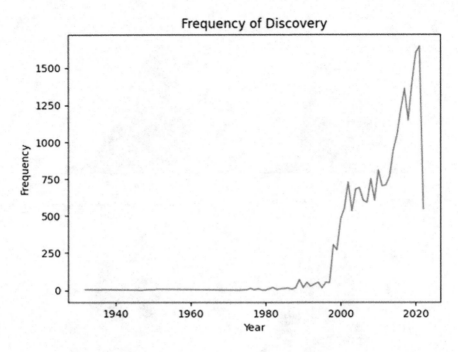

Figure 5. Correlation matrix for the preprocessed Kaggle dataset

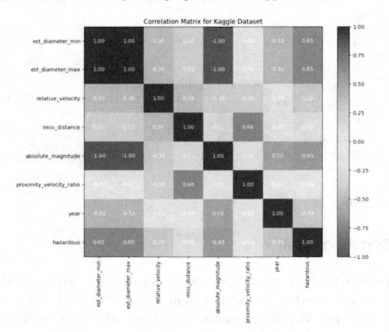

essentially choose to utilise either or both features for the training and testing of the chosen algorithms. In addition, their correlation with the hazardous feature yields a positive value of 0.65. If the value of either diameter features were to increase, so too would the value of the hazardous feature, indicating that those NEOs with higher diameter values are more likely to be hazardous.

Secondly, the absolute magnitude feature also displays a high correlation value, but in the negative polarity of -0.65, with the hazardous feature. This indicates that NEOs with lower values of absolute magnitude are more likely to be classified as hazardous. This is also consistent with astronomy, where lower absolute magnitude values of celestial objects indicate a higher luminosity and thus evidence of a larger celestial object.

2.2.3 JPL Dataset

This dataset has been generated from NASA's Jet Propulsion Laboratory Small-Body Database (NASA/JPL, n.d.). The data was extracted by inputting certain parameters in order to hand-pick features for the classification of potentially hazardous NEO classification, and would perhaps provide a different perspective on what characteristics to focus on for real-world applications. Furthermore, this

Table 2. JPL dataset column names and their descriptions

Column Name	Column Description
spkid	Object primary SPK-ID
pha	Potentially hazardous asteroids (PHA) flag (Y/N)
H	Absolute magnitude parameter
Column Name	Column Description
e	Eccentricity
a	Semi-major axis (a.u.)
q	Perihelion distance (a.u.)
i	Inclination; angle with respect to x–y ecliptic plane
moid	Earth minimum orbit intersection distance (a.u.)
class	Orbit classification
om	Longitude of the ascending node
ad	Aphelion distance
per_y	Sidereal orbital period (years)
epoch	Epoch of osculation in Julian day form

dataset contains certain features that are not available in other ready-made datasets from online sources.

This original dataset contains 32,560 rows and 14 columns before preprocessing. Provided below in Table 2 is a description of the columns names and their descriptions for this dataset.

The target variable for this dataset is the 'pha' column, which stands for potentially hazardous asteroids. It contains string values where 'Y' represents hazardous, and 'N' represents non-hazardous. These values were once again converted to integer values with 1 representing hazardous and 0 representing non-hazardous. This was done to enable the values of this column to be used for classification, as well as to maintain consistency with the Kaggle dataset.

Provided below in Figure 6 is the distribution of true and false values present in the 'pha' feature of the JPL dataset.

This dataset has the 'class' column, which contains categorical values denoting which orbit class the NEO belongs to. The values of this column are Apollo (APO), Amor (AMO), Aten (ATE), and Interior-Earth Objects (IEO). This column is significant as it could display if hazardous NEOs are more likely to be part of a particular orbit class, and if so, which ones. It is not sufficient to take into account only the distance of these orbit classes from Earth, as it does not give us a proper

Figure 6. Distribution of true and false values of the 'pha' feature in the JPL dataset

Distribution of 'pha' feature

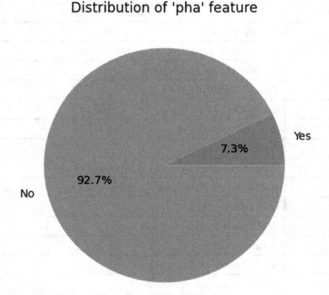

Figure 7. Distribution of orbit classes of the 'class' feature in the JPL dataset

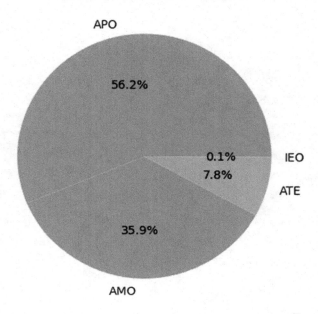

understanding of their potentially hazardous natures, and thus, proper analysis with the chosen algorithms must be undertaken on these orbit classes.

Figure 7 illustrates the distribution of these orbit classes. A majority of the NEOs belong to the Apollo class consisting of 56.2%. The Amor class also contains a substantial amount of NEOs at 35.9%. However, Aten and IEO classes constituted a considerably lesser amount of only 7.8% and 0.1% respectively. Figures 8, 9, and 10 provided below illustrate the distribution of the features before preprocessing has been done.

One hot encoding was performed on the 'class' feature, which generated four separate boolean orbit class features, namely, 'AMO', 'APO', 'ATE', and 'IEO', and finally the 'class' feature was dropped. The 'epoch' feature was dropped as well, as it was highly left skewed and could not be used for computations.

All records with missing values were dropped and outlier removal from the features was done as well. In the case of the 'H' and 'e' features, outliers were detected and removed using the Z-Score technique. The 'a' feature exhibited highly right skewed distribution, and all data greater than five were removed. Further outliers were detected and removed using the Z-Score technique. The 'i' feature displayed highly

Figure 8. Distribution of 'spkid', 'a', 'ad', and 'H' features in the JPL dataset before

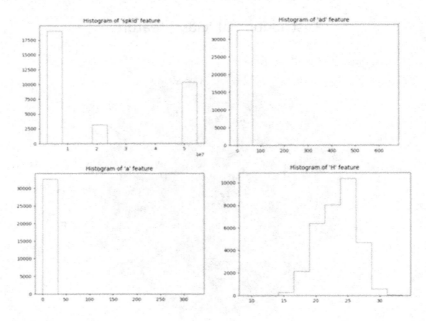

Figure 9. Distribution of 'per_y', 'om', 'q', and 'moid' features in the JPL dataset before

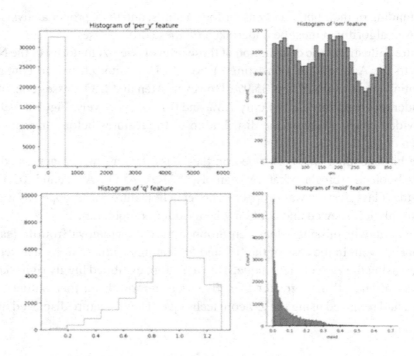

Figure 10. Distribution of 'e', 'epoch', and 'i' features in the JPL dataset before preprocessing

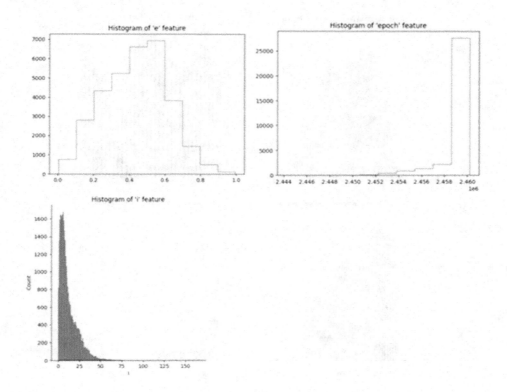

right skewed distribution as well, and all data greater than 80 were removed. In the case of the 'moid' feature, it displayed highly right skewed distribution, and all data greater than 0.5 were removed. The 'ad' feature also displayed highly right skewed distribution, and all data greater than six were removed. In the cases of the 'per_y' and 'q' features, no data removal was done as it would have resulted in elimination of a significant number of true values. Finally, the 'om' feature did not contain any outliers, validated by the Z-Score technique.

Standardisation was performed on all features except for 'spkid', and the dataset was balanced via random undersampling of a 50:50 ratio consisting of a total of 4,598 rows and 15 columns. Provided below in Figures 11 and 12 illustrate the distribution of the features after all preprocessing has been accomplished.

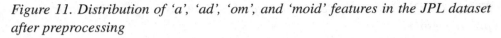

Figure 11. Distribution of 'a', 'ad', 'om', and 'moid' features in the JPL dataset after preprocessing

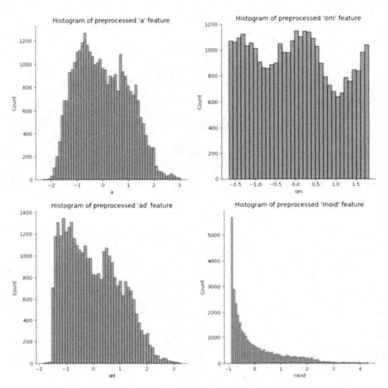

2.2.4 Correlation Matrix

The correlation matrix for the preprocessed JPL dataset illustrated above in Figure 13 contains several points that are worth taking note of. Firstly, the 'H' feature, which is the absolute magnitude of an object, displays a high negative correlation value of -0.61 with that of the target variable 'pha.' This is similar to the Kaggle dataset where the absolute magnitude for that dataset also contained a high negative correlation value.

Secondly, the 'moid' feature, which is the minimum orbit intersection distance also displays a relatively high negative correlation value of -0.43 with the target variable. This feature represents the minimum distance between the orbit of Earth and the orbit of a given NEO. Thus, it can be gathered that a lower 'moid' value would result in a closer approach for the NEO and thus increase its likeliness to be hazardous.

Figure 12. Distribution of 'q', 'e', 'per_y', 'i', 'H', and orbit class features in the JPL dataset after preprocessing

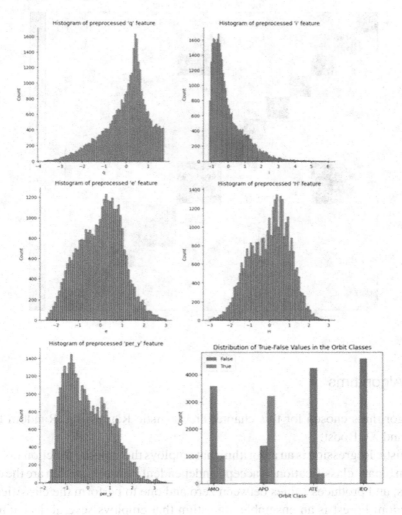

Other interesting points to note are that the 'q' and 'AMO' features also display a relatively high negative correlation value of -0.33 and -0.38 respectively. On the other hand, the 'APO' and 'e' features display a relatively high positive correlation value of positive 0.34 and 0.27 respectively.

249

Figure 13. Correlation matrix for the preprocessed JPL dataset

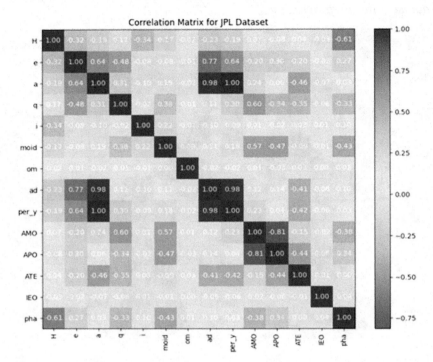

2.2.5 Algorithms

The algorithms chosen for this chapter are Logistic Regression, Random Forest, SVM, and XGBoost.

Logistic Regression is an algorithm that employs the sigmoid function in order to perform binary classification. It accepts independent variables, which are the dataset features, and produces values between zero and one to perform the classification.

Random Forest is an ensemble algorithm that employs several decision trees, wherein each individual decision tree is trained on random subsets of the dataset, and the results of all the trees are aggregated in the end to generate a final prediction as the result. The number of trees, or n_estimators, to be used for this chapter are 100.

SVM is an algorithm that performs classification tasks by attempting to find an optimal hyperplane in order to differentiate between the two classes. This chapter will use the Radial Basis Function (RBF) kernel, since a paper that compared the different SVM kernels in the context of classification of potentially hazardous asteroids found that the RBF kernel was the best performing as compared to the other kernels by a significantly wide margin (Ranaweera *et al.*, 2022).

XGBoost, which stands for Extreme Gradient Boosting, is an ensemble algorithm that combines several decision trees and employs a gradient boosting framework in order to provide an accurate and robust model for classification and other tasks. For this chapter, the n_estimators for XGBoost was also set to 100, with a max_depth of 7.

3. DISCUSSION AND ANALYSIS

Four machine learning algorithms were selected for the task of classifying potentially hazardous NEOs. These algorithms were Logistic Regression, Random Forest, SVM, and XGBoost. To perform this classification, two datasets were chosen, namely, the Kaggle dataset and the JPL dataset. For this analysis, special emphasis will be given to the recall metric to ensure that all models result in relatively high recall scores. This is due to the fact that a low recall score in the specific case of hazardous NEO classification would mean that even if the models recorded high scores in other metrics, it could still potentially result in false negatives for several hazardous NEOs. This would pose substantial risks for real-world applications.

After training and testing were performed, all the models were able to conclude with satisfactory results for both datasets. Provided below in Tables 3 and 4 are the performance metrics of the models for the Kaggle and JPL datasets respectively.

Table 4 shows that all four models have performed exceptionally well with the JPL dataset, with each model except Logistic Regression recording above 95% in

Table 3. Performance metrics of the models for the Kaggle dataset

Models	Accuracy	Precision	Recall	F1-Score	ROC-AUC Score
Log. Reg.	85.41%	80.78%	92.56%	86.27%	85.48%
Random Forest	86.72%	81.78%	94.16%	87.53%	86.79%
SVM	86.87%	79.15%	99.75%	88.27%	86.99%
XGBoost	88%	81.01%	99.17%	89.18%	88.03%

Table 4. Performance metrics of the models for the JPL dataset

Models	Accuracy	Precision	Recall	F1-Score	ROC-AUC Score
Log. Reg.	94.96%	93.11%	97.26%	95.14%	94.92%
Random Forest	99.48%	99.83%	99.14%	99.48%	99.48%
SVM	96.61%	94.75%	98.80%	96.73%	96.57%
XGBoost	99.67%	99.78%	99.57%	99.67%	99.67%

almost all metrics. The performance metrics of the models in the Kaggle dataset shown in Table 3 are relatively lower in comparison, with each model performing over 80% in all metrics except for the precision metric of SVM, which recorded 79.15%.

With regards to the recall metric in the Kaggle dataset, it can be seen in Table 3 that SVM and XGBoost recorded the highest recall scores of 99.75% and 99.17% respectively. It must be noted that these two models had significantly higher recall scores than Logistic Regression and Random Forest, which recorded 92.56% and 94.16% recall scores respectively, but they only performed marginally better than the other, with the difference in recall scores of less than 1%.

With regards to the recall metric JPL dataset, it can be seen in Table 4 that Random Forest and XGBoost had the highest recall scores of 99.14% and 99.57% respectively. Logistic Regression and SVM also performed well, with 98.80% and 97.26% recall scores respectively, only behind the other two models by slightly over 2%.

Furthermore, it can be seen that XGBoost is consistenly the best performing model with both datasets across almost all metrics, especially for the recall metric, recording over 99% with both datasets. Thus, XGBoost should be the algorithm of choice when tasked with classifying potentially hazardous NEOs using machine learning algorithms.

3.1 K-Fold Cross-Validation

K-Fold Cross-Validation technique has been utilised in order to validate the results of the models. K-Fold Cross-Validation is a technique that is used to assess the performance of machine learning models in a generalised perspective. It splits the given dataset into a certain number of subsets or 'folds'. The individual models are then trained and evaluated a specific number of times to be specified in the n_splits parameter, and the results of all the splits are then averaged to give the mean values that results to a generalised view of the model's performance.

In this chapter, the n_splits parameter was set to five, meaning that five folds would be created and the cross-validation process would iterate over five rounds, utilising four folds for training and one fold for testing within each run. Provided below are the mean values that resulted from performing K-Fold Cross-Validation on all the models, with the Kaggle dataset depicted in Table 5 and the JPL dataset depicted in Table 6.

By comparing the performance metrics of the models in Tables 3 and 4, with that of the K-Fold Cross Validation mean results found in Tables 5 and 6, it can be seen that for every model in both datasets, the values are almost the exact same

Table 5. K-Fold cross validation mean results of the models for the Kaggle dataset

Models	Mean Accuracy	Mean Precision	Mean Recall	Mean F1 -Score	Mean ROC-AUC Score
Log. Reg.	85.41%	81.07%	91.66%	86.04%	85.14%
Random Forest	87.21%	82.73%	94.05%	88.02%	87.21%
SVM	87.19%	79.72%	99.74%	88.61%	89.56%
XGBoost	87.68%	80.77%	98.91%	88.92%	87.68%

Table 6. K-Fold cross validation mean results of the models for the JPL dataset

Models	Mean Accuracy	Mean Precision	Mean Recall	Mean F1 -Score	Mean ROC-AUC Score
Log. Reg.	94.91%	93.36%	96.69%	94.99%	94.91%
Random Forest	99.39%	99.47%	99.31%	99.39%	99.40%
SVM	96.95%	95.40%	98.65%	96.99%	99.62%
XGBoost	99.39%	99.47%	99.31%	99.39%	99.40%

across all metrics, with only slight differences in decimal values. This verifies that the models are performing consistently across different subsets of data. It is evidence of, and is a positive indicator for, the robustness of all the model's generalised performance. It denotes the stability of the models and enhances the reliability of their performance metrics.

3.2 Feature Importance Analysis

This chapter utilised the SHAP package available for Python in order to analyse the important or impactful features for classification of potentially hazardous NEOs. It stands for SHapley Additive exPlanations, and it helps to understand the contributions of individual features to a model's prediction. It does so by assigning Shapley values, a concept taken from game theory, to 'players', which are the features in the context of machine learning. These Shapley values indicate a feature's average contribution to a prediction across all possible combination of features. A higher Shapley value would indicate that the feature contributes positively towards a predicted outcome, while lower Shapley values indicate a negative contribution.

The findings are then visualised in a summary plot that ranks the features on the y-axis in decreasing order of the mean absolute value of their Shapley values. The

Figure 14. Logistic regression SHAP summary plot for the Kaggle dataset

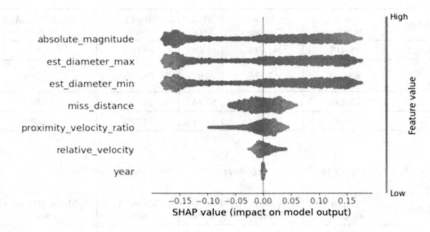

Figure 15. Random forest SHAP summary plot for the Kaggle dataset

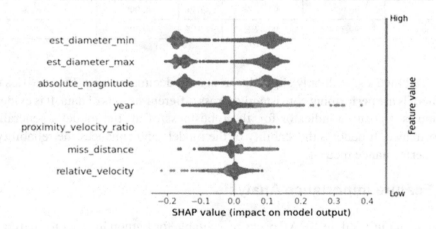

x-axis contains a partition line at x=0, and plots the individual Shapley value for every instance or record of that feature. Values that occur to the right of the partition line indicate positive contributions, while values that occur to the left of the partition line indicate negative contributions. These values are also colour-coded based on each individua data point's original feature value, with red indicating higher original values, and blue indicating lower original values. Provided below in Figures 14, 15, 16, and 17 are the summary plots of each model for the Kaggle dataset.

From the above visualisations, it can be see that the features absolute_magnitude, est_diameter_min, and est_diameter_max were consistently the most important

Figure 16. Support vector machine SHAP summary plot for the Kaggle dataset

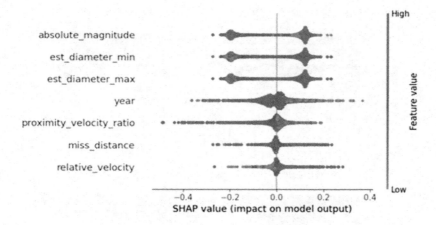

Figure 17. XGBoost SHAP summary plot for the Kaggle dataset

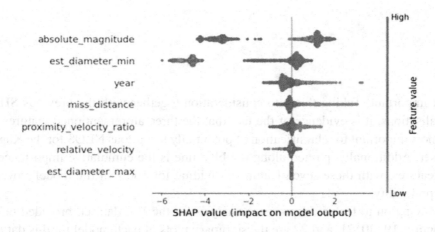

features across all the models. In the case of absolute_magnitude, a majority of the values that occur to the right of the partition line are blue, which signifies that the lower values of this feature contribute more positively towards hazardous classification. The opposite is true for both estimated diameter features, which have their higher values, coded in red, towards the right that contribute more positively towards hazardous classification. This can be further elaborated in below in Figure 18.

This visualisation, plotted based on each feature's Shapley values, illustrates the differences in contributions of each feature, where once again it can be seen that absolute_magnitude, est_diameter_min, est_diameter_max are found to be the

Figure 18. Kaggle waterfall plot of SHAP values

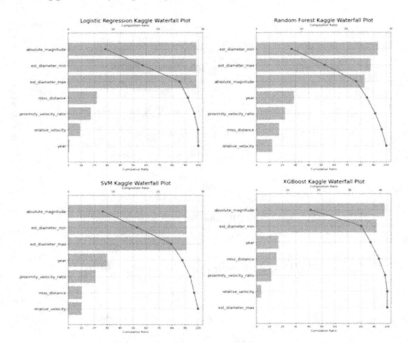

most important. Taking this into consideration together with the previous SHAP visualisations, it is evidence of the fact that the three aforementioned features are the most important for classification of potentially hazardous NEOS for the Kaggle dataset. Additionally, plotted along the blue line is the cumulative importance of the features, with these seven features providing for 100% of the model's overall interpretability.

Moving on to feature importance analysis for the JPL dataset, provided below in Figures 19, 20, 21, and 22 are the summary plots of each model for this dataset.

From the above visualisations, it can be see that the features H, which is the absolute magnitude, and moid, which is the minimum orbit intersection distance, were consistently the most important features across all the models. Similar to the Kaggle dataset, the absolute magnitude feature was the most importance feature for hazardous NEO classification, with similar Shapley value distributions in the summary plot. Additionally, the moid feature also resulted in most of its lower values, coded in blue, occurring to the right of the partition line. Thus, it can be said that the lower values of both the H and moid features contributed positively towards hazardous NEO classification. Once again, this can be further elaborated below in Figure 23.

Figure 19. Logistic regression SHAP summary plot for the JPL dataset

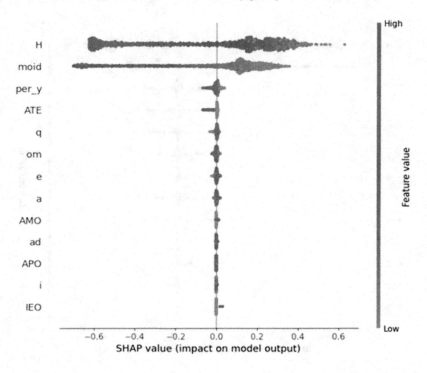

Figure 20. Random forest SHAP summary plot for the JPL dataset

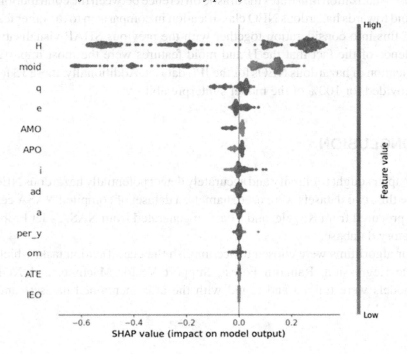

Figure 21. Support vector machine SHAP summary plot for the JPL dataset

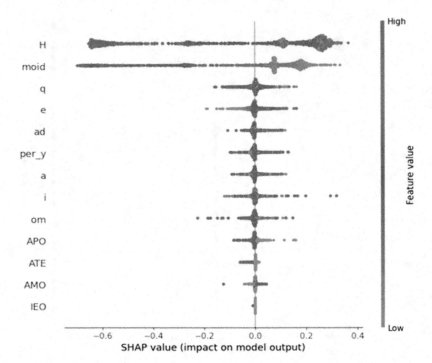

This visualisation illustrates the drastic difference between the contributions of H and moid towards hazardous NEO classification in comparison to the other features. Taking this into consideration together with the previous SHAP visualisations, it is evidence of the fact that the H and moid features were the most important for classification of hazardous NEOs for the JPL dataset. Additionally, these 13 features also provided for 100% of the model's interpretability.

4. CONCLUSION

This chapter sought to classify and accurately detect potentially hazardous NEOs. To achieve this, two datasets were used, namely, a dataset of compiled NASA certified NEOs procured from Kaggle, and a dataset generated from NASA's Jet Propulsion Laboratory database.

Four algorithms were chosen to accomplish the classification task, which were Logistic Regression, Random Forest, Support Vector Machine, and XGBoost. The models were trained and tested with the aforementioned datasets and their

Figure 22. XGBoost SHAP summary plot for the JPL dataset

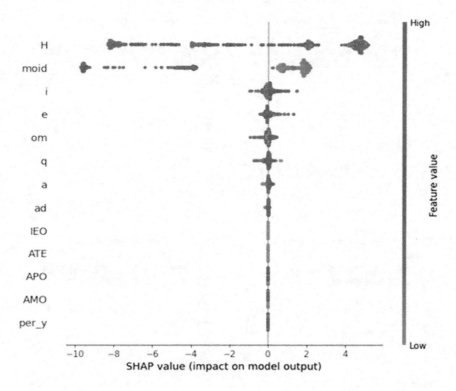

performance metrics were analysed with special emphasis being given to ensure high recall scores for all models.

It was concluded that XGBoost was the consistently the best performing model for both datasets across all metrics, and had also recorded the highest recall scores for both datasets, with 98.91% for the Kaggle dataset and 99.57% for the JPL dataset. However, the other models also performed sufficiently well, recording metrics not too far behind XGBoost, differing only in a few decimal points in the case of some metrics.

Feature importance analysis was done by analysing the Shapley values of each individual feature from both datasets. The implications of these Shapley values were understood with the help of summary plots and waterfall plots. It was concluded that the estimated diameter (both minimum and maximum), absolute magnitude, and minimum orbit intersection distance features of an NEO were the most important for being able to classify whether an NEO is hazardous.

Figure 23. JPL waterfall plot of SHAP values

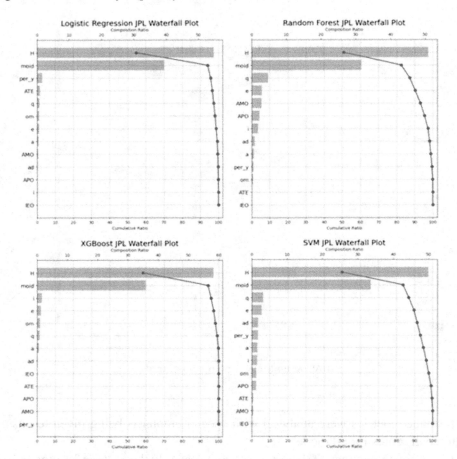

4.1 Datasets

Available from https://github.com/LianSamte/NEOTracker-Datasets

REFERENCES

Bagane, P., Kandula, S. R., Saxena, A., Das, S., Deepak, A., & Rao, S. G. (2023). Intelligent System for Prediction of Potentially Hazardous Nearest Earth Objects Using Machine Learning. *International Journal of Intelligent Systems and Applications in Engineering*, *12*(1s), 71–80. https://ijisae.org/index.php/IJISAE/article/view/3396

Bahel, V., Bhongade, P., Sharma, J., Shukla, S., & Gaikwad, M. (2021). Supervised Classification for Analysis and Detection of Potentially Hazardous Asteroids. *2021 International Conference on Computational Intelligence and Computing Applications.* IEEE. 10.1109/ICCICA52458.2021.9697222

Basu, V. (2019). Prediction of Asteroid Diameter with the Help of Multi-Layer Perceptron Regressor. *International Journal of Advances in Electronics and Computer Science, 6*(4), 36–40. http://www.iraj.in/journal/journal_file/journal_pdf/12-555-156136953136-40.pdf

Bhavsar, R., Jadav, N. K., Bodkhe, U., Gupta, R., Tanwar, S., Sharma, G., Bokoro, P. N., & Sharma, R. (2023). Classification of Potentially Hazardous Asteroids Using Supervised Quantum Machine Learning. *IEEE Access : Practical Innovations, Open Solutions, 11*, 75829–75848. doi:10.1109/ACCESS.2023.3297498

Chhibber, M., Bhatia, M., Chaudhary, A., & Steward, C. (2022). Comparing the Efficacy of Machine Learning Models on Potentially Hazardous Objects. *2022 2nd International Conference on Technological Advancements in Computational Sciences,* (pp. 725-730). IEEE. 10.1109/ACCESS.2023.3297498

Jain, T., Shethia, A., Khanvilkar, S., Patil, L., Devmane, V., & Kodeboyina, S. (2022) Asteroid Detection and Risk Prediction for the Earth. *Advanced Maui Optical and Space Surveillance Technologies Conference.* AMOS Tech. https://amostech.com/TechnicalPapers/2021/Poster/Jain.pdf

McLemore, T. (2022). Classifying Hazardous and Non-Hazardous Asteroids Using Machine Learning. *NHSJS Reports.* https://nhsjs.com/2022/classifying-hazardous-and-non-hazardous-asteroids-using-machine-learning/

NASA. (n.d.). *NEO Basics.* NASA/JPL CNEOS. https://cneos.jpl.nasa.gov/about/neo_groups.html

NASA/JPL. (n.d.). *Small-Body Database Query.* NASA/JPL CNEOS. https://ssd.jpl.nasa.gov/tools/sbdb_query.html

Pasko, V. (2018). Prediction of Orbital Parameters for Undiscovered Potentially Hazardous Asteroids Using Machine Learning. *Stardust Final Conference* (pp. 45-65). Springer. 10.1007/978-3-319-69956-1_3

Ranaweera, N., & Fernando, T. G. I. (2022). Prediction of Potentially Hazardous Asteroids using Deep Learning. *International Conference on Advanced Research in Computing.* IEEE. 10.1109/ICARC54489.2022.9753945

Rao, B. M., Alekhya, G., Aakanksha, J., & Naga Jyothi, K. (2023). Hazardous Asteroid Prediction Using Machine Learning. *2023 2nd International Conference on Vision Towards Emerging Trends in Communication and Networking Technologies*. Springer. 10.1109/ViTECoN58111.2023.10157937

Reddy, T. N., Reddy, G. J., Shashikanth, A., & Anand, V. (2021). A Hybrid Method to Enhance the Prediction of Hazardous Asteroids Using XGBoost Classifier with XGBClassifier Based Feature Selection Method. *International Research Journal of Engineering and Technology*, 8(9), 1704-1707. https://www.irjet.net/archives/V8/i9/IRJET-V8I9244.pdf

Reddy, V. R., Sai, T. N., Sushant, T., Muvva, S., Rani, D. R., & Sahu, A. K. (2023). Hazardous Asteroid Prediction Using Majority Voting Technique, *2023 7th International Conference on Intelligent Computing and Control Systems*. IEEE. 10.1109/ICICCS56967.2023.10142288

Si, A. (2020). Hazardous Asteroid Classification through Various Machine Learning Techniques. *International Research Journal of Engineering and Technology*, 6(3), 5388-5390. https://www.irjet.net/archives/V7/i3/IRJET-V7I31084.pdf

Upender, K., Krishna, T. S., Pothanna, N., & Kumar, P. V. S. (2022). Predicting the Potentially Hazardous Asteroid to Earth Using Machine Learning. *Proceedings of Second International Conference on Advances in Computer Engineering and Communication Systems* (pp. 359-369). Springer. 10.1007/978-981-16-7389-4_34

Vani, S. (2022). *NASA – Nearest Earth Objects* [Data Set]. https://www.kaggle.com/datasets/sameepvani/nasa-nearest-earth-objects

Wang, Y. (2023). Comparison of Machine Learning Strategies in Hazardous Asteroids Prediction. *Highlights in Science. Engineering and Technology*, 39, 201–208. doi:10.54097/hset.v39i.6527

Chapter 13
Optimizing the Benefits of Solar PV–Integrated Infrastructure in Educational Institutes and Organizational Setups in North Eastern India

Jesif Ahmed
Assam Don Bosco University, India

Papul Changmai
Assam Don Bosco University, India

ABSTRACT

In typical Indian organisational settings, users usually rely on the traditional electrical grid and costly, environmentally harmful diesel generators to supply electricity for regular, emergency backup, and transient services. In addition to offering a chance to supply electricity to relocated people, integrating solar capacity into the current grid can result in considerable cost and carbon reductions. Utilising computational energy system modelling and the analysis of monitored demand data, we assess the savings made possible by the integration of solar (160 kW) capacity into the current supply grid of Assam Power Distribution Co. Ltd. (APDCL, India) at the Azara campus of Assam Don Bosco University, India. The authors discover that, over a five-year period, the renewable infrastructure significantly lowers costs and CO_2 emissions. In order to cut costs and emissions and pave the way for sustainable energy practices, organisations should look into ways to integrate renewable energy sources into their current electrical infrastructure and maximise their performance once installed.

DOI: 10.4018/979-8-3693-2260-4.ch013

1. INTRODUCTION

In the rapidly evolving world of energy, the need for sustainable and efficient solutions has never been more pressing. This chapter delves into the transformative potential of integrating solar capacity into traditional electrical infrastructures. In the conventional Indian organizational settings, the primary sources of electricity are the traditional electrical grid and diesel generators. These methods, while reliable, have two major drawbacks. Firstly, they are often costly due to the fluctuating fuel prices and maintenance costs associated with diesel generators. Secondly, they contribute to environmental degradation through the emission of greenhouse gases. This chapter evaluates the cost-effectiveness of integration of solar capacity into existing systems.

The chapter presents a detailed case study of the Azara campus of Assam Don Bosco University, India. Here, a 160 kW solar capacity was integrated into the existing supply grid of Assam Power Distribution Co. Ltd. (APDCL, India) and used as a power source during power cuts. The chapter meticulously evaluates the savings made possible by this integration, using monitored demand data and computational energy system modelling. Over a five-year period, the renewable infrastructure significantly lowers costs and CO_2 emissions while maintaining the generator's present operating strategy. This is a testament to the economic and environmental benefits of RE (renewable energy) sources. Furthermore, the chapter explores an alternate approach using solar water heating, which results in even greater savings compared to heating provided by the grid.

The chapter concludes with a call to action for organizations, especially educational institutions that offer boarding or hostel and other residential facilities. It suggests that these organizations should explore ways to integrate renewable energy sources into their current electrical infrastructure and maximize their performance once installed. This would not only lead to cost and emission reductions but also pave the way for sustainable energy practices.

1.1 Renewable Energy Scenario in India

India is currently creating waves in the renewable energy industry. India has committed to a sustainable future by pledging to reach a 50% cumulative installed capacity of electricity generated by non-fossil fuel-based energy resources by 2030. The nation will have installed an astounding 167.75 GW of renewable energy capacity (including large hydro) by the end of 2022. Furthermore, 78.75 GW of projects are presently in different phases of execution, while an additional 32.60 GW are undergoing bids (*MNRE Annual Report 2022-23*, 2022). On the global stage, India proudly stands fourth in renewable energy installed capacity, wind power capacity,

Table 1. Cumulative RE achievements of India (as on 31.12.2022)

Sector	Installed capacity (GW)	Under Implementation (GW)	Tendered (GW)	Total Installed/ Pipeline (GW)
Solar Power	63.30	51.13	20.34	134.77
Wind Power	41.93	12.93	1.20	56.06
Bio Energy	10.73	---	---	10.73
Small Hydro	4.94	0.54	0.00	5.48
Hybrid/ Round the Clock (RTC)/ Peaking Power/ Thermal + RE Bundling	---	---	11.06	11.06
Sub-total	**120.90**	**64.6**	**32.6**	**218.10**
Large Hydro	46.85	14.15	---	61.00
Total	**167.75**	**78.75**	**32.60**	**279.10**

and solar power capacity (*REN21 Renewables 2022 Global Status Report*, 2022). This demonstrates the nation's commitment to and advancement in using nature's power for a more environmentally friendly future.

The journey towards this achievement has been significant. Large hydropower has contributed significantly to the installed renewable energy capacity, which increased from 76.37 GW in March 2014 to 167.75 GW in December 2022—a gain of around 2.20 times. Even more astounding has been the rise in solar power capacity, which increased by an astounding 24.07 times from a modest 2.63 GW in March 2014 to a formidable 63.30 GW in December 2022., as shown in Table 1 (*MNRE Annual Report 2022-23*, 2022). This progress reflects India's unwavering commitment to renewable energy and a sustainable future.

As per the 2022-23 Annual Report from the Ministry of New and Renewable Energy, Government of India, the nation has successfully tapped into a total of 63.30 GW of solar power. This includes 53 GW from ground-mounted solar facilities, 8.08 GW from RTS (rooftop solar systems), and 2.22 GW from off-grid solar solutions, as of December 31, 2022. In addition, projects with a cumulative capacity of around 51.13 GW are in the pipeline, and projects with a capacity of 31.4 GW are in the tendering phase. It is anticipated that solar power projects with a capacity of approximately 15 GW will be operational during the fiscal year 2022-23. The potential for solar power in the country, considering land availability and solar radiation, is estimated to be around 750 GWp. Table 2 provides a detailed breakdown of the estimated solar energy potential and the cumulative solar installed capacity on a state-wise basis as of December 31, 2022 (*MNRE Annual Report 2022-23*, 2022).

Table 2. State-wise estimated potential in solar energy & cumulative solar installed capacity in India (MNRE Annual Report 2022-23, 2022)

Sl. No.	States/UTs	Solar Potential (GWp)	Cumulative Capacity (MW) till 31-12-2022
1	Andaman & Nicobar		29.91
2	Andhra Pradesh	38.44	4524.72
3	Arunachal Pradesh	8.65	11.52
4	Assam	13.76	147.93
5	Bihar	11.2	192.88
6	Chandigarh		58.69
7	Chhattisgarh	18.27	944.22
8	Dadra & Nagar Haveli		5.46
9	Daman & Diu		41.01
10	Delhi	2.05	211.48
11	Goa	0.88	26.4
12	Gujarat	35.77	8500.74
13	Haryana	4.56	990.67
14	Himachal Pradesh	33.84	87.39
15	Jammu & Kashmir	111.05	48.9
16	Jharkhand	18. 18	94.9
17	Karnataka	24.7	7885.56
18	Kerala	6.11	688.34
19	Ladakh		7.8
20	Lakshadweep		3.27
21	Madhya Pradesh	61.66	2774.78
22	Maharashtra	64.32	3646.13
23	Manipur	10.63	12.28
24	Meghalaya	5.86	4.15
25	Mizoram	9.09	8.02
26	Nagaland	7.29	3.04
27	Odisha	25.78	452.71
28	Puducherry		35.53
29	Punjab	2.81	1153.21
30	Rajasthan	142.31	16340.75
31	Sikkim	4.94	4.69
32	Tamil Nadu	17.67	6412.36
33	Telangana	20.41	4650.93

Table 2. Continued

Sl. No.	States/UTs	Solar Potential (GWp)	Cumulative Capacity (MW) till 31-12-2022
34	Tripura	2.08	16.67
35	Uttar Pradesh	22.83	2485.16
36	Uttarakhand	16.8	575.46
37	West Bengal	6.26	179.82
38	Others	0.79	45.01
	Total	**748.98 GWp**	**63302.49 MW**

Figures 1 and 2 below provide an insight into the solar potential and cumulative installations respectively till 31-Dec-2022 in India's northeastern states (*MNRE Annual Report 2022-23*, 2022).

Figure 1. Solar potential of the northeastern states (as on 31-Dec-2022)

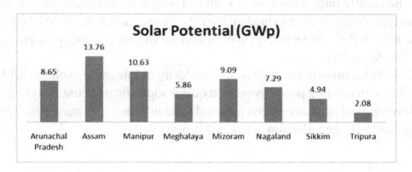

Figure 2. Cumulative solar installed capacity in the northeastern states (as on 31-Dec-2022)

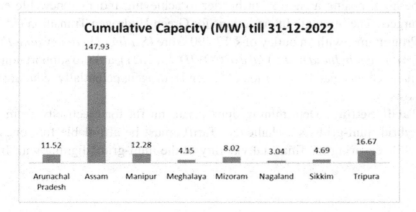

2. CHALLENGES FACED IN RENEWABLE ENERGY INTEGRATION: OPERATING SOLAR HYBRID MINI-GRIDS

The transition to renewable energy sources is a global imperative in the face of climate change. Among these, solar energy has emerged as a promising solution due to its abundance and sustainability. However, the integration of solar energy into existing power systems, particularly in the form of solar hybrid mini-grids, presents a unique set of challenges. In the backdrop of India's ambitious renewable energy targets, as outlined in the latest policy (*Scaling Up Renewable Energy Investment in India in the Wake of COVID-19*, 2021; Verma, 2022; Deb & Kailash, 2023; *Policies And Regulations - Ministry of New and Renewable Energy, India*, n.d.), this chapter takes a deep dive into the complexities of integrating solar energy into existing power systems, particularly in the form of solar hybrid mini-grids.

2.1 Technical Challenges

(a) **Intermittency and Variability:** Solar energy, while abundant and sustainable, is inherently intermittent and variable. This poses challenges for the stability and reliability of solar hybrid mini-grids, a concern that needs to be addressed to meet India's target of 500 GW of non-fossil fuel energy in the energy mix (Deb & Kailash, 2023).

(b) **Grid Integration:** The technical complexity of integrating solar hybrid mini-grids with existing power systems requires sophisticated control systems. The development of standardized protocols and interfaces, as part of the National Green Hydrogen Mission, can aid this process.

2.2 Economic Challenges

(a) **High Initial Costs:** The initial costs of setting up solar hybrid mini-grids can be high, posing a significant barrier to achieving India's renewable energy targets. The Strategic Interventions for Green Hydrogen Transition (SIGHT) Programme, with an outlay of ₹ 17,490 crore (*Scaling Up Renewable Energy Investment in India in the Wake of COVID-19*, 2021), aims to support domestic manufacturing and production of Green Hydrogen, potentially reducing these costs.

(b) **Tariff Setting:** Determining appropriate tariffs for electricity from solar hybrid mini-grids is a challenge. Tariffs must be affordable for consumers while ensuring the financial viability of the mini-grid, aligning with India's commitment to reduce carbon intensity by less than 45 per cent by the end of the decade (Deb & Kailash, 2023).

2.3 Regulatory and Policy Challenges

(a) **Supportive Policies:** The lack of supportive policies and regulations can hinder the adoption and growth of solar hybrid mini-grids. However, the recent policy initiatives by the Indian government, such as the National Green Hydrogen Mission, are promising steps towards addressing this issue.

(b) **Land and Environmental Regulations:** Securing land for solar installations and complying with environmental regulations can be complex and time-consuming, posing additional challenges. Streamlining these processes is crucial to meet India's commitment to reduce total projected carbon emissions by 1 billion tonnes by 2030 (Deb & Kailash, 2023).

3. CHALLENGES IN THE CONTEXT OF INDIA'S LATEST POLICY

The integration of renewable energy, particularly solar energy, into the power grid is a critical aspect of India's energy policy. However, this integration presents several challenges, including resource adequacy, network adequacy, frequency stability, and voltage stability (Hirschhorn & Brijs, 2021). This section will explore these challenges in the context of operating solar hybrid mini-grids in India, in light of the country's latest policy developments.

3.1 Renewable Energy Integration Challenges

(a) **Resource Adequacy:** Resource adequacy refers to the ability of a power system to supply the electrical demand and energy requirements of the end-use customers at all times. The integration of variable renewable energy (VRE) sources such as solar photovoltaic systems introduces uncertainty and variability, making it challenging to ensure resource adequacy.

(b) **Network Adequacy:** Network adequacy is the ability of the power system to transport electricity from generators to consumers. The distributed nature of VRE sources can lead to congestion in the transmission and distribution network, posing a challenge to network adequacy.

(c) **Frequency and Voltage Stability:** Frequency stability is the ability of a power system to maintain its frequency within predefined bounds, while voltage stability refers to the ability to maintain acceptable voltages at all system buses. The integration of VRE sources can cause short-term frequency variations and local voltage issues.

3.2 Solar Hybrid Mini-Grids in India

Solar hybrid mini-grids are a promising solution for renewable energy integration in India. These systems combine solar power with other energy sources, providing a reliable and sustainable power supply (*Solar Mini-Grids: E-Handbook (Version 1)*, 2020). However, operating these mini-grids presents unique challenges, including technical performance evaluation, equipment availability, and resource management (T&D India, 2020). According to Pandey (2023), India has installed about 4,000 solar mini-grids, of which 3,300 are owned or financed by the government. However, only 5% of these grids are operational, highlighting the operational challenges faced.

3.3 India's Latest Policy on Renewable Energy

India's latest policy on renewable energy aims to achieve 500 GW non-fossil-based electricity generation capacity by 2030 (T&D India, 2020). In FY2023-24, India is planning to issue 50 GW tenders for wind, solar, and hybrid projects ("Renewable Energy in India," 2024). This ambitious policy provides a strong impetus for the development and integration of solar hybrid mini-grids.

The Indian government has set an ambitious target to harness 1,00,000 megawatts of solar energy by 2026, with a significant contribution of 40,000 megawatts anticipated from rooftop solar installations (PM – Surya Ghar: Muft Bijli Yojana, n.d.). To streamline the process of residential grid-connected rooftop solar installations, Prime Minister Sh. Narendra Modi inaugurated the National Portal on 30th July 2022. This portal serves as a unified platform for registration and application for Residential Rooftop Solar (RTS) Installation. To accelerate the adoption of solar rooftop systems, the government has rolled out the Solar Rooftop Subsidy Scheme (PM – Surya Ghar: Muft Bijli Yojana). As per the scheme, depicted in Figure 3, residential households are eligible for a subsidy of Rs. 30,000/- per kW for the first 2 kW, and Rs. 18,000/- per kW for any additional capacity up to 3 kW. The total subsidy for systems exceeding 3 kW is capped at Rs. 78,000 (*CFA_structure-Simplifying the Implementation of Rooftop Solar Programme: Subsidy under PM – Surya Ghar: Muft Bijli Yojana*, 2024).

Integrating renewable energy sources into the grid presents a myriad of challenges. However, with the right policy framework and strategic approach, these hurdles can be surmounted. The successful operation of solar hybrid mini-grids in India, under the country's latest policy, stands as a testament to this potential.

Figure 3. Subsidy structure under India's "PM – Surya Ghar: Muft Bijli Yojana"

Suitable Rooftop Solar Plant Capacity for households and subsidy		
Average Monthly Electricity Consumption (units)	**Suitable Rooftop Solar Plant Capacity**	**Subsidy Support**
0 – 150	1 – 2 kW	Rs. 30,000/- to Rs. 60,000/-
150 – 300	2 – 3 kW	Rs. 60,000/- to Rs. 78,000/-
> 300	Above 3 kW	Rs. 78,000/-

4. BACKGROUND STUDY: INTEGRATION OF SOLAR ENERGY INTO ACADEMIC ORGANIZATIONS WITH RESIDENTIAL FACILITIES

The integration of solar energy into academic organizations with residential facilities presents a unique set of challenges and opportunities, which encompasses the technical, economic, and social implications of such integration.

4.1 Technical Challenges

The technical challenges of integrating solar energy primarily revolve around the intermittent nature of solar power and the complexities of grid integration (Shafiullah et al., 2022). These include issues related to non-dispatchability, power quality, angular and voltage stability, reactive power support, and fault ride-through capability. Furthermore, the integration of solar energy systems with building components is highly critical in sensitive heritage contexts (Polo López & Frontini, 2013). Few other issues may present challenges in integrating solar energy in academic organizations with residential facilities (Lehtola & Zahedi, 2020; Kalogirou, 2015; Alshahrani et al., 2019):

(i) **Power System Planning and Risk Management**: The integration of solar energy requires careful planning and risk management to ensure the stability and reliability of the power system.

(ii) **Generation Prediction**: The intermittent nature of solar energy makes it challenging to accurately predict power generation.

(iii) **Energy Storage**: Storing excess solar energy for use during periods of low sunlight (e.g., at night or during cloudy weather) is a significant challenge.

(iv) **Reliability and Security**: Ensuring the reliability and security of the power supply is a critical aspect of integrating solar energy.

(v) **Space Availability**: The availability of space for installing renewable energy systems can be a problem, especially in densely built environments.

(vi) **Maintenance**: Most renewable energy systems require periodic maintenance, which can add to the operational costs.

(vii) **Disruption of Existing Services**: On existing buildings, the integration of solar energy systems may disrupt existing services.

(viii) **Grid Integration**: The integration of large-scale photovoltaic (PV) systems into the grid presents challenges such as voltage regulation and managing the variability of large-scale PV systems.

While these challenges are significant, they are not insurmountable. With the right strategies and technologies, these issues can be effectively addressed.

4.2 Economic and Social Challenges

Economic challenges include the initial investment costs, maintenance costs, and the return on investment. Social challenges, on the other hand, often stem from a lack of awareness and information about solar energy, as well as psycho-social barriers (Polo López & Frontini, 2013).

4.3 Opportunities and Solutions

Despite these challenges, the integration of solar energy in academic organizations with residential facilities offers significant opportunities. For instance, photovoltaic systems can act as characterizing elements and as distinctive architectural materials that can valorize the aesthetic of the entire urban intervention (Formolli et al., 2022). Moreover, solution strategies for overcoming these challenges have been proposed, including grid codes, advanced control strategies, energy storage systems, and renewable energy policies (Shafiullah et al., 2022). The use of alternative solutions such as agri-voltaics, which are compatible with the existing land use, can also help reduce the ecological impact (Formolli et al., 2022).

4.4 Reduction in Greenhouse Gas Emissions

The adoption of the Kyoto Protocol in 1997 signified the beginning of the worldwide community's effort to reduce GHG (greenhouse gas) emissions. This agreement required industrialised countries and economies in transition to reduce their emissions by 18% compared to 1990 levels, therefore operationalizing the United Nations Framework Convention on Climate Change.

However, the Paris Agreement's adoption at the COP21 summit in 2015 marked a dramatic change in the landscape of international climate policy. With the implementation of this pact in November 2016, the purview of accountability was extended beyond industrialised nations. Acknowledging climate change as a worldwide concern, it urged all countries to set emission targets. Although the Paris Agreement has essentially replaced the Kyoto Protocol as the principal legislative framework guiding the global response to climate change, the Kyoto Protocol is still in existence. This development towards the Paris Agreement highlights the growing recognition that climate change is a global issue requiring cooperation across developed and poor countries. The universal approach of the Paris Agreement, which reflects the shared responsibility and collaborative commitment of all nations towards a sustainable future, is a critical advancement in the worldwide battle against climate change.

Countries around the world, are working towards the Paris Agreement for curtailment of GHG emissions. For instance, research by Sterchele et al. (2018) demonstrates that Germany, with its RE (renewable energy) installed capacity at about $100\,GW_{el}$ in 2020, may reduce its energy-related CO_2 emissions by 80% to 95% resp. by the year 2050 if it can raise its capacity by 230–440 GW_{el}. This indicates that a 95% decrease in CO_2 emissions in Germany is possible with a RE installed capacity of around 540 GW_{el} cumulatively, which translates into an annual increase of 8–14 GW_{el} of renewable energy resources.

India's population growth has increased the country's need for water. Being agriculture-dominated, approximately 16.5% of the country's total electricity, mostly from fossil fuels, is used for water pumping (Angadi et al., 2021). This increases GHG emissions in addition to raising the pumps' Life Cycle Cost (LCC). Nonetheless, the integration of renewable energy sources, such solar photovoltaic and wind energy, into water pumping systems has been made possible by new developments in power electronics and drives. A key factor in reducing GHG emissions is the move towards renewable energy.

The field of solar technology is currently witnessing a surge in research activities aimed at its enhancement. For example, a significant contribution to this domain is the work of Changmai et al. (2022), that has proposed an innovative analytical algorithm. This algorithm serves as a valuable tool for photovoltaic (PV) installers, facilitating the estimation of output power from a TCT-connected PV module under diverse shading conditions. Interestingly, aside from detecting temperature and sun irradiance, this estimating method may be carried out without the need for sophisticated measurement equipment.

Although the integration of solar energy in academic organizations with residential facilities presents certain challenges, it also offers immense opportunities for sustainable development. With the right strategies and policies in place, these challenges can be effectively addressed, paving the way for a greener and more sustainable future.

5. LOAD PROFILE OF AZARA CAMPUS OF ASSAM DON BOSCO UNIVERSITY

Assam Don Bosco University, as a part of the commitment to sustainable practices that extend beyond the classroom, has undertaken a comprehensive assessment of its energy consumption patterns, aiming to optimize efficiency and reduce environmental impact (*ENERGY AUDIT REPORT OF ASSAM DON BOSCO UNIVERSITY CAMPUSES AT TAPESIA, AZARA AND KHARGHULI*, 2020). The 2019-20 Energy Audit report of the university presents the following major categories of consumption insights:

(i)   Overall Campus-wide
(ii) Location-wise
(iii) Application-wise
(iv) Equipment-wise

5.1 Campus-Wide Energy Consumption Insights

The university's Azara campus comprises three hostels, an academic complex, and a staff quarter building. A recent energy audit for the year 2019-2020 revealed intriguing trends as shown in Figure 4 and Table 3. Let's delve into the details:

Figure 4. Campus-Wide energy consumption

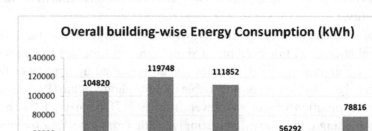

Table 3. Overall building-wise energy consumption of azara campus

Location	Energy Consumption (KWh)
Academic Block	104820
UG Boys Hostel	119748
PG Boys Hostel	111852
Staff Quarters	56292
Girls Hostel	78816
Total	**471528**

Hostels: Among the residential units, the Undergraduate (UG) Boys' hostel emerged as the highest power consumer, closely followed by the Postgraduate (PG) Boys' hostel.

Academic Block: The academic hub, where knowledge thrives, also contributes significantly to the overall energy footprint.

Staff Quarters: The residential quarters of our tireless staff and helpers emerge as a significant load, but during 5 p.m. to 11 p.m. mostly. Their abodes, illuminated by bulbs and powered by appliances, hum with activity.

5.2 Location-Specific Energy Distribution:

A closer look at the location-wise energy distribution reveals fascinating patterns as shown in Figure 5 and Table 4. The residential quarters of staff and helpers account for a substantial portion of energy consumption. Interestingly, the laboratories—despite being less frequented due to student absence for a substantial part of the year—still contribute due to essential equipment like refrigerators that remain operational.

5.3 Application-Specific Energy Utilization

The heart of energy consumption lies in specific applications. As shown in Figure 6 and Table 5, here's a breakdown:

a) **Air Circulation:** A major chunk of energy powers air circulation systems, ensuring comfort and well-being across the campus.

b) **Lighting:** Illumination plays a crucial role, with lighting consuming the next highest share.

c) **Comfort Appliances:** Air conditioners and geysers, essential for maintaining a conducive environment, also contribute significantly.

Figure 5. Location-specific energy distribution

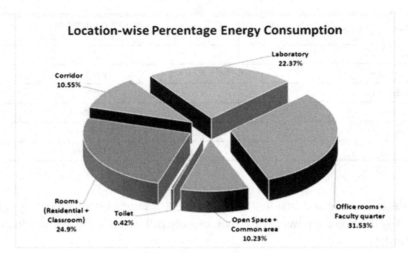

Table 4. Location-wise energy consumption of Azara campus

Locations	Energy Consumption (kWh)	Percentage Energy Consumption (%)
Toilets	1980	0.42%
Rooms (Residential + Classroom)	117403.24	24.90%
Corridors	49764	10.55%
Laboratory	105472.76	22.37%
Office room + Faculty quarter	148656	31.53%
Open Space + Common area	48252.00	10.23%
Total	**471528**	

5.4 Equipment-Specific Analysis

To identify power-intensive equipment within specific application areas, an equipment-specific analysis was conducted as a part of the Energy Audit 2019-20 of the university. The results, summarized in Figure 7 and Table 6, reveal that ceiling fans and wall fans are the primary energy consumers. Their consistent operation across various spaces—lecture halls, offices, and common areas—contributes significantly to the overall load. Often overlooked, wall-mounted fans play a crucial role in maintaining comfort levels. Their localized cooling effect is indispensable, especially in crowded corridors and study zones.

Figure 6. Application-specific energy utilization

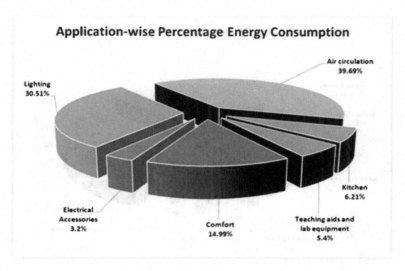

Application-wise Percentage Energy Consumption

Table 5. Application-wise energy consumption of Azara campus

Application	Energy Consumption (kWh)	Percentage Energy Consumption (%)
Comfort	70682.05	14.99%
Electrical Accessories	15088.90	3.2%
Lighting	143863.19	30.51%
Air circulation	187149.46	39.69%
Kitchen	29281.89	6.21%
Teaching aids and lab equipment	25462.51	5.4%
Total	**471528**	

Next, the LED lights follow closely. With their low wattage and extended lifespan, LED lights have become the go-to choice. Yet, their cumulative impact on campus energy consumption cannot be ignored.

The silent workhorses behind climate control, air conditioners strike a balance between comfort and efficiency. Their role in maintaining optimal temperatures during sweltering summers and chilly winters is indispensable. However, their energy appetite—though justified—requires strategic management. Figure 7 and Table 6 clearly show that the air conditioners also draw a considerable share of the campus energy load.

Figure 7. Equipment-specific analysis

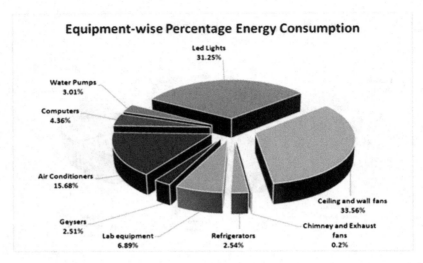

Equipment-wise Percentage Energy Consumption

Led Lights 31.25%

Water Pumps 3.01%

Computers 4.36%

Air Conditioners 15.68%

Geysers 2.51%

Lab equipment 6.89%

Refrigerators 2.54%

Ceiling and wall fans 33.56%

Chimney and Exhaust fans 0.2%

Table 6. Equipment-wise energy consumption of Azara campus

Equipment	Energy Consumption (KWh)s	Percentage Energy Consumption (%)
Water Pumps	14192.99	3.01%
Led Lights	147352.50	31.25%
Ceiling and wall fans	158244.80	33.56%
Chimney and Exhaust fans	943.06	0.2%
Refrigerator	11976.81	2.54%
Lab equipment	32488.28	6.89%
Geysers	11835.35	2.51%
Air Conditioners	73935.59	15.68%
Computers	20558.62	4.36%
Total	**471528**	

6. SOLAR PV INSTALLATION AT AZARA CAMPUS

A 160 KW grid-connected solar photovoltaic power system was installed on 12 June 2018 using the space available on the rooftops of the buildings (Figures 8 and 9).

Table 7 shows a significant saving and an overall trend in energy bills from July 2018 onwards (dotted trend line in Figure 10).

Savings during July 2018 to June 2019 = Rs. 2,36,594.40/-

Figure 8. 160 KW rooftop PV installations at Azara campus of ADBU

Figure 9. 160 kW solar plant data at Azara campus (as on 12-Nov-2019, 4:00 pm)

Power requirement met by renewable energy sources	Total annual energy requirement	Renewable energy source	Energy supplied to the grid
160 kW (peak)	Azara- 471528 kWh	Solar	100% of the energy generated is supplied to the grid

Total Solar Generation at Azara Plant between 12-June -2018 and 12-Nov-2019 = 180636.81 kWH

Taking this as annual average savings due to rooftop solar PV, the total approximated savings from July 2018 to June 2023 = Rs. 11,82,972.00/- (approx.)

Frequent cleaning and regular maintenance of the PV system will definitely result in some more savings.

Table 7. Effects of solar installation on electricity bill at Azara campus (160 kW)

Month	Units Consumed (kWh)	Total Bill Paid (INR)	Effective Rate per unit (INR)	Savings due to PV installation (INR)
Jun-17	23920	231306	8.30	
Jul-17	32320	312534	8.30	
Aug-17	42240	408461	8.30	
Sep-17	36720	355082	8.30	
Oct-17	38600	373262	8.30	
Nov-17	29080	281204	8.30	
Dec-17	16840	162843	8.30	
Jan-18	17272	167020	8.30	
Feb-18	21296	205932	8.30	
Mar-18	26719	258373	8.30	
Apr-18	24680	238656	8.30	
May-18	36754	355411	8.30	
Jun-18	28705	277577	8.30	
Jul-18	**31460**	**304218**	**7.60**	**22022.00**
Aug-18	**41540**	**348474**	**7.60**	**29078.00**
Sep-18	**36715**	**311804**	**7.60**	**25700.50**
Oct-18	**37544**	**318104**	**7.60**	**26280.80**
Nov-18	**28560**	**249826**	**7.60**	**19992.00**
Dec-18	**17970**	**169342**	**7.60**	**12579.00**
Jan-19	**16877**	**161035**	**7.60**	**11813.90**
Feb-19	**22544**	**204104**	**7.60**	**15780.80**
Mar-19	**16580**	**158778**	**7.60**	**11606.00**
Apr-19	**21788**	**198359**	**7.60**	**15251.60**
May-19	**35850**	**305230**	**7.60**	**25095.00**
Jun-19	**30564**	**265056**	**7.60**	**21394.80**

7. CONCLUSION

Effective energy management in higher education institutes with residential facilities can result in significant energy savings, reducing costs and environmental impact.

Figure 10. Effects of solar PV installation at Azara campus

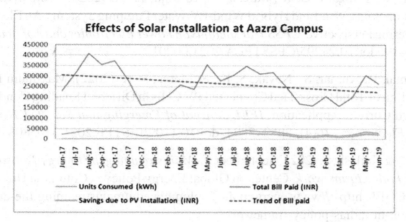

However, achieving these benefits requires a comprehensive approach that considers the unique energy requirements of these institutions.

Despite the various challenges, solar hybrid mini-grids hold immense potential for sustainable energy provision, particularly in remote and off-grid areas. By addressing these challenges head-on, India can pave the way for a more sustainable and resilient energy future, in line with its latest policy commitments. This chapter aims to provide a comprehensive understanding of these challenges and to spur further research and innovation in this field.

This chapter is a must-read for anyone interested in carbon reduction, solar integration, solar heating, and sustainability, particularly in the context of North East India. It offers valuable insights and practical solutions for those looking to optimize the benefits of solar PV-integrated infrastructure. By presenting a successful case study and providing a roadmap for similar implementations, this chapter contributes significantly to the literature on sustainable energy practices in organizational setups. It is a beacon of hope for a future where renewable energy sources are not just an alternative, but the norm.

REFERENCES

Alshahrani, A., Omer, S., Su, Y., Mohamed, E., & Alotaibi, S. (2019). The Technical Challenges Facing the Integration of Small-Scale and Large-scale PV Systems into the Grid: A Critical Review. *Electronics (Basel)*, *8*(12), 1443. doi:10.3390/electronics8121443

Angadi, S., Yaragatti, U. R., Suresh, Y., & Raju, A. B. (2021). Comprehensive Review on Solar, Wind and Hybrid Wind-PV Water Pumping Systems-An Electrical Engineering Perspective. *CPSS Transactions on Power Electronics and Applications*, *6*(1), 1–19. doi:10.24295/CPSSTPEA.2021.00001

Changmai, P., Kumar, S., Nayak, S. K., & Metya, S. K. (2022). Maximum Power Estimation of Total Cross-Tied Connected PV Cells in Different Shading Conditions for High Current Application. *IEEE Journal of Emerging and Selected Topics in Power Electronics*, *10*(4), 3883–3894. doi:10.1109/JESTPE.2021.3105808

Deb, K., & Kailash, S. (2023, September 5). *Mainstreaming the Energy Transition in India's Policy Framework*. Center on Global Energy Policy at Columbia University SIPA | CGEP. https://www.energypolicy.columbia.edu/mainstreaming-the-energy-transition-in-indias-policy-framework/

Energy Audit Report Of Assam Don Bosco University Campuses At Tapesia, Azara And Kharghuli. (2020). DB University. https://dbuniversity.ac.in/pdfs/Internal-Energy-Audit-Report-2020.pdf

Formolli, M., Croce, S., Vettorato, D., Paparella, R., Scognamiglio, A., Mainini, A. G., & Lobaccaro, G. (2022). Solar Energy in Urban Planning: Lesson Learned and Recommendations from Six Italian Case Studies. *Applied Sciences (Basel, Switzerland)*, *12*(6), 2950. doi:10.3390/app12062950

Hirschhorn, P., & Brijs, T. (2021, December 13). *Rising to the Challenges of Integrating Solar and Wind at Scale*. BCG Global. https://www.bcg.com/publications/2021/addressing-variable-renewable-energy-challenges

Kalogirou, S. A. (2015). Building integration of solar renewable energy systems towards zero or nearly zero energy buildings. *The International Journal of Low Carbon Technologies*, *10*(4), 379–385. doi:10.1093/ijlct/ctt071

Lehtola, T., & Zahedi, A. (2020). Technical challenges in the application of renewable energy: A review. *International Journal of Smart Grid and Clean Energy*, *9*(3), 689–699. https://www.ijsgce.com/uploadfile/2020/0415/20200415054706240.pdf. doi:10.12720/sgce.9.3.689-699

MNRE Annual Report 2022-23. (2022). Ministry of New and Renewable Energy, Government of India. https://cdnbbsr.s3waas.gov.in/s3716e1b8c6cd17b771da77391355749f3/uploads/2023/08/2023080211.pdf

Pandey, K. (2023, August 23). *The potential of mini-grids as a sustainable and economical alternative for global electrification.* Mongabay-India. https://india.mongabay.com/2023/08/are-mini-grids-the-sustainable-and-economical-solution-to-achieving-global-electrification/

Policies And Regulations. (n.d.). MNRE. https://mnre.gov.in/policies-and-regulations/

Polo López, C. S., & Frontini, F. (2013). Solar Energy Integration- Challenge and Chance for Conservation Architects. *Advanced Building Skins Conference Proceedings of the 8th ENERGY FORUM. EF ECONOMIC FORUM, Advanced Building Skins.*, (pp. 207–211). Supsi. https://repository.supsi.ch/3068/1/Energy%20Forum_CP_Preprint.pdf

REN21 Renewables 2022 Global Status Report. (2022). REN21 Secretariat. https://www.ren21.net/wp-content/uploads/2019/05/GSR2022_Full_Report.pdf

Scaling Up Renewable Energy Investment in India in the Wake of COVID-19. (2021). IRENA Coalition for Action. https://coalition.irena.org/-/media/Files/IRENA/Coalition-for-Action/Publication/Scaling-up-Renewable-Energy-Investment-in-Emerging-Markets/IRENA-Coalition-for-Action_India_2021.pdf?la=en&hash=E56FB23DF6F70A840CA98B49B04D18040F932BBA

Shafiullah, M., Ahmed, S. D., & Al-Sulaiman, F. A. (2022). Grid Integration Challenges and Solution Strategies for Solar PV Systems: A Review. *IEEE Access : Practical Innovations, Open Solutions, 10*, 52233–52257. doi:10.1109/ACCESS.2022.3174555

Solar mini-grids: E-handbook (Version 1). (2020). International Solar Alliance. https://isolaralliance.org/uploads/docs/17675f3aa6ffa28afa08b186591b17.pdf

Sterchele, P., Palzer, A., & Henning, H.-M. (2018). Electrify Everything?: Exploring the Role of the Electric Sector in a Nearly CO_2-Neutral National Energy System. *IEEE Power & Energy Magazine, 16*(4), 24–33. doi:10.1109/MPE.2018.2824100

T&D India. (2020, October 9). *Smart Power India launches Technical Guide for Solar Hybrid Mini-grids.* T&D India. https://www.tndindia.com/smart-power-india-launches-technical-guide-solar-hybrid-mini-grid/

Verma, K. (2022, February 2). *Union Budget 2022: Impact of Solar PLI Scheme.* Invest Media. https://www.investindia.gov.in/team-india-blogs/union-budget-2022-impact-solar-pli-scheme

Year End Review 2023 of Ministry of new & renewable energy, Govt. of India. (2023). PIB. https://pib.gov.in/ErrorPage.html?aspxerrorpath=/pib.gov.in/Pressreleaseshare.aspx

Chapter 14

Some Aspects of Data Engineering for Edge Computing Using Microservice Design Pattern

Pranjit Kakati
Assam Don Bosco University, India

Abhijit Bora
(iD) https://orcid.org/0000-0002-7754-639X
Assam Don Bosco University, India

ABSTRACT

With the rapid advancement and usage of technology like smart devices, sensors, IoT devices etc. the cloud computing technology is facing challenges of high response time, latency, high load on network due to explosion of data in the recent times. Edges computing technology emerges as solution for this down sides of Cloud computing by bringing the computation and processing of Cloud computing to the edge of the network i.e closer to the source of data. The application developed to run in Edge computing uses Microservices due to its advantages of lightweight, independent deployment, loosely coupled and scalability characteristics. In the research community, the deployment of microservices using microservice design patterns and analysis of performance metrics is an important discussion point. Here, a novel methodology will be proposed in edge computing environment using microservice orchestration. Here, the details of Edge computing and microservice architecture using microservice design patterns will be discussed.

DOI: 10.4018/979-8-3693-2260-4.ch014

Figure 1. Basic edge computing architecture

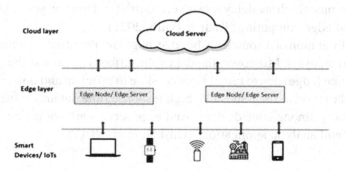

1. INTRODUCTION

With fast pace of advancement of information Technology and 5G communication, smart phones, IoT devices and sensors are becoming more and more popular and important part of our daily life. And that lead to huge increase of data generation and transmission in the network. The role played by centralised data centre or cloud and different services of cloud computing such as google cloud, Microsoft Azure, Amazon Web Services are amazing. Cloud computing has changed the way of our living and working, since its inception around 2005 (Shi et al., 2016). Software-as-a-service(SaaS), Plateform-as-a-service and Infrastructure-as-a-service of cloud computing changed dramatically how we use data and how we work. However, recent advancement of delay sensitive and resource-intensive Internet of Things (IoT) applications like high-definition videos, virtual reality, augmented reality, face recognition etc. are creating difficulty to maintain scalability and resiliency of traditional cloud computing paradigm. In recent times, there is a continuous increase of data generations and the requirement of processing of data in the cloud are diversified, leads to requirement of high transmission bandwidth, minimum response time, energy consumption, latency etc. In this scenario, it is difficult to meet requirements of users maintaining quality of service by cloud (B. Liu et al., 2022). The challenges faced by cloud computing for high responds time, latency and high load in the virtually unlimited resources to delay sensitive applications are reduced by the emergence of edge computing paradigm (Wang et al., 2019).

Edge computing is a recent technology that brings services of cloud computing closer to the end user i.e closer to the source of data and is characterised by fast processing and application response time. The advantage of edge computing is that data generated from the sensors, IoTs or smart devices does not required to transmit to cloud continuously to process and respond, which lowers the bandwidth requirement and energy consumption, improve response time, latency and security. The applications which are delay sensitive, required real time response get maximum advantage of edge computing (Kaur & Batth, 2021).

Due the limitation of resources at the edge, huge amount of data remains underused for potential analysis. Moreover, the data value effectively lost at the proximity of the data source (edge) due to remain inaccessible to efficient and powerful analytics in the cloud to resolve the issues like high response time, latency issue and limited interoperability among edge devices. And edge servers are not resourceful enough to run high end analytic applications (Dustdar et al., 2017).

2. MICROSERVICES IN EDGE

For edge application, deployment of microservice architecture is a suitable approach because of its lightweight characteristic and different design patterns. In microservice architecture for development of applications which are service-oriented is split into small units (Al-Doghman et al., 2023). Microservices are small, independent, loosely coupled autonomous unit of executable codes unlike traditional monolithic architecture and developed for business requirements, where each microservice perform a specific task (Hossain et al., 2023).

Application software is typically designed as a single solution using a monolithic architecture. Few programming languages can be used in this architecture design to create a single application or process that consists of numerous classes, procedures, and packages. The entire application or process is then performed on a single server, regardless of the application requirements. Unfortunately, because any overload in one of its functions might result in a bottleneck and changes to one function can have an impact on other dependent functions, it has poor scalability. Moreover, this design increases the difficulty of resolving the physical heterogeneity problem and the complexity of redeployment and maintenance. The current adoption of microservice design, which divides a single solution or application into smaller, more manageable services, is a means of addressing these flaws. Each and every Microservice carries out a particular task and is separate from the others. Additionally, any computer language can be utilized to implement each offered tiny services. Therefore, the term "Microservice Architecture" refers to the division of a software system into independently deployable autonomous components that cooperate to achieve a specific business purpose while corresponding through lightweight, language-neutral mechanisms. Microservices are now being incorporated into service-oriented architecture in order to overcome issues with the limitations of monolithic architecture. Systems like Netflix, Amazon, SoundClouds are examples of successful microservice architecture. Development, deployment and scaling of

Figure 2. Representation of monolithic vs. microservice architecture

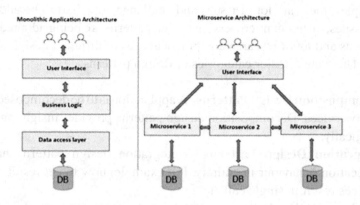

microservices application at the edge for perform data processing locally, different design patterns on the basis of different complexity requirement to be adapted. The success of implementation of microservice architecture depends on suitable use of design patterns. A nos. of patterns have been proposed in few articles, whitepapers, blogs etc. (Akbulut & Perros, 2019). As microservices are still a relatively new trend, it is unclear about the relationships among quality attributes, metrics, and design patterns. The architectural components utilized to build a system are extended by pattern structures to enables fulfilment the quality attributes and satisfy the requirements of stakeholders (Valdivia et al., 2020).

3. MICROSERVICE DESIGN PATTERNS

Microservices architectures are made up of loosely coupled, reusable, and independent units that often work independently of one another. Microservices of an application communicate via application programming interfaces (APIs) and individual microservice perform a specific business functionality or task that makes them more agile, resilient and scalable. Because of independence characteristics, microservices build services that are more fault-tolerant than other architecture. The three main rules that required to be satisfied by a microservice oriented application are –

a) **Independent** – Microservice should be deployed independently
b) **Coupling** – All microservices should be loosely coupled among them so that changes or fault in one microservice should not affect other microservices
c) **Business goal** – Each microservice in an application which should be capable of delivering specific business goal.

The microservice is a complicated architectural paradigm and to fulfil these rules and principles, there are lot of issues and challenges required to be addressed. To solve the issues, different microservice design patterns are being adopted by several organizations and lot of research and practical uses of different design patterns are going on. There are 5 major categories of design patterns.

1. **Decomposition Design Patterns** - A application is to be decomposed in smaller microservices. Decomposition design patterns provides insight on how to do it logically.
2. **Integration Design Patterns** - Integration design patterns handles the application behaviour in entirety. For example, how to get result of multiple services result in single call etc.
3. **Database Design Patterns** - Database design patterns deals with how to define database architecture for microservices like each service should have a separate database per service or use a shared database and so.
4. **Observability Design patterns** - Observability design patterns consider tracking of logging, performance metrices and so.
5. **Cross Cutting Design Patterns** - Cross Cutting Concern Design Patterns deals with service discovery, external configurations, deployment scenarios etc.

3.1. (a) API Gateway - API Gateway is a integration design pattern of microservices. Different microservices in a large application may use different protocols and in such situation, issues arises in communication by users. Implementation of API gateway will make a single entry point for all users to handles all the request. API gateway resides between users and services and provides centralized management of communications between them via APIs.

Figure 3. Representation of API gateway microservice design pattern

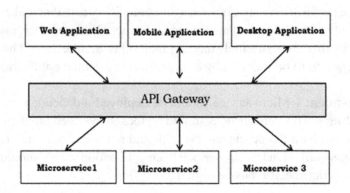

Figure 4. Representation of aggregator microservice design pattern

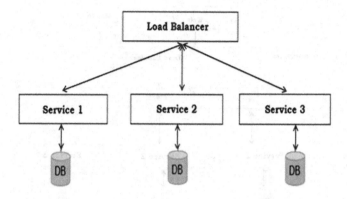

(b) **Aggregator** – In a microservice architecture, a aggregator design pattern which is a integration design is used when the combined result of more than one microservices is required as a output. Aggregator may be act as load balancer which is responsible for calling different services as per user's requirement. This pattern reduces communication overheads between users and services.

(c) **Proxy** – While developing a large application using microservice architecture with lot of microservices often required a unified interface for execution of similar tasks like authorization, validation etc. of user's request. In this context, proxy design pattern will serve as additional layer of control and abstraction in microservice architecture. No business logic is executed by Proxy pattern. Proxy Pattern may be used when there is a requirement of interaction with external service.

(d) **Branch** - Branch is a integration design pattern. In case, in an application one service depends on another service, i.e one service needs output of another service to run, then branch microservice design patterns may be deployed. In branch, one service can communicate more than one services concurrently at a time. This pattern can be used when multiple services have to handle a request or to make parallel calls to multiple services or one service needs output of another service. Moreover, in branch pattern, it is easy to add new microservice in chain in future.

(e) **Shared database per service** – It is database design pattern. Shared database per service may be used when a single database required to be shared among different microservices in an application. Here, each microservice can access the same database and the database have to maintain Atomicity, Consistency, Isolation and Durability (ACID) property.

Figure 5. Representation of proxy microservice design pattern

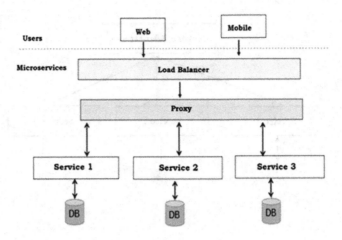

Figure 6. Representation of branch microservice design pattern

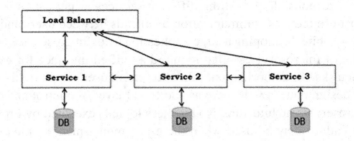

Figure 7. Representation of shared database per service microservice design pattern

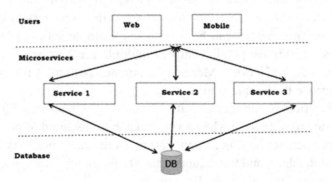

Figure 8. Representation of saga microservice design pattern

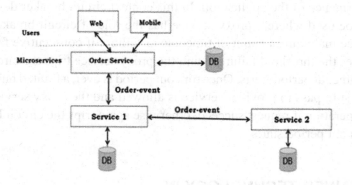

Figure 9. Representation of circuit breaker microservice design pattern

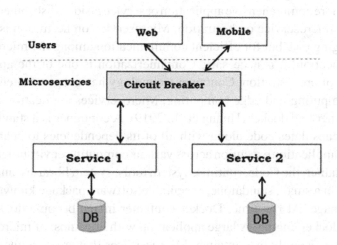

(f) **Saga** – The database design pattern Saga is sequence of transactions where each transaction update a database and triggers an event for next transaction. If a transaction fails, the saga will execute a series of compensating transaction to undo the changes made in the database by the previously executed transaction so that data consistency maintained.

(g) **Circuit Breaker** – In Microservice Architecture, an application is divided into a set of loosely coupled microservices which independently deployed and these services communicate among themselves as per requirement. In some cases, one services may be overloaded or unavoidable and the caller service need to wait or blocked. In such way, if multiple services are blocked then it will hamper the performance of the application. In this context circuit breaker design pattern may be used where a proxy service has the role of circuit breaker. A proxy service maintains a count of timeouts or failure. If consecutive failure count crosses the threshold failure count, the proxy service trips the circuit breaker and timeout period starts. Once timeout period is over, a limited number of test request to pass to provider service is allowed and the proxy service resumed the operation if request succeed, otherwise again trips the circuit breaker and times out period starts.

4. CONTAINER TECHNOLOGY IN MICROSERVICE ARCHITECTURE

The process of managing and arranging separate microservices so that they cooperate to deliver a more comprehensive application or service inside a distributed architecture is known as microservice orchestration. Microservice orchestration is bit complex and challenging task but for efficient communication among the microservices for a large application, it is necessary. Containerization is one of the approaches for deployment of orchestration. Container technology has got great attention recently in cloud computing and edge computing. Microservices application are deployed using container like docker (Huang et al., 2019). A container is a standard software unit that encapsulates code along with all of its dependencies to enable rapid and dependable application execution across various computing environments. In case of Docker container, the Code, runtime, system tools, system libraries, and settings are all included in a small, standalone, executable software package known as a Docker container image. At run time, Docker container image become docker container execute on docker engine. A large application with huge nos. of microservices can be managed efficiently by container. Microservices that are containerized provide lower overhead, more portability, quicker application development, and simpler microservices architecture adoption. (Alam et al., 2018). Unlike a virtual machine (VM), containers do not require to contain image for operating system and that makes containers lightweight and portable and reduces overhead required for hosting. And this is why container technology is most suitable for microservice architecture to manage the microservices in edge computing

Figure 10. Representation of Docker container

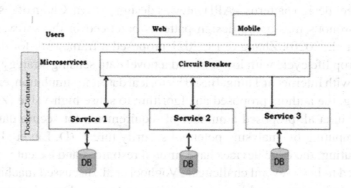

5. RELATED WORKS

In the year 2018, Larrucea et al. discussed about microservice architecture and the methodology to be used to deploy for data processing, (Larrucea et al., n.d.) . However, experimental assessment of the proposed model is lacking in the study. Liu et al. presented an overview for deployment of computational logic using service oriented architecture - monolithic and microservice. Although, the study put light on the key important points against threshold values, but lack of statistical evidence against methodology. Qu et al. investigate policies of deployment for multiple microservices on edge computing platform. The author has used docker container in the microservice architecture and demonstrate performance and interference of microservices. (Qu et al., n.d.). Aitlmoudden et al. proposed a microservices-based framework for computation and data analysis with integration of IoT to build a adaptable, maintainable, fast and efficient data analysis system. The framework will be efficient for faster data processing and data analysis, maintaining fault tolerance. But practical application and validation in real world is lacking in the study (Aitlmoudden et al., 2023). Dustdar et al. propose a unified cloud and edge data analytic platform which is a serverless computing at the edge. (Dustdar et al., 2017). Microservices lead organizations to get the benefits of true service oriented architecture by making more availability of business process and data. Vale et al., 2022 conduct empirical study on practioners perceive impacts on 14 different design patterns of microservices on 7 quality attributes. The authors present a report on interview regarding industry expertise on adaptation of design patterns, architectural trade-offs and metrics used to measure quality attributes (Vale et al., 2022). Valdivia et al. represents review of design of microservices based systems for microservice related design patterns, relative quality attributes and metrics (Valdivia et al., 2020). Akbulut & Perros, 2019 presents reports of obtained performance results related to query response time, hardware usage, hosting costs, and packet loss rate, for three microservices design patterns – API Gateway design pattern, Chain of responsibility and asynchronous messaging design patterns practiced in the software industry (Valdivia et al., 2020). Zhang & Li, 2021 proposed a framework for data sensing for entire crop life cycle with low cost and a novel data sensing strategy using edge computing with Internet of Thing. Based historical data and simulation, environment data sensing, the authors proposed an algorithm to sense high-value (Zhang & Li, 2021). D. Liu et al. proposed a number of requirements for secure data analytics in edge computing by analysing potential security threat. (D. Liu et al., 2019). In edge computing, the edge devices have limited resources and execute applications is considered to have several challenges. Voghoei et al. discussed machine learning method Deep Learning and recent advancement to map Deep Learning in edge computing paradigm (Voghoei et al., n.d.).

6. METHODOLOGY AND DEPLOYMENT STRATEGY

The key objective of the proposed work is to make an experimental setup of edge computing and deploy microservice architecture using microservice design pattern to analyse performance metrics like response time, Throughput and hits/sec. Sensor data has been generated to analyse the performance of edge computing. The generated data if valid, will be fetch by two nos. microservices, developed using spring boot in eclipse integrated development environment (IDE). The microservice execute computation functions and return the result/response. Here, we deploy microservice branch pattern where both the two microservices run parallelly and return values concurrently. Java spring boot is used in eclipse IDE to develop microservices. The execution of microservice is observed using apacheJMeter (Apache JMeter, 2023). The performance metrics response time, latency and his/sec is observed to evaluate the responsiveness of microservice. The flow chart of the system is in Figure 11.

In the experiment, the performance metrics – response time, throughput and hits per second is observed to evaluate the responsiveness of 2 nos. microservices executed concurrently. The performance against increase of thread of 150 consecutive user request are observed individually as well as considering together to observed the co-relation among the metrics. A data sample of 30 records from the thread group of 100 users are considered. The descriptive statistics for the data sample are shown in table 1.

To observe the distribution of the sample data against response time, throughput and hits per second, evaluation of recorded sample using normal probability plot is done. The plot of normalities for the metrics conclude that the data distribution is normal in nature. To evaluate further using Multiple Linear Regression Analysis

Figure 11. Representation of flow chart of proposed microservice architecture

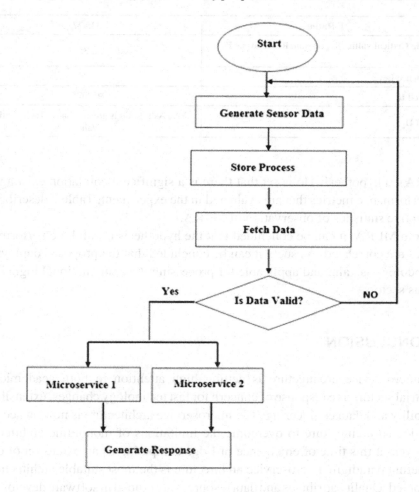

Table 1. Descriptive statistics of data sample

Parameter	Response Time	Throughput	Hits/sec
Mean	5.7	1293.8	8.066
Standard Deviation	0.82	422.06	2.62
Median	5.58	1349.5	8
Mode	5	1429	8

Table 2. Descriptive statistics: MLRA of data sample

F Ratio	345.77
F Table Critical value (Regression, Residual) i.e F(2, 27)	3.35
Confidence Level	95%
Adjusted R^2	95.96%
Accept H_0	Yes, As F Ratio is greater than F Table Critical Value

(MLRA), a hypothesis Ho is set that there is a significant corelation exist against the performance metrics that are evaluated in the experiment. Table 2 describes the descriptive statistics of observation of MLRA.

From MLRA, it can be concluded that the hypothesis is valid, i.e performance metrics are correlated. As such, it can be concluded that the proposed deployment methodology is valid and applicable for processing the computational logic in the various sectors.

7. CONCLUSION

The microservice architecture is getting high attention to both academic and industrial sectors as a response of concern for fast technology changes, extensibility, scalability and data engineering. The microservice architecture is now an accepted and adopted architecture to overcome the limitations of monolithic architecture. Moreover, at this time of emergence of Edge computing as an extension of cloud computing paradigm, microservice architecture is the most suitable architecture to be adopted. Quality attributes and data resources are crucial in software development since satisfaction level has fundamental impact on overall success of a software project. The choice of architecture and selection of design pattern in microservice architecture renders the fulfilment of quality attributes of a software or application. In recent time, cloud and edge computing, microservice architecture are the prime focus area for industrial as well as academic prospect. Further, with the advancement of smart devices and IoTs, edge computing with deployment of microservices for monitoring and performance in the field of agriculture, health, retail etc. is utmost necessary specially in case of time critical and latency sensitive applications. But research on these fields and experimental study is required. There are tremendous scope for study on the insights regarding methods for designing microservice system and experiments on implementation of different design patterns for different problems faced by professionals exist. In this article, the basics of edge computing, microservice architecture, few popular design patterns from data engineering prospective are discussed.

REFERENCES

Aitlmoudden, O., Housni, M., Safeh, N., & Namir, A. (2023). A Microservices-based Framework for Scalable Data Analysis in Agriculture with IoT Integration. *International Journal of Interactive Mobile Technologies*, *17*(19), 147–156. doi:10.3991/ijim.v17i19.40457

Akbulut, A., & Perros, H. G. (2019). Performance Analysis of Microservice Design Patterns. *IEEE Internet Computing*, *23*(6), 19–27. doi:10.1109/MIC.2019.2951094

Al-Doghman, F., Moustafa, N., Khalil, I., Sohrabi, N., Tari, Z., & Zomaya, A. Y. (2023). AI-Enabled Secure Microservices in Edge Computing: Opportunities and Challenges. *IEEE Transactions on Services Computing*, *16*(2), 1485–1504. doi:10.1109/TSC.2022.3155447

Alam, M., Rufino, J., Ferreira, J., Ahmed, S. H., Shah, N., & Chen, Y. (2018). Orchestration of Microservices for IoT Using Docker and Edge Computing. *IEEE Communications Magazine*, *56*(9), 118–123. doi:10.1109/MCOM.2018.1701233

Dustdar, S., Nastic, S., Rausch, T., & Scekic, O. Tu, Gusev, W. M., Koteska, B., Kostoska, M., Jakimovski, B., Ristov, S., & Prodan, R. (2017). *Internet of Things, People, and Processes A Serverless Real-Time Data Analytics Platform for Edge Computing*. AWS. https://aws.amazon.com/

Hossain, Md. D., Sultana, T., Akhter, S., Hossain, M. I., Thu, N. T., Huynh, L. N. T., Lee, G.-W., & Huh, E.-N. (2023). The role of microservice approach in edge computing: Opportunities, challenges, and research directions. *ICT Express*. doi:10.1016/j.icte.2023.06.006

Huang, Y., Zong, R., Cai, K., & Mao, Y. (2019). Design and implementation of an edge computing platform architecture using docker and kubernetes for machine learning. *ACM International Conference Proceeding Series*, (pp. 29–32). ACM. 10.1145/3318265.3318288

Kaur, G., & Batth, R. S. (2021). Edge Computing: Classification, Applications, and Challenges. *Proceedings of 2021 2nd International Conference on Intelligent Engineering and Management, ICIEM 2021*, (pp. 254–259). ACM. 10.1109/ICIEM51511.2021.9445331

Larrucea, M. X., Santamaria, I., Colomo-Palacios, R., & Ebert, C. (n.d.). *SOFTWARE TECHNOLOGY*.

Liu, B., Luo, Z., Chen, H., & Li, C. (2022). A Survey of State-of-the-art on Edge Computing: Theoretical Models, Technologies, Directions, and Development Paths. *IEEE Access: Practical Innovations, Open Solutions, 10*, 54038–54063. doi:10.1109/ACCESS.2022.3176106

Liu, D., Yan, Z., Ding, W., & Atiquzzaman, M. (2019). A survey on secure data analytics in edge computing. *IEEE Internet of Things Journal, 6*(3), 4946–4967. doi:10.1109/JIOT.2019.2897619

Qu, Q., Xu, R., Nikouei, Y., & Chen, Y. (n.d.). *An Experimental Study on Microservices based Edge Computing Platforms*. Open Group. http://www.opengroup.org/soa/source-book/msawp/p3.htm

Shi, W., Cao, J., Zhang, Q., Li, Y., & Xu, L. (2016). Edge Computing: Vision and Challenges. *IEEE Internet of Things Journal, 3*(5), 637–646. doi:10.1109/JIOT.2016.2579198

Valdivia, J. A., Lora-González, A., Limón, X., Cortes-Verdin, K., & Ocharán-Hernández, J. O. (2020). Patterns Related to Microservice Architecture: A Multivocal Literature Review. *Programming and Computer Software, 46*(8), 594–608. doi:10.1134/S0361768820080253

ValeG.CorreiaF. F.GuerraE. M.RosaT. de O.FritzschJ.BognerJ. (2022). *Designing Microservice Systems Using Patterns: An Empirical Study on Quality Trade-Offs*. http://arxiv.org/abs/2201.03598 doi:10.1109/ICSA53651.2022.00015

Voghoei, S., Tonekaboni, N. H., Wallace, J. G., & Arabnia, H. R. (n.d.). *Deep Learning at the Edge*.

Wang, J., Pan, J., Esposito, F., Calyam, P., Yang, Z., & Mohapatra, P. (2019). Edge cloud offloading algorithms: Issues, methods, and perspectives. *ACM Computing Surveys, 52*(1), 1–23. Advance online publication. doi:10.1145/3284387

Zhang, R., & Li, X. (2021). Edge computing driven data sensing strategy in the entire crop lifecycle for smart agriculture. *Sensors (Basel), 21*(22), 7502. doi:10.3390/s21227502 PMID:34833575

Compilation of References

V's Of Big Data – CopyAssignment. (n.d.). PathStream. https://copyassignment.com/3-vs-of-big-data/

Aalborg University. (n.d.). *The Brackish Dataset.* Kaggle. https://www.kaggle.com/aalborguniversity/brackish-dataset

Abbood, A. A., Salih, M. A., & Mohammed, A. Y. (2018). Modeling and simulation of 1 MW grid connected photovoltaic system in Karbala city. *International Journal of Energy and Environment, 9*(2), 153–168.

Abnoosian, K., Farnoosh, R., & Behzadi, M. H. (2023). Prediction of diabetes disease using an ensemble of machine learning multi-classifier models. *BMC Bioinformatics, 24*(1), 337. doi:10.1186/s12859-023-05465-z PMID:37697283

Acharjya, D. P., & Ahmed, K. (2016). A survey on big data analytics: Challenges, open research issues and tools. *International Journal of Advanced Computer Science and Applications, 7*(2), 511–518.

Ahmed, E., Yaqoob, I., Hashem, I. A. T., Khan, I., Ahmed, A. I. A., Imran, M., & Vasilakos, A. V. (2017). The role of big data analytics in internet of things. *Computer Networks, 129*, 459–471. doi:10.1016/j.comnet.2017.06.013

Ahmed, N., Ahammed, R., Islam, M. M., Uddin, M. A., Akhter, A., Talukder, M. A., & Paul, B. K. (2021). Md. Manowarul Islam, Md. Ashraf Uddin, Arnisha Akhter, Md. Alamin Talukder, Bikash Kumar Paul, Machine learning based diabetes prediction and development of smart web application. *International Journal of Cognitive Computing in Engineering, 2*(June), 229–241. doi:10.1016/j.ijcce.2021.12.001

Aitlmoudden, O., Housni, M., Safeh, N., & Namir, A. (2023). A Microservices-based Framework for Scalable Data Analysis in Agriculture with IoT Integration. *International Journal of Interactive Mobile Technologies, 17*(19), 147–156. doi:10.3991/ijim.v17i19.40457

Akbulut, A., & Perros, H. G. (2019). Performance Analysis of Microservice Design Patterns. *IEEE Internet Computing, 23*(6), 19–27. doi:10.1109/MIC.2019.2951094

Akhtarshenas, A., & Toosi, R. (2022). An open-set framework for underwater image classification using autoencoders. *SN Applied Sciences*, *4*(8), 229. doi:10.1007/s42452-022-05105-w

Alam, M., Rufino, J., Ferreira, J., Ahmed, S. H., Shah, N., & Chen, Y. (2018). Orchestration of Microservices for IoT Using Docker and Edge Computing. *IEEE Communications Magazine*, *56*(9), 118–123. doi:10.1109/MCOM.2018.1701233

Al-Doghman, F., Moustafa, N., Khalil, I., Sohrabi, N., Tari, Z., & Zomaya, A. Y. (2023). AI-Enabled Secure Microservices in Edge Computing: Opportunities and Challenges. *IEEE Transactions on Services Computing*, *16*(2), 1485–1504. doi:10.1109/TSC.2022.3155447

Alizadeh, M., & Ma, J. (2021). A comparitive study of series hybrid approaches to model and predict the Vehicle operating states. *Computers & Industrial Engineering*, *162*, 107770. doi:10.1016/j.cie.2021.107770

Alshahrani, A., Omer, S., Su, Y., Mohamed, E., & Alotaibi, S. (2019). The Technical Challenges Facing the Integration of Small-Scale and Large-scale PV Systems into the Grid: A Critical Review. *Electronics (Basel)*, *8*(12), 1443. doi:10.3390/electronics8121443

Al-Zebari, A., & Sengur, A. (2019, November). Performance comparison of machine learning techniques on diabetes disease detection. In *2019 1st International Informatics and software engineering conference (UBMYK)* (pp. 1-4). IEEE. 10.1109/UBMYK48245.2019.8965542

Ambigavathi, M., & Sridharan, D. (2018). Big Data Analytics in Healthcare. *2018 Tenth International Conference on Advanced Computing (ICoAC)*, Chennai, India. 10.1109/ICoAC44903.2018.8939061

Angadi, S., Yaragatti, U. R., Suresh, Y., & Raju, A. B. (2021). Comprehensive Review on Solar, Wind and Hybrid Wind-PV Water Pumping Systems-An Electrical Engineering Perspective. *CPSS Transactions on Power Electronics and Applications*, *6*(1), 1–19. doi:10.24295/CPSSTPEA.2021.00001

Anusha, N., Chaitanya, M. S., & Reddy, G. J. (2019). Weather Prediction using Multi Linear Regression algorithm. *Material Science and Engineering. IOP Conference Series.*

Artificial Intelligence, Machine Learning and Big Data in Finance. (n.d.). OECD. https://www.oecd.org/finance/artificial-intelligence-machine-learning-big-data-in-finance.htm

Bagane, P., Kandula, S. R., Saxena, A., Das, S., Deepak, A., & Rao, S. G. (2023). Intelligent System for Prediction of Potentially Hazardous Nearest Earth Objects Using Machine Learning. *International Journal of Intelligent Systems and Applications in Engineering*, *12*(1s), 71–80. https://ijisae.org/index.php/IJISAE/article/view/3396

Bahel, V., Bhongade, P., Sharma, J., Shukla, S., & Gaikwad, M. (2021). Supervised Classification for Analysis and Detection of Potentially Hazardous Asteroids. *2021 International Conference on Computational Intelligence and Computing Applications*. IEEE. 10.1109/ICCICA52458.2021.9697222

Baitule, A. S., & Sudhakar, K. (2017). Solar powered green campus: A simulation study. *The International Journal of Low Carbon Technologies, 12*(4), 400–410. doi:10.1093/ijlct/ctx011

Baldini, I., Castro, P., Chang, K., Cheng, P., Fink, S., Ishakian, V., Mitchell, N., Muthusamy, V., Rabbah, R., & Slominski, A. (2017). Research Advances in Cloud Computing. Springer; Berlin/Heidelberg.

Barua, S., Prasath, R. A., & Boruah, D. (2017, February). Rooftop Solar Photovoltaic System Design and Assessment for the Academic Campus Using PVsyst Software. *International Journal of Electronics and Electrical Engineering, 5*(1), 76–83. doi:10.18178/ijeee.5.1.76-83

Bastiaanssen, W. G. M. (2015). A new satellite-based methodology for assessing and mapping the impact of floods on rice agriculture. *Agricultural Water Management, 149*, 38–53.

Basu, V. (2019). Prediction of Asteroid Diameter with the Help of Multi-Layer Perceptron Regressor. *International Journal of Advances in Electronics and Computer Science, 6*(4), 36–40. http://www.iraj.in/journal/journal_file/journal_pdf/12-555-156136953136-40.pdf

Benos, L., Tagarakis, A. C., Dolias, G., Berruto, R., Kateris, D., & Bochtis, D. (2021). Machine learning in agriculture: A comprehensive updated review. *Sensors (Basel), 21*(11), 3758. doi:10.3390/s21113758 PMID:34071553

Bethi, S. K., & Deshmukh, S. S. (2023) Challenges and Opportunities for Agri-Tech Startups in Developing Economies. *International Journal of AgricultureSciences, 15*(9), 12661-12666

Bhat, S. S., Selvam, V., Ansari, G. A., & Ansari, M. D. (2022). *Analysis of Diabetes mellitus using Machine Learning Techniques.* 2022 5th International Conference on Multimedia, Signal Processing and Communication Technologies (IMPACT), Aligarh, India. 10.1109/IMPACT55510.2022.10029058

Bhavsar, R., Jadav, N. K., Bodkhe, U., Gupta, R., Tanwar, S., Sharma, G., Bokoro, P. N., & Sharma, R. (2023). Classification of Potentially Hazardous Asteroids Using Supervised Quantum Machine Learning. *IEEE Access : Practical Innovations, Open Solutions, 11*, 75829–75848. doi:10.1109/ACCESS.2023.3297498

Bhavya, M. R., Sanjay, H. C., Suraj, S. K., Savant, A., & Sanjay, M. (2020). Diabetes Prediction using Machine Learning. *IJARCCE, 9*.

Böer, G., Veeramalli, R., & Schramm, H. (2021). Segmentation of Fish in Realistic Underwater Scenes using Lightweight Deep Learning Models. In ROBOVIS (pp. 158- 164). doi:10.5220/0010712700003061

Box, G. E., Jenkins, G. M., & Reinsel, G. C. (2011). *Time series analysis:Forecasting and Control.* John Wiley and Sons.

Breivold, H., & Sandstrom, K. (2015). Internet of Things for Industrial Automation — Challenges and Technical Solutions. *2015 IEEE International Conference on Data Science and Data Intensive Systems.* IEEE. 10.1109/DSDIS.2015.11

Brunton, S. L., Nathan Kutz, J., Manohar, K., Aravkin, A. Y., Morgansen, K., Klemisch, J., Goebel, N., Buttrick, J., Poskin, J., Blom-Schieber, A. W., Hogan, T., & McDonald, D. (2021). Data-driven aerospace engineering: Reframing the industry with machine learning. *AIAA Journal*, *59*(8), 2820–2847. doi:10.2514/1.J060131

Cai, L., McGuire, N. E., Hanlon, R., Mooney, T. A., & Girdhar, Y. (2023). Semi-supervised Visual Tracking of Marine Animals Using Autonomous Underwater Vehicles. *International Journal of Computer Vision*, *131*(6), 1406–1427. doi:10.1007/s11263-023-01762-5

Chai, T., & Dexler, R. R. (2014). Root mean Square error or Mean Absolute Error-Arguements avoiding RMSE in the literature. *Geoscience model devlopment*, *7*(3), 1247-1250.

Changmai, P., Kumar, S., Nayak, S. K., & Metya, S. K. (2022). Maximum Power Estimation of Total Cross-Tied Connected PV Cells in Different Shading Conditions for High Current Application. *IEEE Journal of Emerging and Selected Topics in Power Electronics*, *10*(4), 3883–3894. doi:10.1109/JESTPE.2021.3105808

Charitha, C., & Chaitrasree, A. Devi, Varma, P. C. & Lakshmi, C. (2022). *Type-II Diabetes Prediction Using Machine Learning Algorithms*. 2022 International Conference on Computer Communication and Informatics (ICCCI), Coimbatore, India. 10.1109/ICCCI54379.2022.9740844

Chen, S., Xu, H., Liu, D., Hu, B., & Wang, H. (2014). A Vision of IoT: Applications, Challenges, and Opportunities With China Perspective. *IEEE Internet of Things Journal*, *1*(4), 349–359. doi:10.1109/JIOT.2014.2337336

Chen, X., Yuan, M., Fan, C., Chen, X., Li, Y., & Wang, H. (2023). Research on an Underwater Object Detection Network Based on Dual-Branch Feature Extraction. *Electronics (Basel)*, *12*(16), 3413. doi:10.3390/electronics12163413

Chen, X., Yuan, M., Yang, Q., Yao, H., & Wang, H. (2023). Underwater-YCC: Underwater Target Detection Optimization Algorithm Based on YOLOv7. *Journal of Marine Science and Engineering*, *11*(5), 995. doi:10.3390/jmse11050995

Chung, J., Gulcehre, C., Cho, K., & Bengio, Y. (2014). Empirical evaluation of Gated Recurrent neural network on Sequence Modelling. *arxiv*.

Dakhil, R. A., & Khayeat, A. R. H. (2022). Review On Deep Learning Technique For Underwater Object Detection. *arXiv preprint arXiv:2209.10151*. doi:10.5121/csit.2022.121505

Data Management Study: The Past, Present, and Future of Data. (n.d.). DNB. https://www.dnb.com/perspectives/master-data/data-management-report.html

De Baets, S. (2019). Decision Support Systems in Agriculture: A Systematic Review. *Computers and Electronics in Agriculture*, *157*, 112–125.

Deb, K., & Kailash, S. (2023, September 5). *Mainstreaming the Energy Transition in India's Policy Framework*. Center on Global Energy Policy at Columbia University SIPA | CGEP. https://www.energypolicy.columbia.edu/mainstreaming-the-energy-transition-in-indias-policy-framework/

del Rio, J., Toma, D. M., Martinez, E., O'Reilly, T. C., Delory, E., Pearlman, J. S., Waldmann, C., & Jirka, S. (2018). A Sensor Web Architecture For Integrating Smart Oceanographic Sensors Into The Semantic Sensor Web [Institute Of Electrical And Electronics Engineers] [IEEE]. *IEEE Journal of Oceanic Engineering, 43*(4), 830–842. doi:10.1109/JOE.2017.2768178

Deng, L., & Yu, D. (2014). Deep Learning: Methods and Applications. *Foundations and Trends in Signal Processing Series.* Research Gate.

Dmitry, N., & Manfred, S. S. (2014). On micro-services architecture. *International Journal of Open Information Technologies, 2*(9).

Drusch, M., Del Bello, U., Carlier, S., Colin, O., Fernandez, V., Gascon, F., Hoersch, B., Isola, C., Laberinti, P., Martimort, P., Meygret, A., Spoto, F., Sy, O., Marchese, F., & Bargellini, P. (2012). Sentinel-2: ESA's Optical High-Resolution Mission for GMES Operational Services. *Remote Sensing of Environment, 120*, 25–36. doi:10.1016/j.rse.2011.11.026

Dustdar, S., Nastic, S., Rausch, T., & Scekic, O. Tu, Gusev, W. M., Koteska, B., Kostoska, M., Jakimovski, B., Ristov, S., & Prodan, R. (2017). *Internet of Things, People, and Processes A Serverless Real-Time Data Analytics Platform for Edge Computing.* AWS. https://aws.amazon.com/

Economic Times. (2023). Leadership Challenges in the Digital Age: Navigating Disruption. *The Economic Times.* https://economictimes.indiatimes.com/jobs/c-suite/leadership-challenges-in-the-digital-age-navigating-disruption/articleshow/104625059.cms?from=mdr

El Massari, H., Sabouri, Z., Mhammedi S., & Gherabi, N. (2022). Diabetes Prediction Using Machine Learning Algorithms and Ontology. *Journal of ICT Standardization, 10*(2), 319–338. doi:10.13052/jicts2245-800X.10212

Elgendy, N., & Elragal, A. (2014). Big data analytics: A literature review paper. Lecture Notes in Computer Science (Including Subseries Lecture Notes in Artificial Intelligence and Lecture Notes in Bioinformatics), 8557 LNAI, (pp. 214–227). Springer. doi:10.1007/978-3-319-08976-8_16

ENERGY AUDIT REPORT OF ASSAM DON BOSCO UNIVERSITY CAMPUSES AT TAPESIA, AZARA AND KHARGHULI. (2020). DB University. https://dbuniversity.ac.in/pdfs/Internal-Energy-Audit-Report-2020.pdf

Evwiekpaefe, A E. & Abdulkadir, N. (2021). *A Predictive Model For Diabetes Using Machine Learning Techniques (A Case Study of Some Selected Hospitals In Kaduna Metropolis).* [Master of Science in Computer Science Theses, Kennesaw State University].

Farajollahi, B., Mehmannavaz, M., Mehrjoo, H., Moghbeli, F., & Sayadi, M. (2021). Diabetes Diagnosis Using Machine Learning. *Frontiers in Health Informatics., 10*(1), 65. doi:10.30699/fhi.v10i1.267

Farhan, L. (2018). A Concise Review On Internet Of Things (Iot) -Problems, Challenges And Opportunities. *2018 11ᵀʰ International Symposium On Communication Systems, Networks & Digital Signal Processing (CSNDSP).* IEEE 10.1109/CSNDSP.2018.8471762

Formolli, M., Croce, S., Vettorato, D., Paparella, R., Scognamiglio, A., Mainini, A. G., & Lobaccaro, G. (2022). Solar Energy in Urban Planning: Lesson Learned and Recommendations from Six Italian Case Studies. *Applied Sciences (Basel, Switzerland)*, *12*(6), 2950. doi:10.3390/app12062950

French, G., Fisher, M., Mackiewicz, M., & Needle, C. (2015). *Convolutional neural networks for counting fish in fisheries surveillance video.*

Galletta, A. (2018). A Microservices-Based Platform For Efficiently Managing Oceanographic Data. 2018 4Th International Conference On Big Data Innovations And Applications (Innovate-Data). IEEE. 10.1109/Innovate-Data.2018.00011

Gandhi, P. (2022). Diabetes Prediction using Machine Learning Techniques. *IJRPR, 3*(2), 77-82.

Gitelson, A. A., Chivkunova, O. B., & Merzlyak, M. N. (2009). Nondestructive estimation of anthocyanins and chlorophylls in anthocyanic leaves. *American Journal of Botany*, *96*(10), 1861–1868. doi:10.3732/ajb.0800395 PMID:21622307

Gracious, L. A., Jasmine, R. M., Pooja, E., Anish, T. P., Johncy, G., & Subramanian, R. S. (2023, October). Machine Learning and Deep Learning Transforming Healthcare: An Extensive Exploration of Applications, Algorithms, and Prospects. In *2023 4th IEEE Global Conference for Advancement in Technology (GCAT)* (pp. 1-6). IEEE.

Graves, A. (2012). Long Short time memory. *Supervised sequence Labelling with recurrent neural network*, 37-45.

Guerra, R. R., Vizziello, A., Savazzib, P., Goldoni, E., & Gamba, P. (2024). Forecasting LoRaWAN RSSI using weather parameters: A comparitive study of ARIMA, artificial intelligence and hybrid approaches. *Computer Networks*, *243*, 110258. doi:10.1016/j.comnet.2024.110258

Guo, C., & Chen, J. (2023). Big data analytics in healthcare. In *Knowledge Technology and Systems: Toward Establishing Knowledge Systems Science* (pp. 27–70). Springer Nature Singapore. doi:10.1007/978-981-99-1075-5_2

Gupta, A. K., Singhal, S., & Garg, R. R. (2018). Challenges and issues in data analytics. *Proceedings - 2018 8th International Conference on Communication Systems and Network Technologies, CSNT 2018*, (pp. 144–150). IEEE. 10.1109/CSNT.2018.8820251

Guyon, I. (2006). *Feature Extraction: Foundations and Applications*. Springer. doi:10.1007/978-3-540-35488-8

Haghverdi, A. (2019). Precision Agriculture Irrigation Management Using Machine Learning Algorithms. *Computers and Electronics in Agriculture*, *161*, 280–294.

Hariri, R. H., Fredericks, E. M., & Bowers, K. M. (2019). Uncertainty in big data analytics: Survey, opportunities, and challenges. *Journal of Big Data*, *6*(1), 1–16. doi:10.1186/s40537-019-0206-3

Hastie, T., Tibshirani, R., & Friedman, J. (2009). *The Elements of Statistical Learning: Data Mining, Inference, and Prediction*. Springer. doi:10.1007/978-0-387-84858-7

Hemdan, E. E. D., El-Shafai, W., & Sayed, A. (2023). Integrating Digital Twins with IoT-Based Blockchain: Concept, Architecture, Challenges, and Future Scope. *Wireless Personal Communications*, *131*(3), 1–24. doi:10.1007/s11277-023-10538-6 PMID:37360142

Hirschhorn, P., & Brijs, T. (2021, December 13). *Rising to the Challenges of Integrating Solar and Wind at Scale*. BCG Global. https://www.bcg.com/publications/2021/addressing-variable-renewable-energy-challenges

Hodge, V. J., & Austin, J. (2004). A Survey of Outlier Detection Methodologies. *Artificial Intelligence Review*, *22*(2), 85–126. doi:10.1023/B:AIRE.0000045502.10941.a9

Holmstorm, M., Dylan, L., & Christopher, V. (2016). *Machine learning applied to weather forecasting*. Meterological Applied.

Hossain, Md. D., Sultana, T., Akhter, S., Hossain, M. I., Thu, N. T., Huynh, L. N. T., Lee, G.-W., & Huh, E.-N. (2023). The role of microservice approach in edge computing: Opportunities, challenges, and research directions. *ICT Express*. doi:10.1016/j.icte.2023.06.006

Huang, Y., Zong, R., Cai, K., & Mao, Y. (2019). Design and implementation of an edge computing platform architecture using docker and kubernetes for machine learning. *ACM International Conference Proceeding Series*, (pp. 29–32). ACM. 10.1145/3318265.3318288

Huld, T. (2017). PV MAPS: Software tools and data for the estimation of solar radiation and photovoltaic module performance over large geographical areas. *Solar Energy*, *142*, 171–181. doi:10.1016/j.solener.2016.12.014

Inoue, Y. (2017). Monitoring Rice Growth for Yield Prediction Based on UAV-SfM 3D Modeling and High-Resolution Satellite Multispectral Imagery. *Remote Sensing*, *9*(1), 53.

Islam, M. T., Raihan, M., Aktar, N., Alam, M. S., Ema, R. R., & Islam, T. (2020). *Diabetes Mellitus Prediction using Different Ensemble Machine Learning Approaches*. 2020 11th International Conference on Computing, Communication and Networking Technologies (ICCCNT), Kharagpur, India. 10.1109/ICCCNT49239.2020.9225551

Islam, N. U., & Khanam, R. (2021). *Classification of Diabetes using Machine Learning*. 2021 International Conference on Computational Performance Evaluation (ComPE), Shillong, India. 10.1109/ComPE53109.2021.9751955

Jacob, P., & Mani, P. (2018). Software architecture pattern selection model for Internet of Things based systems. *IET Software*, *12*(5), 390–396. doi:10.1049/iet-sen.2017.0206

Jaggi, A. K., Sharma, A., Sharma, N., Singh, R., & Chakraborty, P. S. (2021). Diabetes Prediction Using Machine Learning. Intelligent Systems. ResearchGate. doi:10.1007/978-981-33-6081-5_34

Jain, T., Shethia, A., Khanvilkar, S., Patil, L., Devmane, V., & Kodeboyina, S. (2022) Asteroid Detection and Risk Prediction for the Earth. *Advanced Maui Optical and Space Surveillance Technologies Conference*. AMOS Tech. https://amostech.com/TechnicalPapers/2021/Poster/Jain.pdf

Jain, A. (2018). A Comprehensive Review on Genetic Algorithm: Past, Present, and Future. *Applied Intelligence, 48*(12), 4333–4370.

Jakaria, A., Hossain, M. M., & Mohammad, A. (2020). Smart Weather Forecasting Using Machine Learning: A Case Study in Tennessee. *Computers & Society*.

James, G., Witten, D., Hastie, T., Tibshirani, R., & Taylor, J. (2023). *An introduction to statistical learning: with application in R*. Springer Nature. doi:10.1007/978-3-031-38747-0

Jones, A., Bruce, E., Davies, K. P., & Cato, D. H. (2023). Enhancing UAV images to improve the observation of submerged whales using a water column correction method. *Marine Mammal Science, 39*(2), 696–702. doi:10.1111/mms.12994

Jones, H. G. (2004). Irrigation scheduling: Advantages and pitfalls of plant-based methods. *Journal of Experimental Botany, 55*(407), 2427–2436. doi:10.1093/jxb/erh213 PMID:15286143

Jones, H. G. (2013). Use of infrared thermometry for estimation of stomatal conductance as a possible aid to irrigation scheduling. *Agricultural and Forest Meteorology, 177*, 129–139. doi:10.1016/j.agrformet.2013.04.031

Justice, C. O., Vermote, E., Townshend, J. R. G., Defries, R., Roy, D. P., Hall, D. K., Salomonson, V. V., Privette, J. L., Riggs, G., Strahler, A., Lucht, W., Myneni, R. B., Knyazikhin, Y., Running, S. W., Nemani, R. R., Zhengming Wan, Huete, A. R., van Leeuwen, W., Wolfe, R. E., & Barnsley, M. J. (1998). The Moderate Resolution Imaging Spectroradiometer (MODIS): Land remote sensing for global change research. *IEEE Transactions on Geoscience and Remote Sensing, 36*(4), 1228–1249. doi:10.1109/36.701075

Jyoti, R. (2020), Diabetes Prediction Using Machine Learning. IJSRCSEIT, 6(4).

Kalinowska, A., Pilarski, P. M., & Murphey, T. D. (2023). Embodied Communication: How Robots and People Communicate Through Physical Interaction. *Annual Review of Control, Robotics, and Autonomous Systems, 6*(1), 205–232. doi:10.1146/annurev-control-070122-102501

Kalogirou, S. A. (2015). Building integration of solar renewable energy systems towards zero or nearly zero energy buildings. *The International Journal of Low Carbon Technologies, 10*(4), 379–385. doi:10.1093/ijlct/ctt071

Karnowski, J., Hutchins, E., & Johnson, C. (2015, January). Dolphin detection and tracking. In *2015 IEEE Winter Applications and Computer Vision Workshops* (pp. 51- 56). IEEE.

Kaur, G., & Batth, R. S. (2021). Edge Computing: Classification, Applications, and Challenges. *Proceedings of 2021 2nd International Conference on Intelligent Engineering and Management, ICIEM 2021*, (pp. 254–259). ACM. 10.1109/ICIEM51511.2021.9445331

Kaur, J. (2023). Robotic Process Automation in Healthcare Sector. In *E3S Web of Conferences* (Vol. 391, p. 01008). EDP Sciences.

Khaki, S. (2019). A Comprehensive Review on Decision Support Systems for Sustainable Agriculture: A Food-Energy-Water Nexus Perspective. *Sustainability, 11*(13), 3532.

Kim, H., Koo, J., Kim, D., Jung, S., Shin, J. U., Lee, S., & Myung, H. (2016). Image- based monitoring of jellyfish using deep learning architecture. *IEEE Sensors Journal, 16*(8), 2215–2216. doi:10.1109/JSEN.2016.2517823

Kim, M. (2016). A Quality Model for Evaluating IoT Applications. *International Journal of Computer and Electric al Engineering, 8*(1), 66–76. doi:10.17706/IJCEE.2016.8.1.66-76

Kopitar, L., Kocbek, P., Cilar, L., Sheikh, A., & Stiglic, G. (2020). Early detection of type 2 diabetes mellitus using machine learning based prediction models. *Scientific Reports, 10*(1), 11981. doi:10.1038/s41598-020-68771-z PMID:32686721

Kumar, A., Singh, M. P., Ghosh, S., & Anand, A. (2012). Weather forecasting model using artificial neural network. *Procedia Technology*, 311–318.

Kumar, N. M., & Subathra, M. S. P. (2019). Three years ahead solar irradiance forecasting to quantify degradation influenced energy potentials from thin film (a-Si) photovoltaic system. *Results in Physics, 12*, 701–703. doi:10.1016/j.rinp.2018.12.027

Kumar, P. (2016). Applications of Artificial Intelligence Techniques in Agriculture. *Annals of Agricultural Science, 61*(1), 31–41.

Kumar, V. N., Gayathri, S., Deepa, S., Varun, C. M., & Subramanian, R. S. (2023, August). A comprehensive survey of machine learning: Advancements, applications, and challenges. In *2023 Second International Conference on Augmented Intelligence and Sustainable Systems (ICAISS)* (pp. 354-361). IEEE.

Kumi, E. N., & Brew-Hammond, A. (2013). *Design and Analysis of a 1 MW Grid-Connected Solar PV System in Ghana.* ATPS (African Technology Policy Studies Network).

Larrucea, M. X., Santamaria, I., Colomo-Palacios, R., & Ebert, C. (n.d.). *SOFTWARE TECHNOLOGY.*

Lehtola, T., & Zahedi, A. (2020). Technical challenges in the application of renewable energy: A review. *International Journal of Smart Grid and Clean Energy, 9*(3), 689–699. https://www.ijsgce.com/uploadfile/2020/0415/20200415054706240.pdf. doi:10.12720/sgce.9.3.689-699

Leonard, D. K., Bloom, G., Hanson, K., O'Farrell, J., & Spicer, N. (2013). Institutional Solutions to the Asymmetric Information Problem in Health and Development Services for the Poor. *World Development, 48*, 71–87. doi:10.1016/j.worlddev.2013.04.003

Li, J., Xu, W., Deng, L., Xiao, Y., Han, Z., & Zheng, H. (2023). Deep learning for visual recognition and detection of aquatic animals: A review. *Reviews in Aquaculture, 15*(2), 409–433. doi:10.1111/raq.12726

Li, L., Dong, B., Rigall, E., Zhou, T., Dong, J., & Chen, G. (2021). Marine animal segmentation. *IEEE Transactions on Circuits and Systems for Video Technology, 32*(4), 2303–2314. doi:10.1109/TCSVT.2021.3093890

Li, L., Rigall, E., Dong, J., & Chen, G. (2020, November). MAS3K: An open dataset for marine animal segmentation. In *International Symposium on Benchmarking, Measuring and Optimization* (pp. 194-212). Cham: Springer International Publishing.

Lin, X., Li, X., & Lin, X. (2020). A review on applications of computational methods in drug screening and design. *Molecules (Basel, Switzerland)*, 25(6), 1375. doi:10.3390/molecules25061375 PMID:32197324

Li, S., Xu, L. D., & Zhao, S. (2015). The internet of things: A survey. *Information Systems Frontiers*, 17(2), 243–259. doi:10.1007/s10796-014-9492-7

Little, R. J., & Rubin, D. B. (2019). *Statistical analysis with missing data* (Vol. 793). John Wiley & Sons.

Liu, H., & Lang, B. (2019). Machine learning and deep learning methods for intrusion detection systems: A survey. *applied sciences, 9*(20), 4396.

Liu, X., Dastjerdi, A. V., & Buyya, R. (2016). Stream processing in IoT: Foundations, state-of-the-art, and future directions. *Internet of Things: Principles and Paradigms*, 145–161. doi:10.1016/B978-0-12-805395-9.00008-3

Liu, B., Luo, Z., Chen, H., & Li, C. (2022). A Survey of State-of-the-art on Edge Computing: Theoretical Models, Technologies, Directions, and Development Paths. *IEEE Access : Practical Innovations, Open Solutions, 10*, 54038–54063. doi:10.1109/ACCESS.2022.3176106

Liu, D., Yan, Z., Ding, W., & Atiquzzaman, M. (2019). A survey on secure data analytics in edge computing. *IEEE Internet of Things Journal, 6*(3), 4946–4967. doi:10.1109/JIOT.2019.2897619

Liu, Q., Zhang, M., Yifeng, H., Zhang, L., Zou, J., Yan, Y., & Guo, Y. (2022). Predicting the Risk of Incident Type 2 Diabetes Mellitus in Chinese Elderly Using Machine Learning Techniques. *Journal of Personalized Medicine, 12*(6), 905. doi:10.3390/jpm12060905 PMID:35743691

Li, X., Shang, M., Hao, J., & Yang, Z. (2016, April). Accelerating fish detection and recognition by sharing CNNs with objectness learning. In *OCEANS 2016-Shanghai* (pp. 1–5). IEEE. doi:10.1109/OCEANSAP.2016.7485476

Li, X., Shang, M., Qin, H., & Chen, L. (2015, October). Fast accurate fish detection and recognition of underwater images with fast r-cnn. In *OCEANS 2015-MTS/IEEE Washington* (pp. 1–5). IEEE.

Lobell, D. B., Hammer, G. L., McLean, G., Messina, C., Roberts, M. J., & Schlenker, W. (2009). The Critical Role of Extreme Heat for Maize Production in the United States. *Nature Climate Change, 3*(5), 497–501. doi:10.1038/nclimate1832

Lowenberg-DeBoer, J. (2012). Precision Agriculture for Grain Crops in the US Midwest. *Plant Science, 18*, 484–491.

Lowery, C. (2016). *Emerging Technology Analysis: Serverless Computing and Function Platform as a Service*. Gartner Research.

Luan, H., Geczy, P., Lai, H., Gobert, J., Yang, S. J. H., Ogata, H., Baltes, J., Guerra, R., Li, P., & Tsai, C. C. (2020). Challenges and Future Directions of Big Data and Artificial Intelligence in Education. *Frontiers in Psychology, 11*, 580820. doi:10.3389/fpsyg.2020.580820 PMID:33192896

Mahdiani, R. M., Khamehchi, E., Hajirezaie, S., & Sarapardeh, H. M. (2020). Modeling viscosity of crude oil using k-nearest neighbor algorithm. *Advances in Geo-Energy Research, 4*(4), 435–447. doi:10.46690/ager.2020.04.08

Mahjan, C., Marathe, S. N., & Choudhari, S. (2023), Diabetes Prediction Using Machine Learning Approach. *IRJMETS, 05*(2).

Malvoni, M., Leggieri, A., Maggiotto, G., Congedo, P. M., & De Giorgi, M. G. (2017). Long term performance, losses and efficiency analysis of a 960 kWP photovoltaic system in the Mediterranean climate. *Energy Conversion and Management, 145*, 169–181. doi:10.1016/j.enconman.2017.04.075

Manev, D., & Dimov, A. (2017). Facilitation of IoT software maintenance via code analysis and generation. *The 2nd International Multidisciplinary Conference on Computer and Energy Science (SpliTech),* (pp. 1-6). IEEE.

Mangal, A., & Jain, V. (2022). *Performance analysis of machine learning models for prediction of diabetes.* 2022 2nd International Conference on Innovative Sustainable Computational Technologies (CISCT), Dehradun, India. 10.1109/CISCT55310.2022.10046630

Manoj Kumar, N., Sudhakar, K., & Samykano, M. (2019). Techno-economic analysis of 1 MWp grid connected solar PV plant in Malaysia. *Int. J. Ambient Energy, 40*(4), 434–443. doi:10.108 0/01430750.2017.1410226

McLemore, T. (2022). Classifying Hazardous and Non-Hazardous Asteroids Using Machine Learning. *NHSJS Reports.* https://nhsjs.com/2022/classifying-hazardous-and-non-hazardous-asteroids-using-machine-learning/

McPadden, J., Durant, T. J., Bunch, D. R., Coppi, A., Price, N., Rodgerson, K., Torre, C. J. Jr, Byron, W., Hsiao, A. L., Krumholz, H. M., & Schulz, W. L. (2019). Health care and precision medicine research: Analysis of a scalable data science platform. *Journal of Medical Internet Research, 21*(4), e13043. doi:10.2196/13043 PMID:30964441

Mercaldo, F. (2017). Diabetes Mellitus Affected Patients Classification and Diagnosis through Machine Learning Techniques. *Procedia Computer Science, 112*, 2519-2528. .(https://www.sciencedirect.com/science/article/pii/S1877050917315880) doi:10.1016/j.procs.2017.08.193

MNRE Annual Report 2022-23. (2022). Ministry of New and Renewable Energy, Government of India. https://cdnbbsr.s3waas.gov.in/s3716e1b8c6cd17b771da77391355749f3/uploads/2023/08/2023080211.pdf

Montgomery, D. C. (2015). *Introduction to Time Series Analysis and Forecasting.* John Wiley & Sons.

Mulla, D. J. (2013). Twenty-Five Years of Remote Sensing in Precision Agriculture: Key Advances and Remaining Knowledge Gaps. *Biosystems Engineering, 114*(4), 358–371. doi:10.1016/j.biosystemseng.2012.08.009

Muzzammel, R., & Raza, A. (2020). *A Support Vector Machine Learning-Based Protection Technique for MT-HVDC Systems.* MDPI energies. Fu Y., Yin Z., Su M., Wu Y. & Liu G. (2020). *Construction and Reasoning Approach of Belief Rule-Base for Classification Base on Decision Tree. IEEE Access : Practical Innovations, Open Solutions.*

Naik G., Birari D., Sonavane, B., & Bhagat, N. (2019). Classification of Iris Flower Species Using Machine Learning. *International Journal for Research in Engineering Application & Management.*

Naik, N. (2017). Choice of effective messaging protocols for IoT systems: MQTT, CoAP, AMQP and HTTP. *Proceedings of the 2017 IEEE International Systems Engineering Symposium (ISSE)*; Vienna, Austria. 10.1109/SysEng.2017.8088251

Nanthini, N., Ashiq, A., Aakash, V. S., & Bhuvaneshwaran, M. J. (2022, December). Convolutional Neural Networks (CNN) based Marine Species Identification. In *2022 International Conference on Automation, Computing and Renewable Systems (ICACRS)* (pp. 602-607). IEEE.

NASA. (n.d.). *NEO Basics.* NASA/JPL CNEOS. https://cneos.jpl.nasa.gov/about/neo_groups.html

NASA/JPL. (n.d.). *Small-Body Database Query.* NASA/JPL CNEOS. https://ssd.jpl.nasa.gov/tools/sbdb_query.html

Nassar, A. K. (2018). Cloud-Based Farm Management Systems: An Overview and Comparison. *Computers and Electronics in Agriculture, 144*, 291–307.

Ngiam, K. Y., & Khor, W. (2019). Big data and machine learning algorithms for health-care delivery. *The Lancet. Oncology, 20*(5), e262–e273. doi:10.1016/S1470-2045(19)30149-4 PMID:31044724

Nguyen, T., Li, Z. H. O. U., Spiegler, V., Ieromonachou, P., & Lin, Y. (2018). Big data analytics in supply chain management: A state-of-the-art literature review. *Computers & Operations Research, 98*, 254–264. doi:10.1016/j.cor.2017.07.004

Ninikrishna, T., Sarkar, S., Tengshe, R., Jha, M., Sharma, L., Daliya, V., & Routray, S. (2017). Software defined IoT: Issues and challenges. *2017 International Conference on Computing Methodologies and Communication (ICCMC).* IEEE. 10.1109/ICCMC.2017.8282560

O'Sullivan, D., & Unwin, D. (2003). *Geographic Information Analysis.* John Wiley & Sons.

Obeidat, F. A., Spencer, B., & Alfandi, O. (2020). Consistently accurate forecasts of temperature within buildings from sensor data using lasso and ridge regression. *Future Generation Computer Systems, 110*, 382–392. doi:10.1016/j.future.2018.02.035

Olta, L. (2021). *Prediction and Detection of Diabetes using Machine Learning.* RTA-CSIT 2021, Tirana, Albania.

Oquendo, F. (2017). Software architecture of self-organizing systems-of-systems for the Internet-of-Things with SosADL. *The 12th System of Systems Engineering Conference (SoSE)*, (pp. 1-6). IEEE. 10.1109/SYSOSE.2017.7994959

Pandey, K. (2023, August 23). *The potential of mini-grids as a sustainable and economical alternative for global electrification*. Mongabay-India. https://india.mongabay.com/2023/08/are-mini-grids-the-sustainable-and-economical-solution-to-achieving-global-electrification/

Pankaj, C., Singh, K. V., & Singh, K. R. (2021). Artificial Intelligence enabled Web-Based Prediction of Diabetes using Machine Learning Approach. *2021 International Conference on Disruptive Technologies for Multi-Disciplinary Research and Applications (CENTCON)*, Bengaluru, India. 10.1109/CENTCON52345.2021.9688236

Pasko, V. (2018). Prediction of Orbital Parameters for Undiscovered Potentially Hazardous Asteroids Using Machine Learning. *Stardust Final Conference* (pp. 45-65). Springer. 10.1007/978-3-319-69956-1_3

Pathan, S. K. (2015). Internet of Things: Architectures, Protocols, and Applications. *Journal of Industrial Information Integration*, *1*, 3–13.

Patra, L., & Rao, U. (2016). Internet of Things — Archit ecture, applications, security and other major challenges. *3rd International Conference on Computing for Sustainable Global Development (INDIACom)*. IEEE.

Perwej, Y., Haq, K., Parwej, F., Mumdouh, M., & Hassan, M. (2019). The internet of things (IoT) and its application domains. *International Journal of Computer Applications*, *975*(8887), 182. doi:10.5120/ijca2019918763

Policies And Regulations. (n.d.). MNRE. https://mnre.gov.in/policies-and-regulations/

Polo López, C. S., & Frontini, F. (2013). Solar Energy Integration- Challenge and Chance for Conservation Architects. *Advanced Building Skins Conference Proceedings of the 8th ENERGY FORUM. EF ECONOMIC FORUM, Advanced Building Skins.*, (pp. 207–211). Supsi. https://repository.supsi.ch/3068/1/Energy%20Forum_CP_Preprint.pdf

Prasanna, V., & Ambhika, C. (2023). A Comprehensive Survey of Deep Learning: Advancements, Applications, and Challenges. *International Journal on Recent and Innovation Trends in Computing and Communication*, *11*(8s), 445–453. doi:10.17762/ijritcc.v11i8s.7225

Psomopoulos, C. S., Loannidis, G. C., & Kaminaris, S. D. (2015). A Comparative Evaluation of Photovoltaic Electricity Production Assessment Software (PVGIS, PV Watts and RETScreen*). Environmental Processes*, *2*(S1), 175–189. doi:10.1007/s40710-015-0092-4

Qu, Q., Xu, R., Nikouei, Y., & Chen, Y. (n.d.). *An Experimental Study on Microservices based Edge Computing Platforms*. Open Group. http://www.opengroup.org/soa/source-book/msawp/p3.htm

Quality data proves critical to business performance. (n.d.). Experianplc. https://www.experianplc.com/newsroom/press-releases/2022/quality-data-proves-critical-to-business-performance

Rajendran, T., Rajathi, S. A., Balakrishnan, C., Aswini, J., Prakash, R. B., & Subramanian, R. S. (2023, December). Risk Prediction Modeling for Breast Cancer using Supervised Machine Learning Approaches. In *2023 2nd International Conference on Automation, Computing and Renewable Systems (ICACRS)* (pp. 702-708). IEEE. 10.1109/ICACRS58579.2023.10404482

Ranaweera, N., & Fernando, T. G. I. (2022). Prediction of Potentially Hazardous Asteroids using Deep Learning. *International Conference on Advanced Research in Computing*. IEEE. 10.1109/ICARC54489.2022.9753945

Ranjith, J., & Mahantesh, K. (2019). *Privacy and Security issues in Smart Health Care*. 2019 4th International Conference on Electrical, Electronics, Communication, Computer Technologies and Optimization Techniques (ICEECCOT), Mysuru, India. 10.1109/ICEECCOT46775.2019.9114681

Rao, B. M., Alekhya, G., Aakanksha, J., & Naga Jyothi, K. (2023). Hazardous Asteroid Prediction Using Machine Learning. *2023 2nd International Conference on Vision Towards Emerging Trends in Communication and Networking Technologies*. Springer. 10.1109/ViTECoN58111.2023.10157937

Rathi, B., & Madeira, F. (2023). Early Prediction of Diabetes Using Machine Learning Techniques. *2023 Global Conference on Wireless and Optical Technologies (GCWOT)*, Malaga, Spain. 10.1109/GCWOT57803.2023.10064682

Raza, I. (2023). Precision Nutrient Application Techniques to Improve Soil Fertility and Crop Yield: A Review with Future Prospect. *International Research Journal of Education and Technology*, 5(08), 109–123.

Reddy, T. N., Reddy, G. J., Shashikanth, A., & Anand, V. (2021). A Hybrid Method to Enhance the Prediction of Hazardous Asteroids Using XGBoost Classifier with XGBClassifier Based Feature Selection Method. *International Research Journal of Engineering and Technology*, 8(9), 1704-1707. https://www.irjet.net/archives/V8/i9/IRJET-V8I9244.pdf

Reddy, V. R., Sai, T. N., Sushant, T., Muvva, S., Rani, D. R., & Sahu, A. K. (2023). Hazardous Asteroid Prediction Using Majority Voting Technique, *2023 7th International Conference on Intelligent Computing and Control Systems*. IEEE. 10.1109/ICICCS56967.2023.10142288

Redman, T. C. (1996). *Data Quality for the Information Age*.

REN21 Renewables 2022 Global Status Report. (2022). REN21 Secretariat. https://www.ren21.net/wp-content/uploads/2019/05/GSR2022_Full_Report.pdf

Roy, D. P. (2014). Landsat-8: Science and product vision for terrestrial global change research. *Remote Sensing of Environment*, *145*, 154–172. doi:10.1016/j.rse.2014.02.001

Saggi, M. K., & Jain, S. (2018). A survey towards an integration of big data analytics to big insights for value-creation. *Information Processing & Management*, *54*(5), 758–790. doi:10.1016/j.ipm.2018.01.010

Salman, A. G., Kanigoro, B., & Heryadi, Y. (2015). Weather Forecasting using deep learning techniques. *International conference on Advanced computer science and information system*, (pp. 281-285). Research Gate.

Saravanan, N. (2014). Spatial data integration for precision agriculture: A review. *Computers and Electronics in Agriculture*, *110*, 1–12.

Saravanan, N. (2014). Spatial Data Integration for Precision Agriculture: A Review. *Computers and Electronics in Agriculture*, *110*, 1–12.

Sarker, I. H. (2021). Machine Learning: Algorithms, Real-World Applications and Research Directions. *SN Computer Science*, *2*(3), 1–21. doi:10.1007/s42979-021-00592-x PMID:33778771

Sathya, D., Sudha, V., & Jagadeesan, D. (2020). Application of machine learning techniques in healthcare. In *Handbook of Research on Applications and Implementations of Machine Learning Techniques* (pp. 289–304). IGI Global. doi:10.4018/978-1-5225-9902-9.ch015

Scaling Up Renewable Energy Investment in India in the Wake of COVID-19. (2021). IRENA Coalition for Action. https://coalition.irena.org/-/media/Files/IRENA/Coalition-for-Action/Publication/Scaling-up-Renewable-Energy-Investment-in-Emerging-Markets/IRENA-Coalition-for-Action_India_2021.pdf?la=en&hash=E56FB23DF6F70A840CA98B49B04D18040F932BBA

Schultz, M. G., Betancourt, C., Gong, B., Kleinert, F., Langguth, M., Leufan, L. H., & Standtler, S. (2020). Can deep learning beat numerical weather prediction'. The Royal Society Publishing, 379.

Sen, P. C., Hajra, M., & Ghosh, M. (2020). Supervised classification algorithms in machine learning: A survey and review. In *Emerging Technology in Modelling and Graphics: Proceedings of IEM Graph 2018* (pp. 99-111). Springer Singapore. 10.1007/978-981-13-7403-6_11

S, G., Reddy, V. S., & Ahmed, M. R. (2023). Type 2 Diabetes Mellitus: Early Detection using Machine Learning Classification. *International Journal of Advanced Computer Science and Applications*, *14*(6). doi:10.14569/IJACSA.2023.01406127

Shafiullah, M., Ahmed, S. D., & Al-Sulaiman, F. A. (2022). Grid Integration Challenges and Solution Strategies for Solar PV Systems: A Review. *IEEE Access : Practical Innovations, Open Solutions*, *10*, 52233–52257. doi:10.1109/ACCESS.2022.3174555

Shahid, M. (2023). *An ensemble learning approach for diabetes prediction using boosting techniques*. Front. Genet. . doi:10.3389/fgene.2023.1252159

Shahid, N., & Aneja, S. (2017). Internet of Things: Vision, application areas and research challenges. *International Conference on I-SMAC (IoT in Social, Mobile, Analytics and Cloud) (I-SMAC)*, (pp. 583-587). IEEE. 10.1109/I-SMAC.2017.8058246

Shamreen Ahamed, B., & Meenakshi, S. (2022). Diabetes Mellitus Disease Prediction Using Machine Learning Classifiers with Oversampling and Feature Augmentation. Advances in Human-Computer Interaction. doi:10.1155/2022/9220560

Shankar, R., & Muthulakshmi, M. (2023, March). Comparing YOLOV3, YOLOV5 & YOLOV7 Architectures for Underwater Marine Creatures Detection. In *2023 International Conference on Computational Intelligence and Knowledge Economy (ICCIKE)* (pp. 25-30). IEEE.

Sharma, E., Chettri, N., Tse-ring, K., Jing, A. B., Mool, F., & Eriksson, M. (2009). *Climate change Impacts and Vulnerability in the Eastern Himalayas*. International centre for integrated Mountain devlopment Kathmandu Nepal.

Sharma, K., & Baalamurugan, K. M. (2021). *A review on Big Data Privacy and Security Techniques for the Healthcare Records*. 2021 3rd International Conference on Advances in Computing, Communication Control and Networking (ICAC3N), Greater Noida, India. 10.1109/ICAC3N53548.2021.9725455

Sharma, N. (2021). Crop Yield Prediction Using Machine Learning Algorithms: A Comprehensive Review. *Computers and Electronics in Agriculture, 180*, 106034.

Sharma, R., & Goel, S. (2017). Performance analysis of a 11.2 kWp roof top grid-connected PV system in Eastern India. *Energy Reports, 3*, 76–84. doi:10.1016/j.egyr.2017.05.001

Shi, W., Cao, J., Zhang, Q., Li, Y., & Xu, L. (2016). Edge Computing: Vision and Challenges. *IEEE Internet of Things Journal, 3*(5), 637–646. doi:10.1109/JIOT.2016.2579198

Shukla, A., Pant, H., Agarwal, A., & Mishra, P. (2020, May). Flower Classification using Supervised Learning. *International Journal of Engineering Research & Technology (IJERT), 9*(05).

Shukla, A. K., Sudhakar, K., & Baredar, P. (2016). Simulation and performance analysis of 110 kWp grid- connected photovoltaic system for residential building in India: A comparative analysis of various PV technology. *Energy Reports, 2*, 82–88. doi:10.1016/j.egyr.2016.04.001

Si, A. (2020). Hazardous Asteroid Classification through Various Machine Learning Techniques. *International Research Journal of Engineering and Technology, 6*(3), 5388-5390. https://www.irjet.net/archives/V7/i3/IRJET-V7I31084.pdf

Sisodia, D., & Gupta, M. K. (2013, September). Modeling And Control Of A Grid Connected Photovoltaic System Using Matlab, *International Journal of Latest Technology in Engineering, Management &. Applied Sciences (Basel, Switzerland), II*(IX), 69–74.

Sneha, N., & Gangil, T. (2019). Analysis of diabetes mellitus for early prediction using optimal features selection. *Journal of Big Data, 6*(1), 13. doi:10.1186/s40537-019-0175-6

Solar mini-grids: E-handbook (Version 1). (2020). International Solar Alliance. https://isolaralliance.org/uploads/docs/17675f3aa6ffa28afa08b186591b17.pdf

Sterchele, P., Palzer, A., & Henning, H.-M. (2018). Electrify Everything?: Exploring the Role of the Electric Sector in a Nearly CO_2-Neutral National Energy System. *IEEE Power & Energy Magazine, 16*(4), 24–33. doi:10.1109/MPE.2018.2824100

Stone, M., Aravopoulou, E., Ekinci, Y., Evans, G., Hobbs, M., Labib, A., Laughlin, P., Machtynger, J., & Machtynger, L. (2020). Artificial intelligence (AI) in strategic marketing decision-making: A research agenda. *The Bottom Line (New York, N.Y.), 33*(2), 183–200. doi:10.1108/BL-03-2020-0022

Subeesh, A., & Mehta, C. R. (2021). Automation and digitization of agriculture using artificial intelligence and internet of things. *Artificial Intelligence in Agriculture, 5*, 278–291. doi:10.1016/j.aiia.2021.11.004

Suchitra, G. (2023, December). Iris Classification Using Machine Learning. *International Journal of Research Publication and Reviews, 4*(12), 4129–4131.

Sun, X., Shi, J., Dong, J., & Wang, X. (2016, October). Fish recognition from low- resolution underwater images. In *2016 9th International Congress on Image and Signal Processing, BioMedical Engineering and Informatics (CISP-BMEI)* (pp. 471-476). IEEE.

Sutikno, T., Stiawan, D., & Subroto, I. M. I. (2014). Fortifying Big Data infrastructures to Face Security and Privacy Issues. [Telecommunication Computing Electronics and Control]. *TELKOMNIKA, 12*(4), 751–752. doi:10.12928/telkomnika.v12i4.957

Swapna, G., Vinayakumar, R., & Soman, K. P. (2018, December). Diabetes detection using deep learning algorithms (2018). *ICT Express, 4*(4), 243–246. doi:10.1016/j.icte.2018.10.005

T&D India. (2020, October 9). *Smart Power India launches Technical Guide for Solar Hybrid Mini-grids*. T&D India. https://www.tndindia.com/smart-power-india-launches-technical-guide-solar-hybrid-mini-grid/

Tagarakis, A. C. (2020). Smart agriculture: A review of technologies in precision farming. *Agricultural Systems, 182*, 102896. doi:10.1016/j.agsy.2020.102896

Talaat, F. M., & ZainEldin, H. (2023). An improved fire detection approach based on YOLO-v8 for smart cities. *Neural Computing & Applications, 35*(28), 1–16. doi:10.1007/s00521-023-08809-1 PMID:37362562

Tariq, N., Asim, M., Al-Obeidat, F., Zubair Farooqi, M., Baker, T., Hammoudeh, M., & Ghafir, I. (2019). The security of big data in fog enabled IoT applications including block chain: A survey. *Sensors (Basel), 19*(8), 1788. doi:10.3390/s19081788 PMID:31013993

Tasin, I., Nabil, T., Islam, S., & Khan, R. (2022). Diabetes prediction using machine learning and explainable AI techniques. *Healthc Technol Lett. 2023 Feb-Apr; 10*(1-2). doi::PMC10107388PMID:37077883 doi:10.1049/htl2.12039PMCID

ThenkabailP. S. (2016). Global Food Security Support Analysis Data (GFSAD) Cropland Extent 2015 Africa 30 m. doi:10.3334/ORNLDAAC/1346

Thenkabail, P. S. (2019). Remote Sensing of Crop Types for Agricultural Supply Management. *Agronomy Journal, 111*(3), 1009–1028.

Tsai, C. W., Lai, C. F., Chao, H. C., & Vasilakos, A. V. (2015). Big data analytics: A survey. *Journal of Big Data, 2*(1), 21. doi:10.1186/s40537-015-0030-3 PMID:26191487

Tucker, C. J. (1979). Red and photographic infrared linear combinations for monitoring vegetation. *Remote Sensing of Environment, 8*(2), 127–150. doi:10.1016/0034-4257(79)90013-0

Unveiling The Future Of Big Data: Insights And Innovations. (n.d.). Avenga. https://www.avenga.com/magazine/trends-and-future-forecasts-in-big-data/

Upender, K., Krishna, T. S., Pothanna, N., & Kumar, P. V. S. (2022). Predicting the Potentially Hazardous Asteroid to Earth Using Machine Learning. *Proceedings of Second International Conference on Advances in Computer Engineering and Communication Systems* (pp. 359-369). Springer. 10.1007/978-981-16-7389-4_34

Uprety, D., Banarjee, D., Kumar, N., & Dhiman, A. (2023). *Smart Sustainable Farming Using IOT, Cloud Computing and Big Data* (No. 10814). EasyChair.

Valdivia, J. A., Lora-González, A., Limón, X., Cortes-Verdin, K., & Ocharán-Hernández, J. O. (2020). Patterns Related to Microservice Architecture: A Multivocal Literature Review. *Programming and Computer Software, 46*(8), 594–608. doi:10.1134/S0361768820080253

ValeG.CorreiaF. F.GuerraE. M.RosaT. de O.FritzschJ.BognerJ. (2022). *Designing Microservice Systems Using Patterns: An Empirical Study on Quality Trade-Offs.* http://arxiv.org/abs/2201.03598 doi:10.1109/ICSA53651.2022.00015

Van Klompenburg, T., Kassahun, A., & Catal, C. (2020). Crop yield prediction using machine learning: A systematic literature review. *Computers and Electronics in Agriculture, 177*, 105709. doi:10.1016/j.compag.2020.105709

Vani, S. (2022). *NASA – Nearest Earth Objects* [Data Set]. https://www.kaggle.com/datasets/sameepvani/nasa-nearest-earth-objects

Vencerlanz09. (n.d.). *Sea Animal Dataset.* Kaggle. https://www.kaggle.com/datasets/vencerlanz09/sea-animals-image-dataste

Verfuss, U. K., Aniceto, A. S., Harris, D. V., Gillespie, D., Fielding, S., Jiménez, G., Johnston, P., Sinclair, R. R., Sivertsen, A., Solbø, S. A., Storvold, R., Biuw, M., & Wyatt, R. (2019). A review of unmanned vehicles for the detection and monitoring of marine fauna. *Marine Pollution Bulletin, 140*, 17–29. doi:10.1016/j.marpolbul.2019.01.009

Verma, K. (2022, February 2). *Union Budget 2022: Impact of Solar PLI Scheme.* Invest Media. https://www.investindia.gov.in/team-india-blogs/union-budget-2022-impact-solar-pli-scheme

Vermesan, O., Bahr, R., Ottella, M., Serrano, M., Karlsen, T., Wahlstrøm, T., Sand, H. E., Ashwathnarayan, M., & Gamba, M. T. (2020). Internet of robotic things intelligent connectivity and platforms. *Frontiers in Robotics and AI, 7*, 104. doi:10.3389/frobt.2020.00104 PMID:33501271

Vermesan, O., Bröring, A., Tragos, E., Serrano, M., Bacciu, D., Chessa, S., & Bahr, R. (2022). Internet of robotic things–converging sensing/actuating, hyper connectivity, artificial intelligence and IoT platforms. In *Cognitive Hyperconnected Digital Transformation* (pp. 97–155). River Publishers. doi:10.1201/9781003337584-4

Villamizar, M., Garcés, O., Castro, H., Verano, M., Salamanca, L., Casallas, R., & Gil, S. (2015). *Evaluating the monolithic and the microservice architecture pattern to deploy web applications in the cloud.* Proceedings of the 2015 10th Computing Colombian Conference (10CCC); Bogota, Colombia. 10.1109/ColumbianCC.2015.7333476

Viswanatha, V., Ramachandra, A.C., & Dhanush, M. (2023). Diabetes Prediction Using Machine Learning Approach. *Strad Research, 10*(8).

Voghoei, S., Tonekaboni, N. H., Wallace, J. G., & Arabnia, H. R. (n.d.). *Deep Learning at the Edge.*

Vresk, T., & Čavrak, I. (2016). *Architecture of an interoperable IoT platform based on microservices.* Proceedings of the 2016 39th International Convention on Information and Communication Technology, Electronics and Microelectronics (MIPRO); Opatija, Croatia. 10.1109/MIPRO.2016.7522321

Wang, H., Han, S., Liu, Y., Yan, J., & Li, L. (2019). Sequence transfer correction algorithm for numerical weather prediction wind speed and its application in a wind power forecasting system. *Applied Energy, 237*, 1–10. doi:10.1016/j.apenergy.2018.12.076

Wang, J., Pan, J., Esposito, F., Calyam, P., Yang, Z., & Mohapatra, P. (2019). Edge cloud offloading algorithms: Issues, methods, and perspectives. *ACM Computing Surveys, 52*(1), 1–23. Advance online publication. doi:10.1145/3284387

Wang, Y. (2018). Remote Sensing for Precision Agriculture: Recent Advances and Future Prospects. *Yaogan Xuebao, 22*(1), 3–23.

Wang, Y. (2023). Comparison of Machine Learning Strategies in Hazardous Asteroids Prediction. *Highlights in Science. Engineering and Technology, 39*, 201–208. doi:10.54097/hset.v39i.6527

Warke, M., Kumar, V., Tarale, S., & Galgat, P. (2019). Diabetes Diagnosis using Machine Learning Algorithms. *IRJET, 06*(3).

Wee, B. F., Sivakumar, S., & Lim, K. H. (2023). *Diabetes detection based on machine learning and deep learning approaches.* Multimed Tools Appl. doi:10.1007/s11042-023-16407-5

Yamini, B., Kaneti, V. R., & Nalini, M. (2023). Machine Learning-driven PCOS prediction for early detection and tailored interventions. *SSRG International Journal of Electrical and Electronics Engineering, 10*(9), 61–75. doi:10.14445/23488379/IJEEE-V10I9P106

Yang, Y., & Yang, Y. (2020). *Hybrid prediction method for wind speed combining ensemble empirical mode decomposition and bayesian ridge regression.* IEEE. doi:10.1109/ACCESS.2020.2984020

Year End Review 2023 of Ministry of new & renewable energy, Govt. of India. (2023). PIB. https://pib.gov.in/ErrorPage.html?aspxerrorpath=/pib.gov.in/Pressreleaseshare.aspx

Zaw, W. T., & Naing, T. T. (2009). *Modelling of Rainfall Prediction Over Mynamar Using Polynomial Regression.* International Conference on Computer Engineering and Technology, Singapore.

Zhang, D., Kopanas, G., Desai, C., Chai, S., & Piacentino, M. (2016, March). Unsupervised underwater fish detection fusing flow and objectiveness. In 2016 IEEE Winter Applications of Computer Vision Workshops (WACVW) (pp. 1-7). IEEE. doi:10.1109/WACVW.2016.7470121

Zhang, R., Li, S., Ji, G., Zhao, X., Li, J., & Pan, M. (2021). Survey on deep learning- based marine object detection. *Journal of Advanced Transportation*, *2021*, 1–18. doi:10.1155/2021/8793101

Zhang, R., & Li, X. (2021). Edge computing driven data sensing strategy in the entire crop lifecycle for smart agriculture. *Sensors (Basel)*, *21*(22), 7502. doi:10.3390/s21227502 PMID:34833575

Zhang, Y., Sun, H., & Guo, Y. (2019). Wind power prediction based on PSO-SVR and grey combination model. *IEEE Access : Practical Innovations, Open Solutions*, *7*, 136254–136267. doi:10.1109/ACCESS.2019.2942012

Zhou, T., Ziging, M., Wen, Q., Sun, L., Yao, T., Yin, W., & Jin, R. (2022). FiLm:Frequency improved legendre memory model for long time series forecasting. *Advances in Neural Information Processing Systems*, 12677–12690.

About the Contributors

Abhijit Bora is an Assistant Professor in the Department of Computer Applications, Assam Don Bosco University, India. Dr. Bora completed his Master of Computer Applications from Jorhat Engineering College, Dibrugarh University in the year 2009. He was awarded Ph.D from Gauhati University in the year 2017. His research interests include web service, software engineering, distributed computing, Grid Computing, Software Reliability and Data Science, Intelligent Systems, Machine Learning, Information Technology and Information Systems. He is currently working on various research-based activities related to academia and industry. He has advised/supervised students for their BCA, MCA and PhD work. He is involved in contribution of many indexed publications of journal, book chapters, proceedings etc. He is the reviewer for different international Journals, Conferences and workshops around the world.

Papul Changmai was born in Ghilamara, Assam, India. He received the B.E. degree in electrical engineering from Jorhat Engineering College, Jorhat, India, in 2008, and the Ph.D. degree from National Institute of Technology Arunachal Pradesh, India, in 2020. He is currently an Assistant Professor in the Department of Electrical and Electronics Engineering, Assam Don Bosco University, Guwahati, India. His current research interests include solar photovoltaic energy, grid integration of renewable energy. Dr. Changmai is also a reviewer of several journals and magazines published by IEEE, Institution of Engineering and Technology (IET), Springer and Elsevier. He has published several international publications including high impact factor SCI journals. Moreover he has a number of Indian patents and successfully completed a set of high valued research and consultancy projects. Dr. Changmai is a recipient of the prestigious National Technical Teacher Award 2022 conferred by Govt. of India.

Mrutyunjay Maharana was born in Balasore, Odisha, India and currently working as a Principal Engineer and Expert in BYD Automotive Product Strategy & New Technology Research Institute, Shenzhen, China. He was a former Assistant

Professor at the School of Electrical Engineering State Key Laboratory Insulation and Power Equipment's (SKLIPE), Xi'an Jiaotong University China. He has received Ph.D. degree from Centre for Energy IIT Guwahati, India in the year 2019. He has completed his M.Tech degree in Mechanical Engineering from IIT Guwahati in year 2014. His research interests include Renewable energy, AI, Predictive modelling, Machine learning, Material Science, Insulation material, dielectrics, nanoengineered materials, condition monitoring, data analysis. He has published more than 30 international publications including high impact SCI research papers. He has granted 3 Indian patent. Dr. Maharana has received young Scientist Award by SERB Government of India in 2018 and prestigious Gandhian Young Technological Innovation (GYTI) award in the year 2019 by Vice President of India.

***

Kathirvel Ayyaswamy, acquired, B.E.(CSE), M.E. (CSE) from Crescent Engineering College affiliated to University of Madras and Ph. D (CSE.) from Anna University. He is currently working as Professor, Dept of Computer Science and Engineering, Karunya Institute of Technology and Sciences, Coimbatore. He is a studious researcher by himself, completed 18 sponsored research projects worth of Rs 103 lakhs and published more than 110 articles in journals and conferences. 4 research scholars have completed Ph. D and 3 under progress under his guidance. He is working as scientific and editorial board member of many journals. He has reviewed dozens of papers in many journals. He has author of 13 books. His research interests are protocol development for wireless ad hoc networks, security in ad hoc network, data communication and networks, mobile computing, wireless networks, WSN and DTN. He is a Life member of the ISTE (India), IACSIT (Singapore), Life Member IAENG (Hong Kong), Member ICST (Europe), IAES, etc. He has given a number of guest lecturers/expert talks and seminars, workshops and symposiums.

B. Yamini has completed her Bachelor of Engineering in Computer Science and Engineering from Mailam Engineering College, in the year 2003. She pursued her Master of Technology in Information Technology from Sathyabama University, Chennai in the year 2007. She was awarded the Doctor of Philosophy in Computer Science and Engineering from Sathyabama Institute of Science and Technology, Chennai in the year 2020. She has published papers in various International and National Conferences and Journals. She is currently working at SRM Institute of Science and Technology, College of Engineering and Technology as Assistant Professor in the Department of Networking and Communications. Her areas of interests include Network Security, Cyber Forensics, Image Processing, and Information Retrieval system, Machine Learning, Deep Learning and Cloud Computing.

Saurav Bhattacharjee, is a lecturer in the Department of Mechanical (Automobile) Engineering, at Kamrup Polytechnic, Assam. He acquired his Master degree in Energy Engineering from Assam Science and Technology University and a Bachelor degree in Mechanical Engineering from Anna University, Chennai. He is also pursuing Ph.D. from the National Institute of Technology, Silchar, Assam. His research interests include Renewable Energy, Machine Learning, Wind Prediction,3d Simulation. His career journey includes roles as a Technical Assistant, Supervisor, and Quality Assurance Engineer. He has pursued certifications in areas such as Residential Solar PV Design, Digital Image Processing, Electric Mobility, and Photogrammetry & Cartography. He has several Indian Patents. He has Organised, attended, and given more than 30 national and International conferences, Seminars, and workshops. He has Supervised more than 20 Students in projects. He is a lifetime member of the Indian Welding Society.

Balakrishnan C. is an Associate Professor in the Department of Computer Science and Engineering, S.A Engineering College, Chennai, India. He has 25 years teaching experience. His research interests include Data Mining, Machine Learning, Big Data Analytics and Networking. He has published many articles in reputed Journals.

Jonti Deuri is working as an Assistant Professor in Assam Don Bosco University from 2022. She has more than 5 years of teaching experience and more than 9 years of research experience.

Bhargav K. Hazarika is a final year student currently pursuing his BCA degree from Assam Don Bosco University, Assam under the Department of Computer Applications.

K. Sudha is an Associate Professor in the Department of Computer Science and Business Systems, since August 2022. She obtained her B. TECH (IT) from SASTRA UNIVERSITY and M. TECH (CSE) from Ponnaiyah Ramajayam Institute of Science &Technology and pursuing Ph.D. in Dr. M. G. R Educational and Research Institute University. She has been in the teaching profession for the past 11 years. Her areas of interest include Design and Analysis of Algorithm, Network Security, Cyber Security Intrusion Detection, Machine Learning. She has published 5 papers in various International and National Journals and 3 papers in various National and International Conferences. She has attended many workshops, Faculty Development Programs (FDPs) and Attended National Level Awareness Quiz on ICT initiatives of MHRD and UGC scored 80%. She is active member in organising various curricular and cocurricular activities of various events and programs and she is the life member of ISSE.

M. Nalini is an Associate Professor in the Department of Computer Science and Engineering, S.A Engineering College, Chennai, India. She received her B.E. in Computer Science and Engineering from Anna University, Chennai in 2010 and M.Tech. in Computer Science and Engineering from B.S.Abdur Rahman Crescent Institute of Science & Technology, Chennai, India in 2012. She was awarded Ph.D. in Computer Science and Engineering from St. Peter's Institute of Higher Education and Research, Chennai, India in 2018. She has 10 years teaching experience. Her research interests include Data Mining, ML, Big Data Analytics and Networking. She has published many articles in reputed Journals.

Lakshmi Haritha M is working is as an Associate Professor in the Department of Computer Science and Engineering, R.M.K. Engineering College, Kavaraipettai and received her Ph.D Degree from JNTUA, Ananthapuramu in the year 2022. She has around 2 years of teaching experience and 2 years of industry experience. Her areas of interests include Information Retrieval, Data Mining, Image Processing and Natural Language Processing.

Siva Subramanian R. is an Associate Professor in the Department of Computer Science and Engineering, RMK College of Engg and Tech, Chennai, India. He received her B.E. in Computer Science and Engineering from Anna University, Chennai in 2009 and M.Tech. in Computer Science and Engineering from Bharath University, Chennai, India in 2013. He has 10 years teaching experience. His research interests include Data Mining, Machine Learning, Big Data Analytics and Networking. He has published many articles in reputed Journals.

Aditya Kumar Rabha is a final year student currently pursuing his BCA degree from Assam Don Bosco University, Assam under the Department of Computer Applications.

Lianmuansang Samte is a final year student currently pursuing his BCA degree from Assam Don Bosco University, Assam under the Department of Computer Applications.

T. P. Anish received his M.E. Degree from the Department of Computer Science and Engineering at Saveetha Engineering College (Affiliated to Anna University), Chennai, India, in 2011. He is currently an Assistant Professor at R.M.K. College of Engineering and Technology, Puduvoyal, India. He is pursuing his Ph.D. degree in Information and Communication Engineering from Anna University. His current research interest includes Machine Learning, Deep Learning and Big Data analytics.

Index

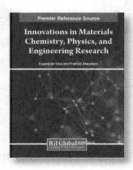

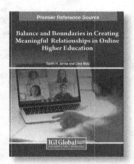

Submit an Open Access Book Proposal

Have Your Work Fully & Freely Available Worldwide After Publication

Seeking the Following Book Classification Types:

Authored & Edited Monographs • Casebooks • Encyclopedias • Handbooks of Research

Gold, Platinum, & Retrospective OA Opportunities to Choose From

Easily Track Your Work in Our Advanced Manuscript Submission System With **Rapid Turnaround Times**

Double-Blind Peer Review by Notable Editorial Boards (*Committee on Publication Ethics* (COPE) Certified

Publications Adhere to All **Current OA Mandates & Compliances**

Affordable APCs *(Often 50% Lower Than the Industry Average)* Including Robust Editorial Service Provisions

Direct Connections with **Prominent Research Funders** & OA Regulatory Groups

Institution Level OA Agreements Available (Recommend or Contact Your Librarian for Details)

Join a **Diverse Community of 150,000+ Researchers Worldwide** Publishing With IGI Global

Content Spread Widely to Leading Repositories (AGOSR, ResearchGate, CORE, & More)

DID YOU KNOW? ## Retrospective Open Access Publishing

You Can Unlock Your Recently Published Work, Including Full Book & Individual Chapter Content to Enjoy All the Benefits of Open Access Publishing

Learn More

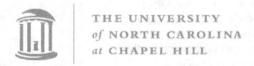